TECHNIQUE AND CULTURE

1 The Growth of Minds and Cultures

WILLEM H. VANDERBURG

The Growth of Minds and Cultures

A UNIFIED THEORY OF THE STRUCTURE OF HUMAN EXPERIENCE

UNIVERSITY OF TORONTO PRESS
Toronto Buffalo London

© University of Toronto Press 1985
Toronto   Buffalo   London
Printed in USA

ISBN 0-8020-2578-1

Canadian Cataloguing in Publication Data
Vanderburg, Willem H.
  The growth of minds and cultures

  Includes bibliographical references and index.
  ISBN 0-8020-2578-1

  1. Science and civilization.   2. Technology –
  Social aspects.   3. Technology and civilization.
  4. Knowledge, Theory of.   5. Consciousness.
  I. Title.

CB151.V36 1985   303.4'83   C85-098799-7

To my parents and to Rita, Esther, and David

CONTENTS

FOREWORD

In this book we find the elaboration of concepts giving insight into culture, its development and transmission. Such an elaboration necessarily leads to one of the essential constituent factors of our society, namely technique. Is it possible to speak of a technical culture? What impact does technique have on culture? How can an adaptation to technique be achieved? These are some of the questions which must be addressed in any large-scale study of technique.

What immediately appears as original in this study is its approach to the subject; it is very different from the customary one, which usually begins with the phenomenon of technique, and from there the question of culture is posed. The approach proposed here begins with man, moves to his relation to culture, and from there technique is encountered. Technique is thus put in second place, but this makes it necessary to consider the retroaction of technique on man and to pose the decisive question as to whether technique modifies the process of human acculturation.

This work is meticulous, intriguing, and unusual in the literature of the social sciences. This is not only because it presents a complete structure, which is rarely done today, and not only because it deals with a question as a whole and does not give way to the trend of specialization, but also because it takes a deliberate position in its interpretation which, it seems to me, is quite remarkable. So much so, that this book has led me to a more general reflection on the development of the sciences. As a matter of fact, this book opposes itself to an older conception of science and also, for very different reasons, to some modern trends. The question of acculturation and the relations between the individual and the culture into which he or she is socialized has been extensively studied, but I know of no research comparable to this. At first glance, this work seems to refer to givens and to

adopt a method which are entirely traditional, but which then appear to be
in agreement with the most recent research and thinking; consequently, it
leads us to call into question the way we usually think about the process of
scientific development, at least in the social sciences. I shall try to clarify
these remarks.

The author places himself in opposition to the traditional positivistic
scientific orientation, which assumed things to be stable and well-defined.
A scientific study could be undertaken only when the object was isolated
from its context and considered to be invariable. Every analysis began with
a strict delimitation of what was studied. It was impossible to study a
complex and unstable ensemble. It was assumed that such an ensemble
could be decomposed into basic elements, and that the whole was equal to
the sum of the parts. The ensemble could then be reconstructed from the
studies of the isolated parts. It was necessary to begin by finding the pure
element, the indivisible particle, or the original group. In ethnology, for
example, the most 'primitive' group was studied as the basic unit, in order
to return to a complex society by combining these analyses of the
'primitive'; the most ancient was considered the simplest and most
original. Since the stability of the basic element had to be assumed, it
stands to reason that no scientific study appeared to be possible if the object
of the observation changed, varied constantly, or if its characteristics
altered during the course of the observation. Therefore, a stable society
was required as an *a priori*, and institutions, structures, and organizations
were commonly so studied. When moving on to the next stage, that of the
reintegration of the parts into a whole, this could be done only in a
mechanistic way. But how could these well-defined elements be combined
and according to which fixed principles? What combination was possible to
get back to the whole from which the parts had been taken? It was necessary
to proceed in such a way that this combination was as rigorous as the
preceding analysis. In other words, there was a kind of 'recomposition
synthesis,' which necessarily excluded the imprecise, the unstable, the
changeable, and in which one had successfully to effect the putting back
together of the parts already studied without anything 'spilling over.' The
different parts were interrelated in a similar way to the parts constituting a
machine. In history, for example, a thorough searching of the archives
should produce, bit by bit, *all* the elements necessary for understanding a
society or obtaining an accurate picture of the politics or the economy of a
given period. It is the outgrowth of this kind of mechanistic reductionism
which is opposed in this book.

The author takes a much more modern position, characterized by the three following basic ideas. One must consider each fact, each given, in relation to its context, along with the other elements making up a whole. That is to say, one must never lose sight of the whole when examining one of its parts. Secondly, what is most important is the system of interrelations and interactions, with the study of the 'flows' and connections predominating. Finally, it must be remembered that the object of the study is on the one hand modified by the observation itself, and on the other hand changes constantly and exists in time. Consequently, an accurate observation at one moment in time may no longer be so at the next. The present work takes into account this new conception of the scientific method, and in this respect does not present anything significantly different. I would not have had to recall these well-known facts if the author had left it at that.

A question begins to present itself when one realizes that the author actually goes beyond this position – unless he is retrogressing. Indeed, what do we see? We start out from the individual experience, that of a person separated from society, the experience of a child, and this is constantly returned to. The author begins with sensation, perception and experience, and goes on to the structure of experience – all this related to the individual. But is this not a falling back into the analytic process separating one part from the whole in order to examine it? A similar approach was common in psychology in the nineteenth century. The psychology of an 'ideal person' was studied and from that a whole set of characteristics was inferred. We will return to this question.

The author claims the existence of the individual subject, in spite of the reservation of many modern thinkers in this regard. Of course, this individual does not remain alone, and this already departs from early psychology where the individual was studied as such, and where the environment disappeared into a kind of fog. In this work the individual is thought of as being in relation with and in constant exchange with his milieu; consequently, what is brought to light is that this subject undergoes pressures, receives stimuli, has experiences, and what is more, builds up his particular being in this context of interrelations. We see here an unceasing effort to demonstrate change *within* continuity. The two must exist together to reveal unity within diversity, which presupposes an endeavour to combine all the components encountered through the increasing complexity but never losing sight of the individual. It is a question of reconstructing a human being's links with the world beginning with the individual's experience of the natural environment and the cultural milieu. One of the strengths of this book is that it shows the indissociable character of this double experience. The natural world is experienced only through a cultural framework but, reciprocally, the experience of this cultural framework builds the culture! Every elaboration of a person's relationship with the world helps build the surrounding culture as well as his own being. The phenomena related to the structure of experience which become more and more complex as a result of the intervention of language, among other things, induce not a pure and simple reproduction but at the same time the elaboration of a diversity; the more complete the experience of the world and the culture becomes, the more the individual becomes determined.

In the same way, Bill Vanderburg is led to present, in a different way from that generally done, the relation between nature and culture and the relation between the biological and the cultural. He avoids the temptation to make a division between what is genetically and culturally acquired. He shows that, during the development of the personality and the coming of discernment, there is an interpenetration of the biological and the cultural, which should not be measured quantitatively but considered qualitatively. His theory thus resolves many problems. But doesn't it also present a considerable difficulty? Here the system built up by the author comes into conflict, as we have said, with a dominant trend in modern sociology. This approach holds that the individual does not exist, the subject does not exist; from the moment of his birth he is part of a whole, he is inseparable and indistinguishable from this whole. It has even been claimed that every being is no more than the sum of his relationships. M. Foucault, for example, argues that what we take to be an individual is nothing but a setting passed over by many currents, or else that 'man' himself is only an ephemeral illusion that is part of an ideology and which will soon disappear. To claim that an individual speaks is to lose sight of the fact that his words are in reality dictated by the whole social ensemble, even to the point that it cannot be said 'I speak,' but '*one*' speaks (through me) or '*it*' speaks! What matters in this sociological approach, what can be observed or considered, are relationships, fluxes, processes, but nothing else – and it is absolutely useless to study a human being as such or to designate a subject, since it is indistinguishable from the world of objects. This approach sets itself up as the new sociology.

The author takes the opposite point of view, and begins with the idea that the individual or the subject exists as such. It should be said that the new approach to sociology gives rise to some problems! We are told that what counts is the 'relationship,' but how can we avoid the question, 'the relationship between what and what?' In short, a relationship cannot exist in itself: in order to have a relationship there must be a transmitter (which exists as such) and a receiver. The subject cannot be dissolved into the relationship.

It is essential not to keep the study of culture to its institutions, but conversely it is going too far to make the institutions disappear, as it were, and to replace them with development and crises. It was certainly a mistake as well to think that the world began with man's experience of it; and the significance of the 'already there' must be stressed, which preceded individual experience, received it, and informed it. Neither was it possible to think of everything in terms of order, equilibrium, and organization. The importance of disorder, of 'noise' in communication, and crisis had to be re-established. Fortunately, there already was an attempt to establish the relationship, without leaving it as noise or disorder only, with, for example, Von Foerster's phrase 'order from noise.' It must be understood that these givens are reciprocal, that is, there is no crisis without an institution, but at the same time there is no institution without crisis. In the same way, there is no communication and information without individuals, and reciprocally there are no individuals without there being information. Finally, the pre-existence of an 'already there' does not negate the subject's existence, but on the contrary it allows the subject to develop. It could even be said that, if we designate the previous given (cultural, political, economic) as 'already there,' it is only with regard to the appearance of a *new* element which joins the established system and which is precisely the subject. If the subject does not appear it is pointless to conceive of the idea of an 'already there.'

Thus the author rejects the idea in vogue that everything is disorder, noise, flux, flow. For him there is a certain order, a language, institutions, a legitimate culture – which is neither oppression nor falsification. To illustrate this, it has often been said in sociological circles that language is terrorist by nature, in that the child is obliged to learn a certain language, and in so doing he is made to take on a certain way of thinking, certain values are imposed on him, he is intellectually conditioned, and so he is no longer free! Of course, the author recognizes the essential role of communication and he deals with it at length but after having posed the subject as such. In the same way he recognizes the importance of disorder, but it is introduced later, to show that the living organism is superior to the machine, in line with Von Neumann, according to whom the reliability of a machine is always inferior to that of each of its components, while that of a living organism is always superior. The living organism, by its ability to transfer functions, to repair itself, and so on, increases its own determinism; that is to say, over and above external determinisms it produces its own determinism, it over-determines itself. In so doing it makes use of uncertainty, chance, ambivalence, and crisis. Disorder is allowed to enter its order, and in that rests simultaneously its specificity and its freedom – a topic which we will return to later. It is this complexity that is analysed and brought to light in this book, but it must be understood that all these factors of disorder appear late in the analysis, when the subject has been well established.

Nevertheless one may be surprised by the author's approach: he begins by explaining, at a very traditional psychological level, the sensations, perceptions, the role of the brain, the process of differentiation, the experience of one's milieu, the appearance of a system of experience, and so on. This seems to take us back to the kind of psycho-sociological studies of at least fifty years ago. It gives the impression of a method which ignores all modern trends and recent work in the humanities, and which falls back on a well-known and outmoded schema. I will show that, while adopting this schema, the author has not only taken account of the more recent studies (which I outlined at the end of the first section), but what is more, he places himself among the latest scientific developments.

This leads me to a brief reflection on the development of the sciences. Their evolution seems to be a kind of spiral. By this I mean that a scientific concept, a hermeneutic principle, or a paradigm may appear 'new' at a certain time, yet strongly resemble a concept, a principle, or a paradigm from an earlier period in the history of scientific thought. At the same time the general context of science, the scientific universe in which they exist, has radically changed, so that they are both similar and different. An obvious example is that of the atom: the concept of the atom of the scientific age has striking similarities to the atom of Lucretius! And when I speak of a spiral-like evolution I mean to say: if I begin with a given point on the spiral and follow it, I will pass a point diametrically opposed to my starting-point, but which is 'higher' with regard to scientific knowledge. If I continue, I will find myself at a point located on the same axis as my starting-point, but the two are not identical with each other because again one is located higher with regard to scientific knowledge. Nevertheless, this concept, hermeneutic principle, or paradigm strictly resembles the preceding one. That is what struck me while reading this book, which begins with the individual and his experience, and in which culture derives from the development of the structure of experience.

Have we not returned to the nineteenth century position, in which the individual was the nucleus from which everything was built up, when all of the organization and development of society was deduced from this qualification of the individual? For example, in political economy Robinson Crusoe's experience was taken as basic, and from this all its principles were deduced. The economy was what it was because under any circumstances the individual pursued his own interests. But later on all this was challenged. A sociology of the masses and averages emerged, complete with statistical methods, just as in economics there was a move to macro-economics and stochastics. The individual could not be considered in these large-scale interpretations. In going back again to individual experience, the author is not at all retrogressing. The process of experiencing, leading to the acquisition of language, and the double phenomenon of acculturation and the growth of culture have nothing in common with traditional individualism. It has been enriched by all the research done on the large ensembles and on culture as a whole. It is thus related to an older given, yet it has been completely renewed by the integration of recent developments.

In returning to the individual the author is not alone, but joins the most recent trend of research in the humanities. I would argue that sociological research using statistical methods is already yesterday's research! The most recent (not shared by everyone) restores to the individual and to his experience a decisive place in the interpretation of sociological phenomena. When, for example, Edgar Morin in his latest book (*Sociologie* 1984) attempts to define society 'in its originality, not as a closed idea but one which is immersed and emerging,' he can conceive of it only as multiple and not strictly determined interactions between individuals. The more of these interactions there are between individuals, the more complex the social organization becomes (which is a positive aspect). This complexity is not that of a machine, but the result of these many individual actions. This brings us back to what should never have been forgotten, namely that 'society is founded on individuality.' Morin opposes the dominant trend in sociology in two respects. In the first place, he observes how surprising it is that sociology excludes the individual from its research, when individualism has never been so highly developed as in modern societies: if we want to analyse sociologically *modern* society (not that of the peoples of the Third World, for example) we must have a theory 'which places the individual at the centre.' His second criticism is that the sociological theories of today are divided between a structural rigidity and a structureless dynamism. Beginning with the individual potential, we need to conceptualize both invariability and the possibility of evolution.

The present work corresponds exactly to what is required. The importance of the connection between the three poles – society, culture, individual – are well set out. On the one hand society depends entirely on culture, it emerges in and through a given culture, but this culture is neither an abstract idea nor an ensemble in itself; it exists only through and in terms of individuals. This perspective is very fruitful because it avoids a common error – namely to define culture or society based on a specific idea, from a fixed point of view, or around a central concept. It should be defined in a polynuclear and polycentric way, the importance of which we will see shortly. In order to conceptualize clearly the system of interactions, specifically human individual events must be taken into account. Take death as an example. In this study the author has taken the experience of a child as the starting point, but he could just as well have begun with death. Death is inseparable from renewal, social rejuvenation, and cultural reproduction. Something of culture is destroyed with the death of each person, both for the individual and the community. It must therefore constantly be transmitted to and reproduced in other individuals. Death necessitates the processes of learning, education, socialization, and acculturation. The question then is: how will these processes develop while integrating the phenomenon of death as an individual event as well as a demand for renewal? The experience of death thus demands the creation of processes for the transmission of culture.

The interpretation presented in this book has several significant implications. I will deal with three of them. The conception of society as an immense self-regulating and self-determining organism leads inevitably to the problem of its relation and resemblance to animal societies – for example, those of insects, which are the most highly differentiated. Although this traditional opposition is an obvious one it takes on new significance in the light of the most recent studies. For example, research on termite societies shows that a strict automatism following an invariable plan appears to control the construction of the termitary (the most skilful and complex of all insect nests). If the specific characteristics of the construction are fixed in the same way as a hereditary anatomical characteristic, then it must be recognized that there is a measure of initiative within the cohesion. The individual tasks achieve a coherent goal only if they are closely co-ordinated. There is an individual automatism, but this is modelled on necessary correlations and by a pattern of behaviour and possibilities of action that individual automatism could not foresee *a priori*. This is the theory of stigmergy. However, human behaviour and access to culture is of a quite different order from stigmergy, and this work implies the vast difference between human behaviour and that of an insect society (no matter how flexible). We might say that human society is a 'hypercomplex' one in which each individual has a high potential (a mind) and in which the division of labour (contrary to that of insect societies) is not somatically inscribed, either in the individual or the social group. Society is hypercomplex in that, as hierarchies shrink, decisions are decentralized and reduced in number, and processes of despecialization begin. There exists a multiplicity of variable and interchangeable social roles, obviously inconceivable in a termite society, no matter how complex! This is due to the dimension of freedom (indeterminism) in human culture.

This work clearly shows, not that the human being and human society are partly determined and partly non-determined, which is much too simplistic, but how the system of culture derived from the structure of experience is 'self-organizing.' It tends to create its own internal determinism, thus distancing itself from external determinisms. There is thus an alliance of sorts between a culture's internal determinism and the kind of freedom it has, which allows one to speak of autonomy with regard to the human cultural system. Society can be defined as an open, complex ensemble made up of highly developed individuals having a measure of autonomy in their behaviour. This presupposes a multiplicity of not strictly determined interactions between individuals, which keeps up with the complexity of social organization, mainly through language, which allows access to this type of culture. The author meticulously demonstrates this in following the cultural development of a child to the double problem of individual diversity in terms of the structure of experience, and cultural unity in spite of and in relation to individual diversity. It is one of the main characteristics of human culture and at the same time the main difficulty which behaviourism has never been able to resolve.

Bill Vanderburg can shed light on another important question: how is it that man has been able to produce cultures that are diverse and yet compatible with one another? One possible answer would be to affirm the existence of a pre-existing, universal human nature. But then we risk returning to a concept of society like that of the termitary; and moreover it is a metaphysical assertion without any proof. What is certain is the extraordinary profusion of cultures developed by man, not only different in form but also incomparable because of their number. Prehistorians are becoming increasingly aware of the existence of miniscule groups of a few dozen individuals, such as lake-dwelling communities. These, however, are neither simple aggregations of individuals nor unstable or disorganized units: no matter how small the number of people, there is always an internal coherence – I would say, cultural coherence – of the group. This has become well recognized today. These lake-dwelling groups vary greatly in detail. Neighbouring lake-dwelling groups in the same milieu, led to settle on the lakes for a variety of reasons, did not give rise to identical cultures; on the contrary.

What seems interesting to me is that the model of culture established by the author can function, in large and complex societies as well as in small groups of this kind, to explain both the coherence and diversity of the group. We should remember that the greater the number of givens a theory can explain, or the greater the variety of different situations to which it can be applied, the more it may be considered as exact.

The last implication which merits our attention is that this theory of culture retains both cultural diversity and the process of acculturation. This is due to the relationship established between culture and its participants, as well as the in-depth definition given to culture. It could be said, without repeating the author's words, that for him culture is a system which establishes communication between the experience of life and a body of organized knowledge which is not peremptorily transmitted. It is to his credit that he takes into account the different definitions of culture without allowing himself to become locked into any of them. Culture is neither a concept nor an indicatory principle, but the way in which the challenge of life is lived. This is never lived as mere acculturation in the strict sense of the word, but the actual reality of learning, development, and evolving makes certain goals set by the group obsolete and creates new ones. By the child's making his way into the culture it may be said that the whole group is modified.

Certain constraints weaken (and we certainly experience it today, but this was the case for every generation!). There is a growing uncertainty about the goals themselves, which is due to the evolving and uncertain nature of the human group. The author's model takes into account this evolving and uncertain character, so that taking it a step further it is difficult to say whether the purpose of society is the individual, or whether the purpose of the individual is society, or whether the purpose of both is mankind. In doing this the author also transcends certain psychological problems such as the change in a child's way of thinking from the fanciful to the rational. He does not use the commonplace idea of 'blockages,' often used to characterize the obstacles to knowledge encountered by the child, attributed to the notion that the child lives by fantasies which direct his understanding of reality. These fantasies cause latent blockages to another understanding of reality; for example, to the development of negative logic necessary for a scientific kind of reasoning. Because of his theory of the structure of experience, the author avoids this kind of problem without disregarding the issues yet providing an elegant solution.

In closing, I would like to point out that this interpretation is all the more important because it situates itself in our rapidly changing world. We are in a so-called hypercomplex society, characterized by a multiplicity of events, or 'virtual newness.' This society is affected by external events to which it must adapt in order to assimilate them, which implies new developments induced from outside. It also itself gives rise to events and divergences, due to internal innovation and because its constitutive elements are related in a rather loose and weakly integrated way. There is thus a constant play between the indispensable continuity and access to this inevitable newness. According to Morin, 'The hypercomplex society maintains a permanent instability, so that the play of social complementarities is simultaneously a play of antagonisms, the play of differences is at the same time a play of oppositions, and its oscillations themselves create real sociological divergences, or crises. Society is weakly culturally integrated; the rigidity of norms and taboos has been weakened; areas of anomie, marginality, and originality are more or less tolerated and constitute areas of sociological divergence, favourable to the creation of new forms.' This book takes this situation into account in its examination of the structure of experience in relation to individual diversity, while at the same time allowing for the possibility of rapid change.

Such interpretations reveal, let me say again, the importance of this work, which encompasses many disciplines. It is, in my opinion, a model of the 'interlinking sciences' envisaged by R. Caillois, which alone can assure a coherent intellectual future in our western scientific culture.

JACQUES ELLUL

PREFACE

The mechanization and rationalization of work during the past two hundred years have profoundly affected the individual, society, and the natural environment. As the application of science and technology continues to spread to new domains, particularly information, knowledge, and intelligence, the rationalization of intellectual work is bound to have even more fundamental consequences, since it will permeate our being much more than did the rationalization of physical work. It is particularly in these most recent developments that the limitations of our understanding of the implications of modern science and technology become apparent. This book is a first step aimed at gaining a unified understanding of the way modern science and technology are transforming human life on the grounds that their overall effect cannot be deduced from the implications of individual technologies or scientific undertakings.

I approach the study of science and technology from a particular vantage point – namely, that of our present culture and time. In the course of their development in Western civilization, modern science and technology have provided us with successive generations of metaphors and analogies that have helped to shape our images of ourselves, society, and nature. As a result, we live in a world in which the methods of the natural sciences, applied sciences, and engineering are thought to be largely applicable to the understanding, organization, and structuring of human activities, institutions, and society. The domain of application of a variety of methods derived from the natural and applied sciences is extended beyond technological systems with little critical awareness of the potential implications. Implicitly or explicitly, it is assumed that the nature of non-engineering systems is sufficiently similar to warrant the extension of the scope of these methods.

I will argue that for living 'systems,' such as human individuals, groups, and societies, this assumption is fundamentally incorrect. The consequences of attempting to understand and relate to living 'systems' on the basis of analogies drawn from non-living systems can, obviously, be far-reaching. Individually and collectively we are literally looking for the living among the dead. If our conception of human individuals and society is essentially mechanistic, even when it is of the most sophisticated kind, it will be impossible to see the deeper implications of the technologies used to render many areas of modern life more rational, effective, or efficient, because many of them are related to the application of methods and procedures developed for non-living systems to living 'systems.'

A first step towards building a new understanding of the roles science and technology play in our contemporary world will therefore consist of examining society as the context and environment for science and technology. Its culture, functioning as a social ecology, names and attributes a value to everything. It assigns everything a place in human life and shapes attitudes accordingly. A detailed knowledge of the role of culture is thus essential for understanding how the members of a society conceptualize science and technology, how they participate in them, and what they expect from them. On the basis of the culture, the activities that constitute science and technology are woven together with many others into a relatively coherent way of life. The members of each new generation grow up with the current patterns of individual and collective life, which profoundly influences the development of their minds. This in turn affects the way they put their cultural inheritance to use, which then moulds future generations, and so on.

When science and technology play a fundamental role within a society, it can be expected that its members will have difficulty treating them critically, given the high value inevitably placed on them by the culture. They are no longer like so many other activities – effective for certain tasks and inappropriate for others. The value a culture has assigned to modern science and technology may even make it very difficult for us to have a fairly neutral conversation about their positive and negative implications. Emotional reactions may, to an outside observer, appear to be surprisingly intense for what is being said. All this is, of course, an essential part of the way a culture allows millions of people to live together with a measure of unity and of the way a society can maintain a measure of coherence during an epoch of history.

We need to be clear, however, about what we mean by culture. A society's tools, techniques, customs, beliefs, institutions, laws, morals, religion, and art – in short, everything that is uniquely human – are a part of a larger totality, namely its culture. It is the basis on which the members of a society interpret their experience and interact with one another, their environment, their past, and their future. The culture of a society may thus be regarded as its social ecology.

The wholeness of a culture has often been taken for granted in the social sciences and humanitites, as if it were little more than the sum of the constituent elements. This state of affairs, however, obscures some of the most important phenomena that underlie a great many events of the past few decades and that are likely to continue to shape events in the near future. Modern science and technology have profoundly influenced human life in the so-called industrially advanced nations and, as their influence spreads, the diversity of human cultures so characteristic of history until recently appears to be declining. The following simple example is paradigmatic. Any face-to-face conversation typically involves an eye etiquette, a set of facial expressions, body language, body rhythms, emotions, and a conversation distance. These are typical of the participants' culture with individual differences in part due to upbringing, personality, and social position. When such a conversation is mediated by a telephone, many of its aspects are externalized since something of the culture and the way human beings express themselves via it has been eliminated. When this kind of transformation happens to a great many relationships in a society, its culture is eroded, resulting in a fundamental mutation in the consciousness of its members, as well as a transformation of its cultural foundation.

These kinds of developments lead to a historically unique vantage point from which to examine the phenomenon of culture. The coexistence of societies in which culturally mediated relationships still predominate, and others where this is no longer the case, offers possibilities of a comparative approach that can enrich our understanding of the implications modern science and technology have on culture and human life. It will offer a key to understanding many of the profound changes in the last half of this century.

While this essay centres on cultures prior to the universalization of modern science and technology, I have in the first chapter elaborated on the historical and social context mentioned above. It joins this essay to forthcoming ones on modern science and technology as integral parts of the first universal subculture and the role it plays in the different cultures and societies currently in existence. They will show how science and technology developed into the larger phenomenon of technique and how technique has taken over a substantial part of the role of culture as social ecology. Yet the role of culture has been so essential in both prehistory and history that this raises some fundamental questions. Can a new civilization emerge which includes technique but is structured on the basis of a culture not permeated by technique? Can a greater distance be created between humanity and technique so that such a civilization can emerge? These are, I believe, the decisive questions of our time with regard to the course human life will take in the decades to come.

The reason for attempting to paint such a vast picture is to make visible some options that may otherwise remain hidden. We appear to be so overwhelmed by the challenges the human race faces that we are increasingly surrendering to the forces of the systems we have created. Our social, economic, political, legal, and religious imagination and creativity seem to be ebbing, to make way for a conservatism on all fronts. Yet it is precisely in the face of considerable problems that we need to gather the moral and religious courage to challenge what appears to be inevitable.

The way a society (or the civilization to which it belongs) meets any challenge depends on what it believes its situation to be. An incorrect perception will almost always lead to a course of action that cannot contribute something decisive. The knowledge base on which our civilization founds its actions is largely built up from research on the frontiers of knowledge. There is only a small contribution from intellectual activities seeking the relationships between the highly specialized knowledge generated by frontier-type research, the implications of these patterns of relationships for human interests, and a unified understanding of our situation. The reason for the imbalance is obvious. No single person has the expertise in all the domains involved in the building of a unified panorama. To attempt such a venture exposes one to being discredited or dismissed because of a misinterpretation of some point. However, in engaging in reflective intellectual work one does not give up the possibility of being scientific. In frontier research, a few experimental points that fall well outside an empirically established relationship can often be attributed to error, and they do not necessarily challenge the newly found correlation. So also in intellectual work one can, by not being a specialist in all fields, be wrong on some points without this necessarily calling the whole panorama into question. Of course, the intellectual-reflective type of research involves a person's stance and commitments to a greater degree than frontier-type research. The present volume and the ones to follow are therefore certainly not the only possible way to paint a picture of our present situation. In mentioning this here, I am inviting the reader to think through his or her commitments and make them an integral part of the dialogue.

I will simply add one personal note. These chapters have their roots in some thinking I began as a graduate student in mechanical engineering. They were developed further during five years of post-doctoral work. As an applied scientist and engineer, I spent this time examining what the social sciences and humanities knew about the roles science and technology play in human life. The guidance of, and dialogue with, Professor Jacques Ellul was invaluable because of his own efforts to gain a unified understanding of these matters as a social scientist. Upon my return to Canada, I continued my research while also teaching courses on the relationship between technology and contemporary society to students in engineering as well as in the social sciences and humanities.

In my research I have become acutely aware of the difficulty of communication between social scientists on the one hand and engineers and natural scientists on the other. Since the purpose of my essays is to stimulate dialogue around one possible unified picture by colleagues and students in all the related disciplines as well as by intellectuals and interested persons outside academia, I have assumed that most of my readers, like myself, will have an expertise in some areas covered by these essays and not in others. The form and style of the essays are therefore designed to facilitate dialogue. My use of the literature in the footnotes, for example, is sometimes illustrative, at other times designed to show that a particular point falls within the accepted spectrum of conflicting theories, or to give the reader not familiar with a particular area an entry point into the literature. In my language I have attempted to recognize the fact that half of the human race are women who should be drawn into these kinds of dialogues to a far greater degree than is currently the case. In all of this I am keenly aware of the fact that both the frontier-type of highly specialized knowledge and the intellectual-reflective kind of knowledge have their unique lacunae. Each can be used to challenge the other. They can also nourish each other by deliberately establishing a dialectical tension between them in one's thinking.

In the course of developing my thoughts during the last ten years, I have been encouraged by many persons. As a graduate student Professor E.L. Holmes was particularly helpful. During my wife's and my stay in France, Professor Jacques Ellul and his wife, Yvette, were an inspiration. Since our return to Canada, on-going contacts and discussions with them are still having a profound influence on my work. At the University of Toronto Professors P.J. Foley, J.M. Ham, M. Wayman, and P.M. Wright continue to be most encouraging. The late Professor J.W. Abrams was, until his untimely death, also most helpful. A very special thanks goes to Professor Ursula M. Franklin for the many ways in which she has encouraged and supported me.

I wish to thank Professor L. Xhignesse and Dr K. Temple for their comments on an earlier version of this manuscript, and my anonymous reviewers for their helpful and encouraging comments. R.I.K. Davidson, of the University of Toronto Press, skilfully guided the manuscript through the system and edited the final version. Of course, my thanks do not mean that the above persons necessarily share the views expressed in this essay, which remains my responsibility.

A special thanks is owing to the staff and volunteers of the Ontario Audio Library Service who recorded a lot of my materials. My research assistants, Monica Franklin and Howard Kwan, also deserve a note of thanks for their special and unique contributions. The response of my students in both engineering and sociology has often given me new courage in my difficult task. Last, but far from least, I wish to thank my wife Rita and our children Esther and David for their understanding. Only other families involved in the writing of a book will fully appreciate what this means.

The research was supported by a NATO Postdoctoral Fellowship and grants from the University of Toronto and the Social Science and Humanities Research Council of Canada. This book has been published with the help of a grant from the Social Science Federation of Canada, using funds provided by the Social Sciences and Humanities Research Council of Canada, and a grant from the Andrew W. Mellon Foundation to the University of Toronto Press.

W.H.V.
January 1985

THE GROWTH OF MINDS AND CULTURES

A UNIFIED THEORY OF THE STRUCTURE OF EXPERIENCE

ONE

Introduction

All through history human groups and societies have interpreted their experiences and shaped the relationships between their members and with the world into a coherent way of life by means of a culture.[1] One of the remarkable things about these cultures is their extraordinary diversity.[2] Apparently the way human beings are linked to reality is genetically determined at birth only to a very limited degree. Whatever determinisms exist are integrated into a culture, with the result that it helps create the roots for the existence of a human group or society in reality. The stability of that existence is assured by building up the foundation beyond the sphere of conscious thought and action in what we will call the metaconscious.[3]

In the twentieth century the diversity of human cultures has shrunk dramatically. There appears to be some phenomenon capable of reaching the roots of traditional cultures in order to transform them in very similar ways. When we search for possible candidates, our attention is soon attracted to science and technology. In the past these elements of human culture did not easily diffuse beyond cultural boundaries and, when they did, they usually underwent some readaptation to another culture. In the present century, however, modern science and technology are increasingly universal. We are witnessing the creation of a knowledge base no longer exclusively linked to any culture, but one that is utilized by a growing number of nations as the basis for a common way of life aimed at economic development. For the first time in human history, all the nations of the world can be classified in terms of their unequal success at achieving a common goal. They are now part of the underdeveloped, developing, or developed nations. The growing importance of computers and the techniques for the accessing, processing, application, and transmission of information will likely reinforce these trends.

We are now able to formulate the basic hypothesis that led to the study of culture presented in this work. Science and technology have become part of a larger phenomenon which increasingly acts as the first universal subculture in human history. As a partial alternative to culture, it affects traditional cultures in their very roots. This situation offers a unique vantage point for the study of culture. Before proceeding, however, we need to make a brief detour to sketch the unique relationship between science, technology, and culture as it has emerged in the twentieth century.

Many aspects of the transformation of the relationships between science, technology, and culture have been studied. It has been noted, for example, that, before a traditional society can take advantage of modern science and technology, it must undergo fundamental changes in its culture and organization.[4] This is evident from the literature on the transfer of technology to Third World societies and indigenous peoples. Some authors have suggested that intermediate or appropriate technologies need to be designed which require fewer and less substantial changes in the recipient cultures.[5] As for those societies already far advanced along the road of economic development, it has been observed that they are taking on very similar socio-economic and political structures.[6] The implications science and technology have for a society are by no means limited to these areas. Typical influences on areas like the arts, language, religion, morality, values, education, leisure, agriculture, and war have also been found.[7] Little work has been done, however, on drawing together the patterns running through these studies in order to establish a theory of modern cultures and their change under the influence of science and technology. Finally, it has also been recognized that science and technology have themselves undergone changes as they began to play new roles within society.[8]

We are thus faced with some important questions. Why are the cultural roles science and technology played in human history so different from their current ones? Why do modern science and technology exhibit a measure of autonomy with respect to human cultures? The answer to these questions lies, we suggested, in the fact that science and technology have become part of a larger phenomenon which they helped to create: what may be called the first universal subculture, in the sense that it is able to interpret experience and establish a network of relationships largely independent from traditional cultures. As such it has helped to create the 'deep structures' for founding a new family of modern societies. While the nature of these societies is still heavily disputed, there is a great deal of agreement on a number of their characteristics.

This universal subculture emerged along with the conviction that the quality of human life can steadily be enhanced by improving the means of our existence. To achieve this goal, every area of life is studied for the purpose of making it function more smoothly and effectively, that is, with greater efficiency and with fewer problems. This takes the form of what will be called the technical operation, comprising the following steps. First, certain aspects of an area of human life are examined in relation to the perceived problem. The results of the study are used to build a model which is, of course, a partial and simplified representation. Next, the model is examined in detail to determine the set of parameters allowing it to function optimally. Finally, on the basis of these findings, the area of human life is reorganized to achieve the highest efficiency demonstrated by the model. The 'one best way' of doing things is thus implemented. In this fashion, technologies have sprung up in virtually every area of human endeavour, including science. The resulting body of knowledge and the techniques for expanding and applying it no longer correspond to what traditionally have been called science and technology. In his work *La Technique ou l'enjeu du siècle*,[9] Jacques Ellul has demonstrated how the technologies, or rather techniques, for achieving the 'one best way' of doing things constitute a new phenomenon he called technique.

The creation of concepts, like technique, to render our world intelligible is absolutely fundamental to human life. Without them we would live our lives on the level of immediate experience the way animals do.[10] The largely artificial urban environment created by science and technology has been made intelligible by means of concepts like the corporation, business, the economy, and the state. In the twentieth century a whole new range of phenomena emerged within this environment such as mass production, mass consumption, leisure, mass media, computers, world wars, an expanding middle class, and so on. At first some of these appeared to be related only superficially, with the result that authors have fairly arbitrarily selected some as characterizing modern societies.

The situation is analogous to the early phases of the so-called Industrial Revolution. As societies began to set out on the road of economic development, many social, economic, political, legal, ideological, and moral changes occurred that appeared to be largely unrelated. They were, however, part of a coherent pattern of change that could be made intelligible by the creation of the concept of capital, although people did this in somewhat different ways depending on their political colours. Capital became the lifeblood of society, and the system it created permeated almost every area of life. In this century, economic development continues to be the goal to which nations aspire, but capital is being displaced as the primary factor of that development. There now exists a new factor that not only structures capital but also the 'deep patterns' of social change. All the new phenomena that arose in the twentieth century directly or indirectly derive from it. By creating the concept of technique, Ellul has sought to demonstrate that what capital was for the nineteenth century, technique is for the twentieth – namely, the key to making a great deal of the world intelligible.

The real significance of the phenomenon of technique for human cultures does not fully come to light until a further stage in its development, namely when it becomes our primary milieu and system.[11] To understand what this means we must break with a well-established mental habit of thinking of technology exclusively in terms of means allowing us to accomplish things that would otherwise be impossible. This is true, of course, but when techniques are the basis for organizing and reorganizing most human activities they not only extend human power but they also become an intermediary between human beings and whatever these techniques are applied to. This is obvious in the case of the telephone mediating between people, or the radio or television mediating between politicians and citizens, between producers and consumers, and between world events and persons. Techniques can also mediate without the use of devices. For example, when techniques of organization are used to have people in a large office work together as efficiently as possible, they also mediate the relationships between them. This mediation is, of course, not total. Spontaneous face-to-face relations based on the personalities and the cultures of the people involved continue to exist.

When techniques so permeate a society that most human relationships are technically mediated, we may speak of technique interposing itself between human beings and the social and natural milieus, thus becoming the primary milieu for human life. As most social relationships in the so-called developed nations are becoming technically mediated, society becomes the secondary milieu. It still exists in those areas of human life which have not been 'technicized' and in the facets of human relationships externalized by the intervention of technique. We are not heading for Mumford's megamachine society[12] nor for Huxley's Brave New World.[13] There, individuals are so totally adjusted to society that they are simply pieces in the social mechanism, but that requires a cultural transformation far more radical than the one we are suggesting.

From the dawn of history until recently, society was the primary human milieu. When it interposed itself between the prehistoric group and nature, the latter became the secondary milieu. Today nature has become the tertiary human milieu in the so-called developed nations. It has slipped far from the centre of human attention to the point that a special effort is required to raise our ecological awareness. There now exists an urgent need to protect and conserve our natural environment.[14]

When techniques permeate the fabric of a society to the point that together they form a milieu, the phenomenon of technique also takes on many of the characteristics of a system. This system is built up from elements taken from nature and society that have been reconstituted by the technical operation. Consequently, so-called developed societies have found a new basis for social cohesion – namely, the system of technique. They depend less and less on the elements of traditional culture, such as institutions, values, morality, and so on. A greater tolerance towards traditional religions and morality in these societies is not the result of these cultures becoming of age but rather the fact that technique has shifted the domain of religion. The traditional means of integrating a society have been largely overshadowed by a new conformity related to the system of technique.

When nature and society constituted the primary milieu and system, they had a profound and unique impact on human life and consciousness. This is not simply because the vast majority of experiences people internalized were related to the primary milieu and system. It is also because a primary milieu and system present a culture with almost everything it needs for its existence as well as with much which threatens that existence. This is obvious for prehistory. When society interposed itself between the small prehistoric group and nature, humanity was better able to defend itself against the dangers associated with the natural milieu. It now provided for its needs through the collectivity of a society with a more or less complex division of labour, but this brought new dangers created by the dependence on the social milieu, such as political instability, economic crises, and war. Today we cannot survive in the urban environment without the complex technical systems providing us with water, food, energy, clothing, transportation, communication, information, social security, and so on, while at the same time technique threatens human survival by furnishing the means for total war or the destruction of the ecosystem.

The introduction of techniques into the cultures of rural or remote societies, indigenous peoples, and the Third World extends the milieu and system of technique. As a result, the integrity of these cultures is threatened because these techniques are not neutral. Thus far they appear to have affected the recipient cultures much more than these cultures were able to adapt them to their own purposes. In the past, the collapse of a culture or civilization did not threaten humanity as a whole. Today, however, there exists a strong tendency for cultural diversity to be reduced as technique spreads across the globe. If the new way of life based on technique would ever collapse, it could lead to an enormous historical tragedy.

From the above quick sketch (which we will elaborate in a later work), it would appear that humanity is on the threshold of a transformation as fundamental as the one marking the transition from prehistory to history. The basic point of departure of our study is now becoming evident. Much of what is currently happening can be interpreted as being related to the interplay between cultures and the first universal subculture. This interplay is bringing to light new aspects of the role culture plays in human life, both individual and collective. In the present work we will examine culture as the social foundation of human existence from our unique historical vantage point. Before proceeding, however, some factors that are likely to colour the panorama need to be examined critically. We must ask ourselves who we are as observers and what kind of intellectual heritage we bring with us to the vantage point. The task is not an easy one because a good deal of this heritage has become an integral part of our being. This makes it all the more important to be critically aware of these limitations. Before undertaking a brief intellectual self-examination in the following sections, the relation of the present study to a larger research project needs to be clarified.

The study of culture presented here evolved as an integral part of a larger study originally aimed at gaining a deeper understanding of modern science and technology and their influence on human life, culture, and society. While it is commonplace to link these activities to social and human progress, the picture that has emerged from careful studies is more ambivalent. The methods currently available to assess the implications of a specific technology or undertaking have significant limitations, but in a society where numerous new technologies and undertakings emerge constantly it is their combined effect that is crucial. This is not simply the sum of the specific effects of each technology or undertaking but a complex non-linear combination of their individual effects[15] which depends on the nature of society, its culture, structure, and institutions as well as its relations with its natural environment and other societies. It is this macro-level of analysis in particular that will allow us to assess the implications for human life. As a result the scope of the study was expanded to the point outlined earlier, namely the interactions between cultures and the first universal subculture of technique.

The complete work is broken down into three parallel but interdependent studies. The first (presented in this book) takes a new look at the process of socialization when children learn to mediate symbolically their relationships with reality on the basis of the culture of their society. It is then possible to examine how a culture creates the social foundation of a society, including the role this foundation plays in the evolution of the society in time. The second study examines professional education as a process of secondary socialization into a community of practitioners, particularly those of science and technology. These communities mediate many of the relationships pertaining to their activities on the basis of unique universal subcultures. Modern science and technology function as a partial alternative to culture in the way they symbolically mediate many of a society's relationships with the social and physical environment. In this capacity they function as integral parts of the first universal subculture of technique.

The possibility of studying science as a kind of culture is implicit in the work of T.S. Kuhn.[16] Every scientific event must be interpreted in the context of a 'paradigm' (what was later called a disciplinary matrix).[17] These paradigms contain many of the same categories of symbolic elements, models, and values found in a culture, but the members of these categories are unique to science and are exclusively acquired by professional education. As a result, this education may be regarded as a process of secondary socialization into the scientific community. The detailed structure of these matrices, and the way they emerge, evolve, and become displaced by others, can be explored further by examining science from the perspective outlined above. This constitutes the first part of the second study.

In the study of technology we encounter a literature with large lacunae. There exists as yet no sociology of modern technology analogous to the sociology of science. Furthermore, the role of 'paradigms' in technology has received relatively little attention. Jacques Ellul, probably more than any other author, has come to terms with the fact that technology has become a part of the phenomenon of technique. He has attributed to technique many characteristics of what we have called a universal subculture. The internal structure and dynamics of technology can be explored further from the perspective outlined earlier, and this will be undertaken in the other part of the second study. Together these parts will constitute the basis for gaining new insight into the structure and dynamics of the new universal subculture of technique.

In the third study we will examine what happens to societies and cultures once technique constitutes a universal subculture within them. The interaction between a culture and the new universal subculture must be examined on a variety of levels. They interact within the minds of professionals, within which the experiences of the secondary process of socialization graft themselves onto, yet do not extend, those of the primary process of socialization into the culture. On the collective planes of analysis the 'paradigms,' social structures, and institutions of the culture and universal subculture interact in ways that are dependent on but not reducible to the interactions in the individual's mind. The fruitfulness of the new theory will be tested by examining its ability to account for the many unique phenomena that have emerged in our time. We will then attempt to develop more comprehensive methodologies for the assessment of the combined effects of technologies and techniques.

The reader should keep this broader context in mind. In the present work, we will be primarily concerned with how human beings individually and collectively symbolically mediate their relationships with reality in the knowledge that technique is transforming this mediation in a profound way.

SCIENCE AND STRUCTURES

Let us begin our study of culture – the symbolic foundation for mediating our relationships with reality – by critically examining some conceptions we have of human life, society and culture. These have been largely shaped by the sciences. The further the social sciences and humanities evolved in the course of their history, the more they subdivided themselves into a host of disciplines each taking charge of examining a particular part of reality. At first sight this may appear as an effective way of subdividing the task of acquiring knowledge about ourselves. If, however, we attempt to piece together their findings into a comprehensive picture of the human phenomenon it is as though we tried to fit together pieces belonging to different jigsaw puzzles. The pieces simply will not fit, and consequently no unified view of human beings, society, and civilization emerges. While there is complementarity of the disciplines in terms of subject area, there is no corresponding complementarity in the contributions they make to a broader understanding of human reality. The situation is similar to the one described by Galileo, who said of the astronomers in his day that they were so 'inconsistent in these (astronomical) investigations that they cannot even explain or observe the constant length of the seasonal year.

With them it is as though the artist were to gather the hands, feet, head and other members for his images from diverse models, each part excellently drawn but not related to a single body, and since they in no way match each other the result would be monster rather than man.'[18]

There are many reasons for this dilemma. We shall examine only a few to illustrate the fragmented picture the sciences have drawn of the human phenomenon. The first reason for the absence of such a view lies in the scientific method itself. Descartes set out a number of rules for scientific inquiry which capture the thrust of the scientific method rather well. He wrote: 'In our search for the direct road towards truth we should busy ourselves with no object about which we cannot attain a certainty equal to that of the demonstrations of arithmetic and geometry.'[19] Another rule for the method of reason was to 'reduce involved and obscure propositions step by step to those that are simpler, and then, starting with the intuitive apprehension of all those that are absolutely simple, attempt to ascend to all knowledge of all others by precisely similar steps.'[20] Implicit in these rules is the belief that the nature of reality must be such that these rules will not distort or mask parts of reality. Consequently they ought to lead to an ever more detailed and accurate uncovering of the structure of reality. This is so only if everything is ultimately controllable, measurable, repeatable, and predictable. If that is the case it ought to be possible to conceive everything in mechanistic terms.[21] The subjectivity of human beings and the unpredictability of life were to be eliminated from scientific consideration. By dismissing the subjective, the qualitative, and the unmeasurable, everything in human experience was either deformed or improverished to fit the mechanistic conception of reality.

All human functions became interpreted in mechanistic terms: the human body operated on the basis of biochemical mechanisms, human behaviour could be explained by the mechanistic stimulus-response model, and meaning became replaced by conditioned response, the nervous system became a telephone system with the brain functioning as its exchange, and so on. Mankind had come into existence by mindless evolution, that is, by chance and blind mechanisms of natural selection. In this mechanistic conception of human beings, it was quite possible to take the 'machine' analytically apart and put it back together again without any loss of information. Any whole was nothing more than the sum of its parts. The various branches of science could isolate the different kinds of mechanisms and study them apart from the whole without the loss of any essential information. In fact, there were no organized wholes in this scientific universe because every complex constituent and phenomenon could be reduced to elementary building blocks. In this universe there existed no meaning or purpose, no fear, joy, wisdom, wonder, anxiety, no hope in the face of life and death, no personality, and no ethical or spiritual dimensions.

While the highly simplistic mechanistic views and theories have long been rejected, their rationalistic and reductionistic orientation has lived on, and this maintains the kind of dilemma described earlier. The lack of external compatibility in the theories of the scientific disciplines dealing with the many aspects of the human phenomenon reflects the fact that in the process of abstraction and reduction important information was lost. This information, even if it were available, could not simply be added on to the existing theories however, for reasons that have to do with the nature of reality frequently expressed in the maxim: the whole is more than the sum of its parts.

The lack of an external consistency of scientific theories, particularly of the various branches of the social sciences and humanities, is to a considerable measure due to their inability to achieve even internal consistency. Unlike the physical sciences, competing schools of thought continue to exist.[22] Competing schools approach the same part of reality in compatible ways, and consequently develop incompatible views and theories of reality. One of the great hopes that people had, particularly during the period of the birth of modern science and a hope which still lives on in the hearts of some, now appears dashed to pieces.[23] This hope was born during the time of the heated debates and wars related to the Reformation and Counter-Reformation when the promise of modern science and the mechanistic world view underlying it appeared extraordinarily seductive. Science would retain only those parts of the human experience of reality that could be shared by all, because what would be retained as scientific knowledge could be verified by everyone simply by repeating the experiments. Hence the new scientific world view would not be socially divisive like the older religious world views because it would eventually eliminate all speculative knowledge that could not be verified and which consequently divided humanity in irreconcilable ways. The persistence of competing schools of thought within many branches of the social sciences and humanities is the most obvious manifestation of the inability of modern science to speak with one objective voice acceptable and convincing to all. Apparently the nature of human reality is not as mechanistic as originally believed, and it certainly does not lend itself to experimental investigations the way physical reality does. It should be emphasized that we are not saying that modern science lacks all unity. We are merely pointing out that its findings cannot easily be pieced together into a coherent view of human reality. Science does have an underlying unity, but it will be found in a somewhat different place from where the philosophy of science has looked for it.

Another reason for the fragmented view of the human phenomenon has its roots in the time of the Industrial Revolution. Before the nineteenth century, the concept of culture as we know it was non-existent. It came about for two reasons: 1) to make a distinction between the intellectual, literary, and artistic (i.e., the cultural) domain and the rest of life; and 2) to reduce the significance of the cultural with respect to 'serious' matters like business, money, the economy, the organization of society, and so on.[24] The cultural domain might help people to reflect occasionally about the larger questions of life and death, but such thoughts and feelings are usually fleeting. As such, culture became a kind of extra and even something superfluous. The message of culture and, in particular, the disturbing indications voiced by art and literature about the new human venture based on industrialization and economic development taking shape during the eighteenth and nineteenth centuries[25] could now be assimilated by society at large. After all, art now became only art and theatre only theatre. They had little or nothing to do with the part of life which really mattered. This was the time when museums and libraries became established, which institutionalized the separation between culture and 'real' life.

The division between the 'useful' and 'essential' on the one side and the 'extra' and 'superfluous' on the other deeply affected the evolution of the sciences. During the early stages of the Industrial Revolution science fell between the two domains. Although its potential technical usefulness was recognized, it did not begin to have a significant effect on technological and industrial development until the latter part of the nineteenth century. Then, beginning with the physical sciences and soon followed by the social sciences, certain branches of science found direct applications in one or another aspect of industrial society, thus entering into the mainstream of life, while others remained on the outskirts. The consequences for the development of science were considerable, but they hardly contributed to making the findings of the various branches of science both internally and externally consistent with one another. It may well be, for example, that certain branches of psychology have contributed greatly to influencing consumer behaviour, but that is not a criterion for evaluating their scientific merit. Yet their funding has often been more influenced by their practical value, their ability to solve commercial, industrial, and military problems than by their contribution to science, and this leads to serious distortions in the development of science. A science has to develop with a measure of autonomy with respect to the vested interests and the exercise of power in a society.

We shall consider one more factor related to the fragmentation of science. A highly subdivided and specialized science is not very responsive to those changes in human reality whose scope transcends the boundaries of a great many disciplines. The reason for this is that the study of these changes would require the collaboration of many scientific disciplines, which is difficult if not impossible owing to their lack of internal and external compatibility. The interdependence between those disciplines changes because of a change in reality. This is not a serious problem for the physical sciences, but it it for the social sciences and humanities. An excellent example is the rise of modern science and technology. There is a widespread recognition that science and technology have permeated almost all aspects of the so-called industrially advanced nations. On the basis of their daily-life experience most people seem to recognize that a concept like industrial society corresponds to something more than just any type of society with a modern industry superimposed on it. Yet there is a great deal of evidence suggesting that this is not reflected in most of the paradigms underlying the scientific disciplines. The social sciences and humanities appear to be able to study the many changes in society and human life with only a casual reference to science and technology, while the physical and applied sciences generally treat their social implications as an afterthought. The following typical experiences of university students bear this out.[26]

It is all too common that engineering students, who as part of their curriculum take a number of courses outside their faculties, do not find this a very relevant experience. While these feelings are no doubt in part due to traditional prejudices against these 'cultural' courses, they can hardly be explained by this. After all, since it is generally recognized that many aspects of our world have been permeated by science and technology, it surely ought to be easy to convince these students that the social sciences and humanities are absolutely essential in helping engineers understand the interactions between technology and society. Despite a growing effort to develop the ability of engineering students to take into account human and social factors in their design work, they continue to fail to see the relevance of many of their non-technical electives. The answer to this paradox lies in the fact that by and large the social sciences and humanities do not as yet consider science and technology as major phenomena affecting the parts of reality which constitute their fields of study. They present the engineering students with views of parts of reality in which science and technology do not play the roles the students think they play; hence these students are presented with fragments from a different world. Regardless of whether the students' view of the world is correct or not, they are unable to integrate these fragments into their world, and as a result these subjects are neither meaningful nor relevant in their eyes.

The situation is not limited to engineering students, however. Students in the social sciences and humanities face the mirror image of the above problem. To them the internal functioning of science and technology is largely a mystery because in general there are few, if any, courses dealing with this subject. This makes it very difficult for them to understand how science and technology have affected the social, economic, political, juridical, religious, moral, and cultural structures of traditional societies, completely transforming them. The result is once again that many of the disciplines in the social sciences and humanities paint pictures of parts of reality in which science and technology play roles that do not correspond to the students' daily-life experience or to the impressions of the world that these students derive from their newspapers and television sets, be they correct or not. They must reconcile this conflict by deciding that either science and technology are simply not as important as some say they are or that much of their course work is simply irrelevant and meaningless.

It is clear that when these students take up their professions they carry these problems with them, with the result that the situation in the university is paradigmatic for the intellectual, scientific, and technical communities as a whole. This situation not only makes it difficult for the industrially advanced nations to effectively meet their challenges, most of which are directly or indirectly related to the way science and technology have permeated them, but it also bars the way to a unified view of ourselves, culture, and society. Yet without such a view we have no points of reference to understand and evaluate the world in which we live, to set a course of action for the future and to live meaningful and responsible lives, being as fully conscious as possible of the reality that surrounds us.

Without going into a detailed analysis of the structure of science, it would appear that the paradigms underlying the scientific disciplines do not imply models of the human phenomenon that are all parts of a larger whole. For example, they implicitly treat economic or social phenomena as manifestations of economic or social mechanisms that are parts of the social machine. A unified science can come into existence only when economic or social phenomena are treated as *dimensions* of the way the members of a society shape their relationships with one another and their environment by means of a culture. This is not a mere play on words. To use a current analogy to be discussed later in this chapter, the paradigms underlying scientific disciplines should ideally be interrelated in the way different areas of a hologram are. Unlike a regular photograph, each area of the hologram contains information about the entire image of the object recorded on it.

The current state of affairs in the sciences with respect to the human phenomenon may be summed up as follows. The mechanistic world view has brought us to a new Tower of Babel. The sciences have failed to build the 'tower of truth' capable of orienting all of humanity. The specialists of different disciplines no longer understand one another very well. Since they consciously and metaconsciously operate on the basis of incompatible paradigms, what is a fact for one specialist is not necessarily a fact for another because facts derive their status from a paradigm. When a paradigm changes, a fact comes to stand in a new context, resulting in its transformation or even elimination.

The point of departure for our study of culture does not lie in the rejection of the sciences, however. On the contrary. A part of our new vantage point is constituted by the current state of affairs in the sciences. We need to recognize that we cannot piece together a theory of culture by fitting together the pieces of the puzzle currently at hand in the sciences. In many cases these pieces must be reshaped and restructured by re-examining a portion of reality in relation to the macro-level views emerging from those pieces already fitted together. In some cases detailed and specialized micro-level analyses may lead to the conclusion that the way the previously considered pieces were fitted together is incorrect and that the process must be started anew. The process must continue to minimize the kind of situation described above by Galileo. The shape and structure of each piece of the puzzle must be compatible with the whole, and the structure of the whole must be compatible with each of the pieces. Because the reality to be depicted by the puzzle pieces changes constantly, this will be a never-ending process, to which we can make only a small contribution, provided we remain critical of our paradigms.

SYSTEMS AND REALITY

Our perception of the world is probably most characterized by the fact that it is difficult if not impossible for us to think of something that exists which is not conceived of as a system or part of a larger system. The universe is now conceived as a system of galaxies containing many solar systems which are systems of suns, moons, stars and planets, constituted in their turn of other systems. The chain can be continued almost indefinitely. At its other end we find molecules which are systems of atoms, while atoms are systems of subatomic particles which may well prove to be systems of still more elementary constituents. On our planet mankind is a part of the ecological system. Mankind itself is a system of civilizations composed of societies which are systems of human individuals. All the higher forms of life are composed of systems of organs, themselves constituted by systems of tissues made up of systems of cells, which in their turn are systems of molecules. Outside the natural world we encounter road and communication systems, computer systems, weapon systems, energy systems, administrative systems, and so on. We could go on multiplying the examples indefinitely. The entire reality as we know it is conceptualized as systems and organized wholes.

All this may appear so self-evident to us that we are led to ask the following questions. Why has this concept of system emerged only so recently in history? How can it symbolize a common aspect of all the different constituents of the universe? Is not the meaning of a concept, claiming to symbolize such an enormous diversity of structures, so broad that it is utterly vague and lacking real substance? Answers to these questions can be found by analysing some elements of our intellectual and cultural heritage in order to determine the context in which the concept of system arose and the reasons for its coming into existence. The meaning of the concept of system, which is fundamental for the present work, can then be clarified.

This concept of system becomes commonplace when Western civilization encounters certain practical and intellectual difficulties. To understand them we go back to the mechanistic world view mentioned above and consider its function not only in science but in Western civilization as a whole.

As we shall examine later in some detail, the world view of a civilization evolves by a process in which it conditions and is conditioned by the experience of reality resulting from a variety of human activities. In these daily-life activities, the members of a civilization impose their intentions and expectations on reality, which in turn impinges on their activities. A world view of a civilization, therefore, implies what might be called a project of existence: the way a society orients its life in reality, complete with an interpretation of the past and hopes for the future. It includes a unique mode of thinking, feeling, and intuiting, in short, a mode of internalizing reality, of acting on it and existing in it. It goes much deeper, therefore, than a philosophy or a Weltanschauung.

The mechanistic world view and the corresponding project of existence came out of the collapse of the medieval world view and its project of existence. The mechanistic view and project of existence presupposed Greek science and the desacralization of nature accomplished by Christianity. Furthermore, they learned from the implications of the failure of medieval civilization to reconcile what it considered to be the three perfections – namely; Christian revelation, Greek philosophy, and Roman law – and from the failure of scholasticism and alchemy (particularly the branch preoccupied with finding the philosopher's stone and the liberation of spirit from matter). The universe was considered to be free from gods and spirits. What a splendid liberation it seemed after a period of wandering in intellectual dead ends! No longer were people dependent on unreliable deities or magical techniques to gain control over what escaped them. Things were now up to man. Ahead was a brilliant future. By means of science everything could be explained and by applying this knowledge, the human situation could be improved. Who would doubt that, when the choices for the future could be rationally and clearly set out, society would not choose good over evil? Man's rational faculty would no longer be impeded by beliefs and religious constraints and he would be the better for it. Progress in all human endeavours could reasonably be expected. There was nothing anyone could think of that could stop material and moral progress. This was the deeply rooted conviction underlying the new project of existence and it gave people new hope and courage to make history. To be sure, what was considered as self-evident at the time did not materialize, as we know from the historical developments that followed.

The universe, desacralized and freed from gods and spirits, became nothing but matter. Its regularity could no longer be disturbed and consequently could be expressed in terms of laws of nature. It was depicted as a gigantic mechanism or clock with God as the great clockmaker who had created it and set it in motion. This paved the way for a whole new way for mankind to relate to reality. Since all the parts of the clock were constituted of basic corpuscles, a concept like system as we have described it was entirely unnecessary. Everything could be understood by resolving it into components involving only the characteristics, motion, and interactions of the corpuscles. People could decompose and recompose the world without any loss of information and without any risks, precisely because no systems or organized wholes had a place in the mechanistic world view. Whatever existed was nothing more than the sum of its parts related by simple causal relationships. Life was reduced to the rational, which affected all spheres of human activities. The road to the development of modern science and technology had been opened up.

The new project of existence emerging out of the ruins of the medieval one produced and was in turn affected by the scientific and industrial revolutions. Eventually a number of internal contradictions arose in the new project of existence, which in our age necessitates a certain transformation. The emergence of the concept of system is a signpost of these developments.[27]

We shall briefly sketch a few of these contradictions. The basic strategy of the sciences had been to reduce all things to their basic elements, in order to discover the universal laws that determine how they combined to produce the things and phenomena being studied. Physics pioneered the strategy and consequently became the model for the other sciences. In physics the search for basic corpuscles seemed to be endless. Each time a group of particles was thought to be the basic building blocks of the universe it was discovered some time later that in fact they themselves were constituted of a number of still more basic particles. The atom, once held to be the most elementary particle of the universe, was later found to be composed of an endlessly growing number of subatomic particles – and there is no reason to assume that the end is in sight. It appears therefore that there are no elementary particles but only temporary limits to how far we are able to investigate subatomic structures. It is more appropriate, therefore, to think of matter in terms of structure and organization than in terms of basic building blocks, in particular when the very concept of particles has become related to the concept of waves.

Similarly, in biology the search for a basic type of living material took an unexpected turn. At one time the basic element was the organism, at another time the cell, and recently certain molecules. In the course of this search it became clear that life had more to do with a unique organization of molecules, as in the cell for example, than with a basic living matter. In sociology society turned out to be more than the sum of its members, and here also the emphasis shifted to social organization and structure. In linguistics structuralism replaced the attempts to explain language on the basis of fundamental building blocks like phonemes. In psychology Gestalt theories opposed reductionism. Structuralism as it exists in the many branches of the social sciences and humanities is an attempt to overcome the limitations of reductionism; hence it is analogous to the systems theory approach in this respect.

Everything has become organization: atoms, molecules, life, society, the solar system, and so on. This shift in emphasis has brought about a methodological problem that is becoming increasingly evident in the sciences. The mechanistic view of reality implied in classical science was that of a diversity of objects in a neutral space. Any object could therefore be isolated from its environment without fundamentally affecting it, and the better one was able to do this the more accurately it could be examined. When an object becomes a part of an organization, however, it can still be isolated, but this process means a limited break-up of the organization. This affects both the object and the organization. The process of abstracting or isolating an object that is part of an organization becomes indissociable from a process of partial disorganization and loss of information. In this sense classical objects no longer exist. Take nuclear physics as an example. Subatomic particles can no longer be determined in space and time, and they interact with the observer. They are both particle and wave and no longer elementary corpuscles. The properties of an atom cannot be explained by the characteristics of its subatomic particles determined by isolating these particles as much as possible. An atom is now seen as an organized whole since the subatomic particles have the traits of the whole more than that the whole has the properties of the subatomic particles. This subtle but fundamental shift in emphasis renders traditional methodology problematic and makes less certain the meaning of the experimental results obtained by it.

The example we have drawn from nuclear physics is paradigmatic of developments in all branches of science. What was possible in the mechanistic world view is now recognized to be problematic. The whole can no longer be known from the parts nor can its behaviour and characteristics be deduced from that of the parts. Since the whole has ceased to be the sum of its parts it can no longer be measured and predicted from them. The parts are now seen as being comprehensible only in terms of the organized whole. This whole is seen as a configuration, a pattern, a Gestalt, or a system, which implies that the parts arrange themselves into a harmonious order, purpose, plan, or organization, and that any changes in the whole must be considered in those terms. We speak of growth, development, or adaptation of the whole, which implies that a whole can maintain its basic character by means of self-regulation and control. In many cases the whole becomes purely qualitative and unmeasurable. Although conceptually the sciences are moving away from the simple mechanistic view of the universe,[28] whenever quantitative measures are sought there is a strong tendency to fall back on the mechanistic heritage.

We have already noted that the impact of the mechanistic world view was not limited to science but that it accompanied a way of relating to and existing in the social and natural environments – in short, a new project of existence. In the daily-life activities that helped make up this new project of existence in the West, certain difficulties arose calling for a different approach. The concept of system may again be regarded as a kind of signpost of these transformations. In traditional societies the scope and power of human actions was on the whole very limited and localized. Consequently they did not generally interact with one another in a substantial way. When science and technology caused a significant increase in the scope and power of human activities, societies became less local. This process began with the industrial mode of production, which ceased to produce merely to satisfy local needs, thus necessitating a series of adjustments to the structure of society. Traditional societies were transformed into industrial societies in which the consequences of economic activities increasingly interacted. A growing number of domains had to be organized and co-ordinated. New problems arose, requiring a kind of systems approach. We shall give a few examples.

When a region has relatively few roads, a new road can be planned on its own. Its location can be selected to serve as many people as possible for an acceptable cost. Its required traffic capacity can then be estimated and its design undertaken. As the road density in the region increases, however, matters change. A new road is no longer only a means to make a part of the region accessible. For example, one of its selections may become a bypass for several existing roads that have too many intersections or that pass through a village. The new road will affect the traffic density on existing roads and its own traffic density will depend on the other roads. The new road must be planned and designed in relation to others so that together they form a coherent whole that we call a road system. Matters may be taken a step further when the road system is co-ordinated with railroad and waterway systems. Each constituent of these systems is no longer viewed only as a new road, a new railroad line, or a new canal but as a link in the transportation system, and this will fundamentally affect its planned location, capacity, time of construction, and so on.

The number of spheres of activity in which the state exercises some form of co-ordination and control has expanded considerably in the industrially advanced nations during the past fifty years. As a result a number of the state's functions began to interact. Unacceptable gaps appeared between them, they overlapped and even contradicted each other, with the result that the state had increasingly to co-ordinate all its functions by making each one a part of an administrative system. As computers became capable of handling a growing diversity of tasks, that is, as the number of components and the density and complexity of their interactions increased, computers became generally referred to as computer systems.

The understanding of many problems we face today requires a kind of systems approach. The impact of our activities on the natural environment has deepened our awareness that it is an organized whole, now known as the ecological system. The whole debate over ecology is centred on the problem of how far we can go with our activities before the disorganization of the ecological system becomes irreversible. Possibly the least disputed aspect of the report, *The Limits to Growth*[29] prepared under the sponsorship of the Club of Rome, was to demonstrate the interdependence of what were considered as the major challenges to humanity (population expansion, depletion of raw materials, pollution, and a potentially inadequate agricultural production). Consequently these require a systems approach for their study. Vacca[30] has shown how the population of our world, by large and interdependent systems for communication, transportation, energy, production, administration, water supply, and so on, entails a considerable risk, particularly for the 'industrially advanced' nations.

The developments are the same in all the above examples. As the scope and power of human activities in a specific sphere expand they form a complex network of interactions. The same holds true for the products of these activities. The result is that each activity or product of that activity depends on all the others, to which they are either directly or indirectly related. At this point their individual characteristics are transformed by becoming a part of a system. We are obliged to reckon with this new reality in whatever we do. We are building a world in which everything is increasingly organized, a world populated with man-made systems.

It is now becoming clear that the concept of system symbolizes a mode of perceiving, intuiting, and thinkng, that is, a mode of internalizing reality which conditions and is conditioned by a way of acting on it. Terms like systems thinking and systems analysis, systems design and engineering, symbolize this in one domain. Reality is now conceived of as an enormous diversity of constituents forming the nodes in a gigantic network of criss-crossing and overlapping relationships of many different kinds. Each constituent of the network can itself be regarded as a network of more elementary constituents. In their turn these constituents can be thought of as being composed of still more elementary constituents, and the only limit to this chain appears to be our scientific and technical capabilities to look deeper into reality.

We should not, however, extrapolate this view too far and conclude that in the final analysis there are only relationships and their structures. The growth of scientific knowledge is non-cumulative, as Kuhn[31] has shown. Hence, as we discover more relationships, they do not simply increase our knowledge of reality. From time to time qualitative changes occur in how reality is conceived, such as the shift from a Newtonian to an Einsteinian view of the physical world. We can conclude, however, that the concept of system is a signpost of a shift away from an atomistic view of the world towards a view emphasizing the interconnectedness of reality. It is not a shift away from a mechanistic world view, but only a shift to a more sophisticated version. As machines became partly self-regulating and were interconnected into systems controlled by computers, reality was also viewed in terms of more sophisticated mechanistic models.

To emphasize the interconnectedness of reality has a number of important implications. In the present work what we perceive as organized wholes are open systems[32] of constituents organized in such a way that they interact and depend more on each other than on the constituents in the remainder of the network of reality, which we shall call the environment. The result is that these open systems behave as single entities in relation to their environments, from which they can be distinguished by their unique phenomenal qualities. These systems attempt to maintain a continuity of identity by resisting disturbances originating from within or without by means of processes of self-regulation and control. Their internal organization is such that a change in one of its constituents affects at least some of the others as well as the whole, while a change in the whole affects the constituent elements. The first implication of considering a particular part of an interconnected reality as an organized whole is that it requires a process of abstracting it out of its environment to which it is related. This involves, at the very minimum, a certain disorganization and reorganization of reality in the mind of the observer, but often also a process of materially disconnecting the part from its environment to reconnect it into a more controlled environment. The process of abstraction therefore implies a certain loss of information.

A second implication is that what an observer takes to be a system distinct from the remainder of reality depends (as we shall examine later in detail) on his culture, training, interests, past experience (i.e., the mental means he has), as well as any external means used to observe and act on reality (i.e., telescopes, electron microscopes, stethoscopes, geiger counters, and so on). The organized wholes experienced by the operator of an electron microscope, for example, are not the same as those experienced with the naked eye, and what the operator can observe with such an instrument depends on his training and prior experience. We must therefore transcend the materialist, idealist, and positivist orientations, since an organized whole perceived by a person is the result of the interaction between what reality is like, the mental structures of the observer acquired from prior experience, and the means employed for observation.

Since any system abstracted from reality is a part of larger systems and is composed of elements which themselves are systems, there is a third implication of emphasizing the interrelatedness of reality. The network of reality can be analysed on various levels, such as that of astronomy, ecology, sociology, psychology, microbiology, chemistry, nuclear physics, and so on. No level of analysis is independent from the others, but neither is it reducible to them. Furthermore, since we by thought and actions create, discover, alter, and destroy constituents in the network of our experience, no analysis of any level is ever complete.

THE ORGANIZED WHOLE

What we have sought to demonstrate is that the concept of system in effect marks a profound reorientation of Western cultures in conceptualizing and dealing with reality. This was reflected in the sciences where concepts like system and structure are signposts of a shift from the first generation of mechanistic world views to a second one based on what might be called a mechanistic holism.[33] Reality is now implicitly considered as a gigantic open system composed of systems, themselves composed of systems. While it is generally recognized that the whole is more than the sum of the parts, reality continues to be conceptualized in mechanistic terms. If we are sensitive to the negative implications this has, it may be tempting to brush our intellectual heritage aside in order to start something fundamentally new or to plunge into some form of mysticism. I do not believe this is possible, however. We have internalized so much of our culture and intellectual tradition that they are an integral part of our being. This does not mean we are trapped in our past, but that genuine change does not come from pretending that a part of ourselves does not exist. In our case genuine change can only come from critically facing the situation to determine how we can go beyond our mechanistic heritage.[34]

The course of action proposed here is no different from the way specific scientific disciplines develop. When the practitioners of a discipline encounter a phenomenon which cannot be explained by their paradigm, they do not throw up their hands in despair and reject their past. Rather, they attempt to make sense of the situation by facing it, and in doing so they implicitly arrive at a new paradigm. We will similarly try to go beyond the second generation of mechanistic world views by describing how one of its central concepts – namely, that of an organized whole – may be used to analyse a reality conceived in terms of interrelated wholes. We will then evaluate this intellectual instrument and seek to transform it in order to overcome its shortcomings.

Since reality now again appears as an interrelated whole[35] of which we can study only a limited part at a time, it follows that we are obliged to at least mentally abstract and often materially isolate a part of reality. In either case the order of complexity is reduced by a process of disorganization, implying a loss of information. This loss is reduced to a minimum when the part of reality to be studied corresponds to an organized whole having a phenomenal autonomy with respect to its environment. Since reality as it is known at this point is perceived as a set of interacting organized wholes on many different levels, the first step on the road of acquiring knowledge about reality involves the art of effectively subdividing the world. Once an organized whole has been selected for study three frames of reference can be used.

The first is that of an observer who places himself outside of an organized whole to study its overall qualities. In some cases this frame of reference can, of course, only be adopted by a process of abstraction. We are as yet unable to observe the solar system from without, neither can we observe a society as a whole. In either case we are nevertheless able to say a number of things about their overall qualities. The qualities of an organized whole are fundamentally different from those of its components or individuals in isolation from one another. Their organization into a whole causes entirely new overall qualities to emerge. Several examples can be given. Water has different qualities from its components, hydrogen and oxygen, which in isolation from each other in the same environment exist as gases. A group of office workers organized to perform a range of tasks by the usual specialization and hierarchization has the qualities of a collective worker, which are quite different from those of a single individual attempting to perform the same tasks. Similarly, a mob has entirely different qualities from those of the same individuals when isolated from each other in daily life.

All of this is usually expressed by the maxim that the whole is more than the sum of the parts. A first frame of reference – looking from the outside – reveals one dimension of an organized whole, namely the qualities that emerge when the components or individuals are arranged in a network of relationships so that together they are more than they would be in isolation from each other. Each component or individual is enriched in some respect by being a part of the whole. The maxim is only one side of the coin, however, since a whole also places some constraints on the components or individuals to prevent itself from breaking up. The first frame of reference must therefore be complemented by others. It reveals only the phenomenal dimension of an organized whole, that is, its extraverted nature turned to its environment. It reveals little about its internal nature.

To use only this first frame of reference gives only a partial understanding of the whole being studied. For example, the organization of a centralized state in ancient Babylon, Egypt, or Rome gave these societies new overall qualities. Some of these qualities permitted them to face certain challenges more effectively and as such aided their citizens. Inextricably bound up with these new characteristics, however, were new forms of repression of both their own citizens and other peoples. In Egypt and Babylon the state organized large-scale irrigation projects to improve food production and liberated a part of its population for other occupations, but it also led to the organization of large human war-machines that conquered other peoples and administrations that oppressed entire sectors of these societies. A study of the new qualities that emerged in these societies must be accompanied by a study of the changes in their internal structures, the impact they had on the people and the people on them.

To examine the internal nature of an organized whole, a second frame of reference is required which places an observer within it. There are many cases in which an observer can achieve this only by means of special instruments that directly extend his senses or do so indirectly because their output can be given a phenomenal interpretation by means of a theory. In other cases it can be achieved only by a process of abstraction and imagination when, for example, we try to picture what the daily life of a member of a past society was like. This second frame of reference permits the study of the structural dimension of an organized whole: how the structure uses the phenomenal qualities of the components or individuals, how the components or individuals interact, how these interactions affect the whole, how the whole affects these interactions, and how the whole maintains its basic structure by making itself partially inert to some influences of its environment and utilizing others by means of self-regulation and control involving both internal and external relationships. The basic types of relationships between the components or individuals are: rigid interdependence, reciprocal interaction, relations via shared constituents, feedback, and communication of information. These relationships exploiting the phenomenal qualities of the components or individuals are interrelated into a structure by means of organization.

The phenomenal dimension examined by means of the first frame of reference is complemented by the structural dimension studied by the present frame of reference. The former reveals the unity an organized whole exhibits in its relations with the environment; the latter shows the structured internal diversity of components or individuals and their interrelationships, which leads to that phenomenal unity. Each dimension is irreducible to the other. The phenomenal dimension is a function of both the structural dimension and the environment. The more complex an organized whole is, the greater are its degrees of freedom, and hence the greater is the distance between the phenomenal and structural dimensions. The structure may permit the occurrence of an enormous diversity of phenomena which, owing to the complexity of the organized whole, cannot be related to external events by a chain of causal relationships. In many highly complex organized wholes there may be a nearly complete separation of the phenomenal and structural dimensions. For example, a human individual acts without knowing what his organs, tissues, or cells are doing while at the same time the cells, tissues, and organs do not know what the person does. A citizen can act without knowing what his society does via the intermediary of the state while the state can act without knowing what all its citizens are doing.

A third frame of reference is required to study the organizational dimension of a whole. This dimension concerns the pattern of interrelationships between the components or individuals. To observe different aspects of this pattern the components or individuals are isolated from each other by placing them in an environment to which they are as inert as possible in order to permit an observer to study their overall qualities. By comparing them to the qualities the same components or individuals have within the organized whole an important aspect of organization emerges – namely, the transformation the components or individuals undergo by virtue of being incorporated into the whole. For example, a child who has spent a crucial part of his life outside human society does not have any of the typical human qualities. We will later examine how people living in societies organized by cultures are transformed from 'natural' into 'artificial' beings. In other words, organization brings about a transformation of the components or individuals. It employs certain qualities and suppresses others. The components or individuals gain some properties when they are organized into a whole but they lose others. Organization is a process that transforms diversity into unity and maintains a balance between the two. Too great a diversity would make unity impossible, while too rigid a unity would eliminate the diversity necessary for the new qualities of the whole to emerge. There is no creation of new unity without diversity, for if all the components or individuals were identical no new organized wholes could emerge.

If a diversity within the unity of an organized whole is not to deteriorate into a homogeneity, the relationship between the components or individuals must be complementary in some respects and antagonistic in others. They must attract in some respects and repel in others. Organization must transform their qualities in such a way that their diversity reinforces unity and their antagonisms strengthen complementarity. It does so by interrelating the components or individuals in a pattern that exploits some of their qualities and minimizes or suppresses others. In an organized whole complementarity is indissociable from antagonisms just as diversity is indissociable from unity. Organization creates both complementarity and antagonisms, and diversity within unity. It must maintain the balance between complementarity and antagonisms on the level of the relationships between components or individuals and also maintain the balance between diversity and unity on the level of the whole. On each level a disturbance of this balance can be exploited for the purpose of self-regulation and control. In other words, organization in permitting some patterns of interaction and in eliminating others creates both order and latent disorder. Disorder is frequently used for self-regulation by means of negative feedback. In these cases disorder actively contributes to the maintenance of the phenomenal and structural character of the organized whole because the organization permits a limited amount of disorder for self-regulation and control, which is the case in living beings. Since, in creating the order that characterizes a whole, organization also creates disorder, all organized wholes can disintegrate and consequently enter into time. Death can come naturally for living beings since all life carries within it latent death.

Some care should be taken not to 'absolutize' the meaning of the concepts of order, disorder, unity, diversity, complementarity, and antagonism. We have used these concepts within specific frames of reference associated with an organized whole. Since this whole is a part of a larger whole and since its components or individuals are also organized wholes, a specific quality or phenomenon can be one thing within one frame of reference and the opposite in another. Consider a group of workers organized around an assembly line. The fact that each worker is able to do far more than the set of simple operations he is charged with is a potential source of disorder from the point of view of the whole organized for the purpose of manufacture, while from the point of view of the human individual this ability is at the heart of human life. Friction is a quality of the components of a motor that its design seeks to minimize, while the design of a brake exploits it as much as possible.

The dialectical tension that we have shown to exist in an organized whole between unity and diversity, between complementarity and antagonism, and between order and disorder shows the other side of the maxim that a whole is more than the sum of its parts. The maxim is true in the sense that organization exploits certain qualities of components or individuals by connecting them in complementary relationships. However, in the sense that organization also suppresses certain qualities of the components or individuals, the sum of the parts is more than the whole. A society enriches the lives of its members but it also represses some of their qualities. The rationalization of work by subdividing it into specialized tasks and hierarchizing these tasks together with the people assigned to them creates an organized whole which behaves as a collective worker. One of the new qualities that emerges is that it can perform more work than if each of its individuals worked in isolation from the others, that is, without the intervention of the process of organization. Each individual in the organized whole gains in efficiency by suppressing many of his other qualities. This is the case for assembly-line work, large administrative systems, and teams of professionals who have received a highly advanced and specialized education. The hierarchization and specialization of work also produces antagonisms between individuals because of the suppression of a great many of their qualities in these organized wholes.

The second and third frames of reference together reveal the constraints an organized whole imposes on its components or individuals – the constraints due to their interdependence and the constraints they impose on the whole. These are the internal sources of potential disorganization. These frames of reference reveal the tensions between complementarity and antagonisms, order and disorder, and unity and diversity, which help constitute the organizational dimension of a whole.

The three frames of reference permit an observer to analyse the phenomenal, structural, and organizational dimensions of an organized whole, which are each complementary and irreducible to the other two. They are all necessary if a fairly complete picture of an organized whole is to be obtained. Together they provide us with insight into: 1) why the constituents or individuals of an organized whole interact with and depend on each other more than on the constituents and individuals in the system's environment, 2) how the whole is affected by the constituents or individuals and how they in turn affect the whole, 3) why the evolution of an organized whole in time is never cyclic, and 4) how an organized whole is able to relate to other systems in its environment and maintain its identity.

The information obtained about an organized whole by means of the above three frames of reference by no means exhausts what can be known about a part of reality. The analysis must be continued in two directions. In the first, we keep on repeating the same type of analysis but each time apply it to the next larger organized whole within which the previously analysed whole is a component or individual. In the second direction, we repeat the same process but this time apply it to the organized wholes that are the components or individuals of the one analysed first. These extensions of the original analysis are necessary since any organized whole is an abstracted part of an interrelated reality. The results of these analyses are not cumulative. They are interdependent since the results obtained in the study of any organized whole are inputs into the analysis of the next larger and next smaller wholes. This makes the analysis of any part of reality dependent on a variety of things not adequately covered by the concept of organized whole.

In the first place, the study of any organized whole is affected by similar investigations of other directly or indirectly related wholes and by what was previously known about reality. In fact, the more a whole is studied, the more the exactness of what was previously known about it will be in question, and the more previously clear-cut causal relationships will be in doubt. These studies will in their turn be affected by later studies. There can be no complete and total knowledge of reality or of its parts. All human knowledge of an interrelated reality is necessarily partial and relative.[36] We can therefore not be sure about the nature of reality, and hence the loss of information involved in using a concept like organized whole cannot be entirely known. The sciences have not been sufficiently critical of the hypothesis of a mechanistic reality.

There is a second way in which human knowledge about an interrelated reality is relative. Any observer is a part of that interrelated whole. We have thus far assumed the opposite. We will later show that any study of reality is the result of an interaction between the persons involved, the means to extend their senses, and what is being studied.[37] All individual knowledge is relative to a paradigm acquired by being socialized into a particular culture and its possible subsequent expansion if a person has undergone a secondary process of socialization in the form of scientific or professional education. These paradigms limit what can be observed and understood. They also determine what will be considered factual and what is not. Since people largely share their paradigms with other members of their culture or scientific and professional community, many personal findings become accepted by the community and added to its knowledge base. There is not necessarily any agreement about the 'facts' between different communities.

From the above two limitations of the concept of organized whole, it follows that a distinction must be drawn between reality and reality as it is known, and that the latter always implies a human observer as well as a community of which he or she is a member. The analysis of any organized whole is necessarily related to this human context. These findings are supported by studies of the historical development of science, which we will briefly summarize to further illustrate the point.

In the course of its development science continues to produce an endless flow of discoveries, and there is no reason to believe that this flow is about to end, at which point the gap between reality and reality as it is known would be closed. Kuhn[38] has shown that we cannot even say whether or not science is narrowing the gap at a particular historical epoch. Through an analysis of the history of science he shows that scientific knowledge is not cumulative. New knowledge of an interrelated reality is necessarily related to already existing knowledge. It interacts with it and transforms it, which is particularly obvious during certain periods that Kuhn calls scientific revolutions. During these periods knowledge is interconnected differently to create new theories. When this happens the meaning of the constituents of these theoretical systems, such as facts and concepts, change in meaning. This was the case for mass and energy, for example, when the Newtonian theory of the physical universe was replaced by that of Einstein. During scientific revolutions some facts and concepts lose their meaning altogether and disappear from science while others may be added. Furthermore, a new range of scientific problems becomes apparent, while some previously identified problems are solved and others cease to be recognized as legitimate scientific areas for investigation.

During these Gestalt switches in scientific theories it is impossible to measure the net gain in scientific knowledge. The only objective standard of scientific progress would be a complete knowledge of reality. In its absence all that can be known is the relationship between reality as it is known at different points in time. Nothing can be said about the relationship between reality and reality as it is known at a given period.

From this perspective, the concept of scientific progress means that today we know more about reality than ever before, but this does not necessarily imply we know reality any better.

Any human knowledge is always open-ended. Human knowledge is never entirely systematic and it bears within itself a number of potential contradictions and sources of disorder from which anomalies can arise. Internal contradictions and new discoveries that prove to be anomalous in relation to what could be expected on the basis of existing knowledge are two sources of non-cumulative growth in human knowledge.

It is evident that no knowledge can be entirely detached from the observer's community to make it objective in the absolute sense of that term. What is held to be factual and objective by scientists fifty years ago is not necessarily accepted as such today. Knowledge is gained in the context of previously internalized knowledge. Processes of primary socialization into a culture and secondary socialization into a scientific or professional community ensure the initial compatibility of the paradigms of their members. Because these paradigms have conscious as well as metacons-cious components, we will later show that the members of a community are normally unaware of the relative objectivity of the knowledge base of their community.

We will give a preliminary summary of our discussion thus far. The hypo-thesis of a mechanistically interrelated reality, implicitly and explicitly embodied in virtually all the paradigms underlying the sciences today, has produced a picture of the human phenomenon that is internally inconsis-tent. Furthermore, the development of the concept of organized whole to study a mechanistically interrelated reality uncovered a number of problems and limitations that could not adequately be dealt with. It would therefore appear that the hypothesis about the mechanistic nature of reality needs to be reconsidered. But how? Having found it necessary to draw a distinction between reality and reality as it is known, it is clearly impossible to approach the problem of the nature of reality directly. What typically happens is that some scientists may begin to sense that somehow reality as they have come to know it does not correspond with what they anticipated on the basis of their paradigms. When these intuitions become widespread new avenues for research open up that were previously denied validity and value by the current paradigm. Out of these explorations a new paradigm may gradually emerge.

Today the hypothesis of a mechanistically interrelated reality is begin-ning to be questioned in a variety of disciplines. What is even more significant is that physics is once again leading the way. Having been central in the development of the mechanistic conception of reality and having pushed this hypothesis to its limits, it is now faced with contradictions.[39] Bohm[40] has argued that the root problem is the incompatibility between the theory of relativity and quantum theory because they imply different conceptions of reality. The search for a new theory is likely to be most fruitful if it is based on what the theory of relativity and quantum theory have in common, namely, the hypothesis of reality being an undivided whole with no separate and independent parts. We then encounter another problem. It is not easy to imagine such a reality, because it is contrary to the mechanistic conceptions that have permeated Western experience and thought for so long.

In attempting to conceptualize a non-mechanistic reality, we need to recall that a mechanistic one is constituted of organized wholes that exist independently, each in their own region of space and time, and that interact by external contact. This is exactly what one finds in a machine. In a living whole, on the contrary, there have never existed any independent 'parts.' Each 'part' has emerged within the whole. They do not interact with the other 'parts' in the same way, and there exist no distinct boundaries between them. In so far as boundaries do manifest themselves, they are likely to shift with the frame of reference employed by the observer and the paradigm he or she has internalized. Think, for example, of the study of human life. No clear boundaries exist between the physiological and psychic components of a person's life, nor is there a sharp dividing line between the social, economic, political, or religious elements in the life of a person or a society. Yet we speak of the economic or political systems of a society as if they have an existence of their own, although we derive them from what in our experience is an undivided whole. It is only on the basis of a mechanistic hypothesis of reality that a society decomposes into functions, mechanisms, systems, and structures. When a society is studied on the basis of a non-mechanistic hypothesis, they become dimensions of an undivided whole. Even what to our senses manifests itself as a largely autonomous whole is in fact a part of the undivided whole of a reality, and science must attempt to account for this undivided wholeness.

Physics has provided us with an interesting analogy for conceptualizing an undivided reality, namely the hologram. When an object is photographed in the usual way, each point on the picture corresponds to one point in the visual field of the camera, that is, to a point of the object placed there. If the film is placed somewhere towards the focal plane of the lens, the information of each point in the visual field of the camera will be stored throughout the picture. What we perceive is an ever more blurred picture as the distance between the new and original position of the film increases. What we are seeing is a record of the wave patterns reflected by an object in the field of the camera. These wave patterns can be read out by transilluminating the film with a coherent light source. The wavefronts captured on the film are then reactivated and a virtual image of the object can be seen by looking towards the film. The image is exactly as 'seen' by the camera at the time of the exposure. It is three-dimensional. If the observer changes the angle of viewing the object, the perspective changes just as it would if the real object were present. Another object in the field of the camera that was partly obscured by the first can be seen in its entirety if the observer moves his or her head to look around the first object. In other words, the visual image has all the properties of the original scene. The photographic record that makes this possible is called a hologram. Each area of a hologram contains information about the entire object recorded on it. As Bohm puts it: 'the form and structure of the entire object may be said to be enfolded within each region of the photographic record. When one shines light on any region, this form and structure are then unfolded, to give a recognizable image of the whole object once again.

'We proposed that a new notion of order is involved here, which we called the implicate order (from a Latin root meaning "to enfold" or "to fold inward"). In terms of the implicate order one may say that everything is enfolded into everything. This contrasts with the explicate order now dominant in physics in which things are unfolded in the sense that each thing lies only in its own particular region of space (and time) and outside the regions belonging to other things.

'The value of the hologram in this context is that it may help to bring this new notion of order to our attention in a sensibly perceptible way; but of course, the hologram is only an instrument whose function is to make a static record (or "snapshot") of this order. The actual order itself which has thus been recorded is in the complex movement of electromagnetic fields, in the form of light waves. Such movement of light waves is present everywhere and in principle enfolds the entire universe of space (and time) in each region (as can be demonstrated in any such region by placing one's eye or a telescope there, which will "unfold" this content).'[41]

Ideas of this kind are by no means limited to physicists. Other researchers have argued that the holographic process may be helpful in conceptualizing some of the functions of the human nervous system, such as perception and memory.[42] Since each area of a hologram contains information about the whole image, it has some interesting possibilities as a memory, for example. Information about the entire image can be retrieved from any part of the hologram and no information is lost if a section of the hologram is damaged. Furthermore, holograms can be superimposed to achieve storage capacities of ten billion bits of information in one cubic centimeter. Non-optical holograms can be created by computer simulations. All of these characteristics make it easier to conceptualize the incredible ability of human memory to retain and recall experiences and not to lose any due to brain lesions.

It is beyond the scope of this work to debate the merits of the holographic analogy for conceptualizing the natures of physical reality or the human nervous system. Nor shall we enter into the fascinating implications of these new notions for other fields of investigation. The point we are making is that the paradigms based on the hypothesis of a mechanistically interrelated reality are almost certainly inadequate. We must be very careful not to take the analogy too far. The mechanistic world view sought to dissolve the whole of reality into basic building blocks. There now appears a tendency to go to the other extreme and to dissolve everything into the undivided whole of reality. Both these extremes are equally disastrous for the study of the human phenomenon. We will therefore attempt to steer a course between these two extremes. There is no question that there is a great deal of enfolding of phenomena related to human existence, but the individual person cannot be dissolved into an undivided reality. The concept of system will therefore be used to designate organized wholes which exhibit a certain measure of autonomy in relation to their environment and yet are partly or entirely enfolded into other systems. Before briefly explaining how this will be attempted, we will need to address one last problem in the mechanistic conception of human life.

Even the most sophisticated models of the human mind as an information-processing and – storing and self-regulating cybernetic device leaves some fundamental questions unanswered. Where is the 'I' that receives the output of this machine? Who is the conscious self receiving information about the world and how does this conscious person live in the world if the 'machine' is self-regulating? Scientific answers to these questions are impossible because they ultimately touch on the mystery of human life itself. Given the necessity of drawing a distinction between reality and reality as it is known, the limits of scientific knowing must be acknowledged.

The approach we propose to follow will not require answers to the above questions because we will assume that the conscious 'I,' able to experience and act on the world (be it at first in a very limited way), is from the very beginning enfolded in a baby. For example, the development of the senses, motor functions, memory, language, or the metaconscious are not the development of the parts in the human mechanism but a complex process of enfolding and unfolding of a semi-autonomous whole enfolded in a society and ecosystem. Each experience is an interaction between the 'I' and the world. It enfolds something of an individual's personality, culture, past experience, anticipations of the future, and the nature of the relationship including its object, purpose, and context. As the experience is internalized, it does not merely passively enter memory but becomes an integral 'part' of a person's life. It becomes enfolded into every aspect of a person's being, including perception, motor functions, language, and memory by means of what we will call the process of differentiation. A process of integration further gives the experience a place in the patterns of a person's life, including those of the subconscious, collective unconscious, and metaconscious. In this manner each experience during the process of socialization enfolds something of a person's social and cultural environment into his or her being. As a result a person is not a part of a society in the mechanistic sense. His or her human potential is unfolded in a life that is both individually unique and enfolded into a society making that life typical of the culture, time, and place to a degree that we can vary from person to person. That is to say, each relationship of a human life unfolds something of the individual as well as the society and culture. Living a human life in reality is, as we will seek to demonstrate, a complex process of enfolding and unfolding the relationships between a conscious 'I' and the world. The concept of system must therefore express what is experienced as an organized whole and the relationships enfolded and unfolded in that experience.

A society may thus be conceptualized as the system of individuals living together in a particular environment within an institutional framework on the basis of a culture. Its members do not dissolve their individuality into the society, and the dialectic between a society and its members is of fundamental importance for a culture. The systematic nature of the individual can best be understood by examining the process of socialization as the enfolding of all facets of a person's life in the development of perception, motor functions, language, memory, thought, intuition, personality, the subconscious, and so on.

The lives of individual members of a society cannot be conveniently split into economic, social, political, legal, moral, or religious sectors. These are at best facets of whole lives even though these lives are subject to contradictions and alienation. On the level of society we do not find autonomous economic, social, political, legal, moral, or religious structures either. Once again, these structures are abstractions from the fabric of a society. In reality they are woven together into one fabric. The action of an individual may, for example, have political overtones, but it remains an expression of his or her personality and aspirations. It will necessarily also have at least some social, economic, moral, and religious implications. We will attempt to demonstrate in the next section that culture underlies all the systems related to the human phenomenon, so that it may constitute a key to a more unified understanding of human life. If this proves true then many of the current theories can be shown to be limiting cases that can be derived from the general theory by some reductionistic assumptions.

The purpose of our study is not to contribute frontier knowledge to the social sciences and humanities but to reinterpret their findings by developing a new conceptual framework for interpreting human life in its social setting particularly for our times. I recognize the risks of such an undertaking. However, as an engineer and social scientist concerned with the situation in the universities described earlier and the implications this has for our ability to address the challenges faced by humanity, a great deal of fundamental conceptual work is required. It is the meeting of this need to which we seek to make a contribution. [43]

CULTURE AS SOCIAL ECOLOGY

Our search for a unified understanding of the human phenomenon will have as its basis and point of departure the realization that we are part of an interrelated reality in which nothing is autonomous or self-sufficient. Hence any knowledge of any part of reality is potentially related to and dependent on all other knowledge. Similarly, the findings of any scientific discipline do not stand on their own; their meaning is partly dependent on all the other scientific findings. When we attempt to fit together into one comprehensive picture the findings of science related to the human phenomenon, we are creating a system (in the sense we have given to this concept) in which a knowledge of the whole cannot be derived from the knowledge of the parts. Each theoretical element, when it becomes integrated into a unified view of the human phenomenon, will affect the knowledge of this theoretical whole, while at the same time its very meaning is dependent on how it is integrated into the whole. Any change in the whole can affect its meaning.

This is not merely an application of what we have learned about systems in the previous section. The history of science shows that the effective development of an area of research occurs only when a diversity of research efforts are enfolded into a theoretical unity which is capable of integrating the many highly specialized studies to show the significance they have in relation to each other. However, the theoretical unity of an area must not merely synthesize the results of the specialized studies but must transcend them to make it capable of guiding future research by pointing to new fruitful areas of investigation. When this theoretical unity of a discipline or a school of thought is violated by a newly discovered phenomenon, it must be recreated. The knowledge of that group of scientists must be systematized in a different way.

When we go one step further and attempt to systematize knowledge about the human phenomenon across disciplinary boundaries based on an interrelated view of reality we can expect much the same thing. Any internal or external inconsistencies in the resulting theories manifest an inadequate theoretical account of an interrelated reality. In view of the distances between reality and reality as it is known, however, these inconsistencies can never be eliminated entirely. Since in some cases various findings of science will need to be reinterpreted before they can be fitted into the body of systematized knowledge about the human phenomenon and since gaps will be found in the existing knowledge, the theoretical unity now underlying some disciplines or schools of thought may be called into question while at the same time new fruitful areas of research may open up.

Reductionisms occur when a domain of scientific investigation is considered as being autonomous from or simply unrelated to other domains. We shall begin by examining some of the interdependencies often ignored in some of the more prominent reductionisms in studies of the human phenomenon.

Humanity is a part of nature, but its primary elements (civilizations, societies, groups, and individuals) are neither totally natural nor totally artificial. Humanity is not totally natural because genetic and evolutionary processes connecting it to nature cannot alone explain the diversity of civilizations, societies, groups, and individuals. But it is equally impossible totally to oppose nature and culture, for if the human biology is nothing but 'raw material' for culture then where does culture come from and how is it related to the remainder of reality? The social, and consequently something of the cultural, is inscribed in nature as is clearly seen with the ants and the bees.

Humanity can be distinguished from the remainder of reality in general and nature in particular by the fact that it is both a natural and an artificial phenomenon and that in its history this dialectical tension is never resolved. As a result biology is not independent from the social, as some sociobiologists have argued.[44] We will reject the new reductionism advanced by some proponents of this new discipline. The fact that human beings and all other forms of life are a part of this same ecosystem requires that biologically they have certain things in common, especially with the highest forms of life, but they are distinguishable from them by their degree of artificiality associated with their culture. This brings us to another reductionism related to intelligence and communication.

Not only has biology ignored the social for a long time, but also intelligence and communication. Human beings, like all other biological organisms, do not only take food and energy from their environment in order to sustain life but also information (negative entropy). Consequently, the natural environment does not affect people through biological relationships only. In conjunction with the larger physical and the socio-cultural environments, it affects the development structure and organization of human beings. Depth psychology, for example, shows that people internalize the experience of their lives in these environments in such a way that the past influences present and future behaviour.

Another reductionism consists of considering human beings as having a bio-natural infrastructure and a psycho-socio-cultural superstructure. However, human beings are whole beings in which the natural, the biological, the psychic, the social, and the cultural are dimensions rather than parts or autonomous substructures. We interact with other members of our society, we internalize in our experience information about the structures of society (scientific, technological, economic, social, political, juridical, moral, religious, and cultural) and the environment (both natural and artificial) in such a way that this information interacts with the structures of our internal environment (sensory and nervous systems, personality, the subconscious, etc.). In other words, to live is to relate to and be interrelated to all reality within the horizon of our experience. All internal and external reality potentially plays a role in our lives by processes of internalizing information in the form of experience and externalizing something of ourselves in our behaviour. The latter impinges on and is impinged on by reality.

Associated with each human life is a unique dynamic network of relationships. As a consequence, when building a unified theory of the human phenomenon no scientific discipline can be ignored. They each make a unique contribution not reducible to that of any of the others. Any reductionism will result in a loss of information and a distortion of the meaning of the results obtained by the various scientific disciplines. A unified view of the human phenomenon can emerge only by a dialogue between all the sciences around the question of who we are. The interrelationships established by this dialogue need to reflect the interconnectedness of reality in relation to the human phenomenon.

In order to build a unified theory of the human phenomenon by establishing a dialogue between the scientific disciplines, we need to employ the concept of system and identify the major systems related to this phenomenon. Humanity may be conceptualized as a system composed of civilizations, in turn made up of societies composed of groups. These are constituted of persons, themselves constituted of various systems. Humanity is a subsystem of the ecosystem, which in turn is a subsystem of the universe.

The sequence in which we focus on the various systems associated with the human phenomenon will affect the severity of the loss of information inevitable in these successive processes of abstraction. Hence some strategic considerations are necessary to determine which sequence will involve a minimal loss of information. It would appear that this loss is minimal if we conceptualize the individual human being and society as the two central systems and deal with the other systems according to their interaction with these two. This is a rather obvious choice, but the next step of deciding between these two systems is not. In fact, a preliminary study of their interrelationships is required before we will be able to focus in on either one without a serious loss of information. Such a study, which will be undertaken in the remainder of this section, will lead us to the heart of the unified theory of the human phenomenon set out in this work, namely the concept of culture as a social ecology.

The key to understanding the relationship between people and society (including the structure and organization of these two systems) lies in the way human beings are linked to reality. Regarding this link, the psychologist C. G. Jung wrote: 'All that I experience is psychic. Even physical pain is a psychic image which I experience; my sense-impressions – for all that they force upon me a world of impenetrable objects occupying space – are psychic images, and these alone constitute my immediate experience, for they alone are the immediate objects of my consciousness. My own psyche even transforms and falsifies reality, and it does this to such a degree that I must resort to artificial means to determine what things are like apart from myself. Then I discover that a sound is a vibration of air of such and such a frequency, or that a colour is a wave of light of such and such a length. We are in truth so wrapped about by psychic images that we cannot penetrate at all to the essence of things external to ourselves. All our knowledge consists of the stuff of the psyche which, because it alone is immediate, is superlatively real. Here, then, is a reality to which the psychologist can appeal – namely, psychic reality.'[45]

The physicist Niels Bohr made the following remark regarding another aspect of our relationship with reality: 'Ultimately we human beings depend on our words, we are hanging in language.' When someone objected that reality lies 'beneath' language, Bohr replied: 'We are suspended in language in such a way that we cannot say what is up and what is down.'[46] Albert Einstein, during a period of crisis in physics, expressed a third aspect: 'It was as if the ground had been pulled out from under one with no firm foundation to be seen anywhere upon which one could have built,' and also: 'It is the theory which decides what we can observe.'[47]

The above quotations point to the three most important aspects of the way we relate to reality. The first refers to the fact that the stimuli received by our senses are *experienced* only when they have taken on a *meaning* in our lives. For example, we hear sounds although our ears detect only vibrations of air and we see colours while our eyes detect only waves of light. From the findings of psychology, social psychology, sociology, and anthropology, to be surveyed later, it will become evident that our links with our internal and external worlds involve the brain. Information about the stimuli received by the senses is transmitted to the brain where it is interpreted largely on the basis of past experience. This experience has been stored in a variety of mental structures including memory, having, as we shall see later, the properties of systems. It is precisely because of this systems character of the mental structures that the elements of information received from the senses can take on a new quality in the brain, namely meaning. The process of interpreting the information is nothing else but having it participate in the various systems. In each of these systems the whole, being greater than the sum of the parts, is enriched by more than just the information received from the senses at any moment, and this is the *meaning* the stimuli acquire from this process of interpretation. Hence the meaning of any set of stimuli is related to the meanings of all previously interpreted stimuli, and together they span the gap between the whole and the sum of the parts.

The second quotation refers to the fact that language plays an important role in the mental structures responsible for interpreting stimuli, with the result that these structures are what Cassirer has called a symbolic medium which mediates between us and the external world.[48] Hence we live in a symbolic universe rather than in a 'real' world. Stimuli can take on a meaning only in the context of the previously acquired mental structures.

Hence the symbolic universe we experience is reality as we know it, as distinct from reality itself.

The last quotations, refer first to the possibility that the mental structures which interpret stimuli can prove inadequate. In such a case a person is no longer sure what is real. But this can only happen because our links with the external world are not direct, so that the conversion of reality into reality as it is known can be inconsistent or incoherent, that is, *non-systematic*. The second point raised is that our mental structures delineate what we are able to experience. We shall later show that the structure of the system constituting the symbolic medium enfolds our personality.

In order for human beings to be linked to reality according to the three characteristics just described, newborn babies, in contrast to animal offspring, should be able to relate to their environment in only a limited way. They should be largely inadapted to their environment at birth so that they can be socialized into a way of relating to and existing in reality that is typical of the culture of their society. In other words, for cultural adaption to an environment to be possible, genetically predetermined adaptation to reality through instincts should be minimal. This in fact is the case. Babies' brains contain far fewer instincts or mental structures passed on by hereditary processes than the brains of animal offspring.[49] Large parts of the brains of babies must organize themselves on the basis of their experience of encounters with the other members of their society. By being born and socialized into a society, children do not in the first place learn its language, customs, manners, skills, institutions, and so on, but rather they acquire mental structures permitting them to relate to reality in a way characteristic of their society.

From this perspective, the human mind develops, enfolded in the brain, by arranging internalized experiences into interrelated patterns. Its systems are enfolded together with the genetically established ones into a larger whole. In some cases the genetically established systems will hardly be affected by the systems established from experience, others may be dominated by them, and still others remain in conflict with them. This has been extensively studied by Freud and others.[50] In the present work we will concentrate on the mind's systems established from experience – which is not to deny the great importance of genetically established systems. We will show, however, that much of what has been called the subconscious and collective unconscious can in fact be explained by a system, built up from experience, that we will call the metaconscious.

Considerable insight into our links with reality can be gained by examining how these links develop from those based on instincts at birth to those mostly based on the mental structures acquired by having grown up in a particular society living in a particular environment. We shall examine this transformation of a baby from a 'natural' being into a 'cultural' being in great detail, but some of its basic features need to be considered here.

Because babies are not genetically adapted to their environment, there exists a constant dialectical tension between the way reality (both social and physical) imposes itself on them and the way they impose themselves on reality. During any activity they internalize information about their internal and external worlds in the form of experience. What is internalized depends on the mental structures which interpret the stimuli received by the senses. It is these same mental systems which increasingly permit babies deliberately to decide on a particular activity and carry it out. As the systems acquired by experience develop, the role of the innate systems recedes somewhat. But as long as their minds are developed to only a limited extent, babies are constantly faced with new discoveries and surprises because reality does not behave as they expected it to. To a large extent this is due to the nature of the process of internalization. Babies slowly begin to interpret stimuli in a systematic way. Since the meaning of a set of stimuli interacts with and depends on the meanings of previously interpreted stimuli, these meanings together begin to constitute a very limited but internally coherent interpretation of reality. But reality constantly proves to be more complex and hence qualitatively different from this interpretation.

Babies orient themselves in the world by the mental structures they have acquired. They can only make sense of those stimuli that can be interpreted by these structures, and this limits the sphere of activities open to them. Whatever behaviour within this range they may embark on, it is impinged upon by reality and particularly by the other members of their society on whom they are dependent. Children never mechanically try out all the possible modes of behaviour in a given event. They are greatly influenced by the way others relate to them and the environment partly because it constantly opens up new possibilities to them. They tend to learn about reality in the way the culture of their society has objectivized the project of existence. In other words, being socialized into a society comprises processes of externalizing something of the development of children's mental structures in their behaviour and internalizing how their behaviour interacts with reality (both material and socio-cultural), leading to further developments in their mental structures. As a result, reality as children know it will increasingly resemble the symbolic universe of their culture, and they will increasingly live their lives in that universe in a way that is unique to their personality and yet typical of their culture and their time.

The mind's systems acquired on the basis of experience mediate all relationships with reality, converting it into a symbolic universe. Within this universe these structures orient behaviour because they imply, as we shall see, certain values, myths, beliefs, etc., with the result that they function as a kind of mental map by which we orient ourselves in reality.[51] Since the process of socialization ensures that the members of a society generally have compatible mental maps, these maps also function as a kind of 'social gyroscope' guiding the lives of the members of a society in compatible directions so that they can exist in reality as a society. The minds of the members of a society are sufficiently different to permit and require communication but not too different to make communication impossible. This dialectical tension is first achieved by means of socialization and later by constant interaction. It is never resolved.

It now follows that culture as acquired by a process of socialization is a way of living in reality based on a certain organization of the mind. Hence a culture may be thought of as the *social ecology* of a society. The customs, manners, beliefs, myths, language, and institutions are in part the phenomenal manifestations of these structures. The meaning of culture as we use it here is, of course, opposed to what culture came to mean as a result of the Industrial Revolution. Rather than dividing the life of a society into two sectors, it now reintegrates them into one whole. We shall later examine the nature of the mental structures associated with a culture by examining the process of socialization and its possible variations from society to society. We will then be able to develop a social psychology of perception, experience, memory, language, thinking, and the subconscious. By examining all these functions and their development in the context of the lives of children in the process of growing up, a more holistic and less mechanistic understanding of them can be gained. Furthermore, since these mental functions together shape the way the members of a society relate to their external environment, the role of culture as a social ecology will clearly come into focus.

It should be emphasized that culture is not an instrument by which reality as it is known to a society is socially constructed in the course of socialization. The reason is implied in what we have already said. A culture develops from the dialectical tension between the way reality imposes itself on the members of a society and the way they learn to impose their customs, values, beliefs, and traditions on reality in daily life. This is why different societies can exist in virtually the same environment, each in a unique way.

Thus far we have focused on culture, primarily taking the individual person as the central system of the human phenomenon. We will next examine it from the vantage point of society. Consider the process of socialization from this new vantage point. The mental structures acquired by being socialized into a culture develop because that culture has been objectivized by previous generations. It pre-exists and transcends individuals. It is a system to which individuals contribute but which nevertheless has a large measure of autonomy from them. The systematic character of a culture is reflected not only in the systematic character of the mental structures acquired by socialization, but also in that of society. A society has the properties of a system with respect to its members because the process of socialization has converted them from 'natural' beings into 'cultural' members of that society. Since the relationships between the members of a society and reality are not predetermined, neither are the relationships between society and reality. They also need to be shaped by culture. This constitutes a cultural order, earlier referred to as a project of existence.

It now follows that the culture of a society may be defined as the patterns of internal and external regularities in the lives of its members, in so far as these patterns are not hereditary in origin. These regularities reflect the cultural order a society establishes as the basis for social life. It thus introduces something artificial into nature that cannot be entirely integrated into it. A cultural order is distinct from and does not evolve with the natural order. By means of socialization, human offspring become a part of the cultural order while never entirely leaving the natural one.

Since the cultural order established by a society is non-natural, it can constantly be called into question by reality. Consequently, a society must continually respond to the challenges to its cultural basis. If it fails to do so successfully it can break down and disintegrate, not because the people have disappeared but because the foundation for social life has collapsed. The genesis, evolution, breakdown, and disintegration of societies must be interpreted in terms of their cultures' functioning as social ecologies on the level of society.

The order established by a culture systematically structures all the relationships a society requires to maintain itself in reality. In other words, the scientific, technological, economic, social, political, legal, religious, moral, artistic, and literary are all dimensions of the way a culture structures and institutionalizes the relationships between the society and reality. The system of these relationships constitutes a project of existence. Just as the mental structures acquired by internalizing a culture mediate the relationship between a person and reality, the project of existence mediates the relationship between society and reality.

According to the findings of our preliminary study, it appears that culture is the key to understanding the two systems central to the human phenomenon. Culture in its role as social ecology also orders the relationships between these two systems by establishing a dynamic equilibrium between the two extreme tendencies. If a society imposes itself too forcefully on its members, the resulting system will be constituted of nearly similar individuals. Hence it seriously weakens its ability to transform itself in order to adapt to new circumstances or challenges arising from within or without. Such a society is headed for collapse. If, on the other hand, a society does not sufficiently impose itself on its members, its unity will quickly be eroded, leading to its collapse as well. In its evolution, a society must constantly find a new dynamic equilibrium in the dialectical tension between the individual and society. This follows directly from what we have said about systems in the previous section.

The character of early Western civilization does in part derive from a unique dialectical tension between the individual and society. After the emergence of the state in history, most civilizations and societies have tended to establish the equilibrium in the tension between the individual and society to the latter's advantage, be it with limited effectiveness due to a lack of means available to the state. When one of the Asian centres of civilization shifted westward in the seventh century BC, this began to change. Crete, the city states of Greece, and Asia Minor were all sea-going commerical economies with many cities being no more than trade centres. The entire Mediterranean became linked, and eventually not even Egypt could maintain its unique identity. The big cities were increasingly no longer continental.

It was in these sea-going economies that a new conception of society emerged which had been largely absent in the older continental empires.[52] The political and spiritual value of the individual was asserted over that of the state because economic development by sea trade was more important than political activities. The state's task was now to help the citizen. This astounding political reversal was possible in the small city-state where each person knew everyone else and where the sea-going economy taught the value and autonomy of the individual. By the time these states declined, the new individualism had spread to Rome and Egypt. The problem of the individual versus the state was never resolved in Egypt and only temporarily in Greece. Rome, however, made it a central problem which it attempted to resolve by juridical means, pushing concern for the citizen and organizational efficiency as far as possible. This then became one of the main three pillars of Western civilization, together with Greek philosophy and Christian revelation.

Our preliminary study has now given us the information necessary to begin a detailed study of the human phenomenon in the chapters which follow. Since culture in its role as a social ecology is at the heart of the systems central to the human phenomenon as well as their interrelationships, the loss of information in abstracting either one of these systems in the perspective set out in this section is expected to be minimal. In the detailed study which follows, we will focus first on the individual and then on society.

Before we proceed, we shall take a brief look at what can be expected in terms of results based on the concept of culture as a social ecology. In relation to the individual, we will be building what might be called a field theory of being.[53] By this we mean that everything entering human experience, because it can take on a meaning in the context of prior experience, is internalized and becomes a part not only of people's minds but of their entire being. Life is a process of being in a network of relationships that form a field of being. Since the members of a society interact, their fields of being overlap considerably, in part because each generation learns to build fields of being from previous generations. A dialectical tension between the individual and society, between the cultural and the natural, and between the symbolic universe and reality are some of the 'magnetic poles' generating the fields of being.

This theory of being is directly opposed to the mechanistic stimulus-response theories of human behaviour which, depending on the degree of sophistication, atomize the holistic character of the structures of the mind. Although these theories are quite successfully used to manipulate human behaviour, they are based on a highly reductionistic view of the human phenomenon. In the mechanistic theories meaning disappeared. We propose to put the striving for meaning which begins with the systematic interpretation of experience, back at the heart of the human phenomenon. This striving is, as we shall see, however, neither philosophical nor theological in nature. It has to do with being in an interrelated reality. We can expect, therefore, to develop concepts to gain a deeper understanding of the human condition in a society because the unified theory we are about to develop will stress the *wholeness* of being, so that forces of alienation and reification will become clearly visible.

On the level of society, the theory can be expected to develop concepts for the making of 'maps' of both contemporary and past societies. These maps are designed to integrate all the specialized and often fragmented knowledge of these societies into a coherent picture by showing how the scientific, technological, economic, social, legal, political, military, moral, religious, artistic, and intellectual are situated in relation to one another. These maps could help reduce the fragmented situation now existing in the universities and many professional communities, as discussed in an earlier section. This situation has arisen because we no longer have an adequate map of modern society. Hence many scientific disciplines suffer a significant loss of information when abstracting, say, the economic or political structures of a society.

In our time, when our means are more and more powerful and when the ends are increasingly determined by the means, the significance of developing such concepts hardly needs to be stressed.

TWO

Our Senses and the World

THE ROLE OF THE MIND

It is generally agreed that our links with the external world are essentially maintained by five senses capable of detecting different kinds of stimuli. The senses transform the stimuli into signals which are transmitted to various parts of the brain via a network of nerves. At this point a conceptual difficulty arises. It is not possible to say that the brain constitutes a multi-dimensional image of the external world from the incoming signals in order to present it to consciousness. Our relationships with the external world are not predominantly the result of an endless chain of responses to the stimuli impinging on our senses. This would make us the mere product of our environment. As members of a culture we individually and collectively explore and act on reality, imposing on it our intentions and expectations. From this perspective the senses act as extensions of the mind. Their functioning is largely enfolded within that of the mind and thus in our whole being.

We experience the external world by consciously establishing relationships with it. Such relationships become a part of our life, causing it to evolve. Usually this evolution does not threaten the integrality of our being. For continuity and change to characterize our life, the relationships with the external world must be lived in the context of our whole being, including our present state of mind, personality, subconscious, metaconscious, the past, and expectations for the future. The meaning a relationship has for us may thus be regarded as arising from its progressive enfolding into our being, and what we experience as the conscious awareness of this process. It is possible to distinguish several stages of enfolding and corresponding levels of meaning. 1) Within a particular dimension of experience associated with one of the senses, a set of stimuli derived from a specific constituent involved in a relationship with the external world takes on a first level of meaning by being placed in the context of and being related to similar perceptions in that dimension of experience. 2) This first level of enfolding takes place in the context of similar processes of interpretation of other sets of stimuli within the same dimension of experience. It constitutes the second level of enfolding. 3) A third level of meaning results from the first two occurring in the context of similar processes in the other dimensions of experience related to the other senses, as well as other processes of the mind. These three levels of meaning associated with the three levels of enfolding will be referred to as those of sensations, Gestalts, and experience Gestalts. We normally consciously experience only the third level of meaning, into which the other two are enfolded.

Shortly after birth and probably just before, we mediate the relationships with the external world primarily on the basis of innate neural structures. As the mind develops within the brain, however, the situation progressively changes and the mediation is increasingly based on mental structures acquired from experience. We will attempt to build up a model of how the mind might accomplish the interpretation of stimuli. First, we will examine those aspects of these functions which are largely involuntary in the sense that they occur below the level of conscious experience and out of reach of an individual's conscious attention. Since there is no direct correspondence between the functions of the mind and the brain, we will not deal with the way the brain executes the functions of the mind.[1] The term 'perceptual apparatus' will be associated with the functions of the mind (based on the brain and the senses) that are related to perception.

We shall begin the study of our links with the world by examining the visual dimension of experience. When we are looking at something, a portion of the light reflected by it is focused on the retina by the optical system of each eye to constitute a set of stimuli. The optic nerves transmit the signals emitted by the retinas to a special part of the cortex where the two sets of stimuli are interpreted, with the result that they together take on a meaning which we have called a sensation. It is possible to create situations in a laboratory where our field of vision contains only one object, with the result that the retinas each receive only one set of stimuli. However, in daily life situations the retinas will each detect as many sets of stimuli as there are objects in the field of vision. These sets will yield sensations as well. By being interrelated in the mind, all these sensations jointly take on a further meaning which we will call a visual Gestalt.

Similar Gestalts emerge from the dimensions of experience related to the external and internal worlds. These are interrelated in the mind, with the result that they jointly take on a still more comprehensive meaning which we have called an experience Gestalt. This is the only one we are normally aware of. The three levels of meaning created in the mind, namely sensations, Gestalts, and experience Gestalts are aspects of experiencing the external world by enfolding a relationship into our life. In this chapter we shall examine the first level, namely the emergence of sensations.

Experiments in visual perception have confirmed that a distinction must be made between a set of stimuli received by the retina and the visual sensation that becomes a part of our experience. In one type of experiment subjects wore goggles that either inverted the field of vision[2] or reversed it from left to right giving its mirror image.[3] They wore these goggles for a period of several weeks. The results obtained were essentially the same in each case, and we will therefore discuss only the latter experiment here. It goes without saying that at first the subjects were totally disoriented, turning right when they wanted to go left and so on. After a while they began to get used to it and, surprisingly, they began to see things normally again in a piecemeal fashion. A building might appear in its real orientation while an inscription on it might appear in mirror writing. Similarly, common words might be read normally but when regarded carefully they became reversed. After this period of transition the entire field of vision was seen as normal again despite the fact that the retinal image remained the mirror image of what they actually saw. When the goggles were removed the subjects had to again go through a period of adjustment.

This experiment clearly shows that a process of interpretation intervenes between the stimuli received by the retina and what we visually experience. After the subjects had begun to wear the goggles the special part of the cortex continued to interpret retinal stimuli in the way it had learned, but since the resulting sensations interrelated into a visual Gestalt were still further integrated into an experience Gestalt, certain inconsistencies occurred. By way of example, suppose one of the subjects who had just begun to wear the goggles was walking down a corridor with an open door on the left and a blank wall on the right. If he tried to pass through the open door he would typically turn right, and as a result run into the wall. The resulting experience Gestalt would be internally inconsistent, because it would comprise a tactile Gestalt from running into the wall, the aural Gestalt of the bang, and a visual Gestalt showing an open door where there was none. Because of the interdependence of the three levels of interpretation, the mind gradually began to adjust a part of its process of interpretation in order to eliminate the inconsistency which had destroyed the systematic character of its operations. It restored it by changing the way it interpreted retinal stimuli. In other words, the mind adjusted a part of its structure acquired on the basis of prior experience as a result of new experiences that were internally inconsistent. But the subjects clearly had no control over the way the mind interpreted stimuli or over the way it learned to do so, otherwise they would have spared themselves the many frustrations. We are normally not conscious of the fact that our visual links with the world are not direct by means of stimuli because we are only aware of what we experience. The process of the interpretation of stimuli carried out by the mind depends in part on our mental structures built up by prior experience.

In another experiment[4] subjects were asked to identify a series of playing cards on short controlled exposures. Some of the cards had been altered, such as a black four of hearts or a red six of spades. Initially the subjects would invariably identify such cards as normal ones without hesitation. For example, the black four of hearts would be identified as either a four of hearts or spades. On increasing the exposure time somewhat the subjects would continue to identify the anomalous cards in the same way but with some hesitation, often saying that something was wrong. A subject might identify a red six of spades as a six of spades but add that the black had a red border. On still longer exposure times they would exhibit more hesitation and confusion until many would suddenly correctly identify the card as a red six of spades. Once one anomalous card had been identified they were soon able to identify all other anomalous cards. Some subjects' minds however, seemed to be unable to change their interpreting of retinal stimuli, so that they were not able to identify all anomalous cards correctly. These persons experienced acute personal distress. One of them exclaimed: 'I can't make the suit out, whatever it is. It didn't even look like a card that time. I don't know what colour it is now or whether it's a spade or a heart. I'm not even sure now what a spade looks like. My God!'[5]

In the course of their daily lives the subjects had learned to interpret neurally the retinal stimuli of playing cards to yield sensations. This was no doubt facilitated by the knowledge that the world of playing cards is populated by four suits. The subjects could rapidly identify any card without conscious analysis. The retinal stimuli of the anomalous cards were at first interpreted like those of normal cards. Upon further exposure to the anomalous cards, the perceptual apparatus that interprets retinal stimuli slowly became aware of the fact that it could not interpret the retinal stimuli of anomalous cards in the way it had learned to interpret normal cards. Although the subjects were not consciously aware of the problem they began to feel something was wrong. They did not know what it was because the part of the mind responsible for interpreting retinal stimuli apparently continued to present them with sensations of normal cards. As the perceptual apparatus began to learn to adjust its interpreting of the retinal stimuli of cards by being exposed to the anomalous ones, some subjects began to notice changes in the sensations they experienced. When the adjustment was completed the anomalous cards could be identified as readily as normal ones. The subjects who were unable to adjust their interpreting of the stimuli experienced a personal crisis because for them reality could, as it were, no longer be trusted. This situation would have been impossible if their visual links with the world had been direct by means of retinal stimuli.

The above experiments are artificial in a certain sense. Yet the same sort of thing happens all the time in our daily lives although it goes largely unnoticed. We all distinguish between situations in which we can or cannot recognize something. A person not familiar with machines may when looking at one see nothing but a mass of metal and wire. If we asked him to describe what he sees he would attempt to describe it in terms of objects he has learned to recognize. He might give the following reply: 'I don't know what it is but it looks to me like a metal cylinder on which a rectangular box is mounted from which a number of wires emerge.' Unable to have a visual sensation of the entire machine, the person begins to analyse whatever visual sensations he was able to derive from the available retinal stimuli. An engineer looking at the same machine recognizes the sensation of a certain type of motor. Similarly a patient looking at an x-ray may say that she sees nothing at all. Although she is looking at something she has no visual sensation of *some thing* but sees only undifferentiated retinal stimuli. Her doctor, on the other hand, may see a tumour. In each of these cases some people have learned to perceive things by means of prolonged experience with a portion of the world, as in medical school, whereas others who have not had this experience perceive nothing meaningful. On the basis of their prolonged and specialized experience their senses have learned to interpret a whole new range of stimuli allowing them to experience meaningful sensations, opening up a new world to them.

The conclusions reached for our visual link with the world can be extended to our links with the world via the other senses. Comparable experiments can be designed to demonstrate that these links are not direct by means of stimuli, but by sensations produced by the involuntary neural interpreting of these stimuli based on prior experience. We shall give one further example for the case of aural perception. An apprentice mechanic listening to a motor may at first hear nothing but a mass of undifferentiated aural stimuli or noise. After additional experience with motors he learns to recognize certain sounds (sensations) that are meaningful to him because they are indicative of actual or potential malfunctions.

In any dimension of experience a sensation may be regarded as an organized whole or system of stimuli. Hence a sensation cannot be reduced to the sum of particular stimuli. This point has been well established by Gestalt psychology,[6] but since it is fundamental for understanding the links with the world via our senses, we will briefly illustrate it by means of the concept of system.

We are able to recognize a cube regardless of the kind of material of which it is made, the colours of its faces, or its environment. What we have learned to see is an organization of retinal stimuli that cannot be reduced to its attributes. In fact, we can make an image of the cube on paper by drawing its visible edges as solid, broken or dotted lines or by colouring the paper in a suitable manner. In each case we experience sensations that are only superficially different despite the fact that they were derived from quite different sets of stimuli. In order to be able to recognize a cube we are not dependent on a particular set of stimuli. The process of interpreting stimuli reflects reality in the sense that the sensation, like the object from which the stimuli were derived, is a system in which the whole is more than the sum of the parts. Similarly, the letters of the alphabet may be printed or handwritten in many different ways. Yet we are consistently able to recognize them because we have learned to see the retinal stimuli as a system.

The same is true for aural sensations. A melody may be considered as a system of notes. It can be transposed into different keys, be played one or more octaves higher or lower, be played on a variety of instruments each producing notes having a highly individualized tonal quality, or be graphically represented on paper. The fact that we can nevertheless recognize the melody shows that it is more than its constituent notes. An aural sensation may be considered as a system of aural stimuli. The same word pronounced by different people will give a different set of aural stimuli due to their different voice characteristics, yet to all who understand the language the aural sensations will differ only superficially. Since there are no chemically pure substances in nature, taste and smell sensations may be considered as unique organizations of the constituent stimuli. These organizations are not totally dependent on their constituents. Quite similar sensations can, for example, be reproduced synthetically with varying degrees of success, as is the case with artificial flavourings and perfumes.

Finally, tactile sensations such as being held by someone or sitting down are clearly complex patterns of stimuli. For the case of sitting on a chair the stimuli will vary greatly depending on the type of chair and the material from which the seat, back, and armrests are made, yet one has the same tactile sensation associated with sitting down. The fact that a sensation cannot be reduced to its constituents does not, of course, exclude the possibility of isolating specific features of its organization or certain attributes, for the purpose of analysis. Such a process of abstraction presupposes the formation of the sensation. It is irreversible because of the loss of information associated with it.

The fact that a sensation cannot be reduced to its constituent stimuli is the key to understanding the operation of our senses. Let us limit our attention to the visual dimension of experience once again. When some of us learned the letters of the alphabet we did so from a specific set of letters typically printed on a chart hung above the blackboard of the classroom. Once we learned to recognize them we could also recognize some letters printed in different scripts or handwritten by the teacher on the blackboard. In other words, once we learned to recognize a set of letters, we learned much more than just to recognize a specific set of retinal stimuli each time they came within our field of vision. To learn to recognize a specific set of retinal stimuli is to establish a model for the involuntary neural interpreting of similar sets of stimuli. As far as the perceptual apparatus responsible for the interpreting of retinal stimuli is concerned, we can say that it has acquired the ability to interpret a new range of stimuli. It has expanded and reorganized its mental structures acquired from experience by adding what we will call a perceptual paradigm for interpreting sets of stimuli that are similar to the set which led to the establishing of the paradigm.

Within any dimension of experience a perceptual paradigm is associated with an expansion and reorganization of the mental structures. It represents a function of the mind that interprets a new range of sets of stimuli to yield sensations that do not differ from one another in a fundamental way. The perceptual apparatus learns to interpret an increasing variety of stimuli by augmenting the number of perceptual paradigms. We recall that the process of interpretation is a facet of experiencing a moment of our life by enfolding it into our being. Thus far we have considered the meaning derived from relating a set of stimuli to prior perceptual experience only.

SENSATIONS FOR THE BABY

The following question now arises. If the involuntary interpreting of stimuli is based on prior experience, how does a newborn baby begin to relate to the outside world without having any direct experience of it?[7] At first the baby's world is virtually totally undifferentiated. The exceptions are the differentiations made on the basis of instincts. A baby's senses perceive mostly a host of undifferentiated stimuli which have no meaning whatsoever; even a consciousness of the possibility of their having a meaning is absent. Let us try to imagine what the baby's situation is like. As far as her sight is concerned the situation can possibly be likened to that of an adult who looks at a photograph which is so badly blurred that he cannot make out what it represents. The patches of colour bear no relationship to one another; they form a random distribution without any order and thus without any meaning. The adult may attempt to interpret the photograph because he knows from prior experience that it must represent something real but until an interpretation is found the photograph yields only retinal stimuli. In the baby's case, however, there is a complete unawareness of potential meaning so that she cannot focus her eyes because there is nothing to focus on. She can only stare blankly. Her other senses are in a similar situation.

We cannot say the baby's existence is meaningless, however, since emotionally she senses that there is a loving care directed toward her. This feeling possibly arouses a sense of curiosity about the world that responds to her. In any case the absence of loving care can greatly retard her development. She will soon discern the emotional tone of her mother's voice from all other sounds and differentiate her responses accordingly. Similarly, she may also begin to note that part of the blur she blankly stares at moves, and that this movement coincides with acts and sounds of loving care. Slowly the baby learns to see the retinal stimuli of people as a meaningful whole – that is, as a sensation. At first this sensation may well be little more than a silhouette.

The baby establishes additional relationships with her environment as soon as the possibility of their having a meaning presents itself. Suppose that she is looking at a suspended uniformly coloured cube against a background of patterned wallpaper. There is no reason why her brain should group the retinal stimuli of the visible faces of the cube together, since they appear to have different shades depending on how the light falls on them. They might just as well be part of the wallpaper. Any grouping of retinal stimuli is equally plausible unless some prior knowledge or further experience with the cube intervenes. When the baby learns to manipulate the cube she experiences it as a whole independent of the patterned wallpaper, thus permitting her to learn to see the cube as a sensation.

In a similar way, an increasing number of visual sensations will emerge out of the background of undifferentiated stimuli as the baby establishes meaningful relationships with her environment. This experience is comparable to one we are all familiar with, namely, the puzzle of finding hidden faces in a drawing in which some of the lines belong simultaneously to the picture and to a face. Once we learn to see some of the lines as belonging to a face, say among the lines representing the leaves of a tree, it is as if the face leaps out from the picture. We have learned to see a new sensation by rearranging some of the stimuli lines of the picture. We have learned to see a face where we saw none before. As the baby learns to recognize an increasing number of visual sensations, the background of anything she looks at will increasingly be made up of sensations also. It will enable her to begin to derive clues about whatever she is looking at from the background context such as relative size, spatial perspective, and so on.

In order to have a visual sensation of someone or something, the baby's mind must be able to separate the corresponding retinal stimuli from the mass of undifferentiated stimuli and learn to interpret them as a whole. In other words, the baby must be able to establish a meaningful relationship with that person or object. This permits a foreground-background distinction between the retinal stimuli so that the baby can learn to see the foreground stimuli as a sensation on the basis of the experience afforded by the established relationships. Since all the senses are involved in these relationships, a context is created in the mind in which the stimuli detected by the other senses can also begin to have a meaning. Once a baby has established a relationship with a constituent of her world she can direct his full consciousness towards it, enabling her to differentiate between various kinds of relationships, such as those that are reciprocal and those that are not, those that involve sounds and those that do not. That she does make such distinctions is evident from her facial expressions and the increasing variety of sounds that she utters. The large variety of baby languages or, more appropriately, sets of baby signals more or less understood by those who regularly interact with her, show that the distinctions are largely her own.

As the child learns to recognize more and more visual sensations among the undifferentiated stimuli because of the development of the mental structures built up from experience, her ability to communicate also changes significantly. At first the phrases adults utter are nothing more than undifferentiated aural stimuli and she may only discern their emotional tone. As the child learns to see facial expressions, gestures, and body posture, things change. The situation becomes more like that of an adult trying to communicate with another adult who speaks a distant foreign language. To communicate anything at all they would have to pay attention to body language (facial expression, gestures, posture, and so on) as well as the emotional tone of the phrases. Any face-to-face conversation between people speaking the same language is in fact facilitated by such cues, but they are normally registered metaconsciously. As the child becomes conscious of body language her ability to communicate improves.

Suppose, for example, that the child has been encouraged to say 'mama.' She may then use the word indiscriminately and call all persons 'mama.' The reactions from everyone but her mother gives her the impression that something is wrong. Since by that time the child has learned to single out her mother by the unique way she behaves toward her, she may put two and two together and use the word correctly. Otherwise the child can only be baffled by the response so that she may temporarily drop the use of the word 'mama' altogether since it cannot have any meaning in her world.

One of the most fundamental aspects of the child's socialization into a society is the learning of the language as spoken by one of its speech communities. To avoid socio-linguistic complications we shall naively define a speech community as a social group within a language community whose speech is relatively uniform as a consequence of its members having a common interpretation of their experience resulting from regular face-to-face interaction. Since their perceptual apparatus functions in part on the basis of prior experience, the members of a speech community will interpret given sets of stimuli in much the same way. Before a child learns to speak, her ability to share her experience of the world with other members of her speech community is severely limited. She must derive her own meaning from the relationships she has learned to have with the constituents of her world. The result is that as compared with the other members of her speech community her perceptual apparatus is able to interpret far fewer stimuli and may interpret any given set of stimuli differently. She lives in a world that only partially coincides with that of the members of her speech community. Her perceptual apparatus only interprets those sets of stimuli that have a meaning to her, so that her world, as limited as it may be, is endowed with meaning. Her world reflects the meaning of the relationships she has learned to have with reality, and her behaviour externalizes the meaning that these relationships have for her.

Once we realize the limitations that a child's perceptual apparatus imposes on the relationships she is able to have, the early phases of her development come to stand in a new light. Given the way she perceives the world, her behaviour now appears purposeful and as 'sensible' as that of an adult. The meaning that can be derived from the physical world by tasting, manipulating, and throwing objects is, after all, quite limited. Playing with a set of keys, for example, has at first no other meaning than the discovery of its shape and the way it feels, sounds, and tastes. When the child learns to walk and follow people around, objects take on a new meaning for her because they are habitually used in specific routines of our daily lives. Give the child the same set of keys and she will imitate the way she has seen them used by others. In imitating the acts that accompany such objects while playing or eating, her perceptual apparatus learns to refine the involuntary process of interpreting stimuli, yielding more detailed sensations of these objects on the basis of this experience. She will, for example, quickly discover by trial and error that only one end of the key can be inserted into the keyhole. Her perceptual apparatus refines the visual sensation of the key, so that after a while she will be able to select the correct end of the key for insertion into the keyhole. Furthermore, there will be increasingly fewer instances in which she confuses keys with similarly shaped objects because she has learned to differentiate them perceptually.

The fact that the daily lives of the other members of the child's speech community are largely composed of a set of shared habits and routines also permits certain aural stimuli to take on meaning because of the regularity with which they are used in specific contexts. While sentences may still be nothing more than a mass of undifferentiated aural stimuli to the child, she nevertheless grasps something of what is being communicated to her, especially when others are particularly expressive with their body language. The social context, the body language, and tone of voice are the general framework for what is being communicated, while spoken language fills in the details, as it were. The child may soon notice that single words or simple phrases are always uttered in specific social contexts and are accompanied by specific body language or acts. She may thus be able to discover a meaning for the aural stimuli, which then become sounds that stand out from other undifferentiated aural stimuli. The child begins to grasp something of the meanings of sounds, the subsequent improvement in her ability to communicate with others may encourage her to pay closer attention to aural stimuli, leading to her learning more words. The meanings these vocal signs may take on in the mind may not fully coincide with the ones shared by the members of her speech community. However, since both the child and the others use words in a daily-life context consistent with how they perceive their meanings, she is able to adjust the meanings of the words she uses in accordance with her interpretation of the way the others react to her usage of a particular word. In the course of these interactions her perceptual apparatus continues to refine its involuntary interpreting of stimuli as she learns to distinguish between words that sound alike and instances of body language that resemble one another.

The child's use of vocal signs can contribute to the development of the way her perceptual apparatus interprets stimuli. If a child grows up in an urban and thus largely artificial environment, she may have noticed the existence of a number of constituents of that environment in spite of the fact that her experience with them was rather superficial. Since they do not directly enter into the daily routines of the members of her speech community, her perceptual apparatus interprets certain sets of stimuli to yield only the most rudimentary sensations. There is no reason to assume that what the child sees when she looks at a tree, which is after all a relatively complex ensemble, is much more than what the average person sees who looks at the engine compartment of a car. In either case there is no prior experience that allows the perceptual apparatus to interpret the mass of stimuli of the complex ensemble, to allow the person to experience visual sensations. When we take the child for a walk and point out a tree to her that is sufficiently isolated in the landscape so that she knows what we are talking about, she may take a closer look at the tree precisely because she senses that the tree has a meaning for other people, and she knows from past experience that the world of her speech community is a world that has meaning. The experience of looking the tree over by scanning it as a whole allows her perceptual apparatus to refine the visual sensation. The very fact that we have called the whole ensemble of the trunk, branches, and leaves by one name helps the child to group the stimuli and detach them from others by better scanning. Naming things thus helps sort out meaningful wholes from the very complex visual world.

Had the child grown up in a 'primitive' clan living in a natural milieu, language would probably not have been necessary in the above case. Trees would have been as much a part of the daily lives of the members of her speech community as a bunch of keys is for the urban child. She has watched others climb trees to pick fruit, gather palm leaves for thatch, break off braches to make sticks – activities which would have provided her perceptual apparatus with sufficient experience to have quite a refined visual sensation of trees without the intervention of vocal signs. Vocal signs may thus help the refinement of the involuntary interpreting of stimuli.

It is now beginning to become evident that a sensation derived from a set of stimuli in any of the five dimensions of experience associated with our external world has two components of meaning. It reflects something of the 'nature' of the constituent in the environment from which the stimuli originated. But since the sensation results from the involuntary interpreting of these stimuli based on prior experience, it also reflects something of the meaning it has in our existence and hence, in the case of adults, the meaning it has in the society of which they are members.

DIFFERENTIATION

To gain further insight into the way perceptual paradigms function both individually and jointly, let us compare the visual sensations provided by ten dogs. When we compare any two sensations all we can say is that they are identical, or different, or similar (that is, partly identical and partly different). If we wish to go into more detail we will have to cease comparing them as wholes and relate them on the basis of their sharing or not sharing components (be they features, elements, or constituents). If we consider the visual sensations of our sample of ten dogs on the level of organized wholes we note that they are neither identical nor totally different, which simply confirms a fact we already knew – namely that, although they are all dogs, they are nevertheless unique individuals.

When we begin to analyse the situation, we might proceed by making a list of all the visible features that we can think of and next list the dogs that share a particular type. Thus the first, third, and ninth dogs may all have long noses, while the second, fifth, sixth, and tenth dogs have flat noses, and the fourth, seventh, and eighth dogs have noses that are both different from each other and different from the other two groups. In repeating this analysis for each feature on our list, we conclude that no two dogs either share all the features on the list or fail to share any feature at all. What we find is a network of criss-crossing and overlapping 'family resemblances' based on explicit criteria.[8] If we tried to increase the rigour of our comparison by introducing a set of measurable variables to characterize each feature, we would find the same result except that the network of criss-crossing and overlapping 'family resemblances' would be transformed into a network of criss-crossing and overlapping relationships based on the sharing of equal or nearly equal values of a particular variable. We can go through a similar analysis with a sample of ten cats and attempt to compare the results with those obtained for dogs, provided that we can manage to compare the features of the dogs to those of the cats.

The question now arises: how did we select the sample of ten dogs from all other animals in the first place? The specialized part of our mind that interprets retinal stimuli could not have learned to resolve the visual sensations of animals into components only to reconstitute them into similarity sets based on members sharing a number of similar components. Our analysis of what the visual sensations of ten dogs had in common implies that the sample could not have been chosen by means of an 'ideal type,' a definition or selection criteria based on a common set of similar components. After all, the visual sensations were related only by a network of criss-crossing and overlapping 'family resemblances.' The special functions of the mind each associated with one of the senses must therefore differentiate between sets of stimuli on the level of wholes by means of a 'logic' of wholes or of systems. We shall refer to this 'logic' as the process of differentiation. In order to come to understand the characteristics of the process of differentiation, we shall examine how a child learns to recognize different kinds of animals.

An urban child who grows up in an apartment complex in which no pets are allowed may have learned to recognize birds in the trees, fish in his father's aquarium, and four-footed animals in the streets and parks. Intuitively he may at first differentiate these animals from their environment because of their mobility. Watching the animals move about affords him the experience necessary to be able to refine their sensations by differentiating relative to each other the positions they assume while at rest or moving about. If this experience is very limited he may not be able to recognize them in pictures, especially those in which the background has been omitted. This could happen if the visual sensation of any animal is as yet sufficiently vague that it is recognized because of the environment it lives in rather than on the basis of its inherent uniqueness. The child may thus at first call an airplane a bird because they both move in the sky. As he continues to be exposed to animals he will eventually be able to recognize them in pictures, which implies that the child no longer differentiates them primarily from their environment. He now differentiates between animals without, of course, having any explicit conceptual knowledge of what an animal is.

Suppose that the first four-footed animal perceived by the urban child is a dog. His attention may be attracted by the dog's movements, which provide the necessary experience for his perceptual apparatus to learn to interpret the retinal stimuli permitting him to experience a visual sensation. Provided that his experience with dogs remains limited to seeing one occasionally on the street, the interpreting of retinal stimuli will remain rudimentary. The perceptual paradigm of dogs in the visual dimension of experience can in such a case be extended to cover the interpreting of the retinal stimuli of cats and horses as well. For the child the visual sensations of cats, dogs, and horses then differ only superficially, as in colour and size. The situation is like that of a Westerner who, having little or no experience with camels, sees them all as being essentially alike, while an Arab camel-driver has a great many names for camels corresponding to the different types he has to be able to distinguish in order to survive. Unless the urban child has some further experience with cats, dogs, and horses, a refinement of the interpreting of their retinal stimuli cannot take place. As we shall see later, things could have been different had the child lived on a farm or had his family kept a cat or dog as a pet, because he would have had a continuous and intimate experience with animals.

The urban child, however, may well have to wait until he begins to use words, which brings his visual confusion of the animals to the attention of the other members of his speech community. When his father points out a dog to him, he will typically use the same name for cats and horses because to him their visual sensations appear to be only superficially different. When his father corrects his identification of a cat or horse as a dog, the child may take another good look at the animal. As he does so he receives the same set of retinal stimuli. He could not possibly mentally compare the cat or the horse with dogs because all cats, dogs, and horses yield visual sensations that differ only superficially. Besides, he is not in any position to analyse these differences to see if in fact they are superficial, because any such analysis presupposes a comparison of features which require mental concepts that he does not have. Even if he did, the logistics of such an approach would be within the reach of only the most intelligent children, and even then the results are, as we have noted, not likely to lead to the perceptual distinction between cats and dogs or dogs and horses. The only possibility that remains open, therefore, is that the mind's interpreting of the retinal stimuli of the cat or horse is refined.

It is important to understand the nature of that refinement. The interpreting of stimuli is largely based on prior experience, so that the refinement must be relative to the child's experience of the three as yet undistinguished animals. The interpreting of the retinal stimuli of cats is increasingly refined in such a way that the resulting sensations begin to exhibit those features that distinguish them from dogs and horses. This is the case because the stimuli are interpreted by the same perceptual paradigm. The same process occurs for dogs and horses. The differences between the visual sensations of cats, dogs, and horses become less and less superficial. This divergence is amplified each time someone corrects his identification. Eventually the divergence becomes so great that it is no longer possible for the perceptual apparatus to continue interpreting the retinal stimuli of these three types of animals in the same way. It now recognizes too many incompatibilities between their visual sensations. At this point the retinal stimuli of these three types of animals are interpreted differently, so that the child now sees three different types of visual sensations corresponding to the three different types of animals.

While the perceptual apparatus now interprets the stimuli of cats, dogs, and horses by means of three different paradigms, it continues to interpret the stimuli of individual animals of each type on the basis of a single paradigm. At no time has the mind learned to see the individual sensations of dogs, for example, as being similar on the basis of a number of shared characteristics. The similarity between specimens of one type of animal is based on the fact that it is unaware of any essential differences. The moment a child begins to notice that, instead of big dogs, thin dogs, long-haired dogs, and so on, there exist essential differences between them, the process described above is busy repeating itself, resulting in his being able to recognize various types of dogs.

Had the child had more intimate experience with cats, dogs, and horses, the intervention of language would not have been necessary. Suppose he had become familiar with a dog. He would have noticed right away that when he tried to play with the first cat he saw in the way he played with the dog, the cat responded quite differently. This exprience would have exactly the same effect as the intervention of the father of the urban child described above.

Because the interpreting of retinal stimuli is based on prior experience, a new perceptual paradigm is always established relative to previously existing ones. To show that this is so, suppose that our urban child who has learned to recognize cats, dogs, and horses is taken to the zoo by his father where he identifies a wolf as a dog. The features of the Gestalts of dogs that must be 'known' by the functions of the child's mind associated with the interpreting of retinal stimuli if it is to distinguish dogs from cats and horses are quite inadequate to distinguish wolves from dogs. The child's father corrects him saying it is not a dog but a wolf, so that he takes another good look at the wolf. When he can finally recognize a wolf he has learned to differentiate wolves from dogs and from the other animals he already knew. He has learned something about wolves relative to dogs and something about dogs relative to wolves. The perceptual paradigm of dogs has broken up into a perceptual paradigm of wolves and a refined perceptual paradigm of dogs. The specialized part of the child's brain now contains the visual perceptual paradigms of cats, dogs, horses, and wolves in addition to the previously established paradigms of fish and birds.

In order to model the system-like nature of these perceptual paradigms we shall use a simple spatial representation. In our model the perceptual paradigms are each represented by a position on a surface. Each paradigm is located on the surface in such a way as to have as neighbours those paradigms which were directly affected as a result of its creation. Thus the perceptual paradigms of cats, dogs, and horses are neighbours within the visual dimension of experience because they resulted from a single paradigm breaking up into three. Any perceptual paradigm may acquire new neighbours whenever it is directly affected by the creation of a new paradigm. This was the case when the creation of the perceptual paradigm of wolves made it into a new neighbour for the paradigm of dogs. Interacting neighbours are indicated by joining them by a line segment. In comparing the sensations that result from the perceptual paradigms when the retina receives the appropriate sets of stimuli, we note that the sensations that most resemble one another issue from neighbouring perceptual paradigms. If we define the function of a perceptual paradigm as the way in which it interprets stimuli, then each perceptual paradigm is directly differentiated from those whose functions most resemble it. Typically, at a previous phase of development the functions of neighbouring paradigms were performed by a smaller number because the interpreting of some sets of stimuli were not differentiated. A group of interconnected and strongly interacting perceptual paradigms form a cluster. An example of such a cluster is the one constituted by the perceptual paradigms of four-footed animals.

It should be remembered that, when the retinal stimuli of four-footed animals were still interpreted by a single perceptual paradigm, the latter was differentiated from the paradigms that interpreted the retinal stimuli of birds and fish. These perceptual paradigms were in turn differentiated from all others not related to animals. All the perceptual paradigms for the interpreting of retinal stimuli acquired by our urban child form a connected network of points on the surface. The complete network includes within it the cluster of the perceptual paradigms of four-footed animals as well as any other clusters or single perceptual paradigms that the child has acquired. The network represents the child's ability to derive visual sensations from the external world which at first was essentially totally undifferentiated. There cannot exist any isolated points on the surface of our model that are not connected to the network, because each newly-formed perceptual paradigm interacts with one or more previously formed paradigms which as a consequence become its neighbour(s).

But what then distinguishes the clusters from the larger network of which they are a part? There are several differences between the network of a cluster and the larger surrounding network, but they all have their root in the way a cluster is formed. The pattern of formation of the cluster of the perceptual paradigms of four-footed animals as described for our urban child is typical of the way the mind organizes the interpreting of retinal stimuli, particularly after a certain level of his development. A cluster begins to form when an established perceptual paradigm, which we shall call the founding perceptual paradigm, divides itself into two or more paradigms. Any one of these may once again divide itself. Each new perceptual paradigm thus reinforces a part of the cluster's network because its formation presupposes the refinement of several neighbouring paradigms relative to itself. Suppose we make the distance between two neighbours in our model proportional to the degree of lack of similarity between the sensations they yield when the retina receives the appropriate stimuli. A cluster within the larger network would then appear in our model as a set of points on the surface that are more closely spaced than are the surrounding points of the larger network. The point in the larger network that represented the founding paradigm has been replaced by a cluster of very closely spaced points. In other words, the sensations produced by the members of a cluster resemble each other much more than any of them resembles any of the sensations produced by the neighbours of the cluster in the larger network.

At any stage in the child's development the network formed by the interacting perceptual paradigms associated with a function of the mind represents his ability to interpret retinal stimuli systematically. This network is the exact opposite of the network of overlapping and criss-crossing 'family resemblances' obtained when we compared the visual sensations of ten dogs because no explicit criteria for assessing similarity or difference have intervened. The former is built up by processes below the level of consciousness from a world that was at first largely undifferentiated, while the latter is arrived at by means of conscious analysis of a world that has already been differentiated. Unlike the network of 'family resemblances' the network of preceptual paradigms is constructed without asking the question about what the visual sensations have in common. The only 'question' that needs to be answered is whether a set of retinal stimuli is essentially different from any other set that has previously been interpreted by any perceptual paradigm in the network. Each perceptual paradigm corresponds to a part of the visual dimension of the external world that has not as yet been differentiated further on the basis of our experience with it.

What the visual sensations resulting from a particular perceptual paradigm have in common is that they are all fundamentally different from the sensations produced by the other paradigms of the network while being only superficially different from each other. In a way, we might say that to a child, within the visual dimension of experience, a dog is what all the other animals he has learned to recognize are *not*. That is, dogs form a part of his visual world that has not been subdivided further, or what dogs have in common is that they have not been distinguished from each other in a fundamental way. The way a network of perceptual paradigms is built up makes it infinitely expandable and each expansion reinforces a part of the existing network. This is not the case for the network of 'family resemblances' based on explicit criteria. If, for example, we changed our sample of visual sensations that are to be compared, the entire analysis would have to be started all over again and the results of any previous analysis risk to be invalidated. For the case of the urban child the sample of visual sensations of ten dogs might first have included any four-footed animal, later any four-footed animal except any he identifies as cats and horses, or still later any four-footed animal except those he identifies as cats, horses, and wolves. At each level of development the network of overlapping and criss-crossing 'family resemblances' of dogs based on explicit criteria would have had to be reconstructed, an effort to which none of the previously carried out comparisons could have made any contribution. Needless to say, if this were how children learned to recognize animals, they would soon be hopelessly bogged down and confused.

As the child develops, the network of interacting perceptual paradigms is increasingly made up of clusters resulting from the break-up of individual paradigms. Once a cluster contains a reasonable number of perceptual paradigms – that is, once the interpreting of the corresponding retinal stimuli is quite refined – an incident like the following may occur. If our urban child sees a giraffe on television he may ask his mother: 'What kind of funny horse is that?' On the basis of his prior experience with four-footed animals the child is able to interpret the stimuli of the giraffe into a sensation that is sufficiently refined so that it clearly does not correspond to any animal he knows. He recognizes its similarity with horses but at the same time senses that the differences between a giraffe and a horse are much more substantial than the superficial differences between various horses. A new perceptual paradigm has formed whch he implicitly recognizes by asking his mother to confirm it by giving it a name. The perceptual paradigm of giraffes was formed relative to horses, which confirms the pattern of cluster expansion we have outlined above.

The network of interacting perceptual paradigms that we have described thus far constitutes what we shall call a system of perceptual paradigms. It represents a function of the mind which interprets retinal stimuli. Gradually, as the child grows up, this function becomes largely a matter of routine on the basis of prior experience. The development of this system is not the same for any two children since it depends on their biographies, even when they are brought up in the same speech community living in a particular environment (rural, urban, etc.). They will eventually largely share the system of perceptual paradigms with the members of their speech community because of their increasing ability to share their experience with them by means of language. The interpreting of stimuli within the other dimensions of experience also occurs by means of systems of perceptual paradigms representing similar functions of the mind. Their development and function is analogous to that of the system of perceptual paradigms of the visual dimensions of experience just described.

THE FOUR DIMENSIONS

The process of differentiation described for the visual dimension of experience is paradigmatic for the other senses and its mode of operation may thus be generalized. We shall do so by specifying its four dimensions of differentiation.

The first dimension of the process of differentiation differentiates the stimuli of something in our range of attention from those of its environment within a dimension of experience. This amounts to drawing a distinction between the foreground (composed of all the stimuli that are to be interpreted as one sensation) and the background (all the other available stimuli). We have already discussed a number of examples such as recognizing hidden faces in a drawing, the child learning to recognize words in spoken phrases that appear at first as a mass of undifferentiated stimuli, and the mechanic learning to recognize meaningful sounds from the background of the noise of a motor.

The second dimension refines the interpreting of a particular set of stimuli on the basis of any changes in the stimuli that are detected by the perceptual paradigm that interprets them. The set of stimuli can then be differentiated relative to itself, resulting in the refinement of the perceptual paradigm. Within the visual dimension of experience changes in a set of stimuli are often due to our mobility, so that we rarely see anything from exactly the same position twice, and sometimes due to the mobility of the source of the stimuli. We can identify a dinner plate regardless of the angle or the distance from which we see it. The same dinner plate appears as circular when seen from above, elliptical when tilted, and still different when seen from the side. The stimuli of an animal change as it moves. Consequently, when we watch it, the process of differentiating its stimuli is refined. Since a perceptual paradigm derives clues about the interpreting of retinal stimuli from the environment of anything we watch, that is, from the other sets of retinal stimuli of the background that are interpreted simultaneously, a changing background may also refine the interpreting of a set of stimuli. Effective use of this fact is made in optical illusions. Changes in the way the light falls on an object will also change the retinal stimuli that we receive. It is because of these constant changes that a continued exposure to anything refines the interpreting of the retinal stimuli associated with it. Similar changes occur in hearing. The acoustic characteristics of the environment, the relative positions of and the distance between a speaker and a listener, the speaker having a cold, his emotional tone, the level of his voice, and so on may change the aural stimuli of the same words spoken under different circumstances. We learn to refine the involuntary interpreting of the stimuli when we are exposed to these variations.

The third dimension is related to the fact that any constituent of our external world is never completely identical with another because they are all unique individuals. As a consequence the sets of stimuli interpreted by a particular perceptual paradigm are all different. Since the perceptual paradigm functions on the basis of prior perceptual experience, it differentiates each new set of stimuli with respect to the sets differentiated earlier. Each time it interprets another set of stimuli it 'learns' something, which translates into a greater variety of retinal sensations. A good example of this occurs when members of one race first meet members of a different race. To a white person black people may at first look so much alike that he has difficulty distinguishing between them. Continued exposure to black people permits his visual apparatus to differentiate them relative to one another, with the result that their sensations are individualized. The third dimension of differentiation creates diversity within the unity of the sensations produced by a perceptual paradigm. It may also result in a perceptual paradigm dividing itself when the diversity of the sensations it yields becomes too great. At this point the fourth dimension takes over.

The fourth dimension breaks up existing perceptual paradigms into two or more paradigms. This was discussed at some length for the case of the child learning to recognize cats, dogs, and horses. As she learned to distinguish between these animals the diversity of the animals in her world increased. A measure of order and unity was created in the new diversity by means of the newly acquired perceptual paradigms. Thus, while the third dimension creates diversity within unity, the fourth dimension essentially brings about unity within diversity. When a set of perceptual paradigms is not expanding, these two dimensions are in equilibrium. When new perceptual paradigms are being added a temporary localized disequilibrium occurs. The four dimensions are completely interdependent and inseparable, constituting one process of differentiation.

In describing the development of our links with the world via the senses, we have concentrated on our sight. This was a deliberate choice, for the modern urban and industrial society lends itself to the primacy of sight over all the other senses since it provides most of the perceptually meaningful data in the form of retinal stimuli. Peoples living in a natural environment employ their other senses more intensely: one only need imagine living in the jungle to realize that many dangers can be heard before they can be seen. Nature produces relatively few aural stimuli that have no meaning because they cannot be related to some aspect of daily-life experience of such peoples. Meaningless undifferentiated aural stimuli (or noise) are characteristic of industrial and urban life. Each culture may therefore have a different hierarchy of the senses.

We began this chapter by suggesting that the meaning a relationship with the external world has for us may be conceptualized as resulting from its progressive enfolding into our being and what we experience as the conscious awareness of this process. This perspective was developed by analysing the role the mind plays in the operation of the senses. At first the ability of babies to make use of their senses appears to be severely restricted by the limited innate structures of the brain. We hypothesized that babies use these structures as paradigms, thus expanding their ability to relate to the world. The resulting experiences are internalized, creating mental structures that are built up from further experiences. These structures built up from experience are grafted onto the innate structures of the brain, thus constituting the mind. The role the mind plays in one of the five senses associated with a dimension of experience was conceptualized as a system of perceptual paradigms whose members represent the specific ability to relate to a range of stimuli. The system operates on the basis of a process of differentiation. We have so far only dealt with the involuntary and thus most mechanistic facets of perception. All the processes we have attempted to conceptualize are, however, embedded in the much larger process of enfolding a relationship with the external world into our life.

As we proceed with the analysis the involvement of our whole being in perception will come to light ...

THREE

The Structure of Experience

Our study of how the mind interprets stimuli is still incomplete. In the last chapter we deferred considering how in daily-life situations the process of interpreting a set of stimuli is affected by the way it interacts with the simultaneous interpreting of other sets of stimuli in the same dimension of experience and how these processes together interact with those occurring in the other dimensions at the same time. In this chapter we shall consider how various perceptual paradigms collaborate to interpret the stimuli received by any one of the senses to yield a Gestalt. Such a Gestalt is, as we have noted, the meaning that emerges when the sensations are interrelated into a system because of the way the perceptual paradigms jointly carry out their tasks.

In the visual dimension of experience it is quite obvious from everyday experience that considerable collaboration between the activated perceptual paradigms takes place. Although we have two eyes we never see two images. Each eye receives slightly different sets of stimuli which are interpreted together to produce a three-dimensional visual experience. Its constituent sensations form a pattern showing how the constituents of the external world which fall within our field of vision are spatially interrelated. To achieve this, a number of perceptual paradigms must not only be busy interpreting sets of stimuli simultaneously but must also interact with one another. Under laboratory conditions it is, of course, possible to have the visual apparatus interpret stimuli derived from a single object exposed to one or two eyes against a neutral background. By introducing this or other limitations to reduce the number of variables, some aspects of how the perceptual paradigms collaborate in interpreting the retinal stimuli can be studied.[1]

The mode of collaboration of the visual perceptual paradigms can be affected by the way we use our eyes to scan something we are interested in. Scanning is frequently necessary, not because the focus of interests falls only partly within our field of vision, but because of the structure of the retina. The retina contains two types of sensitive cells called rods and cones. Cones are situated mainly in the centre of the retina. They enable us to see colours and details of shape in normal levels of illumination, but they do not adapt well to the dark. Rods are situated mainly outside the centre of the retina and adapt gradually to dim light, but they do not permit us to see colours very well. Since the nerve density is greatest in the central part of the retina and relatively low in the outer regions, details of shape and positions of objects are best perceived by cone vision. The area of the cortex which interprets retinal stimuli devotes the greater part of its efforts to stimuli that fall on the central part of the retina. Thus if some of our focus of interest falls within the outer part of the field of vision, we have to scan with our eyes in such a way that each part can be observed with cone vision. The parts of the field of vision that are observed mainly with rod vision tend to form a background. We see what is there, but shape and spatial relationships are not perceived accurately.

When we need to scan a focus of interest we break it up into a sequence of attention areas that are integrated into an overall impression. By resting our eyes on a specific area we determine which perceptual paradigms will collaborate together, and this can have important consequences for the way we perceive a focus of interest. Similarly, the length of time we dwell on an attention area will give it a certain emphasis relative to the others, which affects the way they are integrated into an overall impression. Effective scanning is a complicated affair, and it may be six or seven years before children learn to do it well.

Scanning is a purposeful activity which can significantly affect the way the perceptual paradigms interpreting the retinal stimuli collaborate to yield a visual Gestalt. Consider the situation where we are sitting on a bench in the park watching some children play ball. Our eyes receive a far greater number of retinal stimuli than is necessary for us to be able to follow the game. On the basis of prior experience with this kind of game we scan with our eyes to discriminate between stimuli that are directly relevant to the game and those that are not. As a result, a foreground-background distinction is drawn. The foreground constitutes a network of relationships between the visual sensations derived from the players and the ball, which typifies the game. The background interrelates the remaining sensations that are only indirectly relevant to the game.

To achieve this foreground-background distinction we scanned the available stimuli in an appropriate way. Had our attention been directed to the landscape design of the area of the park where the children play ball rather than to the game, we would have scanned the available stimuli in quite a different pattern to show the plants, shrubs, trees, and so on in their spatial relationships. The remaining information, including the children playing ball, would have been largely passed over and whatever we happened to note of it would have been included in the background. We can go on multiplying the ways in which that same mass of stimuli could have been arranged simply by scanning it differently. The foreground could equally well have been a cat trying to surprise a bird in a tree or simply an unusually shaped tree. It is impossible for us to attend to all these things at the same time. We are constantly being presented with more information than we can pay attention to. It is necessary to select by means of scanning, but this process is not simply a matter of ignoring certain details while paying attention to others. By means of scanning we impose something of ourselves on the way the perceptual paradigms collaborate in interpreting stimuli, and hence on what we see. It is our inability to attend to everything within our field of vision all at once and the imposition of our interests, feelings, and past experience which leads to the available retinal stimuli being interpreted into a visual Gestalt with a foreground-background distinction.

The fact that any given mass of available retinal stimuli can be interpreted in a variety of ways according to our interests, feelings, and prior experience has important implications for the way a particular set of stimuli is interpreted to yield a sensation. Because the foreground of a visual Gestalt interrelates sensations into a system with the remaining sensations constituting its environment, the way any particular set of stimuli will be interpreted will depend on how it relates to the others. For example, we are more likely to observe certain details of one of the ball players if they are relevant to the game, while we are not likely to note them at all if we were looking at the cat trying to catch the bird in the tree because the ball game would then be the background of our visual Gestalt.

There are thus two tendencies in relation to the interpretation of a particular set of retinal stimuli, which can be in conflict with each other. The first is the tendency of a perceptual paradigm, associated with very familiar constituents in our environment usually seen from the same viewpoint, to interpret the retinal stimuli of these constituents strictly on the basis of past experience. The second is to interpret such retinal stimuli to refine the resulting sensations with respect to those details that are important for the system of sensations it will be fitted into and thus largely to ignore the extensively reinforced habitual way of interpretation.

When such conflicts occur several well-known phenomena emerge. We tend to see a tilted dinner plate that we normally look down on as we eat from it, as being more circular than the elliptical image projected on the retina.[2] What we perceive in this case is a compromise between the retinal image and the way the object is usually seen or thought of. This effect is called shape constancy. A similar effect called size constancy occurs also. Normally the stimuli derived from a particular object are interpreted, in relation to those originating from the other objects in its surroundings, to determine its relative size. If an object is quite familiar to us distortions often occur. It is as if with very familiar objects their relative sizes within the spatial pattern of the sensations is partly ignored due to prior experience, leading to distortions. This is a familiar phenomenon to those who have tried to make accurate perspective drawings. We often have to compare the size of an object with that of surrounding objects by holding a pencil at arm's length in order to get the correct proportions in the drawing.

Much of what we have suggested as an explanation for the formation of visual Gestalts can also apply to the emergence of aural Gestalts. As was the case with sight, aural stimuli are detected by twin sense organs, the ears, and interpreted simultaneously but not independently by aural perceptual paradigms. Because of their different spatial position the stimuli received by the ears are slightly different. Yet we hear only one aural sensation. The perceptual apparatus associated with the aural dimension of experience interprets the two nearly identical sets of stimuli to yield a single sensation and some information about the spatial position of the source from which the stimuli originated. This is important when our ears are being stimulated by different sound sources at the same time. It helps the perceptual apparatus separate different sets of stimuli according to their source. Again consider the example of sitting on a bench in the park watching some children play ball. The aural stimuli have been discriminated into the foreground of directly relevant sensations such as what the children shout to each other during the game, and a background that may contain the conversation of the people sitting next to us on the bench, the barking of a dog, and the thunder of a storm looming on the horizon. These aural stimuli could have been interpreted in a variety of ways yielding quite different aural Gestalts. We could, for example, have listened to the conversation of the people beside us on the bench, the distant thunder, or the barking dog, in which cases the aural stimuli of the children playing ball would have become a part of the background of the aural Gestalt. As was the case for our sight, we are unable to pay attention to all the aural stimuli at the same time. As we direct our attention we impose something of our interests, feelings, and prior experience onto the way the perceptual paradigms collaborate to interrelate the sensations associated with some of the sources of aural stimuli into a foreground and to relegate the sensations from the other sources to the background.

The ability to direct our aural attention is particularly crucial in situations like one where we are sitting in a crowded subway car with conversations going on all around us. We can listen to any one conversation only because we are able to discriminate within certain limits between the various sources of aural stimuli by directing our attention, which allows the perceptual apparatus which interprets aural stimuli to interrelate sequences of stimuli from one source more to each other than to the stimuli from the other sources. If we could not direct our aural attention we would not have been able to distinguish between conversations and would hear only a scrambled mass of aural sensations.

In the tactile dimension of experience, stimuli result from contacting a constituent of the external world or one part of our body with another. These stimuli are interpreted to give the meaning of the contact. Here again perceptual paradigms would need to collaborate to interpret complex sets of stimuli distributed over different parts of our body, as when we are seated behind a typewriter. As we type, our fingers are touching the keys, a fly may be sitting on our forehead, and our one-year-old son is tapping our knee. We cannot possibly pay attention to all these things. We need to direct our attention to one of them – in this case our fingers to ensure we are not missing the keys. This becomes the foreground of a tactile Gestalt, while the other sensations receiving only indirect attention are relegated to the background. That such tactile Gestalts are formed is quite evident from situations like the one where we discover a bruise when drying ourselves after a shower and we do not know how and where we got it. We may have been angry or upset at the time or deeply absorbed by something interesting, with the result that we did not notice the incident. Here again our interests, feelings, and prior experience help determine the pattern of collaboration between the perceptual paradigms and hence the kind of tactile Gestalt that results.

Within the dimensions of experience related to taste and smell, similar collaboration of perceptual paradigms appears to occur when different sources of stimuli are present. Once again we can affect the Gestalt by moving our nose closer to one of the sources of stimuli or by the way we manipulate what we are tasting in our mouth. Our interests, feelings, and prior experience will again affect the Gestalts that form in these two dimensions. We may not enjoy good food because we are preoccupied with something else or we may not appreciate the fine bouquet of a wine for lack of experience with wines.

In our analysis of each of the five dimensions of experience related to the external world, it was noted that stimuli are not mechanically processed as by a television camera or a microphone. In each dimension, the pattern of collaboration between the perceptual paradigms interpreting stimuli depends on our interests, feelings, and prior experience. These are reflected in the Gestalts that emerge from each pattern of collaboration. The interpreting of a specific set of stimuli depends on its relation to the Gestalt.

Thus far we have examined the interpreting of stimuli in one dimension of experience in isolation from that in the other dimensions. The external world, however, is not experienced in terms of isolated dimensions of experience. When we dealt with the example of the child learning to recognize four-footed animals we simply assumed that the animals made no sounds. To adhere closely to reality, we should have developed the example considering all five dimensions of experience at the same time. Except for making matters more complex, however, nothing essential would have changed. The fact that the different types of four-footed animals do make different sounds may help the child in learning to distinguish them more easily because each dimension of experience complements and reinforces the others. Eyes and ears collaborate, so the child would have learned to associate any aural stimuli of the animal with the retinal stimuli, since both came from the same position in space. The aural sensation becomes as much a part of the animal as the visual sensation, associating the corresponding perceptual paradigms in each dimension of experience. The result is that when we hear a dog's bark behind a wall he is just as real as if we had seen him quietly watching us without barking.

Any constituent of the external world can be represented in a maximum of five dimensions of experience, but this is rarely the case. Few of us would know many animals by their odours, let alone by their taste. In such cases the animal or any other focus of attention is not represented by a perceptual paradigm in all the five dimensions of experience. Thus birds are usually represented by a perceptual paradigm in only the visual and aural dimensions of experience; food in the dimensions of sight, taste, touch, and smell; perfumes in the dimensions of sight, touch, and smell; cloth in the dimensions of sight and touch; and so on.

However, these associations between perceptual pardigms, each interpreting stimuli from the same source but in a different dimension of experience, are but one facet of the complex patterns of collaboration between the processes that yield a Gestalt in each dimension of experience. When we direct our attention to a constituent of our external world only some of the stimuli are derived from it, and this requires a highly complex process of collaboration between the perceptual apparatus associated with each of the senses. An important characteristic of the mind is that normally it cannot subdivide itself into two or more sections that each work on a different task. (We are, of course, not concerned here with the functions that regulate our organism.) The mind constantly functions as one dynamic whole that is busy with only one thing at a time – namely, that to which our attention is directed.

We might say that the amount that can be attended to per unit of time is fixed. As we broaden the scope of a task, that is, as we distribute our attention over a larger area, the concentration and accuracy with which we perform the task decreases. Under certain conditions we may be able to listen to two things at the same time by alternating our attention between them. Otherwise, while we direct our attention to one thing we may be able to pay some indirect attention to another. For example, while we are sitting in a coffee shop listening to the conversation at our table, we may hear someone at another table mention our name. With our sight this is much more difficult because we may have to shift the direction of our gaze, with the result that one or the other focus of attention usually leaves our field of vision.

It is impossible to have the different parts of the mind associated with our senses function independently by having each sense focus on different things. For example, it is impossible to attend simultaneously to aural and retinal stimuli that come from different sources. When subjects in an experiment had to understand both visual (printed) and aural (spoken) instructions to find points on a map, they always overlooked one or the other, although more of the aural information was overlooked.[3] We have already shown that, in each dimension of experience related to the outside world, our interests, feelings, and prior experience determine the foreground-background distinction and hence the nature of the Gestalt that emerges from the interpreting of stimuli. Since they are the same for each dimension, the various Gestalts represent complementary interpretations of a given situation. Their foregrounds represent only one focus of attention but in different dimensions of experience. We *experience* that situation as a five-dimensional whole which we have called an experience Gestalt. The patterns of collaboration of the perceptual paradigms interpreting stimuli in the various dimensions of experience are in fact part of a larger pattern of collaboration which, as we shall see shortly, involves not only the perceptual apparatus associated with the senses but the entire mind.

Like the Gestalts, an experience Gestalt has the properties of a system. It cannot be derived from its constituent sensations. It is therefore important to emphasize that the process of interpreting stimuli to yield an experience Gestalt is not a two-stage process, first producing sensations which are then combined in the second stage. An organized whole cannot be built up that way since it is more than the sum of its constituents. Our limited scope of attention and the dynamic unity of the mind necessitate a pattern of collaboration of all the perceptual paradigms interpreting stimuli for any given situation. It will include the patterns of collaboration we have examined in each dimension. As a result, complementary foreground-background distinctions are established in each of the dimensions of experience. The foreground of the experience Gestalt is constituted from all the stimuli received from the focus of interest in all the dimensions of experience, while the remaining stimuli constitute its background. Our conceptual model of the progressive enfolding of a relationship with the external world is, as yet, incomplete. We suggested that it involves our present state of mind, interests, feelings, personality, subconscious, metaconscious, prior experience, and our expectations for the future. We will next turn to the incorporation of these facets of the enfolding process into our conceptualization of experience.

STIMULI FROM THE 'INNER' WORLD

An experience Gestalt is not limited to an experience of the external world. To illustrate this, consider once again the situation of sitting on the bench in the park watching some children play ball. Suppose we accepted an invitation to join the game. We would employ our limbs and shout back and forth with the others. Our focus of attention has not changed, but our experience now includes our 'inner' world more directly. The experience of the 'inner' world is also organized into a number of dimensions of experience usually related to the mind via a part of the brain. There are the dimensions of experience dealing with language, thought, imagination, dreams, daydreams, intuition, memory, feelings (related to various aspects of the state of our body) such as hunger, thirst, internal pain, fatigue, and so on, emotions related to our existence (such as joy, excitement, anger, depression, frustration, fear), and the operation and control of our motor and speech functions. In this section we shall discuss the dimensions of experience related to feelings and the operation of the motor functions. The others can be discussed more easily when the theory of culture as a social ecology is more fully developed.

First consider the role the mind plays in the operation of the motor functions. We are able to perform a movement without having the slightest idea (except perhaps if one happens to be a physiologist) which muscles are involved. We do not execute a movement by consciously stimulating each muscle. We execute it on the level of the pattern of stimuli. Examples of these patterns are: turning the head, walking, reaching for an object, and so on. Once we learn a movement the corresponding muscle stimuli become a meaningful pattern that is differentiated from all those previously learned. What the mind has learned is retained in a system of movement paradigms whose structure and development is analogous to that described for the systems of perceptual paradigms. The direction of operation is reversed, however. Rather than interpreting stimuli to yield sensations, a movement is initiated by our will, after which the system of movement paradigms reconstitutes the necessary patterns of muscle stimuli. It does this beginning with a Gestalt which is a set of interdependent movements involved in an activity. For example, when playing ball we may be running and turning our head to keep track of the location of some of the other players. A Gestalt calls forth a pattern of collaboration of various movement paradigms each responsible for generating a pattern of muscle stimuli to carry out the various movements involved in an activity.

The part of the mind that executes the motor functions operates in close co-operation with another part which keeps track of the positions of the body and limbs in space. The information is assembled from a number of sources. By means of the part of the ear called the labyrinth we are able to detect if the head is no longer parallel to the direction of gravitation. The position of the body and limbs is derived from the pressure distribution on joints and muscles and, of course, from what we see. All this information is transmitted to the brain as stimuli which, on the basis of our mind, lead to the formation of meaningful patterns that permit us to control and keep track of our movements.

The functions of the mind associated with the motor functions also collaborate with the interpreting of retinal stimuli. By learning that the environment is stationary we keep on seeing it in the same way despite the fact that by tilting the head the image projected on the retina is tilted also. Regardless of the position of the head we have learned to see the horizontal and vertical directions as being unchanged. A similar compensation mechanism exists for the fact that the image on the retina moves as we turn our eyes. This type of mechanism based on the collaboration between various dimensions of experience remains, of course, unaffected when the mode of collaboration between various functions of the mind changes to cope with a new focus of interest.

The dimension of experience dealing with feelings reflecting various aspects of the state of our body operates in exactly the same way as we have described for the senses. The only difference is that the stimuli originate in the 'inner' world of our body. When they take on a meaning and become a sensation they indicate hunger, thirst, cramp, fatigue, a sprained ankle, or any disorder within the body such as an upset stomach. When a number of these sets of stimuli occur simultaneously a Gestalt forms as a part of the experience Gestalt. The perceptual paradigms interpreting stimuli within the dimension of experience related to feelings will be incorporated into the pattern of collaboration of all the perceptual paradigms active in the other dimensions of experience. If the focus of attention is situated in the external world, then this dimension of experience will contribute only to the background of an experience Gestalt.

It should be noted that for each dimension of experience related to the perception of the 'inner' world, the associated functions of the mind operate on the level of wholes (sensations and Gestalts) which result from the interpretation of stimuli by means of a process of differentiation. In the case of the dimensions related to the motor functions, the same is true except that a set of stimuli is produced from a Gestalt. We have now broadened the concepts of perception, stimuli, sensation, Gestalt, and perceptual paradigm to include the 'inner' world. Stimuli are the consequences of physical, chemical, and biochemical processes detected by the nervous system occurring either within or outside our body, while sensations and Gestalts are the meanings these stimuli take on in the life of a human being. In the case of perception, stimuli are interpreted, while in the motor functions they are generated, both kinds of operations involving functions of the mind.

The concept of experience Gestalt has also been broadened. From our studies of our links with the external world, it is quite obvious that the brain is not a kind of closed-circuit television system reading out an image to the eye of our consciousness. An experience Gestalt enfolds something of our interests, feelings, and prior experience. What now appears evident is that it also involves information about our bodily presence in the world via the Gestalt depicting the position of our body, the Gestalts related to our motor functions which are changing that position by executing various movements, and the Gestalt related to the perception of our 'inner' world. An experience Gestalt will turn out to be much more complex when we later consider the dimensions of experience related to language, thought, imagination, dreams, daydreams, intuition, memory, and emotions. An experience Gestalt results from purposefully interrelating all aspects of our being in a unique way for the purpose of living a moment of our life in reality. It is not simply the result of basic drives for the satisfaction of needs; nor is it purely the result of the imposition of our will. We shall later see that an experience Gestalt is the result of both conscious and unconscious forces, of physical and psychic needs, of personality, of our past, present, and aspirations for the future. It is only then that the concept of 'dimension of experience' will be fully developed. It is, however, becoming clear that the process of enfolding a moment of our life into our being is more than information-processing by means of a co-ordinated effort of interpreting stimuli in all dimensions of expereince. It is the living of a moment of our life because our whole being affects the stimuli that flow simultaneously to and from our minds. This will become increasingly evident as we continue to explore how every aspect of life is enfolded into our being.

THE SYSTEM OF EXPERIENCE

There are a number of reasons to suppose that an experience Gestalt is formed by means of a process of differentiation partly based on prior experience. Consider the example of a child who for the first time watches some people play ball in a park. If he is to understand what is going on, he will have to do more than simply interpret the perceptual stimuli received by his senses to yield sensations. He will have to relate the actions of the ball players to the ball and dissociate them from the cheering, clapping, and waving of a few spectators.

At first this distinction may not be obvious because of incidents like the following: a spectator may kick a stray ball back on the field, an argument may arise between the players causing their behaviour to be less distinct from that of the spectators, and some of the spectators and players may cheer when there is a goal. The child has to interpret all these incidents as being either directly related to the game – that is, to the network of relationships constituting a foreground – or indirectly related to it and thus constituting a part of the background. Without making this foreground-background distinction he will not be able to understand what is going on. If he tries to relate the incident of a few spectators walking away just at the moment that the players advance with the ball in their direction, he will be puzzled when that correlation of events does not reproduce itself later. The child may thus at first constitute a different foreground-background distinction and consequently a different experience Gestalt from that of the other members of his speech community. When this is the case, however, a number of incidents will not make sense because they have not been correctly integrated into the series of experience Gestalts that is associated with the game. The child will continue to adjust his experience Gestalts until the foreground-background distinctions reach an equilibrium position. In the case of complex experience Gestalts the child may never quite reach this equilibrium point before he learns to talk. Once he does, he can ask questions about those incidents that do not quite make sense to him. Language once again helps the child's interpretation of experience to converge to that of the other members of his speech community.

When still later the child learns to play the game, the dimensions of exprience related to the 'inner' world, and particularly the one related to the motor functions, begin to contribute to the foreground of the experience Gestalts. As he learns to play the game better, the Gestalts associated with the movements he carries out will develop in two ways. First, he will learn to execute certain movements with greater accuracy and speed. For example, he will learn to have more control in kicking the ball and to co-ordinate his movements more effectively with those of other players. This will both refine the Gestalts related to his motor functions and help them to become a more integral part of the experience Gestalts. Second, the variety of the Gestalts associated with his motor functions will vastly increase. He will be able to implement and participate in a greater variety of game strategies. The degree to which his mind is able to refine these developments will in part determine how good a player he can become. If the characteristics of his nervous system lend themselves to the development of very extensive and refined mental structures acquired from the experience of the game (with extensive practice and coaching), we say he has a knack for this type of activity. People whose nervous systems are 'naturals' for a specific kind of activity do, when given the chance to develop it, become leaders in that sphere of human endeavour.

The experience Gestalts that the child has learned to form in the course of watching a ball game for the first time can be detached from the specific game, that is, from the specific sensations that constituted the experience Gestalts. He will have no difficulty interpreting the same game when it is played by adults in a stadium although the two games share none of the sensations. What the child has learned in watching the ball game goes beyond the interpreting of stimuli to yield sensations. He learns that the game is a series of patterns of relationships between the players, the ball, and the field. The result is that what he has learned about the patterns of relationships in a specific game can be detached from it and act as a paradigm for the formation of experience Gestalts of the same kind of ball game played by different people on a different field. What the various functions of the mind have been learning is to collaborate in the interpreting of stimuli to form an experience Gestalt on the basis of prior experience.

Suppose we compare ten soccer games in order to find out what they have in common. We may at first be tempted to say that the rules for soccer games define the game. But the rules for soccer only define the permitted relationships between the players, the ball, and the soccer field. This hardly defines the game. Playing the game involves the skill of a team of players to execute new patterns of permitted relationships in order to outmanoeuvre the other team and attempt to score a goal. These patterns cannot be deduced from the rules by the other team or the spectators. There is a strong element of creativity: one can know all the rules and yet be a poor soccer player. When we compare ten games on the basis of the rules we can only say that, when the referee indicates a violation of the rules, the next event in the game can be more or less predicted from the rules. As far as the playing strategies of the ten games are concerned, all we can say is that they are identical, different, or similar (that is, partly identical and partly different). If we wished to go into further details we would have to cease comparing the patterns as organized wholes and analyse them on the level of common features. We would then find that these patterns are related by a network of criss-crossing and overlapping 'family resemblances.' If we next attempted to compare various kinds of ball games, we would again be unable to find a common set of characteristics.

As is the case for sensations, experience Gestalts of ball games are therefore not formed by analysing sets of stimuli, but by the mind's process of differentiation. What the child has learned about the involuntary interpreting of stimuli derived from a particular soccer game is built up as a function of the mind. This ability acquired from the exposure to a particular game functions as a paradigm for the interpreting of stimuli of other soccer games. It will be called an experience paradigm. Among other things, an experience paradigm sets up the pattern of collaboration between the perceptual and movement paradigms which are interpreting or generating stimuli related to a particular moment of existence. It ensures that compatible foreground-background distinctions are made in all dimensions of experience.

As is the case for perceptual paradigms, each new experience paradigm is differentiated from all those previously formed. Together these experience paradigms will be conceptualized as the system of experience. This system is built up in a way analogous to the one described for the systems of perceptual paradigms. We shall briefly illustrate its development with an example. When a young child vaguely familiar with soccer first watches a game of football, she will likely confuse the two. In the same way as described for the case of a child learning to recognize four-footed animals, the existing experience paradigm eventually breaks up into the two paradigms of soccer and football. These may be complemented by experience paradigms of rugby, baseball, volleyball, basketball, tennis, and so on. These experience paradigms then form a cluster of interacting paradigms within the larger network of the system of experience. The spatial model used to illustrate the structure of a system of perceptual paradigms also illustrates that of the system of experience.

The process of differentiating the pattern of collaboration between perceptual and movement paradigms executed by the system of experience has, again, four dimensions. The first dimension differentiates between the perceptual and movement paradigms which are to contribute to the foreground of the emerging experience Gestalt, from those which are to contribute to the background. The pattern of collaboration between the perceptual and movement paradigms may change in time to reflect changes in the focus of attention. In such a case, the second dimension can differentiate the changing pattern with respect to itself, resulting in a refinement of the experience paradigm and hence in the resulting experience Gestalt. Experience never repeats itself. Hence, even similar situations are lived by means of patterns of collaboration between perceptual and movement paradigms that are unique even when they are associated with the same experience paradigm. Each new pattern of collaboration can therefore be differentiated from all the others previously formed by that experience paradigm, because the latter operates on the basis of what it has retained from forming these earlier patterns. This is the third dimension which creates diversity within unity of the experience Gestalts lived by means of the same experience paradigm. It permits us to know more and more differences between similar situations because the experience Gestalts become more refined. It can, of course, happen that the diversity of patterns of collaboration related to any one experience paradigm becomes too large, so that the corresponding experience Gestalts are no longer fundamentally alike. When this occurs, a fourth dimension of the process of differentiation intervenes, resulting in the experience paradigm dividing itself into two or more paradigms. This dimension operates until the patterns of collaboration and the corresponding experience Gestalts associated with each of these experience paradigms are no longer fundamentally different from one another. The fourth dimension thus creates unity within diversity. When the system of experience is not expanding, the third and fourth dimensions of differentiation are in equilibrium with one another.

We have thus far examined the structure and development of the system of experience, but we have as yet said nothing about its mode of operation. The function of the system of experience can be thought of as ensuring an appropriate pattern of collaboration between the various parts of our body and nervous system in order to permit us to live each moment of our existence in a meaningful way. In other words, how and why does the system shift from one pattern of collaboration provided by a particular experience paradigm to another? We shall build a simple model of this self-regulating aspect of the system of experience.

The mind does not, of course, exclusively contain networks and subsystems for the interpreting or generating of stimuli. It also comprises extensive regulatory and control systems. The system of experience can be modelled as one of these systems. It regulates and controls the operation of perceptual and movement paradigms, including some other types of paradigms to be dealt with later, and co-ordinates these functions of the mind with others.

The nervous system and hence the mind, is maintained on a level of alertness ranging from being wide awake to being sound asleep by a master zone of control located in the brainstem, called the reticular formation. It performs this function by sending out non-specific impulses to the cortex and down the spinal cord. These impulses keep the nervous system alert. The reverse situation can also occur, because any stimulation of the senses that passes to the various specialized parts of the cortex has a branch-off to the reticular formation. This is called collateral afference.

When we are sitting in a room with people who are talking about something that does not interest us, we may begin to feel drowsy and doze off. The fact that the others go on talking does not prevent us from dozing. If, however, we suddenly hear our name mentioned we may wake up and pay attention. The mind was stimulated by aural stimuli which it apparently interpreted into sensations even after we dozed off. When the mind interpreted the aural stimuli of our name a sufficiently strong pattern was produced in the mind to cause it to alert the reticular formation, which in turn aroused us by alerting the nervous system: something that the collateral afference of the conversation was not able to do. In the same manner, if we go to bed while our mind is preoccupied with worries, we may have difficulty falling asleep because the cortex keeps on stimulating the reticular formation.

When awake, our interests are often diverted away from whatever happens to be our focus of attention at the time. In most cases, however, the next focus of interest is first a part of the background of the current experience Gestalt, which is why we happen to notice it, be it only indirectly. If, for example, we are back in the park watching the children playing ball, our attention may be drawn away from the game to the cat in the distant tree or the thunderclouds on the horizon. We may also hear footsteps on the path behind us and, hearing our name, turn around to meet an acquaintance. We may suddenly remember we had some shopping to do (thought, as we shall see later, can also contribute a Gestalt to the experience Gestalt) or begin to feel a stomach cramp coming on. In all these cases, indirect attention was first paid to what was to become a new focus of attention. The system of experience was able to anticipate what the next moment of our existence was likely to be on the basis of prior experience, and was therefore able to select a new pattern of collaboration between the perceptual and movement paradigms.

When the anticipations of the next focus of interest prove to be unfounded we are often momentarily startled. Examples of this happening are commonplace. It happens when we step off the curb and it turns out to be about level with the road, or when we try to go up one more step when in fact we have reached the top of the staircase. Someone can sneak up behind and startle us. We may rush to answer the door expecting some close friends we have not seen for a long time, only to find the police. These events show to what degree we depend on anticipating the next moment in our life. The system of experience greatly facilitates these changes in the focus of interest by means of a process of self-regulation based on feedback.

A model of this feedback system can readily be constructed. To any level of attention, ranging from drowsiness to being wide awake, corresponds a certain amount of attention which is distributed to the various perceptual, movement, and other paradigms (related to language, thought, etc.) to form a foreground-background distinction in the experience Gestalt. This can be achieved by an experience paradigm sending out control impulses to these paradigms. It can be supposed that the intensity level of these impulses reflects the amount of attention the paradigm is to have. In other words, the higher the level of intensity of the control impulses received by a paradigm, the more directly will the stimuli it interprets be related to the focus of attention. Perceptual paradigms which interpret stimuli from the same source but in different dimensions of experience will of course receive control impulses of identical intensity. The foreground of the emerging experience Gestalt will comprise the sensations and movements, elements of language and thought emerging from the corresponding paradigms receiving control impulses in the upper range of intensity levels, while the background will be constituted by the paradigms receiving impulses in the lower range of intensity. The control impulses received by the various kinds of paradigms may be thought of as energizing the activities of the paradigms. By means of control impulses of different intensity levels, the experience paradigm links together some functions of the mind more than other functions as necessitated by our limited scope of attention. It reflects what the experience paradigm anticipates the emerging experience Gestalt to be like.

The system of experience must be able to verify whether or not an experience Gestalt resulting from the pattern of collaboration of many different kinds of paradigms corresponds to what was anticipated in its choice of a particular experience paradigm. In other words, the system of experience must check if by means of a particular experience paradigm it has interrelated the various other kinds of other paradigms in a way that appears adequate given the stimuli that have been received. To make this possible we hypothesize that each paradigm can modify the intensity level of the control impulses it receives before it feeds them back to a control unit associated with the system of experience.

We will suggest four conditions that might cause a perceptual paradigm to modify the intensity level of the control impulses. If the level of intensity of the perceptual stimuli received by a perceptual paradigm is quite high, it can raise the intensity level of the control impulses before feeding them back. Bright lights, loud sounds, or a severe internal disorder are some examples of stimuli that can be thought of as having an above-average intensity. Any perceptual paradigm that has been activated frequently in the past because it is related to our work, interests, professional training, or particular circumstances in our past tends to raise the level of intensity of the control impulses when it interprets stimuli. A set of stimuli that proves to be exceptional in any way within the third dimension of the process of differentiation operating on the level of perception (such as those derived from an unusually fat dog or a leaning house) will cause the perceptual paradigm interpreting it to increase the intensity level of the control impulses. The same action is taken by a perceptual paradigm when the set of stimuli it is interpreting is unusual in the context of the stimuli interpreted by the other perceptual paradigms with which it collaborates. In this case the set of stimuli are unusual within the third dimension of the process of differentiation operating on the level of experience. For example, we would be amazed to see a dog in a tree. In each of these three conditions the perceptual paradigm signals the control unit of the system of experience that there is something unusual about the stimuli it is interpreting. By raising the intensity level of the impulses before it feeds them back to the control unit, it requests that more attention be paid to the stimuli it interprets by changing the experience paradigm if necessary.

The fourth condition causes a perceptual paradigm to decrease the intensity level of the control impulses, thereby signalling to the system of experience that it can decrease the attention it gives to it because it is receiving no new information. It takes this action when the stimuli it interprets leave inactive the second dimension of the process of differentiation operating on the level of perception. The intensity level continues to be reduced as the length of time of this inactivity increases. This is a tiring factor of the nervous system. If in such circumstances we force ourselves to continue to fix our attention on a set of stimuli, a number of defence mechanisms of the nervous system may intervene. If we listen to a phrase that is being repeated continuously we begin to hear nonsense syllables and we may find it hard to believe that we were hearing the same phrase all the time. This phenomenon is called the verbal transformation effect. A similar effect occurs when we fixate on something for a long time. Another phenomenon called semantic satiation occurs when we continually repeat a word. It loses its meaningful context of other words and refers only to itself. We may have difficulty using it directly afterwards because it has temporarily lost its meaning.

The model now exhibits some of the self-organizing features that are characteristic of the brain. Suppose that while our attention is focused on some event, a new set of stimuli comes within the range of our perception. If the stimuli were caused by an explosion, an unexpected flash of light, an object with a terrible smell, a sudden internal disorder causing pain, or something related to our personal or professional interests, or to important events in our past, the perceptual paradigm in question may well return control impulses having an intensity level approaching that of the impulses returned by the perceptual paradigms that contribute to the foreground of the experience Gestalt. By comparing the levels of intensity of the emitted control impulses with that of the returned impulses, the control unit can detect that the way attention has been distributed by an experience paradigm is being questioned. The control unit, as it were, receives a request of a perceptual paradigm that the sensation it is producing be admitted to the foreground of the experience Gestalt. Since the experience paradigm has distributed all the available attention, this request can only be met by the system of experience shifting to a different distribution of attention by means of another experience paradigm. If we wish deliberately to ignore the potentially new foreground by concentrating on the existing one, the control unit of the system of experience raises the intensity level but not the distribution of impulses it transmits to the various paradigms that contribute to the foreground. The result is that the intensity level of the control impulses returned to the control unit by paradigms that contribute to the foreground of the experience Gestalts are once again higher than the intensity level of the impulses returned by the perceptual paradigm that produces what was the potential new foreground. The pattern formed by the distribution of intensity levels of the control impulses transmitted by the control unit once again corresponds to that of the impulses returned to it by the various kinds of paradigms. The control unit is therefore able to maintain the experience paradigm, be it at the expense of greater nervous tension. Many people, for example, find it very difficult to study seriously with loud radio music or screaming children in the background.

If we do not deliberately ignore the new set of stimuli our attention will shift. The control unit detects the difference between the patterns formed by the distribution of the intensity levels of the impulses that it transmits and receives back. It seeks to once again match the two patterns by selecting a new experience paradigm on the basis of prior experience.

The process of self-regulation of the system of experience can be affected by redirecting our senses as well as by means of thought. When we are driving home we may be reminded of having promised to do some shopping when we see someone else carrying a bag of groceries. Our thoughts and memory contribute a Gestalt which momentarily becomes the foreground of a new experience Gestalt. As we drive to the store we keep this in mind (as a Gestalt in the background of the experience Gestalt). But more will be said later about the dimension of experience related to thought.

The model of the self-regulating behaviour of the system of experience is, of course, simplistic and incomplete. We have not, for example, considered whether or not emotions and motivation levels affect the operation of the system of experience, nor have we considered how other than perceptual paradigms can modify control impulses. But this was not our intention. We only intended to build a simple model to show how the self-regulation of the system of experience might work.

The self-regulating feature of the system of experience is of considerable importance. One's life has a strong component of routine even though two situations are never quite the same. The system of experience makes use of this fact by making the co-ordination of the functions of the mind and body as much as possible a process based on innate reflexes and prior experience. The advantage is that it leaves us free to direct our attention to the non-routine aspects of an event. While the involuntary neural interpretation occurs beyond the reach of conscious thought and any direct interference, thought can be used to analyse unusual details by means of previously established mental concepts or to compare them to those of previous events recalled from memory. After some thought is given to a situation, it could come to stand in a new light giving the involuntary processes of the mind a chance to refine themselves. The self-regulating feature of the system of experience therefore makes the living of our lives a matter of habit as much as possible, leaving other aspects of our being free to be directed at the non-routine aspects. This greatly enhances our ability to learn.

MEMORY

The systems of perceptual and movement paradigms operate within the framework of the system of experience which oversees and co-ordinates their activities to yield experience Gestalts. As a consequence, memory must receive its input from the system of experience. Experiments have shown that memory is not an isolated storage space but a part of the dynamic organization of the brain.[4] If we associate a memory capacity with the system of experience, a number of known characteristics of memory can readily be incorporated into our hypothetical model. Thus far we have seen that an experience paradigm retains what is necessary to establish appropriate patterns of collaboration in the mind, permitting us to live certain kinds of experiences. The experience Gestalts arising from these events are assumed to be retained in a memory associated with the particular experience paradigm. This leads to an immediate difficulty of interpreting much of the extensive literature on memory. By considering memory as an integral part of the dynamic organization of the mind, the meaning and relevance of information for our existence becomes a crucial variable in the processes of storing, retaining, forgetting, and retrieving information. There is evidence to suggest that within limits the effectiveness of human memory increases as the meaningfulness of information for our existence increases. Yet in almost all experiments on memory this is hardly being considered. Furthermore, this delimits what can be learned about human memory from experiments performed on animals. The introduction of language and thought into the nervous systems of human beings makes them qualitatively different from those of animals.

There are three distinct processes related to human memory, namely the entering of information into memory, its retention, and its retrieval. We will begin by considering the first process. Any information retained in memory was selected from the mass of available stimuli according to our interests, attitudes, and motivations at the time. It also depended on prior experience since any experience Gestalt resulted from processes of differentiation dependent on the levels of development of the system of experience, the systems of perceptual and movement paradigms as well as systems of paradigms related to language, thought, and so on. All these systems are built up from prior experience. Once formed, it is generally thought that the experience Gestalt was momentarily held by a short-term memory which retains a sequence of experience Gestalts for a sufficient length of time so that a long-term memory can be formed. The short-term memory also has the important function of integrating sequences of events lived by means of a single experience paradigm.

As we watch the ball game, for example, successive experience Gestalts are stored by the short-term memory. One such experience Gestalt may be the development of an advance by one of the teams towards the goal of the opposing team, followed by the next experience Gestalt when the pattern is broken off because the defence has intercepted the ball, resulting in a new pattern of relationships. The interaction of the various patterns retained in the short-term memory permits the formation of larger patterns that simplify matters by leaving out a great deal of detail that is less relevant to the larger patterns (a simplification along the Gestalt lines of the larger patterns).

The short-term memory also allows parts of an experience Gestalt that arrive in sequence to be integrated. Suppose we are looking at a painting. When it is too large or too complicated to be taken in at one glance, we scan the picture by letting our eyes rest on a part of it only to move on to another until the entire picture has been covered in a sequence of overlapping attention areas which the short-term memory integrates into an overall impression of the painting. Another example is that of phrases spoken in a conversation. The aural stimuli constitute a sequence which is integrated to produce a pattern of meaning of what is being said. Another function of the short-term memory is to retain incidental information for a brief moment to allow us to perform a task (such as the dialing of a telephone number after we looked it up). Unless this information is reinforced, it is assumed to be trivial. It is probably forgotten by not being transferred from short- into long-term memory.

In our conceptual model we shall assume that experience Gestalts are stored as long-term memory traces, (as long as this term is understood in relation to the mind and not the brain). They are constituted of either single or multiple interrelated experience Gestalts and stored relative to and interact with those traces corresponding to situations lived by means of the same experience paradigm but at different moments in our existence. Any long-term memory trace is therefore affected by traces stored by the same experience paradigm at a later date. The reverse may also occur. If some event brings about the refinement of an experience paradigm it indirectly affects all future events lived via that paradigm, and consequently the long-term memory traces that result from it.

The model of the human memory that we have just described has many of the characteristics of that of the system of experience. Each experience paradigm has exclusive access to a part of the memory surface which retains the experience Gestalts of events lived by it. On the memory surface the experience of our life is then stored as a network of interacting memory traces. The interaction pattern is somewhat more involved than that for the network of experience paradigms, however. Each experience paradigm yields a cluster of memory traces on the memory surface. These clusters do not interact directly with one another but only via the experience paradigms through which they are lived. Within each cluster the interaction between the memory traces is rather complex, and given what little we know about the human memory (at least in the context of daily life), it cannot be conceptualized accurately.

Basically, the memory traces within any cluster are taken to be differentiated from each other on the level of experience. That is, each trace is located adjacent to those from which it was directly differentiated. Since each trace within a cluster shares the same basic Gestalt, it is probable that the traces contain only the information not available from the experience paradigm associated with the cluster. For the purpose of recall they must then be reconstructed by means of the information about their Gestalt retained in the experience paradigm. This economizes memory space. The phenomenon of centring also accomplishes this. As a result of life involving a great deal of routine, some clusters of memory traces may come to contain a great many very similar traces. The refinement of the process of differentiation on the level of experience may approach an asymptote, while the number of similar traces keep on growing. Consequently, we assume that the process of differentiation can eventually no longer keep them apart and they begin to lose their distinct identity and blend together. This is called centring. These enlarged traces may be considered as a single trace. They will still be located on the memory surface adjacent to those from which they are directly differentiated (that is, those which most resemble them and yet can be distinguished from them). Since the traces are thought to be located on the memory surface adjacent to those from whom they are directly differentiated, the memory system, like the systems of perceptual and movement paradigms and the system of experience, is self-reinforcing and infinitely expandable, at least until aging processes begin.

Although the phenomenon of centring is one way in which we forget certain events, it is not the only reason why we may not be able to remember them. To explain this, however, we first need to examine how we recall a situation. This process involves being able to locate it on the memory surface in order to bring it back as a memory Gestalt to form the foreground of the experience Gestalt of that moment. This presents us with an immediate problem. Since the process of differentiation on the level of experience was thought to occur outside the range of our will and conscious thought, we do not know where a particular trace is stored on the memory surface. In order to find it, therefore, there must be other ways of reaching it to make remembering possible. Some of the other ways in which traces on the memory surface are interrelated will therefore be examined.

Each memory trace overlaps the one that preceded and followed it in time. When we discussed how the system of experience shifts from one experience paradigm to another, we noted that it was able to select a new paradigm precisely because the next focus of attention first appeared in the background of the current experience Gestalt. Hence memory traces of events lived by means of different experience paradigms but following each other in time overlap in pairs since the earlier ones contain the focus of attention of the later ones in their backgrounds. They can, of course, be located in quite different areas of the memory surface. A sequence of events may be interrelated further by sharing a Gestalt arising from thought. They may, for example, share a common purpose of going to visit a friend in a distant city and include events like going to the station in a taxi, the train ride, and being met by the friend at the destination. These events and many others more or less related to the purpose of the trip will yield traces scattered over different areas of the memory surface. Another network of relationships between memory traces results from the acquisition of language, but detailed discussion of this will have to be postponed until a later chapter. It is these networks of relationships unrelated to the process of differentiation on the level of experience and hence the position of the traces on the memory surface, which could permit conscious thought to reach into the memory system to recall particular events or series of events.

The recall of an event is thought to presuppose its reconstruction. In part this is because the information in the memory trace must be reintegrated into the information related to its Gestalt as retained in the corresponding experience paradigm. But the trace recalled from memory forms the foreground of an experience Gestalt of the moment of our existence during which the recall takes place. Our present motivations, interests, and attitudes are likely different from those at the time of the event. This could have the consequence that we may be interested in different details from the ones selected in the process of interpretation of the event when it took place, that is, when the experience Gestalt first entered our short-term memory. We recall an event of the past in the context of the present. Recall is therefore probably accompanied by a process of reinterpretation and reconstruction to attempt to recover some details not originally retained. The reconstruction occurs not on the basis of the experience paradigms and concepts we had when we experienced it but by the ones we have at the time of recall. The experience that intervened between the time of the original storage of an experience Gestalt into the memory system and the time we recall it may therefore interact with the information already stored in the memory system and also influence the recall of that information by having affected the experience paradigms and concepts used for reconstruction. Hence our memory is not conceptualized as an isolated storage space but as a complex system that performs its function within the dynamic whole of the mind. It is fully interrelated with the other functions of the mind: for example, it is related to our personality, as we may repress memories to avoid personal conflict or pain.

It is now possible to model some of the processes by which memories of the past may be reinforced or forgotten. Events lived by means of the same experience paradigm but at different moments of our existence can reinforce each other's memory traces, or produce centring leading to forgetting. If the number of such traces is not too high, each new similar event may permit the corresponding experience paradigm to refine itself, with the result that each memory trace can be differentiated more precisely from those already present in the cluster. This may reinforce both the new arrival and the older members of the cluster, helping the traces maintain their individual identities. The reinforcement process is therefore the opposite of the process of centring associated with forgetting. Centring occurs, as we have noted, when the number of a particular kind of trace in a memory cluster becomes so large that the process of differentiation can no longer give a distinct identity to each new trace. In other words, centring which leads to forgetting is, as it were, a limited and localized return to an undifferentiated world.

It is, of course, difficult to say whether or not something is really forgotten. Failure to remember something can occur because the thought used to retrieve it is inadequate. We can after all, remember something later that we could not earlier, or we are able to recall things under hypnosis that are otherwise unreachable. Great care must be taken not to oversimplify the interaction patterns between the memory traces in the system. There appears to be a weak interaction between a particular event stored in the memory system and all the events that intervene between its occurrence and its recall. When sleep is essentially the only intervening activity, there is after about two hours no further forgetting, while with the other intervening activities the amount recalled continued to decrease. Forgetting here appears to be the result of retroactive interference causing a certain obliteration of the old by the new as the events indirectly interact within the memory system. It is likely that this phenomenon occurs mostly or entirely in the short-term memory. Events that have below-average significance for our existence are particularly affected.

When we will discuss the relationship between the system of experience including the memory system and language, personality, and the subconscious, the problem of human memory will become more complex. At that point, the importance of the systems character of human memory and of meaning as an important variable for the system will become even more evident.

The hypothesis of a memory system being associated with the system of experience has important implications for the latter's functioning. We have already seen that experience paradigms organize and co-ordinate the various parts of our body and nervous system in a variety of ways to enable us to live the many different moments of our life. Since these experience paradigms are all constituents of the system of experience and since this system is interrelated with a memory system, it follows that no moment of life is lived in isolation from our prior existence as a whole. When it functions normally, the system of experience prevents human life from becoming a series of unrelated fragments.

To illustrate this, consider once again our spatial models of memory and the other systems as surfaces. On the memory surface is depicted a panorama of our prior life arranged in clusters of memory traces. The clusters are situated in relation to one another according to the process of differentiation. Each cluster is located adjacent to those from which it is directly differentiated (that is, those that once were experienced as not being essentially different). Hence all the clusters related to a particular sphere of our life are located adjacent to each other to form distinct regions within the panorama of our existence. Each of the many different regions are located adjacent to those representing spheres of our life that once upon a time were not differentiated from each other. Within a cluster, the memory traces are again located adjacent to those from which they are directly differentiated.

Let us assume that below the memory surface lies the surface containing the system of experience with each experience paradigm located directly below the cluster of memory traces that were lived by means of it. Below the surface containing the system of experience is assumed to lie a surface containing the various systems of perceptual and movement paradigms which from above can be interconnected in different ways by means of experience paradigms. On the lower side of the surface these systems are assumed to be connected to the corresponding parts of the body (sense organs, muscles, etc.).

According to our hypothetical model, when we are living a particular moment of our life, connections are established between a number of elements located on the various surfaces. But since on each surface these elements are differentiated from all the others, we live each moment of our life in the context of our prior existence on various levels. Below the level of conscious awareness it includes the interpreting or generating of stimuli to yield sensations and movements on one level, the co-ordinating of perceptual and movement paradigms to yield Gestalts and experience Gestalts, the metaconscious experience of storing and retaining experience Gestalts to yield memory traces, and, where applicable, the location and reconstruction of memories. Because each moment of our life is lived in the context of our prior existence, continuity, order, and meaning in life become possible.

The fact that the system of experience is thought to allow us to live each moment of our life in relation to our entire prior existence creates the possibility for another dimension of experience, namely the one related to our emotions. Examples of emotions are hope, anxiety, anguish, anger, rage, laughter, contentment, excitement, terror, pleasure, pride, humiliation, shame, embarrassment, joy, grief, bitterness, disgust, astonishment, jealousy, amusement, and so on. When we analyse such a sample of emotions it becomes immediately evident that all of them express in *holistic* terms something about the relationship between a given moment of our existence and an area of our life or even our life as a whole. An emotion arises when, with reference to all past experience, a relationship stands out.

We will give some examples. When after an hour or so someone has been trying to find a very slow leak in a bicycle tire, she may become very frustrated. Her emotion expresses something of what she has been trying to do for the past hour of her life and each new moment that brings no success. A blind student may be overwhelmed with joy by the news of having been admitted to a professional school because it opens the door to the possibility of eventually being able to pursue a career. Someone may be anxious for weeks until tests show that his fears of a persistent internal pain being symptomatic of some dreadful disease prove to be unfounded. A researcher may be excited for days as she verifies a new discovery. A person can be paralysed with fear when a rattlesnake emerges from a rock he just stepped on. In the above cases, the emotions are all of limited scope. In extreme cases, however, memories that are so upsetting to a person because they call into question one's whole life are often repressed to prevent them from bringing back emotions that are so severe and lasting that they could destroy one's existence. When this defence mechanism fails, an emotional disturbance may result.

In the above examples the course of events or even the direction of one's entire life has taken or could take an unexpected turn. It is possible to detect such turns precisely because experience paradigms relate each moment of our life (experienced as an experience Gestalt) to a part or the whole of our prior existence (as retained in the memory system). Since emotions express something about the relationship between these two *wholes*, they would appear to have their roots in the systems of experience and memory in most cases.[5] The function of the mind associated with the emotional dimension of experience forms Gestalts by means of emotional paradigms which are differentiated from one another to constitute a system of emotional paradigms. These Gestalts emotionally colour the entire experience Gestalts into which they are integrated. Depending on its intensity, the emotional Gestalt can outlast the event that triggered it to affect subsequent behaviour. When it does so it sets the level of a person's motivation in these subsequent events. It can, for example, make someone very passive, taking in a minimum of information from the environment, or it can make someone very active – that is, taking in as much information from the environment as possible in order to interact with it vigorously. It can also fixate one's attention, as is the case when one is paralysed with fear noticing nothing else but the rattlesnake preparing to attack.

Emotions and motivations, therefore, appear to provide us with fundamental indications related to the regulation and control of our more global relationship with internal and external reality. Emotions inform us we are off course and tell us something about the meaning of the corresponding deviation. They make it more difficult for us to go on pretending nothing much has happened, and this is of great practical value for the control and regulation of our being in reality. What is most important, however, is that our emotions give us some indication of the deeper significance of an experience for our life; as such they add to the depth of the meaning of an event.

We learn to control our emotions to various degrees. What we learn to control, of course, is not the formation of the emotional Gestalt or the way it colours the experience Gestalt. These developments are an integral part of the involuntary interpreting and generating of stimuli. What we learn to control is our deliberate and conscious reaction to the object of the emotion. Thus an immediate outburst is often avoided, but a later one provoked by a minor incident is not uncommon. In such a case, the outburst may appear incomprehensible to others unaware of the events preceding it.

Some manifestations of emotions are involuntary. The reason is that the functions of the mind associated with the emotional dimension of experience appear to be interconnected to other parts of the body via the brain in ways that are not controlled by the system of experience. Physical reactions like changes in heart rate, respiration, muscle tension, skin temperature, gastro-intestinal activity, metabolic rate, and so on may be involved. By means of internal perception we experience these changes as our heart leaping in our throat, butterflies in our stomach, or the breaking out in a cold sweat. These are well known and have been extensively studied. Emotions are thus distinct from feelings such as hunger, thirst, internal pain, and so on, which have their origin in physiological processes. Emotions, on the other hand, have, as we have seen, mostly a psychic origin in perception, knowledge, and memory, that is, in the systems of experience and memory. This psychic origin can be further clarified when we show how the personality and subconscious are enfolded within these systems.

Early theories of emotions did not involve the nervous system, later ones involved the peripheral structures and the autonomic nervous system, and still later ones the entire nervous system. Some of the current theories involve the entire organism existing in an environment present, past, and future. Our theory involves the mind, and thus is closest to those of the latter kind.[6] It should be noted, however, that the system of emotional paradigms develops by paradigmatically extending genetically created structures of the brain. Some emotions will therefore be largely 'instinctual.' Our theory also attempts to escape the reductionisms present in the literature on motivation.[7]

THE METACONSCIOUS

On the basis of our conceptualization of the system of experience including the memory system, it is now possible to take another step forward in our understanding of how human beings are linked to reality. Each moment of our life (involving the external world, the 'inner' world of our body, as well as any conscious use we make of our mind) is lived against the background of our prior experience grafted onto the innate structures of the brain. In fact, the experience of a moment of our life flows from a kind of fusion between the various stimuli associated with that moment and our past. The meaning of a moment of our existence appears indeed to be associated with its being enfolded into our life, and our experience appears to be our conscious awareness of this process. The three levels of meaning we have distinguished (sensations, Gestalts, and experience Gestalts) result from enfolding some facet of a moment of our life into the various structures and functions of the mind built up from prior experience. What we can add to our understanding is the role the system of experience and the memory system play as a stable background for our life. It constitutes the meta-experience or metaconscious, which enable each moment of our life to affect our being without generally disrupting the continuity of that being. We constantly change and yet we remain ourselves.

The role of the system of experience and the memory system as metaconscious allows us to shed further light on the role the past plays in the present. The present is clearly not determined by the past. To be sure, our past life is symbolically represented in the metaconscious as we have conceptualized it – but that is not all. On the basis of our past and our imagination we anticipate the possible outcomes of our thoughts and actions.[8] We consciously and unconsciously choose between these possibilities, and these choices condition the present. In other words, by living each moment of our life against the background of a metaconscious, we experience the present in relation to the hopes, dreams, aspirations, fears, and concerns that are woven into our being. The present is, therefore, probably as much conditioned by our anticipations of the future as by our past. This is true even for the most habitual behaviour. Modern depth psychology has neglected this and exaggerated the role the past plays in determining the present. In part this was due to the historical conditions under which this branch of psychology was born and developed, and also the fact that it was heavily based on observations of patients and others whose lives had become stuck in the patterns of the past.[9]

In our conceptualization of experience, we have attempted to correct this problem. Even the involuntary interpreting of stimuli is based on only a paradigmatic use of prior experience. The paradigms within any system of the mind are not fixed algorithms but a relation between stimuli and prior experience in which there is free play to allow a conscious 'I' to be enfolded in every aspect of our being. Each moment of our life requires a more or less large *creative* adaptation of a diversity of paradigms to a situation that is never a repeat of the past. Life is inseparable from creativity. It is tempting to speculate that the processes of differentiation as described thus far can be conceptualized by using the analogy of the hologram; it would, however, make the experiencing of a moment of life too mechanistic in nature.

We have by no means exhausted the study of the way human beings are linked to reality. The role and structure of the metaconscious need to be explored next.

FOUR

The Development of the Mind

CUMULATIVE AND NON-CUMULATIVE DEVELOPMENT

We have been suggesting that something new is created whenever the mind enfolds certain elements into a whole or system and that this has to do with meaning. It happens when a set of stimuli is interrelated in the mind to form a sensation, when sensations are interrelated into a Gestalt, and when Gestalts are linked into an experience Gestalt. The meaning that emerges on each of these three levels depends on the context in which it was formed – that is, on the next higher level of meaning. A set of stimuli becomes a sensation when it first takes on a meaning in the context of a Gestalt, which takes on its meaning in the context of an experience Gestalt. Since the systems of experience and memory allow us to live each moment of our life in the context of our whole existence, it follows that an experience Gestalt takes on its meaning in the context of our prior experience. Through a process of socialization our existence takes on a meaning in the context of the daily life of our speech community, which in turn takes on its meaning in the context of the project of existence and the institutional framework of society. Each level of meaning is both a reflection of reality and the imposition of something human on reality, and hence reflects a dialectical tension between the realistic and idealistic components of culture as a social ecology.

In the previous chapters we have examined the first three levels of meaning – namely those associated with sensations, Gestalts, and experience Gestalts – as well as the development of and interaction between the systems of perceptual and movement paradigms and the system of experience. In examining the memory system associated with the system of experience it became clear that each moment of our life is lived in the context of our whole existence, which points to a fourth level of meaning related to a particular sphere and via it to the whole of our life. We shall now begin to examine this level in order to gain an understanding of the role of the metaconscious. To bring this level of meaning to light we first need to examine how the development of each of the systems affects that of the others and how together they develop as a whole. A systematic study , as attempted by developmental psychology, of how a child grows up is clearly beyond the scope of this work; we shall focus only on some modes of that development.

One preliminary remark is in order, however. If at times the description of the development of babies and young children in terms of the systems of perceptual and movement paradigms and the systems of experience and memory sounds mechanical or behaviouristic, it is not because we hold that to be its true nature. It results from the limitation of the concepts at our disposal. It is impossible to escape entirely from our mechanistic heritage. To depict human development by means of the concept of system is an attempt to give the best possible image of a relational reality in which no simple cartesian causality exists. We must keep in mind the limitations of our theory by maintaining a clear distinction between the theory (reality as we know it) and reality itself in order not to rationalize human life too far.

In a system a change in any of its elements directly affects the others to which it is closely related and possibly the whole. But just as the whole is more than the sum of the parts, so also the development of a system or the joint development of several interacting systems needs to be studied both on the level of the whole and on the level of the constituent elements. We shall begin with the joint development of the mind-body systems built up from experience (focusing on the systems of perceptual and movement paradigms, the system of experience, and the memory system) on the level of their constituents. Suppose a set of stimuli regularly coincides with a particular experience Gestalt. We may then become conscious of this coincidence, in which case the experience Gestalt forms a framework able to give a meaning to the stimuli. When this occurs a new perceptual paradigm is formed and incorporated into the appropriate system of perceptual paradigms by means of the process of differentiation related to the perceptual apparatus responsible for the interpreting of the stimuli in question. A set of stimuli thus takes on a meaning to become a sensation when it can refine an experience Gestalt.

The case is in some ways analogous to the one where all but one or two pieces of a jigsaw puzzle have been fitted into their proper places. They then form a context from which the position that the last one or two pieces must take becomes quite evident; once fitted into place the pieces show the picture more clearly. In the same way all the dimensions of experience into which the world was resolved by our senses regain their proper interdependence within the experience Gestalts, permitting each dimension of experience to take on its full meaning in the context of the others.

While an experience Gestalt facilitates the transformation of the stimuli into sensations, it is at the same time affected when this occurs. The sensation contributes something new to an experience Gestalt. As a result the corresponding experience paradigm is able to refine itself. If the refined paradigm disturbs the equilibrium of the third and fourth dimensions of differentiation between it and its neighbours in the system of experience, it will break up and a new experience paradigm will be formed. When this is not the case, the refined paradigm will interact with its neighbours, but no new experience paradigm will result. The same pattern of development occurs in the interaction between the systems of movement paradigms and the system of experience.

There exists a minor variation of the above mode of joint development of the systems of perceptual or movement paradigms and the system of experience. An experience Gestalt can also form a context in which a new aspect of a previously known sensation can become evident. A consequent refinement in the corresponding perceptual paradigm then occurs. If the refined perceptual paradigm disturbs the equilibrium between the third and fourth dimensions of differentiation between it and its neighbours within the system it will break up, resulting in a new paradigm to be added to the system. When this does not occur the refined perceptual paradigm will only interact with its neighbours. The consequences of the refinement of the perceptual paradigm for the system of experience are as described above.

From the above description it is evident that joint micro-level development of the mind's systems built up from experience can be cumulative or non-cumulative. A cumulative micro-level development occurs when something new is discovered which merely adds to the reality as it was known prior to the discovery – that is, when no existing paradigms in the mind's systems break up. Non-cumulative micro-level developments occur when a new discovery does not merely add something to reality as it was known up to that point, but when it also causes parts or all of it to stand in a new light. This happens when the third and fourth dimensions of differentiation are disturbed in one or more of the systems, with the result that one or more paradigms break up. During the cumulative micro-level developments, the prior experience of interpreting or generating stimuli is borne out by the new discovery which merely adds something to it, while for the other case it needs to be altered in a non-cumulative way. To use the analogy of the jigsaw puzzle once again, we can say that cumulative developments amount to fitting new pieces into place; they interlock with and hence confirm the positions of the previously interlocked pieces. In the non-cumulative developments it is as if we tried to add pieces of another puzzle; they do not fit, and if we wish to interlock them we will have to change the contours of some of the previously interlocked pieces.

On the macro-level the joint development of the mind's systems built up from experience is more complex. Any moment of our life involves many sets of stimuli, each of which gives rise to the kinds of micro-level developments described above. Any experience can therefore involve both cumulative and non-cumulative micro-level developments, but the latter are necessarily limited in scope. If they were not, there would be no stable framework in the context of which sets of stimuli could take on a meaning for the first time or change their meaning in a non-cumulative way. This also means that when non-cumulative changes occur in an experience paradigm their scope is necessarily limited. There is therefore an extraordinary continuity and stability in human life. Non-cumulative developments on the micro-level require the predominance of cumulative ones.

This does not mean, however, that over a period of a person's life joint macro-level development of the neural systems built up from experience is always predominantly cumulative. In the systems of experience and memory, non-cumulative micro-level changes can begin to link together to bring about a change in the very framework within which all stimuli are interpreted or generated. In such a case all prior experience slowly comes to stand in a new light as the frame of reference provided by the systems of experience and memory changes. When this occurs the joint macro-level development of the neural systems built up from experience is predominantly non-cumulative, even though the non-cumulative changes on the micro-level remain in the minority during any single moment of experience. This follows directly from the characteristics of a system because its elements are interrelated in such a way that a change in any of its elements can affect the whole, while any change in the whole affects all the elements.

The developments just described do not need to take place uniformly throughout the systems of memory and experience, however. In order to bring this clearly into focus we shall introduce the concept of a subsystem. A subsystem is a part of a system whose elements interact more with each other than with the remaining elements, with the result that it tends to act as a kind of composite element within the system. Within the mind's systems built up from experience examples of subsystems are a cluster of paradigms of any kind, a cluster of memory traces, or a part of the network of such clusters related to an area of a person's life (such as her profession, marriage, or interests). On the macro-level it is now possible to conceive of the joint development of the neural systems built up from experience in terms of interdependent developments of all the subsystems, each related to an area of a person's activities. The macro-level development of any one subsystem can be either cumulative or non-cumulative. It is cumulative if as a whole it develops predominantly cumulatively, and non-cumulative if it does not. The various kinds of developments related to different areas of a person's life do, of course, interact within the systems of experience and memory. The non-cumulatively developing subsystems tend to yield many memory traces having a strong emotional colouring, because the course of events in these areas of life is constantly upset or full of new and exciting possibilities. As a result, the subsystem in the systems of experience and memory will dominate the others and hence a person's whole life, at least for a certain period. An example of such an occurrence would be a physicist deeply involved in what Kuhn[1] has called a scientific revolution. In such cases we will speak of a non-cumulative joint macro-level development of the mind's systems built up from experience.

With babies and young children such joint non-cumulative macro-level developments of the mind-body systems built up from experience is more common than with adults for two reasons. Although they are relatively unfamiliar with the world, they have few startling experiences. The reason for this is that they are protected from an excess of novelty simply because reality slowly unfolds itself to them by means of sets of stimuli taking on a meaning in the context of their prior experience. It is as if the world were slowly put together before their eyes. They adopt a playful attitude towards the world, particularly when they receive much love and guidance from their parents and when they also learn to trust others that introduce them to it. They have nothing to fear from that world and hence creatively open themselves to it. There is, therefore, an endless flow of non-cumulative micro-level developments that eventually lead to non-cumulative macro-level developments. In the second place, non-cumulative macro-level developments related to one area of activity easily affect other areas to permeate the entire systems of experience and memory and hence their whole existence. This is because, unlike adults, babies and young children have very limited neural systems built up from experience and hence no well-developed subsystems. Macro-level developments in children are therefore more uniformly cumulative or non-cumulative throughout the systems.

Is it then possible to study the development of human offspring in terms of stages, that is, in terms of periods of cumulative joint macro-level development of the mind-body systems built up from experience? The most developed stage theory is derived from Jean Piaget's studies, but some authors[2] have pointed out some difficulties in such a theory. In the present work the development of human offspring will be shown to be simultaneously cumulative and non-cumulative. During what has been called a stage in the development of a child, the joint macro-level development of the mind-body systems built up from experience is cumulative because the non-cumulative micro-level developments in the various systems are as yet not linking together to the point where they affect the framework within which stimuli are interpreted and generated. Hence these non-cumulative micro-level developments do not as yet externalize themselves very noticeably in a child's behaviour. They remain almost hidden until they begin to link together to the point of affecting the systems of experience and memory at the level of the whole. At that point the framework within which stimuli are interpreted and generated begins to change. A period of transition sets in during which these developments begin to externalize themselves in the child's behaviour. As a result these developments are reinforced until they have fully permeated the systems of experience and memory, bringing the transition period to an end and ushering in another period of cumulative joint macro-level development of the mind-body systems acquired from experience. What has been called a stage of development, therefore, is a period of cumulative joint macro-level development, while behind the scenes non-cumulative micro-level developments are almost imperceptibly preparing for the next transition period. During a transition period these micro-level developments reach the level of the whole of the system, while cumulative micro-level developments prepare the way for the next stage.

Each stage prepares the way for the next transition period and to a lesser degree for the stages and transition periods to follow later. There is one further complication which makes a simple stage theory impossible. As a child grows older and as the mind's systems built up from experience begin to develop subsystems, a variety of only weakly interdependent developments, both cumulative and non-cumulative, happens in the subsystems. Furthermore, the development of the neural systems built up from experience becomes more and more complex as new systems related to language and thought are added. New frontiers for development open up, each of which can develop cumulatively and non-cumulatively. Hence the concept of a stage of development becomes virtually meaningless as the child grows older, unless it is used only for a particular aspect of the child's development.

The concept of stage also needs to be related to the distinction we have made between reality and reality as it is known. Reality as it is known is not the same for all cultures. It is not the same for all speech communities, social and professional groups within a culture, or for their members. This is in fact one of the sources for the dialectical relationships which are necessary if these groups and societies are to continue to develop and without which they would stagnate and collapse.[3] We shall have to deal with these matters in greater detail later. For the moment it is important to realize that the development of babies and young children in a large measure comprises the closing of the gap that exists between reality as they know it and reality as the adults of their speech community know it. Stages may therefore be considered as phases in the development of culture as a social ecology in the life of children.

From our findings in earlier chapters it follows that the first stage in the development of babies is largely characterized by the paradigmatic expansion of their limited innate ability to relate to reality. Their active explorations of the environment leads to the development of the mind and its enfolding into their being. We suggested that some of these developments may be conceptualized in terms of the systems of perceptual and movement paradigms, the system of experience, and the memory system. Despite the limited abilities of self-expression, no two babies behave in the same way, but their development (at least within a particular culture) nevertheless has many shared features. We now focus on some of them, particularly the transition from one stage to the next.

METACONSCIOUS KNOWLEDGE IN CHILDREN

In order to illustrate the cumulative and non-cumulative development of the mind-body system resulting from experience and the interdependence between macro- and micro-level developments, we shall briefly examine various periods within the lives of babies and young children. Long before birth, a baby's existence is already deeply enfolded into that of her mother. The experiences of her mother's body help constitute the beginnings of the various systems built up from experience. These are therefore fundamental for the developments that take place after birth. Although the way a baby's and a mother's life are enfolded together changes fundamentally as a result of the birth process, the baby does not now explore the world on her own. Her life typically remains deeply enfolded into that of her mother, and her experiences of the world are lived by means of a structure of experience largely built up from her experiences in the womb. The baby's existence is therefore profoundly social from the beginning, even though it is very different from that of older children or adults. Her experiences are not egocentric, as has so often been thought. They are lived from the perspective of a highly enfolded being with an extremely limited self-awareness.

The developments after birth begin to change the nature of the way her being is enfolded into that of her mother and other people. These new relations affect her structure of experience and her perception of herself, which in turn permits her to expand the network of relations associated with her being. In other words, when we speak of a baby in the pages that follow we speak of a human subject whose self-awareness is very different from ours, so that terms like 'he,' 'she,' 'his,' 'her,' and so on must be interpreted with this in mind if we are not to fall into the egocentric interpretation of a baby's development. There are no terms in our language to describe these ways of being in the world; hence many sentences should be read as though they had been put in quotations, if they are not to be interpreted as egocentric actions of the baby.

Initially a baby's world is largely undifferentiated. The distinctions she has learned to make are either innate or learned as a being whose existence is deeply enfolded into that of her mother. The experience of that world slowly unfolds a differentiated world to her. The endless playful discovery that the world as she knows it is only a glimpse of reality is the mainspring of her development.

She is presented with a variety of stimuli related to being hungry or well fed, or being tired or wide awake. These stimuli are registered and differentiated in her mind as she experiences them. In her behaviour she externalizes the distinctions she learns to make, so that her ways of crying soon vary depending on the cause. As she learns to differentiate various feelings, some relationships with the outside world take on a meaning as they become associated with changes in her feelings. Each time she is being fed she experiences (by means of the systems of experience and memory) a gradual change in her hunger feeling and a complex set of tactile stimuli related to her being held to be fed. Slowly these sets of stimuli begin to take on some kind of meaning in each others' context. The baby becomes conscious of a new experience and the tactile stimuli become a sensation related to being held to be fed. The differentiated experience of her 'inner' world allows her to begin to experience consciously some of her relationships with the outside world.

The baby's existence is increasingly characterized by the establishment of somewhat more voluntary relationships with the world. If she is to experience other relationships not directly associated with feelings derived from the states of her organism, she must become more aware of her own existence. The baby has to learn something of the difference between her body and the rest of the world. A simple series of events that together constitute a stage in her development gradually lead to this distinction.

As she moves her limbs in a random and largely uncontrolled way, the baby produces a new series of events. When she waves her arms in the range of her sight, she learns to interpret the retinal stimuli as they move together against the static background. The process of differentiation yields a new addition to the system of visual perceptual paradigms. While waving her arms around, she may happen to touch the one with the other, which produces tactile stimuli that are different from those produced when she touches her crib. In the former event her mind detects two sets of tactile stimuli while in the latter it receives only one. As she learns to follow the movements with her eyes, the tactile stimuli coincide with the visual sensations in different experience Gestalts. When after repeated occurrences the baby becomes aware of these coincidences, the tactile stimuli take on a meaning in this context and are consequently transformed into sensations. In a similar way the functions of the mind that control the motor functions learn to constitute patterns of muscle stimuli, resulting in new movement paradigms that enable the baby to execute different movements at will.

To gain a deeper understanding of these events, consider the developments that take place on the level of the systems of experience and memory as the baby plays with her limbs. When the baby's movements are still largely uncontrolled she does not distinguish between the different events in which by waving her limbs around she touches nothing at all, her body, or an external object. They appear to her as being essentially alike and hence are lived via a single experience paradigm that is differentiated from other paradigms associated with being fed, changed, played with, and so on. As new stimuli begin to take on a meaning the variety of experience Gestalts increases, with the result that the experience paradigm associated with the baby's playing with her limbs begins to break up. A cluster begins to form which expands until the equilibrium between the third and fourth dimensions of the process of differentiation on the level of experience is no longer disturbed.

At first the baby may well distinguish two events in a manner that is not borne out by further experience. If, for example, she has not yet distinguished by sight her hand from her foot, she might try to move her hand by kicking her foot. This in no way prevents the proper development of the cluster, because what matters is not how individual experience paradigms temporarily interpret a particular range of events but eventually how the cluster as a whole depicts the particular sphere of activities. Many paths of successive distinctions made in a system-like manner will lead to the same final cluster because the process is, as we have already noted, fully self-correcting and self-reinforcing.

The way experience paradigms or memory traces are interrelated within clusters and via these clusters within systems is very important for the development of the baby. It permits her to learn a great deal more about the external world and herself than she could have if the networks of interrelationships had been absent. In the latter case she would simply have made unrelated distinctions between various experiences two at a time, which would imply nothing more than that they are different, provided we stop short of analysing these differences as we did in an earlier chapter. In any case, the baby is unable to analyse them since she lacks the necessary mental concepts which she acquires only later when she learns a language. If, however, by means of a process of differentiation, the local micro-level distinctions are interrelated within a network of experience paradigms and a network of memory traces, a great deal of information slowly becomes implied in the structure of these networks.

This is clearly evident in the structure of the cluster of experience paradigms and the clusters of memory traces resulting from the baby's playing with her limbs. When the equilibrium between the third and fourth dimensions of the process of differentiation is no longer disturbed by new events, the micro-level distinctions have linked together to establish a macro-level distinction related primarily to the difference between her body and the external world. The cluster of experience paradigms contain some paradigms that allow her to live events in which she touches nothing (involving no tactile sensations), in which she touches her body with one of her limbs (yielding two tactile sensations), or in which she touched an external object (yielding only one tactile sensation). Some experience paradigms are associated with events in which she could control the movement of what she saw (a limb) and others in which she could not (an external object). Once these experiences begin to be differentiated in this manner they increasingly imply some information about the baby's body and how it is different from the external world. Long before she has any conscious knowledge of this, this information derived from playing with her limbs is building up in the structure of the clusters.

But is this information available to the baby? It is, of course, not accessible to conscious thought because the structure of the clusters is determined by the process of differentiation. In this sense the information is metaconscious. The baby does, however, involuntarily and metaconsciously utilize it via any of the experience paradigms in the cluster whenever she plays with her limbs. She interprets stimuli and executes movements by means of the process of differentiation operating on the basis of the structure of the systems of experience and memory. This leads either to a refinement of this structure or its modification if the equilibrium between the third and fourth dimension of differentiation is disturbed. As a result, it is constantly being refined or modified in a manner that is self-correcting and self-reinforcing. The baby's behaviour soon begins to show that she draws distinctions, implying a partial and preconceptual metaconscious 'knowledge' of the difference between her body and the external world. As she continues to play with her limbs, the local micro-level distinctions between experience paradigms and memory traces link up to form what may be called a Gestalt of metaconscious knowledge of her body and of how it is different from the external world.[4] We will see later how this Gestalt contributes to the formation of the explicit concepts of body and external world acquired when she learns to speak.

The formation of Gestalts of metaconscious knowledge also occur in other clusters of experience paradigms and the associated clusters of memory traces. We shall consider the formation of some other kinds of Gestalts of metaconscious knowledge. It is helpful at this point to broaden the meaning of two concepts. The way our life is depicted in the systems of experience and memory will be called the structure of experience and the information implied in it will be called metaconscious knowledge. It is the formation of metaconscious knowledge that brings about the non-cumulative macro-level developments in babies.

When the developments described above approach their completion, the baby can produce at will any event related to playing with her limbs. The element of chance diminishes. Soon there are no more new discoveries or surprises. These developments depend on many others occurring simultaneously. As the baby begins to use her movements, a certain self-awareness emerges. The 'things waving in front of my eyes' become 'something that can do things I want them to do' and eventually simply 'my arms.'

A new phase in the baby's development can now begin. She seeks out new experiences and turns her attention to the objects suspended above her crib. She may have accidentally touched them before, but at that time the resulting stimuli could not yet take on a meaning because the levels of development of the systems of perceptual and movement paradigms and the system of experience were inadequate. When, for example, the baby wiggling in her crib accidentally touches a rattle hanging above her, she is surprised and delighted by the noise and movement. In an attempt to repeat the effects, she begins to wiggle her body more energetically. Because the tactile stimuli she receives when she touches the rattle do not have any meaning for her, she associates the noise and movement of the rattle with the wiggling of her body. To use the analogy of the jigsaw puzzle again: some intermediary pieces have to be fitted into place first before the present pieces can be interlocked with the completed part of the puzzle.

She can now begin to interpret the new stimuli on the basis of what she has learned from playing with her limbs. New perceptual, movement, and experience paradigms will result from the manipulation of objects. Since new events are interpreted on the basis of prior experience, the newly formed experience paradigms will at first attach themselves to the cluster built up from the playing with her limbs. As the baby continues to manipulate objects, the cluster will eventually break up into two as further metaconscious knowledge develops related to her body and how it is different from the external world. One cluster will interpret and execute events involving only her own body, while the other will interpret and execute events in which she acts on the external world.

There are some details of the developments just described that merit special consideration. Once the baby begins to manipulate objects she can look at them from different directions and grasp them in different ways. She must learn to associate the different sensations that may result as representing the same object. In such cases, perceptual paradigms are neither refined nor broken up. Their scope is expanded – that is, the range of stimuli that they can interpret is enlarged. At the same time, activities like watching herself trace the contours of an object with her fingers help the baby to integrate the visual, tactile, and movement dimensions of experience within experience Gestalts. The baby begins to learn to co-ordinate her senses of sight and touch with the movements of her limbs. Different patterns of co-ordination are learned from other events. The baby gradually learns to co-ordinate the different functions of the mind and the dimensions of experience associated with them. She is, as it were, learning to put the different parts of her body and nervous system together. Each dimension of experience can take on further meaning in the context of the others. All these developments continue as the baby learns to move herself about her crib, to crawl, and later to walk. We shall note one last detail: the visual perceptual paradigms undergo a further expansion in scope as she learns to identify with any object the visual sensations of seeing it at different distances.

The developments we have described above are, of course, only abstracted parts of the baby's experience. They interact with other developments such as those resulting from the baby's contact with human beings. No matter how rudimentary the experience Gestalts from these relationships may be at first, she soon distinguishes them from all the others because they bring about changes in her life. She no longer feels hungry or wet, she is carried about, played with, and so on. Once again a range of stimuli begin to take on a meaning. We have already suggested how the tactile stimuli related to being held to be fed become a meaningful sensation, and how she may learn to see her mother because of the way the visual stimuli move together against the static background. Other stimuli such as those related to her mother's facial expressions, body language, and speech can in turn take on a meaning and be transformed into sensations. These sensations refine the experience Gestalts, with the result that their variety increases. Social relationships add new clusters of paradigms to the various neural systems acquired from experience. These developments accelerate when social relationships become more recipro- cal, as the baby uses what she has learned about her body to externalize something of herself in her body language and her behaviour in general for the purpose of communication.

Each social relationship involves the baby, another member of her speech community, whatever is transacted, and the context of the relationship. This does not appear to cause the process of differentiation to waver between whichever of these four aspects it must take as the basis for differentiating these relationships. They are differentiated on the basis of the meaning they can have in the child's world. The interpretation gradually builds up in complexity when sets of stimuli take on a meaning as metaconscious knowledge implicit in the structure of experience develops.

As an example of how the interpretation of a social relationship may develop, consider the experience Gestalts that result from the baby being fed. At first her interpretation of this event may simply be 'that which makes the hunger feeling disappear.' When she learns something of the distinction between herself and the external world it may become 'that which makes *my* hunger feeling disappear.' When the baby learns to recognize her mother and distinguish her from other people it may become 'I am being fed by the person who always feeds me' or 'I am being fed by somone I do not know' or 'I am being fed by the person who usually only plays with me.' As more stimuli take on a meaning, she may begin to notice things about the food she eats, and the meaning of the experience Gestalt may now become 'I am being fed by my mother as usual but I don't like the food.' As other sets of stimuli take on a meaning, the baby may notice that she is being fed in a different room.

At an early stage in the baby's development, the cluster of experience paradigms derived from her social relationships may contain paradigms associated with events in which she is being fed, changed, played with, and so on. As stimuli continue to take on a meaning, the experience Gestalts of these events become more elaborated, with the result that each event of a certain type becomes more unique relative to other events of the same type. This was illustrated in the description of how the baby's social relationships during feeding develop. At the same time a certain type of event becomes increasingly distinct from all the others. Eventually different types of social relationships come to be regarded by the baby as being fundamentally different. The original cluster of experience paradigms associated with social relationships will then have broken up into several. One may be derived from contact with the other members of her speech community during feeding, another from contacts while the baby is being changed, and a third from being played with. These clusters are established along with others, some of which have already been mentioned.

When we examine the structure of the clusters of experience paradigms including the corresponding parts of the memory system built up from social relationships, it becomes clear that a great deal of metaconscious knowledge is being acquired. The structure differentiates between events of a particular type in which various people behaved differently and between events of that same type in which a specific person behaved differently. Thus the structure of experience of social relationships implies what the usual behaviour of the baby's mother is in a particular instance and how that behaviour is typical of her mother, that is, different from other people. As the variety of events that a child can distinguish becomes very large, it is clear that the structure of experience contains metaconscious knowledge of her mother's personality and the personality of other people she meets frequently. It also contains metaconscious knowledge of the social roles of these people. The baby learns to see the behaviour of her mother and father, brothers and sisters, relatives, friends, and strangers towards her as being unique, as each person's behaviour is differentiated from that of the others via specific events.

As the child grows up, she will learn to deal with people according to the social role they play, such as a policeman, teacher, or doctor. She differentiates the form these social relationships take from all other social relationships as well as how various people acted in similar events, and acquires metaconscious knowledge of the range of acceptable and unacceptable behaviour. The structure of experience thus gradually implies a metaconscious knowledge of the social structure of the child's speech community and society, what constitutes normal, customary, and acceptable behaviour in particular circumstances and what does not.

As a child acquires metaconscious knowledge of the personality of significant others in her speech community and the social roles occupied by them and people she meets only occasionally, she also acquires a metaconscious knowledge of herself. These relationships are constituted by her own behaviour and how others behave towards her. The structure of experience differentiates between similar events in which the child behaved differently. Each type of event is in turn differentiated from all other types. As a result, the structure of experience shows the child's typical behaviour in all the events she has learned to interpret and differentiate from the others. The structure of experience therefore also contains metaconscious knowledge of the personality of the child.

During the first stages of the baby's development many of the social relationships centre around her physical needs and the way her being is enfolded into that of her mother. Hence the image of the self implied in the structure of experience overemphasizes its physical aspects. This metaconscious knowledge interacts with and is complemented by that derived from her playing with her limbs and the manipulation of objects. As the baby's social relationships gradually become reciprocal, the social aspects of the self implied in the structure of experience grow in scope and importance. Both the physical and social components of the metaconscious knowledge of the self are of fundamental importance for the proper development of the baby. If, for example, the significant others ignore her or show little love, the structure of experience implies that she is not lovable, with the well-known disastrous consequences for the child's development. Her relationships with other people act as a mirror to show her who she is. To a lesser degree this is also true for her relationships with animals, plants, and objects.[5] All this is an integral part of the way children move from one kind of enfolded existence to another.

The way animals, plants and objects and the environment as a whole enter into the social and other relationships brings out what we may call their cultural identity. The structure of experience differentiates how they enter into the various relationships that are typical of the culture of the speech community and the society in which the child grows up; that is, it contains metaconscious knowledge of the meaning they have in the life of that culture.

In all these aspects of the development of children, metaconscious knowledge develops when the micro-level distinctions between neighbours in one or more subsystems of the systems of experience and memory begin to link together into a Gestalt. Although this Gestalt is not directly available to conscious thought, it affects the macro-level structure of these subsystems. To use the analogy of the jigsaw puzzle once again, it is as if several sets of a few interlocked pieces, hitherto seemingly unrelated, can suddenly be fitted together. All the remaining pieces then readily fall into place. When a metaconscious Gestalt begins to take shape, the framework within which stimuli are interpreted and generated begins to change. In this manner, micro-level developments in the mind's systems built up from experience eventually reach the macro-level.

METACONSCIOUS KNOWLEDGE IN DAILY LIFE

Metaconscious knowledge continues to play an important role in the lives of people after they have been socialized into a culture. Consider face-to-face conversations, for example. Because many of these kinds of experiences have been enfolded into our being, we have learned a great deal more about how to conduct ourselves in these situations than we are generally aware of. Metaconscious knowledge emerges from differentiating countless face-to-face conversations. Its role becomes particularly obvious when two people from different cultures talk together.

By growing up in a particular culture, a person has learned to stand at a certain distance when talking to someone else. If he or she stood a little too close or too far away, the experience typically involved an emotional reaction. The other person might find us too reserved and distant or too pushy. By differentiating these experiences from all others, North Americans metaconsciously learn to stand at about two feet from each other while South Americans stand much closer. When a North and South American have a friendly conversation, they will typically, without knowing it, attempt to maintain what for their culture is the normal talking distance. If the North American succeeds the South American will move closer, which causes the former to back up, and so on. The result is the two persons slowly moving in one direction as the one keeps backing up while the other advances.[6] If they have several of these experiences, sterotypes of the other culture may result. The North American may feel that South Americans are pushy, while the latter may feel that the former are a distant and unfriendly people. These sterotypes often emerge whenever people are not aware of the role metaconscious knowledge plays in face-to-face encounters.

A face-to-face conversation also involves other kinds of metaconscious knowledge. Facial expressions, eye movements, and body language may be used by a culture to form the framework for what is exchanged by means of language. They can communicate the listener's level of interest and attention to the speaker, who can utilize this information to cut short or elaborate a particular topic. They can also act as traffic signals to allow the speaker to indicate that it is time for the listener to respond. In some cultures, for example, the speaker will glance at the listener during pauses in her speech, usually at the end of a sentence, to see if the listener is following. The listener, on the other hand, spends much more time looking at the speaker so as to be able to signal interest whenever the speaker looks his way. When she is finished talking, the speaker gives the listener a significantly longer glance to signal she is awaiting a response.

Other cultures may have developed somewhat different ways of handling the non-verbal aspects of face-to-face conversations. Eye behavior, for example, can vary considerably.[7] Arabs often look intently into each other's eyes when they talk, while in other cultures it is rude to look at one another. Once again, when members from different cultures meet, they can easily misinterpret each other's signals because they generally have no conscious knowledge of their precise roles. Westerners may be very uncomfortable under the steady gaze of an Arab and find a person who does not even look at them rude or emotionally disturbed. But these impressions are erroneous because we interpret the signals from the members of other cultures not on their own terms but on the basis of our culture. These problems can also arise between members of the same culture. In cultures where eye signals play an important role in conversations, people may be quite reluctant to talk with visually handicapped persons. They might better understand their reluctance if they attempted to carry out conversations without all the signals depending on sight by using a blindfold.

Most people have, of course, some conscious awareness of the eye etiquette of their culture. But there is yet another type of metaconscious knowledge involved in face-to-face conversations which can best be detected by using high-speed movie cameras. Conversations involve body rhythms which are shared by both a speaker and listener. This phenomenon is called interactional synchrony.[8] For example, as a speaker moves her hand, the listener may move his head to the left. When the hand motion reverses itself, the head may follow suit and begin to shift in the opposite direction. If the one speeds up, the other may too, or the rhythm may be picked up by the body or limbs.

Interactional synchrony creates metaconscious messages related to the degree a speaker and listener are in tune with one another. If the listener's attention fades, synchrony weakens or even disappears. A feeling of great rapport may be created when both parties put their whole being into the conversation, as it were, by having their entire bodies participate in the interactional synchrony, while moderate involvement may be indicated by having perhaps only the head or one limb involved. Interactional synchrony illustrates the enfolded character of these aspects of our being. This is weakened or delimited when mental problems occur of an emotional or physiological origin. Schizophrenics, autistic children, people with aphasia, mild epilepsy, and Parkinson's disease often do not establish a rhythm that is consistent for their entire bodies. One hand may, for example, move with the rhythm of their speech, while the other hand or the head moves out of phase. When such people engage in communications with others not having these problems, intuitions will arise that make communication very difficult. Even when schizophrenic children establish a measure of interactional synchrony with their parents, it appears, at least in some cases, that the latter will shift their body posture and rhythm away from synchrony. They metaconsciously express the fact that they cannot establish a normal rapport with the child and therefore want to keep their distance, particularly when they are unable to love the child and they accept the disability only with difficulty.

The time aspect of social relationships is also handled quite differently by various cultures. As a result, there may be quite different notions of punctuality. Being an hour late in one culture may be the same as being five minutes late in a Western culture; but unless Westerners know this, they may feel insulted when they are kept waiting for an hour. By having differentiated people's reactions in respect to being late, we have acquired a metaconscious knowledge of what is acceptable and what is not. When kept waiting our emotions reflect our 'cultural clock' without the intervention of any conscious thought.

Other kinds of metaconscious knowledge that play an important role, not only in face-to-face conversations but in any social relationship, are associated with our own personality and those of others. The latter is evident when a person declares that 'I did not expect her to do that' or 'that is typical of him' or 'I don't know what's the matter with her; she does not seem to be herself today.' If someone asked the person to be more specific or to justify her remark, she would have to try to recall all previous experiences of the other person and try to fit them into patterns that can be described by some personality trait or type. On the basis of this analysis, she would then be able to evaluate how typical the experience in question was. It is clear that this is not an easy talk for many people. In any case, such an analysis is not the basis for the above kind of remarks. They can be based only on a metaconscious knowledge obtained by differentiating the experiences of the person in question. The metaconscious knowledge of others may be erroneous. For example, a too rapidly formed initial impression may be projected on subsequent encounters, distorting the metaconscious image of the relationship.

Our metaconscious knowledge of another person is not exclusively the result of direct encounters with him. We may have talked about the individual with others or he may have been the subject of our thoughts, and these experiences contribute to our metaconscious image of the other person. These images help determine the emotions and motivations associated with social relations.

In our dealings with others we may also depend on a metaconscious knowledge related to certain social roles. For example, what it is to be male and female in a culture is derived from a wide range of differentiated experiences. All these Gestalts of metaconscious knowledge do not exist in isolation from one another. What it is to be female in a culture is relative to what it is to be male and vice versa. Since our relations with others do not occur in a vacuum, they also draw in our metaconscious knowledge of the 'nature' of time, the group, and the environment as perceived by our culture.

While a great deal of knowledge as to how we are to conduct ourselves in social relationships in our culture may exist both on the conscious and metaconscious level, only the latter is utilized in spontaneous behaviour. What we tend to do automatically, without thinking, is executed solely by the process of differentiation operating on the basis of the structure of experience. Once we understand that different cultures structure face-to-face conversations differently, we may keep our spontaneous reactions in check, think things over, and modify our usual behaviour accordingly. However, even the most carefully thought-out behaviour still needs to be executed on the basis of the process of differentiation; hence it will still contain a substantial metaconscious component. The role of culture as a social ecology is therefore extensively based on metaconscious knowledge.

The role of this knowledge is, of course, not limited to social relationships. It enters into any relationship, but we will not pursue that here.

Instead let us turn to a different kind of role that it plays. Intuitions express something about relationships established beyond the level of consciousness as one or more experiences are enfolded into our metaconscious. Intuition is called our sixth sense by some, while others deny its existence. Both these positions can now be understood. By interrelating our past experience by means of a process of differentiation and by deriving information from the resulting structures, new insight can be created. Yet we did not directly acquire it via any of the dimensions of experience. Intuitions signal the creation of significant metaconscious information by presenting our consciousness with some clue.

The phenomena associated with intuition derive from the properties of Gestalts. Patterns can be more or less complete or detailed and still be recognizable. This is evident from sketches. Some people are able to communicate the essentials of a situation or object with a few pencil lines. If the sketch is then shown to various people, their reactions could vary considerably. To some the sketch may communicate nothing, while others may be able to elaborate it with countless details. The various elaborated sketches may, however, communicate little more than the original. The differences between them would, among other things, reflect the prior experience of those who worked them out. In a sense the human mind does the same thing. The same stimuli may give rise to a variety of sensations, Gestalts, and experience Gestalts, depending on the prior experience of the person. Similarly, depending on their sensitivity, some people may form Gestalts of metaconscious knowledge where others can as yet form none.

The situation is somewhat like fitting a curve through a set of scattered experimental points on a graph. Some investigators may intuit what the curve is going to be somewhat earlier than others, but none of them will need data points for each point on the curve before they can discern the relationship. Our minds are able to deduce Gestalts of metaconscious knowledge from incomplete 'data' because they are able to interpolate and extrapolate, and this gives rise to various kinds of intuitions.

Intuitions give us a feeling that somehow there is more to a given situation than what our senses tell us. We can now understand their source. The experience Gestalt of the situation takes on its meaning in the context of the structure of experience by means of the process of differentiation. It also participates in metaconscious knowledge on a variety of levels; on one of these levels it may allow for a new Gestalt of metaconscious knowledge to form. It is like watching someone make a quick pencil sketch of an unknown object. A certain number of pencil lines may have been made on the paper, but we as yet have no clue as to what they mean. Then the artist adds one more line and suddenly we have an idea of what it might become. When a new experience Gestalt creates this kind of situation, our mind may give us an intuition. We have the feeling there is a potential of further meaning because of the new Gestalt of metaconscious knowledge which is beginning to form, but only additional relevant experience Gestalts (often created by analysing the situation) allow the intuition to be confirmed. They either permit the Gestalt of metaconscious knowledge to establish itself and hence place the event that triggered off the intuition in a new light, or they destroy the embryonic Gestalt by not fitting into it. Here are some examples.

Consider a group of students taking notes in a lecture. Their notes will differ considerably, particularly if the professor does not use the blackboard. Each student has interpreted the aural stimuli by means of a process of differentiation which operates on the basis of structures acquired from previous experience. The result is that each part of the lecture is seen in relation to what the students already know, and this can vary considerably from one individual to another. At one point some of them may suddenly catch on when a number of things fall into place as they form a Gestalt. There is another reason, however, why the notes of the students differ: some may suddenly have an intuition. They have sensed something in the stimuli being interpreted that cannot possibly be deduced from them. By placing the stimuli in the context of the structure of experience by means of the processes of differentiation and integration it is possible to intuit something of their potential meaning or significance that can normally only become evident from a more extensive experience with the subject at hand. Intuition utilizes the metaconscious to derive information about a particular situation or phenomenon that can only be verified by more extensive exposure to it.

We may come home one day, walk into our living room, and get the distinct feeling that something has changed without knowing what it is. Within its third dimension the process of differentiation operating on the level of experience has detected that the stimuli are different from what they usually are. It is able to do this because of the metaconscious knowledge implicit in the structure of experience. The functions of the mind acting below the level of consciousness can only transmit such findings by means of an intuition, however. Once we learn to interpret these intuitions we will begin to pay closer attention to the situation and analyse it as best we can. We may try to recall what we can about the room and compare it with what we observe. In the days when instruments to detect danger were virtually non-existent, an experienced miner could supposedly smell danger. What in fact he felt was that something was not quite as usual. This, of course, did not necessarily mean trouble, but under the circumstances it is obvious that he would take these feelings seriously and investigate the situation.

There are situations in which babies appear to experience similar feelings. Because the members of their speech community share a common culture and because of the general regularity in their behaviour due to their personalities, babies' lives usually have a dominant component of routine. This greatly facilitates their learning to interpret stimuli. As long as things happen in their usual routine the baby can learn to interpret new aspects of basically familiar events. When the routine is totally disturbed he becomes uneasy at not being able to interpret the events on the basis of prior experience. The baby is not consciously aware of what comprises his daily routine since that knowledge is implicit in his structure of experience. He cannot make it conscious by recalling and analysing experience Gestalts the way adults can. He shows his frustration by long crying spells. When babies and young children cannot as yet recall experience Gestalts from memory they are nevertheless able to recognize familiar events, people or objects by means of the process of differentiation and the metaconscious knowledge implied in the structure of experience.

Intuitions are not uncommon when we are trying to solve some problem. We may have some intuition regarding the direction in which we should search for a solution based on metaconscious knowledge derived from our structure of experience. We begin to follow it up by using our past experience. Typically the solution does not immediately present itself. As we keep on trying, the scope of one or more existing experience paradigms is extended within the third dimension of the process of differentiation – that is, we try to look at the problem as if it were like one we already know. This effort permits the process of differentiation to 'learn' by extending existing paradigms (be it directly by means of experience paradigms or first by perceptual or movement paradigms which then in turn affect the experience paradigm). If the equilibrium between the third and fourth dimensions of differentiation of neighbouring experience paradigms is disturbed, a new paradigm will be formed. By means of the new paradigm we suddenly see the problem in a new light, which may or may not confirm the intuition. The structural changes in the systems of perceptual and movement paradigms and the system of experience break into conscious-ness via a particular experience Gestalt. The consequences are often limited in scope, as was the case with the subjects in the playing-card experiment learning to recognize anomalous cards and in the case of the baby playing with her limbs.

The consequences can also be rather extensive if the disturbance of the equilibrium between the third and fourth dimensions of differentiation of neighbouring paradigms in turn disturbs the equilibrium between their neighbours to pave the way for a kind of chain reaction. Such situations typically occur when a great deal of exploratory work has been done, which has pushed the scope of many experience paradigms to the limit. The paradigms are on the verge of breaking up, with the result that the stability of a part of the structure of experience has been sufficiently weakened so that the break-up of a single experience paradigm can trigger off a chain reaction. Before the chain reaction occurs, aesthetically sensitive persons may feel that somehow things are ready for a change. The histories of art, science, and religious movements provide many illustrations. Initially a researcher may be impressed with the beauty of a theory because of its elegant mathematical formulation and the way it accurately models a wide variety of phenomena. After working with the theory for a period of time he may begin to detect weaknesses in it. He stretches it to the limit by making many minor modifications, causing the theory to become less coherent and hence less aesthetically pleasing. The researcher may then begin to feel that a new theory could perhaps represent the same set of phenomena more simply and accurately. Whether or not he has this feeling, he may one day suddenly see a whole new range of possibilities. It may be the beginning of a scientific revolution, as Kuhn has described it.

A similar situation occurs when an artist begins to paint in a different way. She has come to see reality in a new light. Somehow she feels that reality as she knows it has changed and that it can no longer be represented in the same way.[9] Another example is furnished by religious conversions. One of the more spectacular historical examples is possibly the conversion of the Mongolians to Buddhism, which changed them from one of the most warlike people of the time to one of the most peaceful. They had come to see the reality of their existence in a different way. Individual conversions are usually provoked when people intuit that there is more to life than what their structures of experience imply. They begin to search for other sources of meaning, which weakens the equilibrium of a part of their structure of experience. They are then susceptible to conversion.

A structural chain reaction cannot occur spontaneously, however. The structure of experience is self-organizing and self-reinforcing only as it functions, that is, as experience paradigms interpret stimuli. It cannot be changed in any other way. The chain reaction takes place step by step. When an experience paradigm in the domain of the structure of experience, whose structural equilibrium has been weakened, happens to break up as it interprets stimuli, the newly formed paradigm may then disrupt the weakened equilibrium. Only the particular situation at hand comes to stand in a new light by means of the new paradigm. However, because the equilibrium of the whole region has been disturbed, some people may intuit that there is more to the change than meets the senses. All the other experience paradigms involved in the disturbance of the structural equilibrium are not interpreting stimuli and hence cannot reorganize themselves. These persons must therefore look over and reflect on the events in that domain of experience once more or work through the problems again, using the intuition they had to direct the process of differentiation and integration. It is only as they use the other experience paradigms in the course of these activities that the full-scale restructuring of a part of the structure of experience is accomplished, as the paradigms activated by stimuli reorganize themselves while they interpret them. We then regard the domain of experience with a new intelligence.

A good illustration of an interrupted chain reaction is provided by Western-style mass religious conversions, often provoked by deep emotions and the pressure of the crowd or mass media on the individual. When the emotions wear off, *no new intelligence with which to see the world* (the meaning of the Greek word for conversion) has developed, either because these people have not been told that they must individually and together work out the new intelligence for their daily lives, or because, once left to work things out, they are unable to do so, or because the new religion creates a dualism in them of a spiritual and a profane realm. The result is that despite their sincerity, their conversion leads to little concrete change. This is a sociological reality of many religious movements springing up today and of many Christian crusades. Whether in art, science, or religion, conversions from one type of structure of experience to another are therefore not truly revolutionary; they must be painstakingly worked out over a period of time. The intuitions must be made durable.

During a period in which a part of the structure of experience is transformed, two patterns of metaconscious knowledge can coexist. A new pattern may be beginning to link up without the former one having been displaced. The old pattern disintegrates as the new pattern takes on more definite shape because it loses some of its components which are starting to reorient themselves to form the beginnings of the outline for the new pattern. During the period of transition both patterns may be recognizable. Intuition permits a person to detect new patterns of metaconscious knowledge before they are completed. He has a glimpse of the potential significance of a phenomenon or an event by sensing something of the consequences it may have for the metaconscious knowledge implicit in part of the structure of experience. When an intuition is followed up by an attempt to verify it, it may, if it proves to be well founded, accelerate structural changes. In the absence of intuitions a smooth transition from one structural pattern to another occurs, as is well illustrated by the transition from one stage of a child's development to the next. Intuition permits someone to see something in a situation or an event, of which others are as yet unaware. A particularly sensitive person can intuit something of the new patterns of metaconscious knowledge that are constantly linking up because of the endless dynamic changes in the structure of experience. It is possible, therefore, that someone can sense something happening which will only be fully evident to others at a later date. By means of intuition a person can sense something of what is to come in the future because its beginnings are already there in the present. These people are often ahead of their time, as is the case with famous artists and scientists.

Some phenomena related to intuition are, of course, closely linked with creativity and imagination. From the preceding chapters it is evident that creativity and imagination are a fundamental part of the lives of children. There is an ever-present component of creativity in the way they learn to interpret and relate to their environment. Out of undifferentiated stimuli their minds create sensations, Gestalts, and experience Gestalts in the course of their encounters with that world. They creatively and imaginatively explore and experiment as they try to make sense of their surroundings. When they become adults their creative ability does not stop. Life is full of unexpected situations which cannot be met on the basis of prior experience and consequently demand some measure of creativity. Without it, people and their society would quickly alienate themselves from reality. From the discussion above, it is clear how the metaconscious plays an important role in human creativity.

The most spectacular way in which metaconscious knowledge can be intuited is by the relatively rare flash of inspiration. It may occur when the structural equilibrium of a number of experience paradigms has been seriously weakened, which initiates a structural transition. As a result, a new Gestalt of metaconscious knowledge begins to link up and the flash of inspiration reveals something of that new pattern. Of course, the flash of inspiration must be worked out to give the experience paradigms the opportunity to adjust themselves.

A flash of inspiration can also occur after the person has temporarily ceased all activities in a domain of experience. When someone has been working on a problem he has internalized it via a set of experience Gestalts. Since our memory is a dynamic system, the resulting memory traces interact with one another and with traces formed either previously or subsequently. As a result, a range of experiences relating to the unsuccessful attempts to solve the problem, which were confused and unclear, may later start to fit together and permit a Gestalt of metaconscious knowledge to form. When this happens people with a strong aesthetic sensitivity may experience a flash of inspiration which, when worked out, causes the pieces to fall into place. After the fact, things then typically look so simple that the person wonders why he did not see it right away. There are many accounts of creative flashes, and they have received the attention of psychologists. One of the best-known accounts of such a moment is by the mathematician Poincaré.[10] While stepping on the bus one day during a geological excursion he suddenly had a new idea about a mathematical problem he had not thought about for several days.

Before considering another range of phenomena related to intuition one matter needs to be clarified. Provided a society is not stagnating, the structure of experience of its members may include metaconscious knowledge in three coexisting Gestalts: the remnants of disintegrating patterns of the past (the now obsolete aspects of the culture), the current and hence best-developed patterns, and the patterns of things to come which are beginning to link up. Intuition draws on the latter patterns. An intuition can be very trivial, in which case it is founded on a small fraction of the structure of experience and as a consequence can easily prove incorrect. At the other end of the spectrum, an intuition is an exceedingly complex affair when it is solidly founded on a large part of the structure of experience. It may then be impossible to communicate except in an indirect way as in music, art, and myths. Its message rarely proves unfounded or insignificant. This is confirmed by the complete reversal in the Westerner's attitude towards the myths of past civilizations: until relatively recently they were considered as proof of the religious naivety and lack of scientific rationality of past civilizations, but the existential depth and validity of myths is now widely recognized. What now appears naive is not the myths but the narrow rationality with which they were judged in the West for some time.

Members of a speech community, group, or society whose daily lives interact directly or indirectly share many experiences and hence possess structures of experience that exhibit a significant measure of unity within their diversity. As a result they share a considerable part of their metaconscious knowledge. Because it is not available to them at will, the parts of it that have surfaced into consciousness will vary from person to person.

Another range of phenomena related to metaconscious knowledge is based on those differences which permit some members of a speech community, group, or society who have special training or above average sensitivity to help others to become aware of what metaconsciously already lives within them. The other members will then have the feeling of somehow having known or experienced these things all along without realizing it. Upon being confronted with the explicit formulation of a meaning of a domain of experience that until now lived only as metaconscious knowledge within them, they are able to recognize it as being something of themselves.

Examples are frequent in children that are growing up. Members of the child's speech community can explain something as much as they like, but if she is not ready for it – that is, when there is not even a partial support of metaconscious knowledge within the child – she will be unable to grasp it. When she enters school she is able to differentiate people, animals, plants, and things although she has never formulated these distinctions in the form of concepts. She knows they are different and what these differences mean in her daily existence. Her teacher can readily appeal to this as he teaches her the concepts of people, animals, plants, and things, which renders the metaconscious knowledge conscious.

The same phenomenon can occur within a society. Although existentialism had been established as a philosophy well before the Second World War, it was practically unknown outside philosophical circles. As the nations of Europe lived through the war years, people experienced many terrible things that metaconsciously prepared the way for looking at life differently. When Jean-Paul Sartre expressed it in his plays and novels, existentialism suddenly swept the continent. Many recognized in Sartre's work something of their own feelings that they had been unable to express so far. The same phenomenon can occur when something of the time in which a society lives is expressed in the form of art or music. (When the message strikes too close to the heart of a society, however, it is often rejected by means of complex defence mechanisms.) Another example is psychoanalysis, which is designed to help a patient uncover and understand some conflicts and problems that are implied in his structure of experience so that he can overcome their influence.

The other side of the coin is the possibility of psychological manipulation. While brain-washing attempts to force a kind of religious conversion on people by attempting to convert their structure of experience, some techniques of psychological manipulation do not attempt to change that structure but to exploit it for a particular end. In other words, the purpose of these techniques is not to have people accept certain ideas but to interfere with the normal functioning of their structures of experience to lead them to do things that they would otherwise not do.

A first example of this type of psychological technique is modern advertising. Advertisers employ what lives within people's metaconscious by means of advertising symbolism, which has been studied by several authors.[11] People respond to advertising symbolism because of what already exists within them. Baudrillard[12] has shown that indeed modern consumer goods are not mere objects without a meaning other than the purpose for which they are designed, because they symbolize something in the metaconscious to which advertising symbolism can appeal. Galbraith[13] has demonstrated that the traditional assumption of consumer sovereignty in classical economics can no longer be maintained because of the impact that modern advertising has on the consumer. What Galbraith does not analyse sufficiently, however, is that advertising only exploits, but does not seek to modify, the structure of experience, which means that the cultural context limits producer sovereignty. The producer-consumer interaction by means of modern advertising occurs within the domain traced out by a culture founded on the structures of experience of the people that share the culture.

On a different plane, a second example of techniques of psychological manipulation is integration propaganda, which threatens the political sovereignty of the citizen in modern democratic states. Just as advertising has become a necessity for the technically advanced sector of the economic system, so integration propaganda has become a necessity in the modern state.[14] Both techniques function in essentially the same way. For the moment it is not important that the reader understand the relationships between the economic and political systems of the modern state on the one hand and the structure of experience of its citizens on the other. We have not yet developed all the prerequisites for such a study. These relationships are simply cited to illustrate the daily-life consequences of what is being examined here.

The last phenomenon to be noted by which metaconscious knowledge surfaces into consciousness is dreams. Research on sleep[15] would appear to suggest the following explanation. There are two kinds of sleep. The first, which is most frequent during the night, is called orthodox sleep or non-rapid-eye-movement sleep. After falling asleep a person spends on the average seventy minutes in orthodox sleep followed by a twenty-minute period of the second kind of sleep called paradoxical or rapid-eye-movement sleep, thus making a ninety-minute cycle.

During orthodox sleep existing cells and tissues in the body are renewed or replaced by new cells. The cells in the brain are never replaced, however, and this is probably one of the reasons why the second kind of sleep exists. During paradoxical sleep the blood-flow to the brain rises, while it falls sharply in the muscles. The heat output of the brain also rises, indicating increased chemical activity. A few weeks before and after birth, when cortex thickness increases considerably, a baby spends twice as much time in paradoxical sleep as the average adult. Mentally retarded children, whose brains develop more slowly, have less paradoxical sleep. After a drug overdose causing brain damage, paradoxical sleep duration increases. Senility, caused by a decrease in brain renewal which thus produces a shrivelling of the brain, is also accompanied by a reduction in paradoxical sleep. All this appears to indicate that paradoxical sleep is associated with the brain's need to have its cells renewed or with brain growth. There are even some claims that paradoxical sleep increases with learning and that it is important for the synthesis of durable memory proteins.

We may thus imagine that as repair work is in progress, as it were, on the brain, the networks of relationships in the mind may be affected. Patterns may arise because certain parts of the networks are activated as they are checked out or as new connections established during the previous day are reinforced. It would then be possible, that, as in the case of flashes of illumination, these patterns can break into consciousness when they have a particular significance. Dreams have been the object of serious investigation, and their potential existential significance seems undeniable.[16] Whatever these reductionistic theories can tell us about the biochemical aspects of dreams, they cannot explain their contents.

THE SUBCONSCIOUS AND THE METACONSCIOUS

According to the way we have conceptualized the structure of experience, it is now possible to distinguish five levels of consciousness: besides that of conscious awareness, two are related to the subconscious and two to the metaconscious. First consider the subconscious. We have already noted that, based on innate structures of the brain, babies can establish a variety of instinctual relationships with reality. We will assume that implied in these structures is a certain amount of knowledge, as was taken to be the case for the structures acquired from experience. Subconscious knowledge includes the information implicit in the structure of the brain into which the innate structures are enfolded. It may also include some information implied in the structure of the body into which the brain is enfolded as well as the self as it is enfolded into the whole. In so far as these innate structures and subconscious knowledge are shared by all human beings, they are analogous to what Jung has called instincts and archetypes respectively. We will therefore also call this level of consciousness the collective unconscious.

Since the individual and collective existence of the members of a culture is grafted onto the collective unconscious, it continues to play a unique role during a person's entire life. We do not believe, however, that this role is as extensive as Jung has portrayed it. As our analysis advances, it will become clear that much of what Jung relates to the role of the collective unconscious can in fact be attributed to the role of the metaconscious.[17]

A second level of consciousness is the personal unconscious. It can be distinguished from the collective unconscious because its contents are derived from experience. It mostly contains experiences that cannot be recalled or that are repressed and thus withdrawn from consciousness. In other words, the contents of the personal unconscious do not participate in the structure of experience in the way other experiences do. Particularly in relation to the metaconscious their role is fundamentally different. The hypothesis of the metaconscious causes us to part ways with Jung and Freud on a variety of issues. We will briefly consider a few of them here.

Experiments have shown that adults can only very rarely recall events that happened before they were three or four years old.[18] For the exceptions, there is the possibility that the subject had been told about it later, which can easily be confused with actually recalling the original event. The explanation which suggests itself in the light of the present study is that we are unable to reconstruct these experiences because the memory traces depict the situation from an 'existential' viewpoint that is no longer available from the current experience paradigms.[19] The experience paradigms via which the events of early childhood were lived have been totally transformed, which is probably the reason why the reconstruction of the events is nearly impossible. Even with considerable thought and analysis, the interpretation of events on the basis of a system of experience in which the social self is implied in only a rudimentary fashion cannot be imagined easily. It would appear, therefore, that Freud's thesis that we repress early childhood experiences when we are socialized because they are so selfish and pleasure-seeking is not necessary to explain childhood amnesia. Because these experiences cannot be recalled from memory they form a part of our personal unconscious.

When an event is profoundly upsetting to the point that it threatens an aspect of a person's existence, it is often repressed. This may be regarded as a kind of defence mechanism to protect the social self enfolded into the structure of experience. Destroying the relative coherence of the social self would make existence impossible because the systems-like character of the systems of experience and memory would be damaged, leading to serious mental disorders. Amnesia of the event thus protects the personality. In extreme and very rare cases when the threat cannot be resolved in this way, the structure of experience may break up, creating a multiple personality. This will be discussed later. For now, we simply note that any repressed memories also form a part of the subconscious contents of the structure of experience.

The degree of repression can vary. Weakly repressed memories may be recalled in disguised form in dreams or in the fantasies of day-dreaming when repression weakens. They can also be uncovered by association tests. In such tests, a psychoanalyst calls out a word to which the subject is to respond with the first word that comes to his or her mind. Long delays in the responses are taken to be a function of the degree of association with repressed memories. By scanning an area of experience in this manner, patterns may be formed by the response words which were particularly slow in coming. This permits the psychoanalyst to get a glimpse of the psychic dimension of the structure of experience, including nuclei of repressed memories. We will interpret the degree of repression as an indication of the level to which experiences are withdrawn from normal participation in the structure of experience.

Jung has argued that the personal unconscious also contains sense impressions that did not quite reach consciousness. This can be explained in terms of our model as due to the fact that at the time they did not really make sense and hence could not be interpreted into a coherent experience Gestalt, or because the stimuli were not present for a sufficiently long time to allow the mind's systems to complete their interpretation. Similar phenomena occur when something in the background does not receive enough attention for its stimuli to be fully interpreted to reach consciousness. The latter phenomenon is abused in modern advertising. Since the perceptual and movement paradigms involved in these cases are affected and since these effects participate normally in the operations of the structure of experience whenever these paradigms are activated, we will include in the metaconscious the information built into the structure of experience as a result of these events. The subliminal sensations and elements of experience participate in the structure of experience in the usual way, and they will therefore be included in the metaconscious also. It is obvious, however, that the distinction between the subconscious and the metaconscious cannot be drawn clearly.

The role the personal unconscious plays in a structure of experience will largely depend on its structure. If its elements constitute a system, it will play a semi-autonomous role, but, if they are only weakly associated with each other, it cannot play such a role. Particularly in the case of childhood experiences, the former appears likely according to our model, and the extensive literature on depth psychology would appear to confirm this. The personal unconscious can function with a measure of autonomy in relation to a person's being. What cannot be enfolded into our being in the usual manner is enfolded together into our personal unconscious.

Two levels of consciousness are associated with the metaconscious. We have already noted that various aspects of human behaviour can be explained by hypothesizing that Gestalts of metaconscious knowledge can be derived from the way experiences have been structured in relation to each other by the process of differentiation. What this means is that enfolding a moment of our life into our being does not stop with the process of differentiation. Experiences are further enfolded into our life by being integrated into patterns yielding Gestalts of metaconscious knowledge. The systematic character of these processes of integration link these Gestalts into another system of the mind that we have called the metaconscious. The process of differentiation and integration are fully complementary in allowing us to experience each moment of our life by living it in the context of our whole being.

The processes of integration associated with the metaconscious occur on a variety of levels which can be understood by introducing the concept of metaconscious depth. The depth of a Gestalt of metaconscious knowledge will be said to increase with the scope of the structure of experience from which it is derived. On the level of least metaconscious depth we find Gestalts of knowledge derived from a single cluster of memory traces lived by means of the same experience paradigm. On the next lower level we find Gestalts derived from a cluster of experience paradigms and the associated clusters of memory traces, while on still lower levels we encounter Gestalts derived from entire subsystems of the systems of experience and memory. The greatest level of metaconscious depth is reached when the structure of experience is taken as a whole. These Gestalts depict, as we will see later, the project of existence of a culture, provided a person has lived his or her entire life in it. By way of example, we can say that the Gestalts of metaconscious knowledge related to the personalities of friends lie less deep than the one related to one's image of one's own social self.

The Gestalts of metaconscious knowledge on the same or different levels of depth are interdependent and constitute a system. This can be briefly illustrated as follows. Thc Gestalts having the greater depth presuppose at least a rudimentary form of Gestalts with a lesser depth; this follows from the fact that there is not just one component of metaconscious knowledge implied in a particular part of the systems of experience and memory. Each part can contribute to various Gestalts of metaconscious knowledge. For example, the parts of a child's structure of experience related to her social relationships with her mother yield metaconscious knowledge of her own and her mother's personality, the role of mothers in that culture (by differentiating her mother's behaviour from that of other mothers), what it is to be male and female in that culture (by differentiating the role of mother and other female roles from those of males), and so on. This presupposes the metaconscious knowledge related to her physical and social self and how they are different from the remainder of the world.

There are some important differences between the various levels of metaconscious depth. The levels with the least depth mostly contain Gestalts that are largely unique to the individual. Next are the levels with Gestalts largely shared by the members of a primary group, followed by those with Gestalts shared by a speech community, social stratum, or class, depending on the social structure of the society. The levels with the greatest depth are almost always shared by all the members of a society, and we will therefore refer to them as the collective metaconscious as opposed to the somewhat more personal metaconscious. It is clear that the structure of the metaconscious depends on the structure of a society.[20] We will return to this problem in great detail when we examine the role of culture as a social ecology from the point of view of a society.

The metaconscious can be incorporated into the simple spatial model of the structure of experience developed earlier. It can be added as a series of parallel planes located above the plane containing the memory system. Gestalts of metaconscious knowledge having the same depth can be imagined as being located on the same surface, each one directly above those parts of the systems of experience and memory from which the process of integration derived the experiences. The greater the metaconscious depth, the higher the plane on which it is located. As a particular area of a child's structure of experience begins to develop, the Gestalts with the least metaconscious depth will begin to form along with those having a somewhat greater depth, but the latter's development will necessarily lag behind the former. As the various parts of the systems of experience and memory develop further, Gestalts of still greater metaconscious depth begin to form, until finally the collective metaconscious begins to develop on the highest surfaces. Gestalts having a greater depth presuppose at least a rudimentary form of metaconscious knowledge represented as Gestalts having a lesser depth.

The distinctions we have drawn between the five levels of consciousness (namely the collective unconscious, personal unconscious, conscious awareness, the personal metaconscious, and the collective metaconscious) are not largely a distinction between structure and content of the mind. We have shown that there can be no experience Gestalts or memory traces without a larger framework and no larger structure without experience Gestalts and memory traces. Furthermore, the different levels of consciousness overlap and interpenetrate as they are all enfolded into one being. For example, a great deal of conscious knowledge has metaconscious roots; when metaconscious knowledge breaks into consciousness there exists a conscious and metaconscious version of that knowledge.

The role of the metaconscious can be distinguished from that of the subconscious largely on the basis of their varying contribution to the meaning which a moment of our life has as it is enfolded into our being. The processes of integration directly complement the processes of differentiation in that process of enfolding. Each sensation, Gestalt, and experience Gestalt derives a component of meaning from both processes. The subconscious, on the other hand, is not enfolded into the structure of experience the way the other systems of the mind are, because its contents either could not be enfolded or ceased to be enfolded into one's life in the ways we have described.

The component of meaning which the metaconscious contributes to every moment of our life can easily be illustrated by two examples used by John Welwood[21] in a different context. We cannot access Gestalts of metaconscious knowledge the way we can recall memory traces, but we can feel a relationship: 'If you ask yourself how you feel now, what you get when you first refer inwardly to your felt sense of your present situation, is a blurry whole. Or try referring to your inner felt sense of a person in your life. What is your overall feeling about your father, your whole sense of him? Let yourself feel the whole quality of your relationship to him, without concentrating on specific thoughts or images. Notice that this whole sense has no definite form, but is a very global "feel quality". If what came to mind first was a particular image, see if you can let it broaden out into a blurry whole felt sense.'[22]

The metaconscious allows us to feel a relationship in a global kind of way. These feelings arise before we get a chance to analyse them or the associated experience. It is this ability based on the memory system and the metaconscious that we associated with the formation of emotional Gestalts in the previous chapter. Welwood suggests that: 'Felt meaning can be seen as an experiential manifestation of holographic compression, where many bits of information function all together as a whole. For example, go back to your felt sense of your father. Now notice that not only can you have this global sense of him apart from any particular image, memory, emotion or thought about him, but also your felt sense actually includes all of the ways you have ever experienced or interacted with him. This felt sense is like a holographic record of all the aspects of your relationship to him (interference patterns). All of your joys, hurts, disappointments, appreciations, angers – all of your whole experience with him is holographically compressed in this one felt sense. The felt sense is blurry in that it includes all of this *implicitly*. This implicit is not focal or sharply defined, but always functions as a global background. When we attend to an implicit felt sense in this way, we are using a scanning type of attention that does not single out specific focal objects one at a time. This global type of *diffuse attention* allows us to sense a holographic blur all at once, without imposing a preconceived grid, filter or focus on it. When we attempt to focus or pinpoint it, then we begin to make aspects of it *explicit*.'[23] The same analogy is applied to the building up of a metaconscious image of one's father: 'All of your experiences with your father have been "folded inward" in your felt sense. How you act and respond to him from moment to moment will largely be affected by this global felt background sense (which, however, is not static but keeps changing).'[24]

Given the highly interrelated and enfolded character of the structure of experience, each relationship directly or indirectly involves a great many aspects of our being, that of others, our culture and environment, in addition to the particularities of a given moment. Our feelings of the situation involves all of these. The metaconscious may be regarded as the order of our life into which all of our experiences are enfolded and which is unfolded to a limited degree in our behaviour. In counselling or psychotherapy stuck patterns and hidden meanings may be unfolded from the implicit order of the metaconscious. Once we become conscious of some of these aspects of our life, they come to stand in a different context so that their meaning is affected. Similarly when we suddenly feel 'I've got it' when trying to solve a problem, we do not know any of the details. All we have is a blurry intuition the contents of which need to be unfolded.

In so far as the holographic analogy helps us to conceptualize the highly enfolded character of human existence it is quite useful. It cannot help us understand how our structure of experience functions, however. Since a human person, a conscious 'I,' is enfolded into our being, no mechanism or mechanistic analogy can help us understand life without introducing the reductionisms we are trying to break away from. Holograms operate on the basis of interference patterns and function – as far as we know – according to certain laws, so no conscious 'I' can be enfolded into them.

It is now becoming evident that a great deal of what in human behaviour has been attributed to the collective unconscious, personal unconscious, or subconscious can in fact be explained by the metaconscious. (There is no space here to work out the implications of the hypothesis of a metaconscious for the theories of Jung, Freud, and others.) As far as intuition is concerned, it is now largely but not exclusively associated with the metaconscious. It is likely, however, that during the early stages of development of babies and in some people with certain types of mental disorders, intuitions and dreams derived from the collective unconscious play a very important role in their being.

BEING IN REALITY

Our point of departure has been that nothing in reality is autonomous – that is, everything in our universe is related to and affected by its environment. In this sense, to live in reality is to relate and to be related to it. It is from this perspective that we will develop some of the findings of our study.

The way babies learn to relate to reality is greatly facilitated by the way their senses, restricted self-awareness, and the way their being is enfolded into reality limit both the number and complexity of the relationships they are able to have at any point in their development. The worlds of babies are never private because of the way their being is enfolded with those of others. They are populated with only those constituents with which they have been able to establish a relationship with some kind of meaning. They know each constituent of that world in so far as they are able to incorporate it into their being via their structures of experience. It is not a question of the degree to which their minds can mechanically process stimuli into Gestalts or perform the reverse operation, because the self is inextricably bound up with these processes. This became quite evident in the case of human memory. The inclusion of emotional Gestalts in the memory traces and the possibility of repressing those traces that are too threatening to the self show that what is stored in memory is not data from the encounter with reality but personal knowledge.

In order to bring this into focus more clearly, let us consider the role of the self in the development of children. We have already noted that from the very beginning there is a unique human being enfolded into babies. Because we are most familiar with its biological dimension does not mean that this is all that is knowable about it.[25] To deny this would be to assert a belief in reductionism which, as we have seen, distorts our view of reality. The self weaves a structure of experience between itself and reality, permitting the formation of metaconscious knowledge of its physical, socio-cultural, and psychic expressions of its being in reality and the way it is enfolded into the being of others. The growing self-awareness paves the way for it to extend the scope of its being in reality and hence for the formation of new metaconscious knowledge related to the self. As new relationships become established and existing ones are transformed, a further round of developments becomes possible in an endless chain.

Growing up is therefore not merely closing the gap between the reality as it is known by babies and children and the reality as it is known by the members of their speech community, but primarily a transformation of the way their being is enfolded into that of others and the world. Their worlds are therefore never private because they reflect the way their existence is both 'naturally' and culturally enfolded into those of others. For the same reason, the utterances of babies and young children are not private. Both their world and their language are gradually enfolded into the world and vernacular of their speech community respectively, reflecting the way their being is enfolding into the culture.[26]

We might say that a structure of experience functions as a mental map of the world. It symbolically represents its contents. In this sense, it is like a road map except that the journey is not along a series of roads but through reality itself. Babies and children interpret this map playfully because they metaconsciously know it is incomplete. On it they chart the endless flow of new discoveries that trickle into 'their' world from beyond the horizon of their experience where reality as yet manifests itself only as undifferentiated stimuli. The limitations of their structures of experience (including their self-awareness) ensure that these discoveries do indeed trickle in at a manageable pace with limited degrees of freedom of interpretation. This brings the systematic interpretation of reality, essential for a coherent life, within reach of all children regardless of their level of intelligence. This is quite remarkable given the complexity of this task!

The structure of experience is more than just a map for life's journey, however. The reality that has been mapped is the reality in which babies and children have become enfolded. Their maps are full of emotional colours and repressed regions. It is not an objective view of the world charted by someone observing it from the outside. Children are deeply involved in 'their' world and build their whole being in relation to it. Each set of stimuli becomes a Gestalt only when it can be enfolded into their structures of experience on which it leaves its mark. The result may be in the form of the extension of the scope of an existing paradigm, the addition of new paradigms, and a contribution to metaconscious knowledge. In this sense, we may say that something can exist in the worlds of children only if they can pour something of themselves into it by giving it a meaning in their lives. All knowledge is inseparable from a person's being in reality, which does not mean, however, that it is determined by it. Much of what we have argued for here would, when applied to the domain of human knowledge, yield conclusions analogous to the ones formulated by Polanyi.[27]

A structure of experience is therefore more than a mental map for our being in reality – it is that very being in the world. This will be elaborated further in the next two chapters, but it is already evident that the perceptual apparatus and psychological structures develop together within one structure of experience. As a result, the worlds of babies and children are meaningful and not overwhelming, which is of fundamental importance for their emotional and psychic stability. They can live in reality with a childlike playfulness. The unknown is not threatening to them, particularly when they play within reach of their parents, whom they know will watch over them and help if a new situation perplexes them. The slow unfolding of the world allows babies and children to learn to be themselves in it and to retain their inner equilibrium.

Because an experience Gestalt reflects the meaning an event has in the child's life, it is existentially just as adequate, valid, and factual in his world as the experience Gestalt derived from the same event by an adult in the adult's world. Since most of what children learn becomes a matter of routine by frequent repetition, their conscious attention is free to direct itself to new and unusual things. It reduces psychological tensions and allows them to learn more easily. The regularity in the behaviour of the members of their speech community that arises from a shared culture also facilitates the interpretation of their social relationships. Without all this, no coherent being with a well-integrated personality could emerge.

Any relationship that can be routinely grasped on the basis of the structure of experience will be called a normal relationship. It may include something new, which can be dealt with by the refinement of existing perceptual, movement, and experience paradigms or by the creation of new ones. Non-normal relationships that totally baffle children because they cannot be interpreted on the basis of prior experience are rare, since the children are protected by their limited perceptual capabilities and self-awareness. As they grow older, these limitations slowly fall away, creating the possibility for non-normal relationships to occur more frequently. As this occurs, however, children acquire means to deal with them. The acquisition of language permits them to analyse non-normal relationships by means of mental concepts or by asking the other members of their speech community for an explanation.

At each stage in the development of children, they expand and refine the network of normal relationships that are constantly reinforced in the course of daily life. A set of limitations characterizes each state of development; they constrain the expansion of the network of normal relationships and hence the structure of experience. These constraints reflect the various stages in the transformation of the way their being is enfolded into those of others and the world. The important ones in the development of babies and young children are limited perceptual and motor functions, limited integration of the various functions of the mind, limited self-awareness, and limited ability to communicate. We still need to examine how children overcome this last major constraint as they acquire language.

FIVE

Language

THE SYMBOLIC BASIS

Although language is fundamental in constituting the socio-cultural environment of babies and children, it has not played a corresponding role in our account thus far of the development of their minds. The role it has played may in fact have appeared to be little different from that of a set of signs, such as those used by some animals or in information-processing or cybernetic devices. Within the human context the structures of experience of babies pave the way for the beginning of language. Language cannot, as we will attempt to show, be reduced to the communication of information. The next stage in the development that we will examine is characterized by the transformation of the set of signs acquired previously into the symbolic system of language. The acquisition of language fully launches the transformation of children from 'natural' into cultural beings. The relationships with others and their being in reality are fundamentally transformed. The world of immediate experience recedes as they enter into the world of their culture and begin to participate in its history.

Given the radical character of the transformation that language brings to the lives of children, it is useful to reinterpret everything we have said thus far about the development of their minds as leading up to the acquisition of language. In other words, we will examine the symbolic character of the structure of experience as conceptualized thus far. This includes the symbolic character of the systems of perceptual and movement paradigms, the systems of experience and memory, the subconscious, and the metaconscious. Language is founded on the symbolic character of these systems which it develops and extends, leading to a transformation of the ways in which they are used. In the previous chapters we have suggested how these systems may be built up by enfolding each moment of the lives of babies and children into their whole being. In order to examine in what way their development constitutes a prerequisite for language, we will now look at the other side of the coin. The problem then becomes: given that stimuli are interpreted in the context of a person's whole being, how do the resulting sensations and experience Gestalts symbolize a person's life on the one hand and the reality of the immediate situation on the other?

Whatever exists within or outside of us manifests itself as stimuli when detected either directly by our senses or indirectly via instruments extending the range of our perception. When these stimuli can be related to our structure of experience, they will take on a meaning which increasingly symbolizes the role the source of the stimuli will play in our life. Take a simple example: when a baby visually perceives his mother walking into the room, he may smile and turn toward her. Clearly the visual sensation symbolizes not only his mother but also something of his experiences with her as reflected in his emotions and other behaviour. Although a sensation lies within one dimension of experience, it symbolizes the entire constituent of the world from which the stimuli are derived.

A set of stimuli derived from a constituent of the world first takes on a meaning in the context of an experience Gestalt which symbolizes the relationships between it and other constituents and the observer by means of a pattern that relates the sensations representing these constituents. As a consequence, when a set of stimuli is transformed into a sensation it symbolizes the reality of the constituent unfolding itself in the relationships portrayed by the experience Gestalt. Since any subsequent refinements of the sensation also occur in the context of an experience Gestalt, a sensation symbolizes the reality of a constituent of the world as it has unfolded itself by participating in the network of normal relationships a person has learned to establish with the world. It is in this matter that it symbolizes something of his or her prior experience.

By way of illustration, consider once more the relationships a person may have with keys at different points during his lifetime. We have already noted that at first keys are nothing more than objects to which he relates by manipulating, tasting, or throwing. The meaning of these relationships is restricted by the limited development of his perceptual apparatus. When some time later he learns to walk and follow the other members of his speech community around in their daily activities, he is able to observe the relationships they have with keys, which he imitates when he gets hold of a set. The experience Gestalts of his relationships with keys now take on an entirely different meaning which approaches that of the intended functions of keys. The shape of the key begins to make sense as it becomes related to its intended use, permitting the visual sensations to be refined in the context of the experience Gestalts. He learns to use keys correctly.

If still later the person becomes a locksmith, his network of normal relationships is no longer only that of a user. His normal relationships with keys now also include the relationships between keys and lock mechanisms, with the result that the experience Gestalts and hence the sensations take on new meanings. He now notices things about keys that excape people who only use them. His visual sensations of keys no longer symbolize the relationships of a user only but also the relationships between keys and locks. A locksmith can, for example, tell from a glance at a key what type of lock it opens. Because he can distinguish between different types of keys that to the user look more or less alike, the visual sensations that he derives from the stimuli of keys must be more refined than those of the user.

When someone designs or creates an object, he does so by means of his structure of experience. He therefore unfolds something of himself and, being a person of his time and culture, he unfolds something of his culture.[1] Archeology uses this fact to gain insight into civilizations long disappeared, by studying objects found in excavations. This means, returning to the example of keys, that it is impossible to say that the locksmith has closed the gap between the reality of keys and the reality of keys as he knows it. Had the person become an art historian he would have noticed things about keys that reflect the relationships between its non-functional aspects and the aesthetic conceptions of the culture to whom the craftsman belonged. Once again the visual sensations would be different for they would symbolize the aesthetic aspects of keys more precisely. Most people may only notice that the shape of a key is particularly elegant or ugly.

Keys reflect many other relationships, however. Had the person become an engineer specializing in mechanical design, manufacturing, metallurgy, or burglar-proof devices, he would have interpreted the retinal stimuli of keys to yield sensations that symbolize still other relationships of keys and locks and the mechanical concepts they embody, the methods used to produce them, the materials employed, or the lock-picking skills of burglars. Everything that ever happened to a key, from its conception in the mind of a designer to its manufacture and use, affects its form in one way or another and hence leaves perceptually recognizable traces. A policeman may even attempt to discover something of the relationship between a key and its recent users by examining the fingerprints it bears. We are, however, primarily concerned here with what a person notices about a key at a single glance and not so much with what can be discovered via a process of thought and analysis.

A key is the result of a whole series of relationships which are partially symbolized by its form. A number of them are reflected in what can be visually perceived. Each of the above persons interprets the retinal stimuli of keys in ways that permit them to see things that escape others or that others are unable to see because their perceptual apparatus lacks the necessary prior experience. This was also the case in the anomalous playing-card experiment described earlier. Initially the relationship between the subjects and the cards was that of users only, which was evident from the way they interpreted the retinal stimuli.

The case is no different from the natural constituents of the world. The way they are perceived depends on a person's prior experience as well as on their 'nature,' that is, their internal structure of relationships. The natural constituents interact with and are affected by the relationships they have with other constituents of the world. The average adult and a botanist will derive significantly different sensations from the retinal stimuli of a tree because their normal relationships with trees are different. When a botanist studies the structure of the internal relationships of trees, she may discover things that have perceptually observable consequences. She then learns to see something where she before noticed only undifferentiated stimuli. Although the examples so far have been drawn from visual perception, the same case can readily be made for the other dimensions of experience.

. Thus far we have demonstrated that because stimuli take on and refine their meaning by being interpreted in the context of our being, their meaning necessarily symbolizes our life in some ways. What is true for sensations, however, is equally the case for Gestalts and experience Gestalts. Together the systems of perceptual and movement paradigms, the systems of experience and memory, the subconscious, and the metaconscious symbolize how we have enfolded our being into reality. What characterizes a structure of experience is that each of its elements takes on its meaning in relation to some of the others, which in their turn take on their meaning in relation to yet other elements. In other words, something of a person's life is enfolded into every element of experience; there are no parts and no wholes in the mechanistic sense. As a result each element of experience symbolizes something of a person's life and something of that life unfolds itself in every experience.

Any element of experience can so dominate and permeate a domain of a person's life that it represents some of the deeper patterns of meaning in the metaconscious that underlie a person's and a culture's existence. The power of symbols varies according to the depth of the patterns of metaconscious knowledge they represent. The greater the domain of experience they symbolize, the greater their power. An obvious example of a symbol in our culture is the car because it has deeply permeated and structured a good deal of our lives, so that it is no longer a mere means of transportation. This is equally true of many other consumer goods in our society.[2] Some symbols can represent patterns of great metaconscious depth reaching even into the collective metaconscious. An example is the national flag – or, still deeper, the swastika in Hitler's Germany. Such symbols are capable of eliciting a religious response. But they lose their power when they become largely conscious and when the metaconscious patterns they can reach begin to weaken or break up.

The symbolic function of our structure of experience expresses itself most clearly in creating the world of our dreams. It is this world that plays an important role in the development of children, and particularly in the acquisition of language.[3] The adults of a child's speech community do not live on the level of the experience immediately available to their senses. This is only a small part of reality as they know it. But children do live in the world of their immediate experience until they acquire language. As the symbolic functions of their structures of experience begin to develop well before they acquire language, they are confronted with another world, namely the one of their dreams. When they wake up, for example from a bad dream, they move from that world into their daytime world. Gradually they begin to learn to differentiate the two. These experiences help them to take distance from daytime reality. They learn that there is more to the world than meets the eye and this helps them go beyond immediate experience by means of imagination and creativity. Children now begin to explore their human potential more fully. The world of immediate experience recedes and they prepare to enter the world of their culture. Language is the gateway to this world. But they cannot acquire a human language before the symbolic nature of their structures of experience is sufficiently developed to form a foundation for language.

LANGUAGE AND INFORMATION

Since we live in a society in which technique has greatly devalued language,[4] we should focus briefly on what exactly human language is. We tend to reduce language to the transmission of information, typically conceptualized in mechanistic terms. Although the communication of information is an aspect of language, it is not its most important one. Language is so deeply enfolded into the being of nearly all persons that it cannot be separated from that being without introducing serious reductionisms. It is not our purpose here to deal with the phenomenon of language as a whole[5] but to point briefly to a few elementary aspects that will help us understand the radical transformation its acquisition has for the development of the mind.[6]

Language comes into being through human relationships. It exists within and for those relationships. It is by means of language that we transcend the world of immediate experience to create one that cannot be directly derived from it. It is this latter world that we consider to be the 'true' one into which we enfold our being. When we use language in our relationships with others, something of our being is unfolded in it. When we use the word 'father,' for example, it symbolizes the relationship we have with our father, the fathers of friends and others, and perhaps our own role as father, our heavenly father, the fathers we see on television, and so on. The blurry feeling we have of all our experiences with fathers is symbolized when we use the word. For the listener our saying 'father' in a conversation evokes a different blurry feeling based on other experiences. Few or none of these may be shared with the speaker. Language respects and requires individual differences, and we can each enfold our life into it. If the speaker and listeners live in the same society, their blurry feelings of fathers will not be so different that communication becomes very diffuclt. What is true for particular concepts is even more true for entire phrases and whole conversations. Language does not transmit information constituted of signs that have one and only one meaning. In a conversation it helps bring two or more people together who are different and yet similar. What they say to each other always carries more of their being than they realize or intend, and it is never entirely understood. It is less precise than information since every word and sentence symbolizes something of our being. It can only function in the context of being related to and yet separated from another person.

Language carries the relationship between human beings beyond immediate experience to another context. It weaves together the meaning of individual lives into a collective being of a group or society. It brings that collective being into time and without it there would be no history. Within that collective being, language respects the freedom of the members of a culture: they can each communicate different things by using the same language. They each decide how much of themselves they want to reveal by what they say and how much of what others say will be enfolded into their own life. At the same time, the enfolding and unfolding of their being in their relationships is always richer than they may be momentarily aware of. In this chapter we discuss the collective being created by language only in terms of the developments of the minds of children who acquire language, leaving until later chapters the examination of the role of language from the point of view of a society.

There are no sets of signs as used by animals or in 'languages' used in information-processing devices or cybernetic systems that have any of the above characteristics. Language introduces us to the mystery of saying more than we know and the hearing of more than we understand – that is, the mystery of our being and that of others. We need to keep the distinction between language and information in mind as we begin our study of the influence language has on the development of children and the way their being is enfolded in reality, in particular in their socio-cultural environment.

THE EMERGENCE OF LANGUAGE

The paradigm-based interpretation of stimuli unfolds to children a world with an intelligible complexity.[7] Before they acquire a language, their perceptual paradigms organize the world into classes of constituents and phenomena whose members are perceived to differ only superficially from each other while they differ fundamentally from the members of other classes. These developments below the level of consciousness form one of the prerequisites before children can learn some vocal signs. Take the simple example of a child learning the meaning of the word 'dog.' Before she can learn what this sound means, she must see dogs and hear their bark as differing only superficially from one another while differing fundamentally from all other animals, so that it makes sense to call them by one name. She must also hear other people pronouncing the word 'dog' as saying the same thing despite their different voice characteristics.

There comes a stage in the child's development when the interpretation of familiar events requires no particular attention, permitting the process of differentiation to focus on the language component of the encounters with other members of her speech community. She may then notice that some experience Gestalts involving dogs coincide with someone pronouncing the word 'dog.' The experience Gestalts provide a context in which the aural stimuli can take on a meaning. Once this happens the resulting sensation is included in the foreground of the experience Gestalts. The experience paradigm learns to associate the newly formed perceptual paradigm that interprets the aural stimuli derived from someone pronouncing the word 'dog,' with all the other perceptual paradigms that interpret stimuli derived from dogs in any dimension of experience. Consequently, when the child hears a dog barking behind a wall she will know that there is a dog behind the wall because the aural sensation symbolizes a dog. In the same manner the aural sensation of someone saying the word 'dog' will come to symbolize a dog to the child, and she will look for one even when she cannot perceive it. At this point the vocal sign 'dog' is on the way to becoming a symbolic concept because it has become detached from any specific experience Gestalt that contains for example, the aural sensation of a dog in its foreground.

The learning of a language begins with the acquisition of a number of vocal signs, but their mere accumulation does not constitute a gradual qualitative transition from a set of vocal signs to a symbolic language. The symbolic aspect of the sensations resulting from spoken words is no different from what has been described for other sensations. This situation will not change simply by a child learning more vocal signs. To use the analogy of the jigsaw puzzle once again, we might say that the child can heap up puzzle pieces indefinitely without finding out that they constitute a puzzle. It is not until he realizes that each piece has a relationship to at least one other piece and that together they form an interlocking whole that he realizes the significance of the other pieces. Not before he has seen a completed puzzle forming a picture will he know what a puzzle is and what the significance of each piece is. It is only then that he will be motivated to fit a puzzle together himself because the situation now has a meaning. What he regarded before as a heap of unrelated bits and pieces now appears as a puzzle that he can fit together to form a picture.

The situation is exactly analogous for children having learned a number of vocal signs. Vocal signs are transformed into symbolic concepts when they become pieces of a language puzzle, and once again the metaconscious makes this transformation possible. When the patterns of metaconscious knowledge have reached a sufficient depth, children begin to have some intuition of the continuity of space and time and the wholeness of the world in which they live. As they then acquire an increasing number of vocal signs, their structures of experience begin to contain some metaconscious knowledge of what language is all about – namely, that each spoken sound has a meaning and that each thing or event has a name, so that language can symbolically represent the world in which they live. As this metaconscious knowledge related to language develops, it soon begins to affect the behaviour of children. They no longer quietly interpret their experiences and increasingly become interested in language.

Among the first vocal signs acquired by a child we find a number of verbs indicating actions and relationships. When the child's world is as yet little differentiated, relationships and actions are not clearly differentiated from the constituents involved. A considerable development of the structure of experience is required before an experience Gestalt makes a distinction between subject, object, and the action that relates them. Initially the verb may be the fundamental element in relation to which everything else is organized. Gradually children become interested in the names of things and events, and the fact that they rarely forget one once they have learned it shows that they are not mechanically learning lists of names but that a new world is opening up to them. Vocal signs become symbolic concepts, and they begin to intuit that words spoken in succession are in fact interlocking pieces of the language puzzle.

The vocabulary of a language is fundamentally different from a set of vocal signs because of the absence of the characteristics of a system in the latter. The meaning of any vocal sign can be changed often without its affecting that of the others. This is not the case for a language. To illustrate this, let us again consider our earlier example of a child learning the names of four-footed animals. Suppose that a child growing up on a farm had learned to distinguish cats, dogs, horses, and cows from the way they behave in general and towards him in particular, and that he distinguishes them from birds and fish. When his father teaches him the word 'dog' the child can take it to mean 'dog' or 'four-footed animal' – that is, he can attach the word 'dog' either to dogs only or to cats, cows, and horses as well. It is not until he learns the names of the remaining three kinds of four-footed animals that the possible ambiguity is eliminated. Other kinds of ambiguities are also possible. He could take the word 'dog' to mean everything that has a furry appearance, for instance. The possibilities could be multiplied, but the point becomes evident: it is because everything has a name that eventually the meaning of each word is delimited by those of others, so that the meaning of each word can be described in terms of other words as in dictionaries. Increasingly, as the child's vocabulary expands, the words do not attach directly to elements of experience. Together they form a system which symbolically represents the world of a speech community, with the result that they are attached to that world via the system they form.

In earlier chapters we have shown that reality as it is known cannot be grasped on the level of sensations but only on the level of experience Gestalts, because the latter depict the relationships between the constituents and phenomena of reality from which the sensations are derived. For the same reason, language cannot symbolize reality as it is known by means of a vocabulary whose elements, like sensations, can symbolize only constituents and phenomena. Consequently, it is by means of sentences or phrases symbolizing interrelationships that language can represent more complex aspects of reality as it is known. Sentences and phrases are organized wholes whose meaning cannot be reduced to that of the words they contain, because they symbolize relationships. We can therefore refer to sentences and phrases as language Gestalts. Once a child grasps something of the meaning of language – namely that virtually every sound people utter has a meaning – he will also begin to understand what phrases and sentences are all about. Since communication by means of language generally employs language Gestalts, words soon begin to take on a meaning in the context of others, thus accelerating the conversion from a set of vocal signs to a system of words.

The short phrases, sentences, and isolated vocal signs that first take on a meaning to a child are those that coincide regularly with specific events. Once a child notices the association, the aural stimuli can take on a meaning in the context of the experience Gestalts that she derives from these situations. A few examples are: the way her mother greets her after her naps, what she says, when she cuddles her, or what she says when she spits out her food. In each of these cases what the child's mother says is a natural extension of the foreground of the experience Gestalt, which enables the child to deduce more or less correctly the meaning from the context. In a great many cases the connection between the meaning of what is said and the foreground of the experience Gestalt derived from the physical here and now is far less direct.

When the child is a little older her father may ask her at the dinner table what she did that afternoon, or tell her that he will take her to the doctor tomorrow, or inquire how she likes the new game she got for her birthday. It is impossible to deduce the meaning of these questions from the context of the physical here and now of these situations. The experience Gestalts of the above situations would have been quite similar had the child as yet not acquired some language skills. Their foreground would have contained something related to the physical here and now and everything else, including the aural stimuli of any conversation, would have constituted the background. Due to the language component, however, the foreground of the experience Gestalts created by the father's first question relates to the child's activities of that afternoon, the foreground of the second experience Gestalt relates to an event in the future, while the foreground of the third relates to the child's relationship with an object absent from the physical here and now. Because what is being said is not directly related to the situation, the meaning of the aural stimuli resulting from the child's father talking cannot be grasped by means of the process of differentiation operating on the level of experience as we have described it thus far. New mental structures are required to interpret the aural stimuli of speech.

In order to appreciate the radical transformation of the way children are linked to reality once they acquire a language, let us briefly consider some aspects of language and what additions and changes are required in the various systems of perceptual and movement paradigms and the systems of experience of children learning a language. A language may be conceptualized as a system that can, by means of its grammar, be employed in an infinite variety of ways to represent symbolically any aspect of human experience. Each element takes on its meaning in relation to all the other elements of the system. The system as a whole takes on its meaning in relation to the experience of reality. Phrases and sentences interrelate the symbolic elements in specific ways to form organized wholes, the symbolic meaning of which cannot be derived from their components.

The interpretation of spoken language occurs on three interdependent levels. On the first level, the aural stimuli of words must be directly differentiated from one another and indirectly from all other aural stimuli. Initially the perceptual paradigms that interpret aural stimuli derived from language are differentiated from all the other paradigms within that dimension of experience. Since the perceptual paradigms are directly differentiated from the ones that most resemble them, the perceptual paradigms resulting from the speech of others soon become directly differentiated from one another and hence only indirectly differentiated from all the other paradigms. Gradually a cluster of perceptual paradigms related to language begins to form within the system of aural perceptual paradigms. These developments are reinforced and eventually transcended by the development of Gestalts of metaconscious knowledge beginning to show something of the meaning of language. Telling stories to children at this point in their development even though they do not yet understand their meaning will teach them that these stimuli do not directly refer to the physical here and now and that they must be interpreted in terms of themselves – that is, by means of processes of differentiation based on the prior experience of language. Progressively the cluster of aural perceptual paradigms related to language becomes first a subsystem and eventually a system when children begin to master their vernacular. We shall conceptualize it as a system of perceptual paradigms related to language.

When children learn to read, they will acquire another system of perceptual paradigms related to language in the visual dimension of experience in order to permit them to recognize letters, numbers, and other related symbols. People who cannot use one or more of their senses may acquire such a system in another dimension of experience, as is the case for a blind person learning to read braille or a deaf person learning sign language. When a system of perceptual paradigms related to language is located in the visual or tactile dimensions of experience it in fact comprises two subsystems: one to differentiate the letters and another to differentiate frequently encountered groups of letters, words, and even groups of words. Some educators prefer to have children learn to read by developing the latter subsystem first, teaching them to recognize simple words and only later the letters of the alphabet. The subsequent two levels of interpretation can derive their input from any one of these systems.

Unlike other kinds of stimuli we considered in earlier chapters, the aural stimuli of spoken words are not directly derived from the constituent of reality which they symbolize. Hence there is no direct link between them and their meaning, and a second level of interpretation is required to differentiate them according to their meanings. This ability is represented by the system of concepts. The components are not paradigms but the concepts themselves. Each concept is directly differentiated from those with similar meanings. But how and where does this system arise in the structure of experience? To answer this question we need to go back to what we noted earlier, namely, that the paradigm-based mode of interpreting stimuli introduces children to a world with an intelligible complexity. Some constituents and events of that world are perceived as being essentially alike and fundamentally diferent from others. Such classes of constituents or events are symbolized by perceptual paradigms in the various dimensions of experience, and these paradigms are interrelated so that together they form a pre-language concept within the metaconscious.

For example, the perceptual paradigms related to the visual Gestalts of dogs, their bark, touch, and smell are interrelated across the dimensions of experience to form a pre-language concept of dogs which can be symbolized by a sensation in any dimension of experience. The pre-language concept of dog takes on another aspect when children learn the vocal sign of 'dog.' When the word 'dog' becomes a symbolic concept it can be used to symbolize the pre-language concept of dog even when no dog is present in the physical here and now. In the same way, the clusters of perceptual paradigms related to four-footed animals as located in the various dimensions of experience together form a pre-language concept of four-footed animals which can later be symbolically designated by a collective name. The example can readily be extended to include experience paradigms such as the ones related to ball games. A part of the system of concepts is therefore a direct reflection of the developments that have taken place in the metaconscious.

Many concepts of a language are less directly related to metaconscious developments and require the intervention of intellectual operations. Classes of constituents can be grouped together or they may be analysed by isolating aspects for special consideration. Common features can be abstracted and be named, such as the parts of animal bodies. Relationships between the constituents or events of reality as it is known can also give rise to new concepts. A house in relation to a family gives the concept of a home, and money in relation to work can form the concept of a wage. The more abstract a concept becomes, the less directly it is related to one or more perceptual paradigms existing in the metaconscious. These concepts can, when children learn them, shift their meaning without affecting any perceptual paradigms.

To illustrate how children acquire abstract concepts, consider how they learn what 'freedom' is. A child may one day pose the question as to why people in prison cannot go home. His father may then give an explanation to the effect that the guards keep the doors locked because these people are not allowed to go free, since they have done something wrong. Some time later he may ask his parents to take him to the beach, to which his father may reply that he would like to but that he is not free that day since he has to work. Yet another time the child's teacher may tell the class that tomorow they will be free from school.

We must guard against rationalizing the situation of the child. The above examples of human situations are not presented in sucession with the suggestion that he should try to find out what these situations have in common in order to discover what freedom is all about. By abstracting these examples out of his daily life we have already destroyed something of what is really happening, for these situations are encountered along with a host of others. The very existence of the word 'free' already suggests that there are other situations that are not free and still others where the concept is simply meaningless. We cannot say that the child is learning to attach the word 'free' to human existence nor that he is learning rules for using it correctly. The child has already learned to differentiate a great many human situations on the level of experience. He now learns to reinterpret and symbolically designate them by means of a cluster of concepts. The human situations become differentiated on two different but interdependent levels: that of experience and that of language.

The beginning of the learning of a concept like freedom is greatly facilitated by the fact that the interpretation of stimuli unrelated to language is now much less frequently affected by language than at an earlier stage of development. At that time the intervention of vocal signs led to such changes as we saw in the example of the child learning to recognize four-footed animals. The intervention of others by means of language now permits the system of concepts to adjust the way it differentiates its components.

The child's cluster of concepts containing the concept of freedom converges to and soon largely corresponds to that of the other members of his speech community. At no time has the child been given a definition of what freedom is. He has learned its meaning relative to a number of other concepts that together form a cluster which depicts a range of human situations.

The child expands his system of concepts in the course of learning to share his daily experience with the members of his speech community. Each new discovery of the material world and our existence in it adds new concepts that are differentiated from all those previously acquired. The equilibrium between the third and fourth dimensions of differentiation in the system of concepts is disturbed each time the child is corrected for his use of language or when what he says does not appear to convey to others what he intended. The system of concepts then seeks to restore its internal equilibrium by shifting the way it differentiates concepts. It is by countless shifts and refinements that a child's system of concepts increasingly resembles that of the other members of his speech community. It is the constant search for a coherent (that is, systematic) interpretation of experience that permits the child to learn what he does in such a relatively short time. Each shift does not simply change the meaning of one concept but a part of the system of concepts. These developments demand, of course, that there is no substantial change in the child's systems of perceptual paradigms and his system of experience. This in fact is often the case at the stage of development in which a child acquires language. Nevertheless the process of differentation on the level of language does, as we shall see later, lead to refinements in the process of differentiation on the level of experience and even perception.

In some ways, the dictionary of a language is a reconstruction of the information contained in the system of concepts of the members of a language community. The meaning of each word is given by relating it to other words in phrases or sentences or by giving synonyms. Together these relationships show how the vocabulary of a language reflects reality as it is known. The system of concepts attaches itself to reality in the same way. When a set of vocal signs acquired by a child begins to be transformed into a system of concepts, the words begin to take on a meaning in the context of others, with the result that they begin to symbolize something in reality via that system of concepts.[8] But this can only happen when on the first level of interpretation a system of perceptual paradigms related to language begins to constitute itself, while on a third level of interpretation yet another kind of system develops.

Since phrases and sentences are not simple cumulations of words but carefully organized wholes or language Gestalts, the interpretation of language requires a third level of interpretation. Simple phrases first take on a meaning in the context of an experience Gestalt to which they then contribute a language Gestalt. As children learn the meaning of more phrases, a cluster of experience paradigms forms to differentiate language Gestalts. They begin to be able to understand phrases unrelated to the physical here and now by differentiating them on the basis of their prior experience of language. At this point the interpretation of stimuli related to language becomes largely independent of the interpretation of other stimuli. In a situation where language is unrelated to the physical here and now, the language Gestalts form the foreground of the experience Gestalts while everything else, including the facial expressions and body language of the speaker, constitutes the background. When language is related to the immediate situation, a language Gestalt will be a part of the foreground of the experience Gestalt together with the other Gestalts, provided the listener pays attention to it. If this is not the case, the language Gestalt will be integrated into the background.

As these developments begin to happen in a child's structure of experience, a cluster of experience paradigms related to events with a substantial language component becomes a cluster of language paradigms. As the child increasingly masters his vernacular, this cluster of language paradigms develops into a subsystem and eventually into a system of language exclusively responsible for interpreting language Gestalts. The latter are integrated into experience Gestalts by means of the system of experience. Language paradigms perform the same function with regard to concepts as experience paradigms do in relation to perceptual paradigms. Just as experience Gestalts depict the meaning of the relationships between sensations, so language Gestalts depict the meaning of the ways concepts are related in sentences and phrases. By differentiating the language paradigms from one another, a child is able to learn implicitly the minutest subtleties of the structure of the vernacular.

The metaconscious knowledge implied in the structure of the system of language comprises, when rendered explicit, the grammar of the language. The models of language built up by modern linguistics are attempts to render this information explicit.[9] A child first learns the grammar of his vernacular implicitly, simply by interpreting sentences and phrases by means of a process of differentiation based on her prior experience of language. She will later be taught the grammar explicitly, which teaches her the 'official' form of her language. Yet the metaconscious knowledge implied in the system of language can never be rendered entirely explicit. A person teaching her vernacular to an immigrant may one day correct him by saying that, although she does not know exactly what is wrong with what he said, one simply does not say it that way. The person, by means of the process of differentiation on the level of language, does not recognize the language Gestalt the immigrant has used and hence she knows it just is not said that way.

The three levels of differentiation associated with language are interdependent and evolve together. Increasingly this joint development is characterized by language taking on a meaning directly in the context of the prior experience of language and only indirectly in the broader context of experience. At first, words and simple sentences take on a meaning for a child in the context of experience Gestalts, but as the system of concepts and the system of language begin to form, new concepts increasingly take on a meaning in the immediate context of phrases or sentences and only indirectly in the context of experience Gestalts via the sentences. The system of language expands as the variety and complexity of the sentences that have a meaning for children increases. This allows the refinement of the meaning of previously acquired concepts as well as permitting new words to take on a meaning, which refines and enforces their system of concepts. The reverse interaction occurs when the expansion of their vocabulary stored in the system of concepts permits new sentences to take on a meaning, thereby adding new language paradigms to the system of language.

In the course of children acquiring language, we see that in various dimensions of experience new systems begin to form that gradually become less dependent on the previously formed systems out of which they emerged. Together they constitute what is essentially a new dimension of experience related to language. Until this point, the sphere of attention of children was limited to the physical here and now except for the world of their dreams. They could recognize persons or things when they perceived them – that is, when their senses received the appropriate stimuli – but they were not able to bring these people or things to mind when absent from the physical here and now. The new dimension of experience related to language allows children to transcend the world of the physical here and how with respect to time, space, and the social. They can reach into their own past or imagine their future. It permits them to benefit from the experiences of previous generations. They can learn things about places and people both past and present, of which they have no direct experience. They are able to learn about matters not directly accessible to their senses, such as atoms, bacteria, cells, distant stars, and so on. Furthermore, the world of the imagination, fairy tales, fiction, poetry, and the mythology of other cultures all become accessible because of language.

It should be noted that the way we are linked to reality allows nearly all children to learn their vernacular regardless of their level of intelligence. Had these links been direct via stimuli, similarity sets would have had to be constructed within each dimension of experience by means of conscious analysis. These sets would then constitute the prerequisite for language. We have already suggested the enormous difficulties this would present – if indeed it would not make the lives of many children downright impossible, because they would be unable to interpret their existence coherently with the obvious psychic and emotional consequences. We only need to recall the consternation of the subjects in the playing-card experiment who could not identify the anomalous cards, in order to begin to realize the consequences if this situation became a fact of daily life rather than an extreme situation produced in a laboratory.

As the systems related to language develop, children also learn to speak. As they do, they develop yet another system. They build up a system of movement paradigms that directs and controls the speech function. This happens in a manner analogous to the one described for a baby learning to move his limbs and to grasp and manipulate objects. When children learn to speak, they learn to use the system of language and the system of concepts in the reverse direction. A thought yields a language Gestalt which then translates into a sequence of concepts uttered by means of the appropriate movement paradigms. These paradigms possibly correspond to one or more phonemes.

LANGUAGE AND EXPERIENCE

Although the stimuli derived from spoken or written language are received by the senses just like all the others, they are unique in that they can be entirely unrelated to the physical here and now. We therefore need to consider the relationship between the simultaneous interpretation of these two kinds of stimuli. After watching a television program a husband may ask his wife what she thought of it. If, however, the next morning at work he wishes to ask his colleagues the same question he must specify the 'it.' He may ask them if they watched the show on channel 17 at eight o'clock the night before and, if they answer him in the affirmative, he is able to repeat the question he asked his wife. When a person begins a subject of conversation that is unrelated to the physical here and now, he must signal to the other participants that he is doing so and create a new frame of reference within which the conversation can continue. Each person has learned to do this. The other participants have learned to interpret these signals and in turn place themselves in this new frame of reference. The experience paradigms can take the language Gestalts emerging from the system of language as the foreground of the experience Gestalts, while the directly relevant experience of the physical here and now, such as the facial expressions and body language of the speaker, is placed in the background.

In conversation, a speaker can take advantage of the fact that she shares the experience of the physical here and now with the people she is talking to, by shifting her frame of reference with only the slightest warning. The person walking down the street with a friend may suddenly interrupt the subject of the conversation with the remark, 'Did you see that?' By using the past tense she signals her friend that whatever attracted her attention is no longer a part of the physical here and now, and she assumes that whatever attracted her attention also attracted that of her friend. She knows her friend sufficiently well to be sure that she would also have found the event noteworthy enough to give it momentarily her undivided attention. Had the person been in the company of someone whom she did not know very well and whose interests were unknown to her, she probably would have indicated what attracted her attention. Had the person been accompanied by her boss with whom she was discussing the possibility of a raise as they walked to his car parked along the street, she might have said to her boss, 'Did you see that man almost get hit by a car?' As a kind of apology for interrupting the conversation, not being sure how her boss felt about such an event, she might have added, 'It never ceases to shock me that we who consider ourselves so civilized, put up with all the deaths and injuries on the roads.' In face-to-face conversations, children gradually learn to interpret the signals of how they are to relate language to the physical here and now, which determines what the relationships between the processes of differentiation operating on the levels of language and experience will be.

Had the person written a story that included the above events, the situation would have been different. Neither does she know the people who read it, nor does she know what experiences she shares with them, nor does she share with them the physical here and now. People reading the story know that its meaning is entirely unrelated to the physical here and now, with the consequence that the process of differentiation operating on the level of experience delegates the task of constructing the foreground of the experience Gestalts to the process of differentiation operating on the level of language. The writer must now introduce her readers to the world she is writing about in order to establish a common frame of reference. To do so effectively, she needs to imagine who her readers are likely to be or to write for a particular public. She must have language perform the functions which in face-to-face communication are performed by the reader's process of differentiation operating on the level of experience. All this gives the impression that written communication is more objective and precise, while oral communication has, by contrast, been regarded by some as highly subjective, non-logical, and lacking precision.

Those who frequently communicate in writing may in fact have a conversational style that has been heavily influenced by the way they write. Since this is generally the case for those in the higher levels of the social hierarchy, this style symbolizes a certain status and is often considered superior to the purely conversational styles.[10] In fact, this is not at all the case. The differences between oral and written communication derive from the fact that they are adapted to, and hence most effective in, quite different situations. In oral, unlike written, communication, the meaning of language can be extended by the context of the physical here and now and the speaker has direct contact with the others. Modern technology has created new modes of communication, to which the use of language must be adjusted, and so too must the mode of collaboration between the processes of differentiation operating on the levels of experience and language. This is the case for radio and television, the telephone, and the telephone with a viewing screen.[11]

The impact of language on the structure of experience is considerable, with the result that the acquisition of language affects the interpretation of stimuli unrelated to language. First, consider the consequences for the way a child interprets his world by means of the systems of perceptual paradigms and the system of experience. Even when a child is learning the meaning of a few words that are as yet only vocal signs for him, the impact of language on these systems can already be noticeable, as was evident from the example of the urban child learning to recognize four-footed animals. In order to focus on some other aspects of the impact of language, we shall examine a similar example of how a child learns to distinguish colours.

At first children identify objects according to shape rather than colour, to which they pay little attention. They learn the names of objects before they learn to identify colours. Accurate perception of colours generally does not come about until a child learns to name them. Before that, he may be able to match them if the colours are simple and primary.[12] A child frequently learns to identify red colours first and later blue. For a certain time blue may be anything that is not red.[13] These developments are analogous to those we have described for the recognition of four-footed animals. In general, people differentiate colours much better than they remember them. Colours that are named are generally better remembered than intermediate shades that are not named, probably because of the fact that the named colours form a cluster of colour concepts that correspond to a cluster of visual perceptual paradigms whose paradigms have been centred on these colour concepts by the impact of language. The retinal stimuli of unnamed colours are interpreted by one of the members of the cluster of perceptual paradigms. Because of the paradigmatic function of the perceptual paradigm, an unnamed colour is seen as rather like one of the named colours. Since the unnamed colour is not clearly distinguished from the named colours, it does not have an individuality on the level of perception and hence it is not well remembered.

The variation of colour perception of different cultures is rather remarkable. In the presence of the rainbow, members of different cultures have learned to have different visual sensations. Consider how several Greek and Roman authors described the colours of the rainbow.[14] Xenophon in the sixth century BC only distinguished red, yellow-green (as one colour), and violet; Artistotle in the fourth century BC distinguished orange as well; Seneca in the first century AD distinguished red, orange-yellow (as one colour), green, blue-indigo (as one colour), and violet; Marcellus in the fourth century AD distinguished red, orange-red, yellow, green, blue-indigo, and violet. The variations in colour perception of different cultures has been noted by many anthropologists, and particularly the colour perception of the so-called primitive peoples has been widely discussed.

When a language has only one word for two colours, their perception may be confused. The Fiji Islanders use the same word for blue and green but they have another word for green that is only used for plants. They also emphasize the dark quality of some colours, and both dark red and dark blue may be referred to simply as 'dark.' The question of knowing whether or not the members of a culture recognize a colour is complex, for tests must not teach the colour distinctions they are attempting to determine.

The meaning of someone saying that something is yellow depends on the other colours he has learned to name, because no name attaches directly to reality as it is known. The cluster of colour concepts together represent the world of colour. Once a child learns something of what colours are all about – that is, once he distinguishes colours from other attributes of the constituents of reality – a new world (of colour) is opening up to him. The distinctions he makes between colours are coextensive with the world of colour. When he has learned to recognize the colours red and blue, all colours are seen as being variations of red or blue. When he learns a third colour concept, the world of colour is made up of variations of these three colours, and so on. This is exactly the case in the examples we have given. Each way of differentiating the colours in the rainbow represents reality as science has come to know it sufficiently well so that the members of these cultures could render their experience of the world of colour intelligible without encountering anomalies. The latter would certainly have arisen had the world of colour not been represented in a manner compatible with reality. The colour distinctions of a particular culture are borne out in the daily lives of its members. Their knowledge of colours appears factual and objective to them until it is challenged by a new discovery, an anomaly, or contact with another culture which perceives colours differently.

Suppose that a member of a culture that had learned to distinguish green from yellow visits a culture that does not make this distinction and whose language is unknown to her culture. She will then have no other alternative but to learn the language in the context of daily experience. When a member of her host culture points out something yellow and later something green, the visitor notices that in both cases the same colour name was used. If she was unaware of the fact that our links with the world are not direct by means of stimuli, she would equate perceived reality with reality itself. She would have to conclude that the native had made a mistake, that he was slightly colour-blind, or that she misunderstood. What is objective to members of the host culture is made into a subjective peculiarity of the persons involved, and the matter is probably not given another thought. History gives many examples of this happening. Colour blindness appears to have gone unnoticed until first reported by John Dalton in 1794.

Colour blindness is caused by defects in the structure of the retina, such as a lack of cones. A child who is partially or totally colour-blind is simply not aware of things having certain colours or any colours at all. When he encounters the words for colours when learning his language, he draws from them whatever meaning he can in his experience. A colour-blind child can learn the meaning of the word 'blue,' for example, in the context of language as being 'what the sky is.' The situation is analogous to someone who knows what a dinosaur is without ever having seen a picture or model of one. If a particular colour concept cannot take on a meaning in the child's world, he will avoid using that concept. This makes colour blindness hard to detect in the context of daily life because the child's system of concepts, although not identical to that of the other members of his culture, remains compatible with it. Some systematic testing is required if its existence is to be detected.

Owing to the impact of language, our links with the world via our structure of experience are affected by the culture in which we grow up. Our relation to the world of colour is typical of our relationship to the world as a whole. Let us return to the example of a child's relationship with the world of four-footed animals. If the culture of his speech community despises dogs, as in the Near East, its members will shun dogs and pay little attention to their differences. The language of these cultures originally distinguished very few kinds of dogs by name, and consequently the way the members of these cultures perceived dogs was little refined. In Western cultures, whose members generally consider dogs to be their best friends among the animals, the unique characteristics of different types of dogs have caused the languages of these cultures to distinguish a great many types of dogs by name, with the result that their members' perception of dogs is on the whole quite refined. The reverse is true for camels, which the Westerner only sees in zoos or when he travels. Hence Europeans distinguish very few, if any, types of camels by name and consequently have a less refined perception of these animals. Variations can also occur within a culture. Someone who is interested in animals or who works with them, such as a farmer, will distinguish more of them by name than the average urban resident, with the same consequences for his perception.

The vocabulary people have is related to their experience, which it represents symbolically. Because of the impact of language on the systems of perceptual paradigms and the system of experience, a child learning his vernacular increasingly perceives reality as he knows it in a manner that is compatible with the way the members of his speech community perceive reality as they know it; that is, the child increasingly lives in the same world as the members of his speech community.

SYMBOLIC UNIVERSES

What is the world of a culture like and how does it vary from culture to culture? To find a preliminary answer to this question, we need to continue our examination of the impact language has on experience beyond that of the physical world. We have seen that when children first grasp something of the meaning of language, their system of concepts and their system of language are largely a reflection of the development beyond the level of consciousness of perceptual, movement, and experience paradigms, which are designated symbolically with names. However, no human language ever had a vocabulary that was a mere inventory of the constituents and events of the world and the relationships between them in so far as they are represented in the systems of perceptual and movement paradigms and the system of experience. Even the languages of the materially most destitute peoples living in very homogeneous environments have extensive vocabularies.[15] This is an important clue to the real meaning of language. Language is not merely a convenient means of communicating. It expresses the meaning of living in reality as it is known, which goes far beyond what can be perceived.

No so-called primitive people or any other society totally immersed in nature has ever lived simply on the level of immediate experience. They never lived as though reality as they knew it was nothing but a collection of unrelated constituents and phenomena. There was more than just the ground, trees, clouds, stones, animals, water, flowers, insects, and so on, as well as some isolated interrelationships between these constituents such as clouds that give rainwater, animals that eat plants, plants that die when taken out of the ground, and so on. On the level of immediate experience, these constituents appear to have little in common and to be only superficially related. However, by becoming interrelated in experience Gestalts, the systems of experience and memory and the metaconscious point to deeper levels of meaning by means of intuitions.

The lives of the members of so-called primitive societies were totally embedded in the natural milieu, and nearly every experience was permeated by it. Everything these societies needed for their sustenance as well as everything that endangered their existence came from that environment. The deeper patterns of metaconscious knowledge that developed in the minds of such people, as a result of living a life largely immersed in a natural milieu, form the basis for a pre-language concept like nature. When a member of such a society intuits this, they may give it a name. Some concept (quite different from that of nature) may then quickly find its way into the language as other members recognize its validity and significance because it corresponds to something living deeply within their metacons- cious. Once such a concept enters into the language, it helps to pave the way for a society to elaborate its meaning and to help shape its entire way of life. We shall briefly indicate some possibilities.

The way in which a society elaborates a concept for what we call nature conditions and is conditioned by such activities as the gaining of knowledge of the world, utilizing it for human ends, and finding answers to the questions posed by life and death within it. For reasons we shall analyse in a later chapter, nature was commonly regarded as populated by spirits, powers, and deities who had jurisdiction over specific constituents or phenomena. Typically, this jurisdiction was spatially delimited. There was no purely material world, and this made science as we know it impossible. After all, what guarantee would one have of reproducing an experiment if the powers that control the relevant phenomena could have been angered for one reason or another, causing them to intervene? Clearly the regularity of nature implicit in a mechanistic world view would be unthinkable. The science and technology of the so-called primitive people was therefore inseparable from magic and religion. Nature could be counted on only if the powers concerned willed it to be so. The Aztecs, for example, thought that the return of the sun the next morning could only be guaranteed by making a contract with the sun gods whose co-operation was assured by religious rituals involving human sacrifice.

A specific concept of nature also underlies modern science. It too is based on a conviction that natural reality is not just a collection of constituents but a whole interrelated in ways that mostly transcend immediate experien- ce.[16] The new conception of nature is now purely material with a mechanistic regularity. As a result the relationship between science and religion has changed and traditional magic has disappeared. The limits traditional religions placed on knowing and exploiting nature have been pushed back and the notion of material progress by the unlimited possibilities of science and technology leading to moral and spiritual progress have paved the way for new secular religions. Once again the elaboration of a concept like nature conditions and is conditioned by a whole range of activities, and each natural constituent and phenomenon takes on its meaning in the context of these activities.

What a concept like nature does in one domain of human existence, concepts like freedom, education, the state, humanity, the arts, literature, and so on achieve for other domains. The experience of the physical here and now is transcended and each moment of our life is experienced as part of a sphere of activities which in their turn take on a meaning in terms of being part of a way of life established by a culture. The fact that a human society is more than a collection of individual lives already manifested itself in the patterns of metaconscious knowledge. Language permits human beings and their culture to elaborate this wholeness above the level of immediate experience. The systematization of experience into a coherent way of life permeates all action, thought, and communication. The way is then opened up for consciously affecting the course of our lives and that of our culture. Each moment of our life now takes on its meaning more directly in the context of our individual life and the collective being of our society as opposed to immediate experience.

The above developments are well illustrated in children as they are being socialized into a culture. When children learn an abstract concept in the context of language, they are learning something new about human experience symbolized by the concept. At this point only the system of concepts is immediately affected. The next time they experience what the concept refers to, they may direct their attention to the situation differently, with the result that an experience paradigm and some perceptual paradigms may adjust themselves to include whatever perceptual consequences the new concept implies. Such is the case for a medical student who, after theoretical studies, learns to see things on x-rays that he never saw before. Some retinal stimuli that were meaningless to him now take on a meaning because they symbolize something he learned from his textbooks. The very same process occurs in the case of the child learning what freedom is. The examples could be multiplied indefinitely.

Language by means of concepts can affect the way a child interprets the world because the concepts have an indirect impact on the systems of perceptual paradigms and the system of experience. These effects diffuse throughout these systems because any of the processes of differentiation operate on the basis of prior experience including that already transformed by language.

As another example of how language changes the world in which a child lives, consider the concept of time. Nowhere does one encounter time the way one encounters the constituents or events of the world. Yet the concept of time that each child acquires by means of language permeates his whole existence because it becomes an existence within that time. The concept of time establishes relationships that cannot be directly perceived but which permeate reality as it is known. The structure of the grammar in relation to verb tenses and what the vocabulary can and cannot say about time are only some of the ways a culture transmits its mode of time perception from generation to generation. Westen civilization conceives time in linear mechanical terms. Time creates order and is related to progress towards a goal. Wasted time marks off experience that did not achieve a goal. We live to reach planned goals that will be achieved in time. This may be an immediate goal, as in the case of an assembly-line worker who works to reach payday or the weekend, or a distant one such as reaching retirement. Other cultures do not perceive time in this fashion. A few cultures still live in a present that is thought of as repeating the past; they do what their forefathers did. Some cultures live in a present that excludes all things that can just as well be done tomorrow. Time perception has been extensively studied, and by comparing the time perception of various cultures its permeation of daily life becomes evident. The concept of time, like concepts of nature, relates events and constituents of the world in ways that are not evident from immediate experience and that are acquired by a child largely by means of language.

It should be stressed that the relationships and organizations of relationships that result from language and thought do not form a kind of superstructure erected on the infrastructure of the perceived constituents and events of the world and the perceived relationships between them. The meaning that any constituent or event of the world takes on in human experience is, as we have noted, derived from the relationships that it enters into. Whether these relationships result from immediate experience, thought, or in learning the concepts of a language matters little because it is the relationships and not their origin which are a source of meaning. As a consequence, the relationships and organizations of relationships derived from language and thought so permeate reality as it is perceived that it is impossible to speak of an infrastructure and superstructure.

It is impossible to separate experience into two components: the first comprising what can be perceived, and the second what cannot be perceived because it springs from language and thought. There is thus no domain of 'empirical facts' and no domain of 'theory.' There exist no facts, apart from a structure of experience in relation to which they become facts, and there exists no structure of experience not permeated by facts. For decades many able philosophers of science have unsuccessfully attempted to construct a theory of science based on the distinction between observation and theory, and neither could they succeed in creating a neutral observation language that was to deal with experience on the level of observation only.[17]

This leads us to two important conclusions. First, the acquisition of language radically transforms the reality as it is known by children since the constituents and events of their worlds expand their meaning in the context of new relationships established by language. Without these relationships they would continue to live on the level of immediate experience as animals do. Second, the adults of the child's speech community do not live in the mere material reality as they know it, but in what we shall call a symbolic universe. Interacting speech communities which together constitute a society generally live in the same symbolic universe even though they may speak different dialects or other variations of a common language.

The symbolic universe of a culture is much more than a representation of reality as it is known. This will become evident when we examine the role of culture as a social ecology from the point of view of a society, but it is also apparent from the way language permeates the structures of experience of children. This permeation does not limit itself to the systems of perceptual and movement paradigms, the system of experience, and the memory system. Language helps to expand the personal metaconscious and allows for the formation of the patterns of ever deeper Gestalts of metaconscious knowledge. The gradual formation of the patterns of the collective metaconscious is particularly significant since they are the deepest and most comprehensive patterns of meaning in the lives of children. They increasingly represent the project of existence of the culture as experienced by a child from a particular position in the social hierarchy. In other words, language enfolds the order of the lives of children as it develops in their collective metaconscious into the project of existence of their culture. More than ever before, the development of the minds of children becomes inseparable from their enfolding their lives into the collective being of their culture.

As a result of the way language helps build the collective metaconscious in children, each concept used by them increasingly symbolizes something of how the project of existence of their culture orders their lives as well as an individually unique range of experiences. The concept of mother, for example, can symbolize any mother they have experienced directly or indirectly via stories or television. It also represents the typical role of mothers in their culture and what good or bad mothers are like, largely arrived at metaconsciously by integrating the experiences related to mothers. Children do eventually develop their own thoughts on the matter, but these are always in reference to the order of the culture. They may be ahead of their time, behind their time, or atypical of their time, but they never entirely escape the time and culture. By extending this argument to language as a whole, it is clear that the symbolic universe of a culture is the world of everyday life. It is the way reality appears to the members because their lives have been enfolded into the collective being of their society.

Language converts the structures of experience of children into mental maps by which they orient themselves in the world. Unlike geographical maps, these maps colour life with emotions, hopes, fears, expectations, norms, values, beliefs, customs, and, as we shall see, myths. Once children acquire these maps, they can meaningfully participate in the project of existence of their culture. The similarities and differences in their life maps allow the members of a culture to evolve together as if they were kept on a common course by a cultural gyroscope. This will become particularly evident when we consider the role of culture as a social ecology from the point of view of a society.

Language also creates the world of myths. What, after all, is the basis for the symbolic universe of a culture? What makes it the 'true' world of daily life, the world of our existence? Why do the members of a culture trust this world as the 'real' world as opposed to the world of immediate experience? People do not live as if there is any essential difference between their symbolic universe (reality as they know it) and reality. The discoveries that are made are taken for linear extensions of their world. Yet it is clear that the symbolic universes of different socities or those of the same society at different historical epochs are not identical, and their differences cannot be explained as resulting from a process by which humanity progressively acquires a better knowledge of reality. Like scientific knowledge, everyday knowledge of reality does not grow cumulatively. Hence a new discovery could be anomalous with respect to the symbolic universe of a culture and call into question its coherence. This would plunge a society into total chaos. As we shall examine in a later chapter, this can indeed happen but only very slowly in the course of many generations. The reason for this, as we shall see then, is that a symbolic universe is highly resistant to anomalies because it is founded on a system of myths. These myths, when alive and well in a society, give its members the sense that their individual and collective being has a firm foundation. Their symbolic universe is real, reliable, and true, and in that sense it constitutes their culture's symbolic home in reality. When, on the other hand, these myths weaken in any way, some members of a culture may begin to have a sense of being adrift, of having no firm roots – that is, a feeling of *anomie*. If the myths continue to weaken, a society disintegrates as its symbolic home in reality collapses.

Some aspects of the role language plays in creating a system of myths along with the symbolic universe have already become apparent even though we have not yet examined the role of culture as a social ecology from the point of view of a society. As long as reality as it is known to a culture is not coextensive with reality, there are necessarily aspects of our knowledge of the world and our being in it that are mythical. Language helps to create and transmit the myths every culture requires. As we saw from the worlds of colours, four-footed animals, and playing cards, the distinctions we have learned to make as members of a culture 'cover' an entire domain of life. Things simply cannot be different. There is an absence of knowledge beyond reality as we know it. The experience of a domain of life has been so extensively reinforced, without any adjustments in the process of differentiation being necessary, that metaconsciously we begin to sense that this is the way the world is. The experience of a domain of life is thus metaconsciously extrapolated to cover all possibilities. This implies certain metaconscious assumptions being imposed on reality. The unknown is now nothing but some details of the known that remain to be discovered.

In a way this is how language helps create myths. It is also evident now why the playful attitude babies and children have to the world eventually comes to an end when the set of myths of their culture is well developed within their structures of experience. As adults we cannot live without myths.

When we analyse the role of culture as a social ecology from the perspective of a society, we will see how language helps to put the symbolic universe of a culture on a firm foundation. The gap between reality and reality as it is known is closed because the latter is transformed into the former by a set of myths. The gap between reality and the symbolic universe of a culture becomes nothing else but the as yet unknown aspects of the symbolic universe. We will later show that the subconscious and metaconscious bases for the processes of differentiation and integration and hence the structure of experience can be called into question only very slowly in the course of generations. The role myths play is entirely metaconscious. Aspects of current myths are unfolded in commonplaces such as 'time will tell' or 'history will judge.' It is via language that the set of myths of a culture is transmitted, maintained, developed, and destroyed.

It is quite clear that, contrary to many modern theories, language cannot be reduced to the transmission of information or to structures of signs. A language as spoken, written, and interpreted by the members of a culture enfolds their experiences into the order of their individual and collective being while, at the same time, something of that order is unfolded in their experiences. Each language Gestalt enfolds and unfolds something of the meaning of a person's individual being as well as something of the collective being of his or her culture. Hence each concept and each sentence will not symbolize the same thing for different persons and yet mean sufficiently similar things that communication within a culture is possible. Because each language Gestalt designates a range of past experiences as well as the metaconscious knowledge associated with them, both talking and listening enfold and unfold some aspects of our individual and collective being that we are not consciously aware of. We can be misunderstood or, when listening to a tape of a conversation, we may notice things about what we said and heard that we were not aware of at the time. Similarly, we may write something and come back to it a few days later and make similar discoveries. Here we encounter the source of the ambiguity and complexity of human language. People can use exactly the same words and yet mean quite different things. Each element of a sentence has both cumulative components that help build the language Gestalt and non-cumulative components that derive from language being enfolded into every aspect of the person's individual and collective being. The latter component would be noise from the point of view of the transmission of information, but from the point of view of a culture it constitutes a vital background to each and every language Gestalt without which the various roles of language as described earlier could not function and without which human culture, at least as we have known it in history, cannot maintain itself. No other so-called languages related to animals or machines have any of these characteristics.[18]

The relationship between language and the developments below and above the level of consciousness ensures that the language of a society evolves along with its symbolic universe that it helps to structure. These on-going evolutionary processes are, of course, not uniform throughout a language community. In general we can say that language lags behind the developments in the metaconscious of the members of a language community to varying degress.

By way of illustration, consider the role of artists in a language community once again. Although new patterns of metaconscious knowledge may be linking up in the minds of many members of a language community, artists may be the first to respond. Being aesthetically very sensitive to the patterns of the collective metaconscious, artists may begin to see things differently. If the evolution of the symbolic universe causes its constituents and phenomena to stand in a new context, there is a shift in meaning. When this permeates perception every so slightly, an artist sensitive to these shifts may begin to try to express this in his work. If successful, other artists may recognize that this work somehow corresponds to something that lives within their metaconscious although they are as yet unable to express it. They may then begin to model their work after that artist, leading to the formation of a new school. Poets and novelists may also sense these metaconscious developments and begin to try to use language to express them. Eventually all these developments in the collective metaconscious of a people will become more and more pronounced and enter into everyone's perception and usage of language. The art and literature which captures something of these changes will then find widespread recognition.

One of the ways in which a language evolves can now be readily understood. When metaconscious knowledge implicit in someone's structure of experience happens to break into consciousness and is worked out, or when a person has an idea and thinks it out by relating it to constituents or events in the symbolic universe, they may be led to formulate new concepts. If the person's contemporaries find that these concepts help them to better understand the world they will adopt them. The new concepts may then find their way into the language. There is, therefore, a lag between the time that the need for a new concept is first experienced and the time it is accepted into a language – that is, when it finds widespread acceptance among the members of a language community. The same lag between the evolution of experience and language occurs due to new scientific and technical discoveries, new theories, philosophies, political or religious developments, and so on.

When the evolution of a society is extremely rapid, each generation may find that its vernacular is in certain respects an inadequate symbolic framework in which to suspend its experience. This situation may cause each generation to develop its own jargon or even slang, which, because it emerges in relation to its experience, does not necessarily have a significance for other generations. The diffusion of such jargon or slang into the language community is then limited, as is its impact on the language itself.

Because of the lag between the evolution of the experience of a language community and the evolution of its language, the meaning of the names of concepts and the grammatical structure of the language may be lost in the course of centuries. The names of many concepts are relatively arbitrary today. At the time they were first introduced into a language, they often had a significance in terms of the symbolic universe of the language community, and the choice of a name for a new discovery was an event of deep significance in some cultures. In many cases, the significance of these names can be found by means of etymological studies. The Greek word for moon, for example, denotes its function to measure time, while the Latin word refers to its lucidity or brightness. What appears to a culture as the most characteristic attribute of something frequently reveals its dominant preoccupations. The significance of an object may vary accordingly. The Greeks were preoccupied with measuring time, the creation of the cosmos, the gods, and so on. The Romans did not share this interest at all; apart from the Jews, they were the only culture interested in history. For the Romans, history began with the founding of Rome and everything was related to Rome, making their central preoccupation a political one. The Greek metaphysical preoccupation and the Roman political preoccupation clearly manifest themselves when their myths are compared.

As we have already noted, to know what a constituent of the world (such as the moon) is, we do not need to know a long list of its attributes elaborated with scientific rigour, by which it is distinguished from all the other constituents of the world. The reality of the moon as it is known to a society is the relationships it enters into within its symbolic universe, which springs from the way the members of that society exist in reality via their structures of experience. Within the system of concepts the meaning of the concept of 'moon' is directly differentiated from that of stars, planets, and comets. The discovery of something new about a constituent of the world may change these relationships, which may lead to some constituents being transferred to a new or different class of constituents and becoming designated by the name of that class. Such transfers occurred when it was discovered that the moon is not a planet, creating a new class of constituents designated by the name 'moon.' Although the choice of a concept name is relatively arbitrary and rarely shared by any two languages, once it is adopted it symbolizes a position (that is, a set of relationships) in the system of concepts, and this is its real meaning. The grammatical structure of a language may also still reflect how a culture once conceived the structure of its symbolic universe. The verb tenses, for example, may symbolize how a culture conceived time.

For the members of a language community to live in a coherent symbolic universe, their perceptual and movement paradigms, the system of experience, the memory system, the subconscious, the metaconscious, the system of concepts, and the system of language must each be internally consistent and externally consistent with its environment made up of the other systems. These systems permit the members of a language community to interpret the world in a consistent manner by reducing its complexity to an intelligible one. Because of language, all the members of a language community live in the same symbolic universe – that is, their experiences of the world are relatively consistent with one another. The learning of a vernacular is thus inextricably associated with a process in which all the systems of children become compatible with those of the other members of their language community. This compatibility of the systems of the members of a language community does not mean, of course, that they are exactly identical. While they develop from unique experience, the structures of these systems become very similar under the influence of language.

In order to achieve this, the structures of experience of children need to be quite open to change, while those of adults must be more resistant. The structures of experience of children undergo constant adjustment and hence are reinforced to a far lesser degree than those of adults. Children behave as if they know from the unending flow of new discoveries and corrections that their world is neither coextensive nor identical with that of the other members of their speech community. The situation of adults is quite different, partly because they have acquired a set of myths. When adults know a part of the world fairly well, the parts of the various systems that they use to interpret it have been so frequently used and thus reinforced that they have become rigid and not open to new things. When reality appears to be different from what they expect it to be, as was the case in the anomalous playing-card experiment, they will at first not notice the anomaly. Some of the adults did not in fact manage to shift their systems of perceptual paradigms, which resulted in an emotional crisis. This would not have happened had these people been unfamiliar with playing cards, for the perceptual paradigms would have been less reinforced and thus more fluid and open to discoveries. Whether an anomaly or a discovery occurs depends largely on how well the various systems have been reinforced.

THE REALM OF THOUGHT

Our structures of experience mediate our links with the external and internal worlds in two directions. At first we focused primarily on the direction related to the interpretation of incoming stimuli. This led us to an understanding of the process of mediation in the reverse direction, when a structure of experience is used to carry out a movement, to utter a phrase, to focus or redirect our eyes, and so on. In other words, some of the experience and language paradigms can apparently function in the reverse direction as thought paradigms initiating an activity. A toddler coming home from a walk may run to his toy shelf in another room; he has thought of playing with a toy and utilizes an experience paradigm in the reverse direction to go and get it. By means of thought, he is able to transcend the physical here and now and go on to create another situation.

In babies and young children, it is probably that 'thought' comprises little else than utilizing paradigms in their structures of experience to execute behaviour not called for by their inner or external worlds. As they learn to distinguish between their own bodies and the external world and become more aware of themselves, this begins to change. Paradigms utilized for both directions of mediation will break up to yield two separate ones corresponding to the two directions of mediation. Gradually two clusters of paradigms will be constituted. In the system of experience, a cluster of thought paradigms emerges. This development is reinforced by the experience paradigms resulting from dreaming. Dreaming will help alter the direction of the emergence of intelligence from being more or less directly related to the motor functions to gradually including more abstract thought quite unrelated to the physical here and now. The cluster of thought paradigms gains in its relative autonomy from the remainder of the system of experience along with the related clusters in other systems, such as the cluster of movement paradigms.

These developments are greatly accelerated by the onset of language. Language paradigms can also be used in two directions and, as children learn that they can be detached from the physical here and now, they help pave the way for more abstract thought. Eventually a system of differentiated thought paradigms emerges which is able to contribute a thought Gestalt to an experience Gestalt in the same way as the system of language is able to contribute a language Gestalt. When we are thinking about something, a thought Gestalt forms the foreground of an experience Gestalt while it is a part of the background when we are keeping something in the back of our mind.

The evolution of intelligence in children has been extensively studied by Piaget.[19] He defines five stages of thought development. Until the age of two, children primarily develop their perception and motor functions. They cannot internalize their actions symbolically. We have examined this in earlier chapters. From two to four years, the acquisition of language causes the onset of symbolic behaviour: imitation, make-believe, going beyond the physical here and now. This too we have already examined. From four to six years, the solution to problems is largely dependent on what children perceive. Suppose, for example, that two identical glasses are filled with an equal number of marbles by dropping a marble alternately into a glass. If the contents of one of the glasses are transferred to another glass that is taller and thinner, children in this age group might say that the taller glass contains more marbles than the shorter one. If the marbles continue to be transferred to an even taller and thinner glass, they may say at some point that now the glass has fewer marbles because it is too narrow. Their reasoning is determined by the perceptual features of the glass. They do not dissociate themselves from the immediate situation to think back to the beginning, when the marbles were transferred, in order to realize that their number has not changed.

Between eight and eleven years, children begin to be able to combine logical operations, and they begin to grasp some mathematical concepts and classification operations. Children now begin to have a notion of the concepts of time and space. Activities become related in time and space in a common-sense way. They accept that the lengths or areas of two differently shaped objects can be the same. All reasoning is still limited to concrete actions and situations. They cannot perform actions abstractly in thought. Between the ages of eleven to fourteen, reasoning can go beyond concrete situations. Children are able to produce theories and test hypotheses, make inferences that go beyond the concrete situation, and do some mathematics. A child's logical and mathematical concepts grow out of basic activities which permit the system of thought paradigms to form and expand in the same way as the previously described systems.

The system of thought clearly evolves in the context of a structure of experience of which it is a subsystem.[20] As such, it affects and is affected by the other systems. We will discuss some of the most important interactions.

The emergence of the system of thought has a major impact on the function the memory system performs within the structure of experience. In order to locate a memory trace in the system, we need to designate symbolically the experience paradigm by means of which the event was lived. This could be achieved by thinking of a concept or language Gestalt that represents the experience paradigm, such as 'going to work.' But this designates a host of memory traces associated with an experience paradigm, and since it is not possible to recall more than one memory trace at a time, and since the structure of the relevant cluster of memory traces is inaccessible to thought, nothing can be recalled in this manner. To be able to recall a specific memory trace, we need to think of further characteristics of the particular memory trace, such as 'yesterday when going to work.' In other words, a process of symbolically reconstructing aspects of an event by means of thought and language is necessary to locate a trace in the memory system. Once an embryonic symbolic representation has been thought up, the memory system can be scanned to locate memory traces that resemble it.

This is perhaps accomplished by differentiating the memory traces with respect to the Gestalt reconstructed by means of thought and language in order to find a trace that resembles it. Recall fails when the Gestalt produced by thought is inadequate, possibly because the event was not interpreted quite that way at the time. Consider the following example.

To help a friend recall a particular incident that they went through together, a person will give a description and relate it to other events. She might say, 'Remember that beautiful dog we saw downtown last week? My brother got one yesterday just like it.' If this language Gestalt does not permit her friend to recall the dog, she may add, 'It was the morning we had a flat tire on our way to work just turning onto Main Street.' Since the first language Gestalt did not permit her friend to recall the dog, she tries to have her recall one of the events that took place that morning. Once the friend can recall one memory trace, she may recall the ones that followed it, because each one contains in its background what became the foreground of the next experience Gestalt. The friend may in this way be able to relive the sequence of events until she recalls the dog. The reason for the friend not being able to recall the dog by means of the first language Gestalt suggested to her may be due to the fact that she directed her attention to the original event quite differently, and consequently included the dog in the background of the experience Gestalt. Since the recall of an event always occurs in relation to the current situation, the Gestalt which she forms and uses to attempt the recall is influenced by the situation at hand. It is therefore possible that she might not be able to recall an event which some time earlier under different circumstances she was able to recall.

From the above example, it follows that the emergence of the systems related to language and thought lead to an extension of the roles children's memories play in their structures of experience. The reciprocal interaction leads to an expansion of the systems related to language and thought. Children learn to think through events of the past, to analyse and compare them, and to draw generalizations from them. The result is an expansion of the scope of existing paradigms related to language and thought or the creation of new ones. All these developments help to integrate their lives more consciously into the present and hence to strengthen the coherence of their being.

There is also a considerable interaction between the systems related to thought or language and the metaconscious. We have already noted earlier that intuitions derived from the formation of patterns of metaconscious knowledge need to be worked out and to be given form by means of language and thought. The reciprocal interaction also occurs. When children learn to think out an event, it may come to stand in a new light. Depending on the role this event plays in their lives, existing patterns of metaconscious knowledge could be affected or new ones created when subsequent similar events are lived differently.

But there is another important role that the metaconscious plays in thought processes. By differentiating the events in our lives, we learn that some events are more related than others. By forming patterns of metaconscious knowledge, the metaconscious derives what information it can from this differentiated panorama of our life as contained in our memory systems. When someone has an intuition related to the formation of a new pattern of metaconscious knowledge, he may work it out in the form of a concept like the economy, the state, industry, science, technology, and so on. This process requires thought.

Within the structure of experience there exist interrelated and complementary forms of knowledge. Consider the structures of experience of the members of a highly differentiated society. Their memory systems will differentiate between clusters of memory traces which correspond to what might be designated as the social, economic, political, and legal domains of life, to mention only a few. By integrating the traces within each cluster and the clusters themselves, Gestalts of metaconscious knowledge form that depict criss-crossing and overlapping family resemblances. These Gestalts can be intuited and symbolically designated by concepts that are learned in the course of daily life without any definition being necessary. It is only later by means of thought that children can articulate what the social, economic, political, and legal relationships are. This will be done quite differently by the members of a culture. In other words, the system of thought can develop the implications of the remaining systems in the structures of experience to yield a range of interpretations. This explains the diversity of ideas, world views, and ideologies which can coexist in a society despite the highly similar patterns of the collective metaconscious. We will later show why this does not threaten the unity of a culture but rather helps create the vitally important dialectical tensions without which a society could not evolve. This role of the system of thought is therefore extremely important.

The realm of thought is not unlimited, however. We have already noted that, by forming a symbolic universe, language creates an individual and a collective field of being. It includes the past and expectations for the future as well as the universe of thought and ideas generated by the members of a society. Language, through the structure of experience, limits the field of being of the members of a culture. It is difficult to experience or think of things that cannot be reached by language because of the latter's influence on the structure of experience. Language therefore helps to create a highly stable horizon for human existence and thought. This is well illustrated when two cultures contact one another. When Westerners encountered so-called primitive people, the latter were not able to make sense of many objects and customs of the former and vice versa, because these came from beyond their horizon of experience.

There is one final role of the system of thought that we have already referred to in an earlier chapter, and that we will therefore simply mention. When we routinely live a moment of our life by means of a previously acquired experience paradigm, the situation may turn out to be different from what we anticipated on the basis of that paradigm. At this point we are not stuck because the system of thought allows us to think through the situation. This is equally true for highly complex activities such as flying a plane.[21]

SIX

Individual Diversity

The inadequacy of the current mechanistic conceptions of reality in general and human life in particular has led us to consider the diverse ways in which the being of a person is enfolded into a variety of systems which in turn are enfolded into one another. The development of babies and children as described thus far may be regarded in terms of the enfolding and unfolding of their being in relation to these systems. The variety of ways in which this occurs is an important source of individual diversity while its limits ensure the unity of the human phenomenon. We shall begin our study of individual diversity by briefly highlighting a number of systems, including their interactions, which are central for human life.

A first system contributing to human individuality is the genetic, which is fundamental in maintaining the diversity of individuals and races within the unity we call humanity. It is increasingly recognized that this system does not function mechanistically. There is no complete determinism in genetic transmission. We have a genetic inheritance, but the 'mechanism' is so complex that the possibilities are enormous. Some possible outcomes can be predicted, but a strong element of indeterminism remains.[1] It would be too simplistic to picture the functions of the genetic system as generating a diversity of 'biological' selves, into which the human persons are enfolded. Biological individuality may be regarded as one manifestation of the presence of an enfolded being. In any case, this individuality is fundamental. For example, some of the difficulties encountered in transplant surgery arise because an organism seeks to preserve its biological individuality by rejecting whatever foreign tissue or organ is transplanted into it. Research into these problems has shown how fundamental this individuality is. The real issue here is to give biological individuality its full weight, and to do this we should reflect for a moment on the meaning of the term 'biological.'

Modern biology has shown that there is no special living matter, but only living systems that organize matter. A cell, for example, organizes a very large number of molecules into a self-organizing and self-regulating system. Living systems do not just take food and energy from their environment. Any system, living or not, contains constituents, events, and relationships which are outside its organization; this results in disorder and noise. In any non-living system the amount of disorder or entropy can only increase until the system eventually breaks down.

In living systems, on the other hand, the opposite usually happens. When disorder goes beyond certain limits, measures are taken to reduce it, which take the form of processes of self-organization. These processes force the living system to evolve because it can only deal with disorder by reorganizing itself into a greater complexity. For example, an organism tolerates a certain disorder in the form of foreign germs or viruses, but if the disorder goes too far it tries to reorganize itself, which, if successful, may produce a certain immunity to a specific type of disorder. To achieve reorganization a living system must be open; that is, it requires a constant flow of information from its environment to be able to maintain itself (negative entropy). When a living system is unable to cope with the disorder which constantly threatens it, it disintegrates and dies. It evolves in spite of and by means of disorder. In highly complex living systems like the human body, the components (molecules, cells, tissues, and so on) can degrade, while the ensemble is in a permanent process of reorganization to decrease momentary disorder and maintain its unique identity.

The environment may be considered as co-organizer and co-regulator of a living system. Both the living system and its environment are open. Each one is enfolded into the other while, at the same time, each also constitutes a whole in itself. The more autonomous a living system is, the more dependent it is on a complex diversity of relationships with its environment. The autonomy of an open system is therefore inseparable from a dependence on its environment.

What all this means is that, in generating a diversity of biological organisms within the unity of a species, the genetic system creates a diversity of living systems that can develop only in relation to an environment. This development is anticipated by the genetic system, which evolves by interacting with the other systems into which it is enfolded. The organization of each living organism generated by the genetic system contains in it the potential for these interactions. As for the human phenomenon, the genetic system helps perpetuate both the unity of the human phenomenon and the diversity of its individual members within that unity.

A second system contributing to human individuality is the brain, composed of such elements as neurons and synapses. A discussion of the structure of the brain, however, is beyond the scope of this work. We have noted that the functioning of the human brain is characterized by the fact that the genetic system equips it with relatively few modes of behaviour built into the brain from birth. Thus most behaviour is learned from experience. The genetic system helps create human brains that are adapted to being organized to a great extent on the basis of experience. As a result human beings require a long period of socialization. The enormous size and complexity of the human brain as compared to those of animals help make human beings both more autonomous and relatively more dependent on their environment. Since the mind enfolds itself into the brain as it develops, the characteristics of the latter greatly affect the former. The diversity of human brains created by the genetic system manifests itself by varying abilities to carry out different kinds of mental operations. Some people, for example, excel in those related to creativity, others to intelligence, and still others in relation to the metaconscious. We shall return to the subject later in this chapter.

A third system contributing to individual diversity is the structure of experience or the mind. As it develops within the brain, it increasingly becomes the heart of a person's existence. It is via the mind that a person's being unfolds itself in relation to the systems central to human life while it is at the same time enfolded into them. All these systems begin to take on an individual and collective meaning in the context of the lives of the members of a culture by means of their minds. It is tempting to liken the distinction between the mind and the brain to that between computer software and hardware, but the fundamental opposition between living and non-living systems makes this analogy misleading.[2] The 'language' of the mind is that of meaning, which is at the centre of human existence. It is possible to speculate on the relationship between our theory of the mind and the findings of neurophysiology, chemistry, and biology, but the gap between these two levels of research is still vast. However, the findings of the latter are not incompatible with our interpretation.

Both the brain and the structure of experience contain disorder in view of the fact that they are open systems. When disorder in the brain becomes too great due to the invasion and growth of a virus, microbes, or the introduction of any other object foreign to its organization, it must defend itself or risk deterioration and death. Disorder in the structure of experience has other sources. One of them is a constant tension between the mode of getting at the meaning of experience by the interacting processes of differentiation and the complementary mode that attempts to achieve the same objective by integrating the elements of experience into patterns. This may happen when an experience Gestalt is anomalous in relation to certain metaconscious patterns of experience. Cultural evolution of the society is another source of disorder, since it causes new patterns of experience to link up while older ones disintegrate. The coexistence of fragments of old and largely disintegrated patterns, the current and hence most developed patterns, and fragments of new patterns in the process of linking up is another source of disorder. This disorder is both a threat to cultural coherence and a necessary prerequisite for cultural evolution.

While the brain combats disorder by means of biological processes, the structure of experience can do so by means of its intellectual, creative, and imaginative faculties, for example and in extreme cases, by repressing memories. When the amount of disorder becomes too great, the structure of experience loses its wholeness, causing a certain fragmentation. In this case, it lacks the integrality necessary to interpret experiences coherently and to generate coherent behaviour patterns – in short, to permit a person to lead a normal existence. When that coherence is lost, mental 'illness' results, which originates not in the brain but in the mind. The reverse can also occur. A serious disorder in the brain can cause a deterioration in the structure of experience.

The remaining systems that contribute to individual diversity and the unity of the human phenomenon are the ones that constitute the environment open to the structure of experience. The body, its growth largely controlled by the genetic system, constitutes a fourth system affecting human development. What concerns us most is the way the senses located within it become enfolded into the mind when they begin to help constitute the dimensions of experience. The detection of stimuli and their transmission to the mind via the brain becomes an integral part of a person's being. This in turn paves the way for the 'inner' and external worlds of a person to be enfolded into his or her existence. Both worlds comprise many systems, but we highlight only the most important ones for the study of individual diversity: the socio-cultural system constituted by a society to which a person belongs (a fifth system), the artificial environment (a sixth system), the ecosystem (a seventh), and the universe (an eighth system). These systems are also enfolded into each other in a variety of ways. They become enfolded into a person's existence via the mind. During the very earliest stages of human development the being of a person is enfolded into the body, including the brain. As that being begins to unfold itself, the mind develops and increasingly the centre of the enfolding and unfolding of human existence shifts to the mind. This shift marks the transformation of a person from a largely 'natural' to a predominantly cultural being.

The socio-cultural system constituted as a society is an important mode of self-organization of the relationships between people and between them and their environment. Societies occur in both the animal world and humanity. The difference between animal and human societies is that the former are largely structured by the instincts placed in the brain by the genetic system and a system of signs acquired from experience.[3] A society is a largely non-natural system organized by means of a language and culture acquired by socialization. Societies are highly complex and dependent on a rich diversity of relationships between their members and between these societies and reality. Because of this complex diversity of relationships, the cultural unity of a society is, as we will see, constantly threatened with considerable disorder, forcing it to evolve or to collapse.

As far as the remaining systems are concerned, the increasing mechanical interdependence and systems-like character of our urban environment and the inherent potential risk to human survival have been pointed out by Vacca.[4] The systems-like character of nature has become painfully obvious by research into the consequences of our intervention in the ecological system. The ability of the ecosystem to deal with disorders and the alarming way in which disorders in that system are increasing are well known.

The systems-like character of the universe has become apparent from the ways in which scientific knowledge evolves. An anomaly can necessitate a complete transformation in the way science depicts reality as it is known. If the constituents and phenomena of reality were not extensively interconnected, no such revolutions would be necessary, because anomalies could be coped with by sets of cumulative additions to scientific theories.

To conceptualize the ways the above systems are dynamically enfolded into one another is a difficult task, particularly since the mechanistic conception of matter appears to be in doubt. We have already referred to this problem in more general terms in the first chapter. It is almost impossible to describe systematically the patterns of interaction between these systems[5] or the way variations in them help create an individual diversity within the unity of the human phenomenon. Each system affects individual persons differently and consequently contributes to the unfolding of a person's unique individuality. We have already seen that the genetic system organizes the innate structures of the brain and that onto them are grafted structures acquired from experience. The experiences of a person enfold and unfold something of a person's being, the socio-cultural system, the ecosystem, and the way these systems are enfolded into the universe. The socio-cultural system helps structure the mind. It in turn affects how the members of a society live in reality to create what for them is a meaningful non-natural milieu. In helping to create the human condition in a society, this milieu can affect the genetic system and ecosystem. The latter influences the genetic system, and both affect the socio-cultural system. The interrelationships are numerous and complex, and we will be able to examine only a few of them in relation to the creation of an individual diversity within the human phenomenon.

THE WILD BOY OF AVEYRON AND OTHER EXTREMES

The processes by which human beings enter into the symbolic universe of their culture can be regarded from the perspective of the interaction of the above systems in the life of a person. The unique nature of these interactions is woven into the fabric of each person's life, which helps create individual diversity. In fact, a culture's process of socialization tends to produce the diversity of individuals necessary to sustain its way of life, while at the same time it limits this diversity so as not to threaten its coherence.

We will examine a number of cases selected to illustrate the crucial importance of a symbolic universe in the lives of human beings. This can most readily be appreciated when we come into contact with people in whose childhood the processes described in the previous chapters were interrupted after only a few years or rendered extremely difficult, or who, after having learned to share the symbolic universe with their speech community, later became unable to do so. These cases will furthermore illustrate the participation of the brain and the structure of experience in the links with our external world, the importance of language, and the fundamental role played by the metaconscious.

The first case is that of a boy who was estimated to be eleven or twelve years old when he was captured in the woods of Aveyron in France in the year 1800. He was entirely naked and fed himself with roots and acorns. He appeared completely at home in his natural environment, shunning all contact with human beings. He was ferocious, biting and scratching those who held him captive, and indifferent to everything in the human world from which he constantly attempted to escape. The child aroused considerable public interest and a government minister ordered him to be taken to Paris. There, the directors of a national institute for the deaf and mute entrusted him to Dr Jean Itard for medical attention. After carefully observing the child, Itard came to suspect that the boy's behaviour could not be explained by presupposing deafness or madness as his contemporaries did, nor did he believe that the child had been abandoned by his parents just before he was captured. Further research revealed that the child had been seen in the woods five years earlier, fleeing the people that approached him. He then already appeared to be entirely adapted to his natural environment. According to Itard, this meant that the boy must have been abandoned at least two years earlier, which he estimated to be the minimum time interval necessary for the child to adapt to his new environment.

For Itard, this confirmed the conclusions he had reached from his careful observations, namely that the boy's solitude for at least seven years in a natural environment explained his initial indifference to everything in his new social milieu (indoors protection, clothing, furniture, social pleasures, etc.) and his love for the woods and open fields to which he constantly tried to escape. At first the boy could not walk normally, but only trotted or galloped. He did not eat meat, and his body was covered with scars, indicating animal bites and other signs of a long existence in nature. He did not make sounds and hated to sleep in a bed. According to Itard, to have been able to survive in nature for at least seven years, the boy must have been four or five years old when he was abandoned, but the long period of solitary existence had wiped out all traces of socialization from his mind. The explanation of the boy's behaviour was to be found in the conditions under which the child had lived for so long. It was on the basis of this hypothesis that Itard designed a program of education for the boy which has inspired many of the methods used in the Montessori system to this day. He described his observations of the boy after his capture, his educational program, and its results in two reports,[6] some parts of which we shall discuss in the light of the theory of the structure of experience. Itard's first report made him famous all over Europe.

While the boy lived a solitary existence in nature, his structure of experience learned to interpret the stimuli related to that existence. Due to the absence of social relationships, his metaconscious patterns of experience implied no images of other human beings or a social self. The parts of his structure of experience related to language and thought acquired during his early years completely disintegrated from lack of use.[7] Once the boy was captured and brought into a completely different environment, his structure of experience encountered a whole new range of stimuli which could not have any meaning for him. He had entered a social and material milieu that made no sense to him and that overwhelmed him. This indeed corrresponds to the description Itard gives of the boy's behaviour after his capture and before the program of resocialization had begun to take effect.

A few examples of the way his senses responded to stimuli clearly show the crucial role the structure of experience plays in what is perceived. The boy's ears appeared the least sensitive of all his senses, and many had concluded that he was deaf. A pistol shot unexpectedly fired just behind his head drew only a slight response while a second shot drew no response at all. His eyes were without expression, wandering from one thing to another without stopping. He did not fixate and hardly seemed to be able to distinguish a picture from the real object. He was totally indifferent to what for other people are very distasteful or pleasant smells. He touched objects only to hold them. The boy uttered only one uniform sound which was not used for the purpose of communication.

The boy's insensitivity to temperature was remarkable. He was perfectly content to be outside for hours in the cold wind, rain, or snow, seeking no protection even when he wore no clothing. Only his basic needs appeared to be able to capture his attention, but even they were at first unable to induce elementary intellectual activities such as opening a door or climbing a chair to reach food. There was a total absence of any body language for the purpose of communication. Emotional changes appeared to be random and excessive. He was totally indifferent to his own filthiness and would not even get up to satisfy his bodily needs. Affection from others met with no response, and his only pleasure seemed to be eating something he knew. His behaviour was not even like that of an animal because it was void of any social aptitudes found among animals due to their socialization into animal societies. He knew only how to eat, sleep, run through the fields and woods, and be idle. In his report Itard refers to the boy as a 'man-plant.'

His growing convictions about the reasons for the boy's behaviour caused Itard to treat the child quite differently from the way others had. Itard designed a five-stage program to resocialize the boy by 1) attaching him to social life more than to his former life, 2) awakening his nervous sensibility by strong stimuli and affection, 3) extending the sphere of his ideas to give him needs and to multiply his relationship with others, 4) teaching him language by making it a necessity, and 5) developing mental operations via things that were necessary to him. The whole approach was based on respecting the boy's habits as much as possible while at the same time attempting to develop and socialize them. To put it in the language of our model of the structure of experience, it was a strategy of expanding existing paradigms and establishing new ones by having established paradigms break up into two or more. The boy was taken for long walks in parks, put to bed regularly at dusk, and so on.

Itard's convictions about the boy allowed him to observe things others never noticed because they had stereotyped him. It is these observations which show that the boy had a structure of experience developed by and corresponding to his solitary existence in nature. He was able to respond normally to any set of stimuli which could have a meaning to him. His hearing, for example, permitted him to respond to the sound of a nut falling from a distant tree. When he was in his room (an environment that meant nothing to him at first) he would sway monotonously while sadly looking at the woods outside, or place himself in the draft from the open window. He did, however, respond to changes in the weather. A wind that suddenly came up or the sun being covered by a cloud made him laugh loudly and want to go outside, while at other times it made him furious and dangerous. When it had snowed one morning he escaped into the garden only half-dressed to happily heap the snow into his hands and roll himself in it. On the whole, he seemed more peaceful and at rest in the garden. At night he could spend hours standing in front of his window looking at the moonlit landscape. These are not the responses to nature of a deaf and mentally deranged child, but of someone who was held captive in a new milieu which made little sense to him. He longed to be free and recover the meaning of his existence in the milieu he knew and in which he had grown up.

To illustrate briefly Itard's strategy for resocializing the boy, consider his insensitivity to temperature. Apart from his ability to live in nature without clothing, he could take potatoes out of boiling water with his bare hands, place them in the fire, and retrieve them moments later to eat them, or pick up glowing cinders that had rolled out of the fireplace and put them back without any hurry. Itard extensively used warmth in the form of hot baths lasting several hours and warm clothing to get the boy's senses used to new stimuli. This treatment made him more sensitive to cold, which in turn led to his acceptance of clothing. Left in the cold beside his clothes, he soon learned to dress himself. He began to appreciate a clean dry bed and learned to get up to satisfy his bodily needs. When one day the boy did not like the temperature of his bath he took the hand of this governess to show her by dipping it into the bath. These are some typical results of as fundamental an activity as resocializing the boy's senses.

While the resocialization of touch, smell, and taste advanced steadily, the resocialization of his sight and hearing did not advance at all at first.

This can readily be understood from our model of the structure of experience. The mental structures associated with sight and hearing are much more complex partly because they involve two sense organs. We shall not discuss the ingenious methods Itard used to resocialize these senses, but simply remark that they were also based on the principle of expanding existing paradigms to have them break up to constitute new ones.

After a period of nine months Itard's efforts had brought about an enormous change in the boy's condition. He now seemed almost a normal child, yet all the functions of the structure of experience that lie beyond the level of differentiating experience Gestalts never developed. The few words he learned to utter appeared to be more an expression of his emotions at the time than vocal signs related to communication. He later learned to read a number of words, showing that he understood what they represented, but he never grasped the meaning of phrases either spoken or written, which would have required a process of differentiating language Gestalts. His communication was limited to what can be achieved by a structure of experience that does not go beyond the differentiation of experience Gestalts. If, for example, he wanted to be driven around in the wheelbarrow, he would lead someone from the house and place him between the handles of the wheelbarrow and then hop into it. If that brought no results, he would get out and demonstratively drive it around himself and hop into it again. His social relationships with others always remained very elementary. Not only was he unable to go beyond the physical here and now by means of language; neither could he do so via his imagination, with the result that he never learned to play with toys.

A number of explanations can be given for the blockage of the boy's development. It is, of course, possible that Itard had socialized him to roughly the same level as did his parents and that neither had been able to go any further due to a brain defect. It is equally possible that his structure of experience sustained permanent psychic damage after a traumatic experience.

Whatever the explanation for his condition, in the natural environment in which he lived there was no meaning other than that of the physical here and now in so far as it was relevant to his basic needs. There was no adult world whose meaning transcended that of his own and in the larger context of which his experience could take on new meaning. He lacked the constant stimulation of the symbolic universe of a speech community to teach him that there was literally more to experience than what meets the eye. The absence of a second world would have largely brought the development of his imagination to an end and led to the deterioration of what imagination he may have had. In his world, there was no reason for his structure of experience to be anything more than an instrument to find food and detect danger. The 'myths'[8] implied in his rudimentary metaconscious patterns of experience were that there was no more to life than biological survival and that he was nothing more than a biological organism. To teach the boy language and to reactivate his intellectual, creative, and imaginative faculties required a transformation of what the patterns of his metaconscious implied about life and about himself. To undo all the effects of the past at age eleven or twelve proved to be impossible.

The boy's new socio-cultural milieu was interpreted on the basis of his prior experience. While Itard was able to change a number of perceptual and experience paradigms, the changes were evidently not significant enough to alter the deeper patterns of metaconscious knowledge. Yet these patterns needed to be changed to make a new kind of life. No new paradigm could imply the existence of a social self, with the result that the boy was locked into the 'man-plant' existence based on the deep structures of his metaconscious. Itard could make the boy enter the symbolic universe of his culture in so far as it could be made into an extension of the boy's original world, that is, a world essentially void of the social. This is not the case for a child whose world, due to its constant interaction with the symbolic universe of the members of his speech community, is dependent on it for its meaning. The symbolic universe is a transcendent source of meaning which acts as a reference and stimulant that permits a baby to become a cultural being rather than a natural one. How the boy came to what he was may never be known, but the case is an exceptional illustration of the role the structure of experience plays in the functioning of our senses. It also illustrates what happens to it in the absence of a socio-cultural system leading to an individuality that was quite different from what we consider 'normal.'

We will next examine a range of cases where people's links with their external world are extremely limited, as for blind deaf-mute children. These cases are fundamentally different from the preceding one in that there is no absence of the socio-cultural system, and these children often enter into the symbolic universe of the culture in which they grow up. However, the process is extremely difficult and drawn out because their experience of the outside world is derived from only three dimensions of experience, namely touch, smell, and taste. This means in fact that their contact with the symbolic universe of their speech community must be made almost exclusively via tactile sensations. Again we encounter teachers who, like Itard, firmly believed that there was a human potential which could be developed even when their contemporaries considered that all evidence proved the contrary. The cases of Helen Keller and Laura Bridgman have been well documented.[9]

Their teachers used the manual alphabet to spell the names of things to them. The developments related to language, which for other children begin in the aural dimension of experience, can for blind deaf-mute children take place only within the tactile dimension. These developments necessarily proceed in the same fashion as described earlier, but they are a great deal more difficult because the links these children have with their external world are very much restricted. They are much less open to their external environment and particularly to the symbolic universe of their speech community. Language cannot take on a meaning in the context of facial expressions, tone of voice, body language, and the general situation at hand. For these children, most experience Gestalts are nothing more than some tactile sensations.

The odds against blind deaf-mute children entering the symbolic universe of their speech community appear overwhelming. At first there is a total absence of the possibility that the names of things spelled by the manual alphabet can have a meaning. The spelling of the names of things at first appears to these children as an unrelated act. They must intuit the meaning of language as a whole because its significance cannot be derived from the parts.

One day Helen Keller suddenly discovered the meaning of language. Helen's teacher has recorded the circumstances in which this occurred. One morning while washing, Helen wanted to know the name for water, by patting her teacher's hand and pointing to the water. This was not unusual and the teacher thought nothing of it. Later that morning as she pumped water while Helen held her mug under the spout, she again spelled w-a-t-e-r into Helen's free hand as the cold water gushed into the mug and over Helen's hand. Helen seemed startled, dropped the mug, and stood as though transfixed. A new light came into her face as she spelled water several times to her teacher. She next dropped to the ground and asked for its name, and continued to ask for the names of everything around her. Suddenly the meaning of names had been discovered, which was the first step to understanding the meaning of language. This is the point of entry into the symbolic universe.

Despite the limitations imposed by a direct knowledge of the world via tactile sensations, Helen Keller reached a high degree of mental development and culture. She is the author of children's stories and an autobiography. The fact that she was able to enter the symbolic universe of her speech community in spite of the limited quality of her sensations shows that we must not regard the symbolic universe as a superstructure determined by the systems of perceptual paradigms. If this were the case, the symbolic universe of her speech community would have remained largely inaccessible to her because she was unable to acquire perceptual paradigms in several dimensions of experience.

When the development of a child is retarded due to special circumstances, as was the case for Helen Keller and Laura Bridgman, some of the phases in the development of symbolic thought become clear. Such children have a great deal of difficulty at first imagining hypothetical cases and figures of speech. Laura Bridgman, for example, would react to an arithmetic problem as if what is supposed really did happen. When her teacher presented her with a problem out of a textbook one morning, her first reaction was to inquire how the man who wrote the book knew she was there. The problem was as follows: If you can buy a barrel of cider for four dollars, how much can you buy for one dollar? Her reply was that she could not give much for cider because it was very sour. She was as yet unable to detach thought from the concrete situation. Aphasia patients have the same difficulty. They are unable to shift from the immediate concrete situation to an imaginary one. If one asks a patient who is paralysed in his right hand to repeat a phrase to the effect that he can write with his right hand, he will be unable to do so, while he will have no difficulty repeating a phrase saying that he can write with his left hand.[10]

In both these cases, language and thought extend the situation of the physical here and now without being able to detach themselves from it completely. Neither thought nor language can be used to create an entirely hypothetical situation because the processes of differentiation on the levels of experience and language cannot be completely detached from each other. The result is that these people live in the shrunken world of each instance, which with other instances do not fully connect into a symbolic universe. To be able fully to enter the symbolic universe of a culture, a person must be able to transcend the situation of the physical here and now. The inability to do so may be temporary, as is the case for most children, or permanent because of a brain defect, as with aphasia patients.

Some patients suffering from schizophrenia never learn to share, or after a severe emotional shock cease to share, the symbolic universe of their speech community. We shall briefly consider the case described by Herbert Kohl.[11] The child in question would become extremely disturbed when anything upset his daily routine. When one day the boy entered his classroom in the special school he attended, he noticed that another boy who was the closest thing he had to a friend was absent. He went to pieces; he fell on the floor screaming, 'The day is all broken, the day is broken up, they broke the day!' He was completely uncontrollable until his classmate walked in, twenty minutes late. Upon seeing him, the boy said, 'The day is all fixed,' and set out to do his work as if nothing had happened. Similarly, if the story period was shorter than usual, he would become anxious saying, 'The day's going backwards, the clock's going backwards.'

Once again we see that our links with the world are not direct but that they require a structure of experience which interprets the stimuli derived from reality. Reality as it was known to the boy by means of his structure of experience was not the same as the symbolic universe of his speech community. He lived in a world of his own with a concept of time entirely different from that of the culture in which he lived. Life was perceived by him as a cycle of events having a fixed character and a fixed length. Each day was a kind of solid object that could not change in any way without shattering or going out of control. Reality as perceived by the boy did not allow for human existence the way we know it, and he indeed did not seem to be aware of his unique self. He could not be taught to say the words 'I,' 'he,' and his name, Dennis' correctly. The boy conceived of his existence in terms of the phases in his routine, the building blocks out of which his rigid world was constructed. As a consequence, he would use 'I hungry,' 'he hungry,' and 'Dennis hungry' interchangeably.

The limited awareness of his own existence made relationships with other people virtually impossible. The boy hardly seemed to feel pain. He lived in a sort of private symbolic universe that was internally consistent, but insufficiently externally consistent with the symbolic universe of the society in which he lived. The problem with the boy's structure of experience may have been due to the metaconscious patterns not having developed normally or having been unavailable to the child for one reason or another. In either case these patterns could not play a crucial role in the boy's development. Each time he realized that reality was anomalous with respect to his private world, he also became aware of his inability to resolve the anomaly. This would trigger off a deep personal crisis. The situation is somewhat analogous to that of the subjects in the playing-card experiment who could not resolve the problem of the anomalous cards. Their situation, however, had been created artificially because normally reality is compatible with their symbolic universe. It is clear that the processes by which a culture generates a symbolic universe cannot be called the 'social construction of reality' because this very term seems to presuppose a conscious intention which is totally absent.

To conclude our brief look at some special cases, consider a range of cases in which a part of a person's structure of experience is repressed. The repressed part is withdrawn from normal participation in the functions of the structure of experience, with the result that it is split into two semi-autonomous parts. Repression appears to be an involuntary act of self-defence on the level of a person's structure of experience. A deeply disturbing event causing intense anxiety can be blocked from voluntary recall to prevent an emotional crisis. The repressed part of the structure of experience appears not to be destroyed in the act, however. The repressed events can sometimes be relived to the minutest detail at the expense of normal consciousness in a dream or a trance (the occurrence of which is completely forgotten when normal consciousness returns) or brought out under treatment with drugs, hypnosis, or free association tests. Even the attempt to recall a repressed experience frequently brings on anxiety, headaches, or nausea. Repression therefore appears to be not a once-and-for-all act but a continuous process that requires a constant expenditure of psychic energy.

The extent of the repressed part of a structure of experience may vary greatly. It may be a name, a word, a phrase, a particular skill (such as how to write, stand, walk, or drive a car), or a range of events occurring over a short or long period which are related to a specific event or sphere of activity. It should be noted that, in the case of a skill, the repression typically affects only the movement paradigms necessary for the function involved, so that the limbs can be used for all functions controlled by the other movement paradigms.

As noted earlier, an experience Gestalt contains an emotional dimension which expresses its relationship to the structure of experience as a whole. When this emotional dimension has an extreme intensity, it flows over to all other events that are related to it because of their interconnectedness within the structure of experience. The repressed part may constitute a sort of mini-structure of experience that in extreme and rare cases develops into a multiple personality which may begin with the sudden loss of personal identity. This results in what is called a fugue (literally, flight) which designates an extended period of acting as a different person.

In times of war, for example, a soldier carrying out a dangerous mission may face an internal conflict between his being a person like anyone else and being a soldier. This conflict can come to a head owing to a violent incident such as a narrow escape from death by a shell explosion. As a person, he wants to abandon the dangerous mission and flee to safety, while on the other hand as a soldier he is aware of his responsibilities, such as the risk to the lives of his companions if he abandons his part in the mission. In civilian life, such a conflict could result from an excessive tension between one's life as a hard-pressed business person and one's private life with family and friends. It should be noted that in both cases the structure of experience contains two domains corresponding to the two principal sectors of the person's life, which have taken on a relative autonomy from each other because the density of interrelationships of their constituent components drops off sharply near their boundaries. They are both in that sense a sort of gigantic cluster, each of which is internally more interconnected than it is connected to its surroundings.

If the tension between two parts of someone's life reaches a point of crisis and if the situation appears absolutely hopeless, the person may try to commit suicide or 'psychological suicide' in repressing his identity.[12] When in the latter case, these people recover their identity under treatment, they often repress all memories of their fugue. Fugue appears to be an alternative to suicide and nervous breakdown. In a fugue a person is lacking in identity but a new identity can evolve from the part of the structure of experience that is not suppressed. If this happens, a double personality may develop.

Whatever may cause the development of a double personality, the structure of experience typically breaks up into two relatively independent systems. Although they seem to share the systems of perceptual and movement paradigms, the system of concepts, the system of language, and the system of thought paradigms, each appears to have its own system of experience related to the periods of the person's life in which either one or the other personality interprets experience and helps determine behaviour. Each part of the system of experience leads to a set of metaconscious patterns of experience including an image of a social self. There may occur even more rare cases of triple personalities with complex interrelationships. For example, the first personality may be entirely unaware of the other two by repressing both of them when it determines conscious behaviour. The second personality may be aware of the existence of the third and be able to recall some of its experiences, while the third is unaware of the other two.[13] There are even cases in which one personality acts consciously while another functions subconsciouly. The subconscious personality may manifest itself because the person, without being aware of it, writes out messages of a style and content quite different from his consciously controlled writing while he carries out a conversation with someone on an entirely unrelated issue. The cases of multiple personality vary a great deal, and it is not our purpose to examine them in depth. They do, however, appear to confirm the systems-like character of the structure of experience as we have described it in the previous chapters.

The above range of mental illnesses, whether they have a physiological origin in the system of the brain or a psychological origin in the structure of experience, create abnormal individualities in the sense that they do not belong to the normal individual diversity associated with the symbolic universe of a culture. At the same time, however, the complexity and diversity of these cases, as well as many others documented in the vast literature on the psychology of abnormal persons, must remain a constant warning against rationalizing the model of the structure of experience too far. The concept of system as we have utilized it is only a means of grasping some aspects of reality. Since the complexity of reality constantly exceeds what was supposed, we are endlessly obliged to further the development of the concepts which form our intellectual instruments. The results of this brief exploration of the relationship between some types of mental disease in relation to the structure of experience and the symbolic universe of a culture are therefore at best preliminary.

The special cases of people whose lives were lived on or beyond the fringes of the symbolic universe of their society illustrate the vital importance of culture for human existence. The individualities of these people are not 'normal' – that is, they lie outside the individual diversity that, as we shall see in the next chapter, finds its cohesion in the unity of a culture. These special cases also show that, whichever of the systems may be the causes of abnormal individuality, it is the way the system affects a person's structure of experience that is of vital importance. Of all the systems contributing to our individuality, the structure of experience is the only one open to all the others. This makes it the heart of our existence and the place in which all aspects come together to give our lives coherence and meaning. It is by means of our structures of experience that we transform the stimuli derived from reality into a symbolic universe endowed with meaning and that our unique selves develop in relation to that universe to become indissociable from it. We become people of our time and culture, which sets us apart from other times and other cultures, but it also gives us a unique identity within the unity of a culture to create a diversity of individuals within that unity.

FUNCTIONAL INDETERMINISM

We have noted that, of all the systems involved in human existence, the structure of experience is the most central. Its examination will help us understand individual diversity as well as some of the contributions the other systems make. To facilitate the analysis let us recall that the meaning of any relationship with the external world can involve four relatively distinct functions of the structure of experience: they are perception, thought, feeling, and intuition. Their differences and complementarity may be briefly summarized as follows.

Perception, involving the senses, the systems of perceptual paradigms, the system of concepts, the system of language, and the system of experience, is thought to be based on the process of differentiation. It yields an experience Gestalt (with or without a language Gestalt in the foreground or background) which does not mechanically depict the immediate situation. Because the process of differentiation is paradigm-based, it reflects and must be directed by the person whose being is enfolded into the structure of experience. The experience Gestalt does not exhaust the potential meaning of the relationship; it can be complemented by the other functions.

The function of thought based on the system of thought paradigms permits a person to shed further light on a relationship with the external world by placing some of its aspects in the context of other elements of experience past or present, real or imagined. Thought cannot relate experiences in their totality, so that a process of abstraction intervenes. It is able to shed light on aspects of a relationship that are inaccessible to the process of differentiation associated with perception.

The feeling function relates the experience Gestalt of a moment of our life to our existence as a whole or parts thereof as depicted in the metaconscious. The result takes the form of an emotion created by the system of emotional paradigms. We can feel something about the relationship as a whole. Interpersonal relations are highly dependent on the feeling function. It enables a person to evaluate an encounter with someone else against the background of previous ones with the same person, the experience Gestalts of which encounters have constituted a metaconscious image of that person and his relationship with him. By means of the feeling function, the metaconscious forms a background that goes beyond specific encounters to act as a sort of 'meta-social' structure which permits human relationships to take on a depth and continuity that would otherwise be impossible to achieve.

The feeling function helps a person determine her behaviour towards someone else by going beyond the meaning of the immediate situation. For example, someone meeting her friend may notice his reserved behaviour towards her. Rather than concluding that their friendship is deteriorating and responding coolly, she may feel that her friend is not himself and make a special effort to behave warmly towards him in order to gain his confidence and ask him what is wrong. She could, of course, have arrived at a similar conclusion by recalling previous encounters one by one and comparing them by means of the thinking function. It is clear, however, that in the course of an encounter this procedure would be impossible under the pressure of time. In our rational civilization, the feeling function is considered to be more developed in women than in men. This is possibly inborn or the result of extensive experience with young children with whom they often have to feel a relationship, particularly before the child has acquired language.

Another example of the feeling function would be when someone says to a friend, 'I feel this job might be really good for you.' He relates the job to the metaconscious image of his friend implied in his structure of experience. The entire relationship between the image of the friend (involving a great many experience Gestalts) and the job can only be felt, although he can also analyse the situation by unfolding something of his metaconscious image of the friend to obtain a sense of his friend's personality type and compare it to the skills required for the job. The feeling function complements the thought function.

The feeling function helps to produce a hierarchy of values. When two or more entities are compared as organized wholes, their relationship can only be expressed in terms of values. A person may remark that he feels this car is better than another without having used a process of thought which abstracts a number of common characteristics from each one of them in order to analyse them. Since an organized whole cannot be reduced to the sum of its parts, the functions of feeling and thought typically operate on two different levels, the former on the level of organized wholes and the latter on the level of the constituent parts or characteristics. The values generated by the feeling function interact within the structure of experience, which results in a hierarchy of values whose foundation we examine in the next chapter.

The fourth function – intuition – can alert us to an established relationship having further potential meaning in addition to that revealed by the other three. We intuit this potential when the experience Gestalt of the relationship appears to permit the formation or further development of a pattern of metaconscious knowledge. The intuition needs to be confirmed by thinking it out, which yields a series of further experience Gestalts that either confirm the metaconscious developments that led to the intuition or show them to be unwarranted. Like the feeling function, intuition is associated with the metaconscious.

The four functions can affect each other in a variety of ways. Intuition may guide the way attention is directed in a given situation, while an unfavourable feeling about it may lead to selective inattention. The functions of intuition, feeling, and perception may spur someone to think through a situation, and feeling or intuition may guide that process in a limited way.

It should be noted that, since the four functions are enfolded into a person's structure of experience, they are affected by any facet of that person's being. We shall give a number of examples.

Perception is frequently affected by concepts and prior experience associated with them. In daily life a person often gives something his attention just long enough to recognize it. Once he is able to name it, he knows what it is and there is no use in continuing to give it attention. In this process, he substitutes prior experience in the form of an idea associated with the concept for further perceptual attention – that is, he projects the idea onto what he recognizes. The collaboration of the systems of perceptual paradigms and the system of concepts is such that he is generally incapable of later recalling what he actually perceived and what he projected from prior experience. This was clearly demonstrated in an experiment in which subjects were presented with ambiguous drawings of things for very short periods of time. At the same moment the drawings were named. When subjects were later asked to reproduce them, they did so according to the kind of figure commonly associated with the name rather than according to the original figures.[14]

It might be expected that formal education would make perception more objective and factual by supplementing it with a more precise system of concepts and by teaching students what to look for and what to select perceptually. A simple experiment has shown that this is not necessarily the case. When experts were presented with a number of chest x-rays, they varied considerably in their interpretations. For example, one picked out 56 of them as indicating tuberculosis while another selected 100. When they received the same x-rays two months later, they made still different assessments.[15] Evidently, despite formal education, their structures of experience functioned quite differently and this functioning was not constant over time.

Expectations may also affect what a person perceives. Two groups of subjects were presented tachistoscopically with groups of letters such as 'sael' and 'wharl.' Those who were told they would be presented with words related to boats read the letters as 'sail' and 'wharf,' while those who were told they would be presented with animal names read 'seal' and 'whale.' Such results may also occur out of force of habit, as in the anomalous playing-card experiment.[16]

Motivation can also affect perception. When hungry subjects were presented with blurred pictures of food items together with other household articles at varying intervals after their last meal, they perceived an increasingly large number of items related to food up to about six hours of fasting. After this period there was a decrease, and also an increase in the number of times no response was given at all.[17] This is possibly due to the fact that, as the subjects became hungrier, their frustration increased to the point where they no longer bothered to respond. In another experiment, hungry and thirsty people perceived pictures of articles of food and drink as being relatively brighter than those in a control group did.[18] These experiments also occur outside the laboratory. When something has made a person extremely happy, she may experience the world to be brighter, either because she notices more bright colours or because she projects something of her feelings onto what she perceives.

In an investigation of the effects of reward and punishment on judgements of length and weight, the subjects were first asked to estimate them. In a second phase, the subjects were rewarded by being given money in association with certain percepts and it was taken away in association with others. When they were again asked to estimate length and weight, the subjects exhibited significant shifts in their estimations in the direction of the percepts which had been rewarded.[19] Perception can also be affected by one's beliefs and prejudices. When subjects were asked to read two short texts at a one-week interval, one being favourable and the other opposed to communism, the subjects having clear political convictions absorbed more from the text which matched their poltical beliefs.[20]

In a similar experiment, subjects were presented first with one and later another description of a factory worker which were identical except for one detail. In the first, the worker was described as intelligent, but this detail was omitted in the second. The subjects who were prejudiced against factory workers found it difficult to form an idea of the person described in the first portrait.[21] In both these experiments, the subjects were presented with an account of something which was anomalous in relation to a part of reality as they knew it or as they believed it to be. In the second experiment, the subjects could resolve the anomaly by 1) overlooking the fact that the worker was described as intelligent by selective inattention, 2) restructuring the portrait to render this personality trait insignificant, 3) rejecting the portrait as being incoherent, or 4) modifying their sterotypes of factory workers. These are just some of the means people use to protect their beliefs or self-esteem when they are threatened.[22]

This sample of typical experiments drawn from a considerable literature on the subject suggests the following conclusion about the functioning of a structure of experience. It is not organized according to a rigid hierarchy of its constituent systems. Instead it is a highly decentralized ensemble of systems, each of which carries out a set of operations. These operations complement one another in a variety of ways, permitting our structure of experience to interrelate all the different aspects of each moment of our life into a coherent experience Gestalt in the context of our whole existence. The four basic functions are the result of some operations collaborating more with each other than with other operations. Together the four functions are directed by our interests, motivations, and beliefs, even to the point of protecting us to some extent from information harmful to ourselves. In their functioning and collaborating, they are an expression of our person and our culture. Some attempts have been made to correlate the characteristics of the perceptual function to personality traits.

The way we internalize a situation and our response to it are never determined by the stimuli received by our senses, because of the contribution the 'inner' world can make to the experience Gestalt. We can intervene in instinctive reflexes or interrupt routine responses simply by contributing something of ourself, which then calls for a different pattern of self-organization of the structure of experience. This functional indeterminism of our structure of experience with regard to the external world establishes a certain distance between the world and ourselves. In animals this distance is significantly smaller, since the contributions of the 'inner' world are a great deal more limited and less varied owing to the larger number of instincts and no real self-awareness. The functional indeterminism of our structure of experience is the most powerful defence we have against all the external influences seeking to determine us.

It now becomes evident that the role of culture as a social ecology presents us with two contradictory but inseparable phenomena. On the one hand, it determines us by making us people of our time and culture, and, on the other, it provides us with a defence against becoming totally determined by our environment. Studies of persons in situations that leave the individual little freedom, such as prisons, mental institutions, or the assembly-line factory, bear this out. Assembly-line workers, for example, defend themselves against a highly monotonous, repetitive, and therefore meaningless environment by day-dreaming and fantasizing. There are, however, real limits to the resources of their 'inner' world, with the well-known disastrous consequences.

We have already noted that each moment of our life is lived by means of patterns of self-organization of the structure of experience. These patterns must relate our needs, motivations, interests, past experience, or any other manifestations of the self enfolded into the structure of experience to the experience derived from our material and social environment. The antagonisms that frequently occur between them must be resolved by giving some aspects of a moment in our life more weight than others, causing them to be included or excluded from the foreground of an experience Gestalt. As children grow up, they learn to develop, modify, and replace patterns of self-organization of the structure of experience to live as meaningfully as possible under the circumstances. The acquisition of paradigms of all sorts and patterns of metaconscious knowledge allow for a great deal of routine behaviour. However, the functional indeterminism of the structure of experience in relation to the external world makes purely mechanical routines impossible. Even during the most routine events, normal behaviour will vary because conditions originating from within have changed, possibly requiring the intervention of the creative, imaginative, and intellectual faculties. This intervention becomes anticipated in many of the paradigms.

The functional indeterminism of the structure of experience in relation to the 'inner' world can be demonstrated by using arguments analogous to those used for the basic functions related to the external world. This is not to deny the influence of the genetic system, but to recognize its limits. It rules out the possiblity of considering human beings as essentially rational because the intellectual faculties always function in the context of the structure of experience, reducing the rational function to the status of one among many. Neither are the structures of experience functionally determined by physical, biological, or culturally induced needs, which dooms to failure all attempts to explain human behaviour and history exclusively in terms of survival or the economic structures governing the production and distribution of what is necessary for human needs. The existence of a constant human nature is equally impossible, as is the belief in an infinitely adaptable and perfectible humanity.

The functional indeterminism of the structure of experience allows for the human person enfolded into it to unfold him / or herself by means of the will.

However, human freedom is a freedom from being totally determined by the various systems enfolded into human existence. It is dialectically related to powerful determinisms. Without them, human freedom would have no meaning.

SOME PSYCHOLOGICAL DIMENSIONS

The functional indeterminism of the structure of experience makes totally mechanistic relationships with the world impossible. Babies already unfold something of themselves in every relationship, and any stimuli that they cannot enfold into their beings are meaningless. They begin to establish a field of being within the symbolic universe of their culture. At the heart of this process lies the development of a structure of experience, which is the key to understanding how the 'natural' diversity created in each generation of human offspring by the genetic system develops into a cultural diversity of individuals.

The 'natural' diversity is affected from the very moment babies begin to develop structures of experience. At this point, all the other systems to which a structure of experience is open start making a contribution to a baby's individuality. These systems never play exactly the same role in the lives of any two babies; each lives a unique life. Consequently the 'building blocks' (internalized experiences) of their structures of experience are different. Even when they are older and have the same stimuli available to them, they will not interpret them in the same way. To be sure, they increasingly live in the same symbolic universe as the members of their speech community, and this places real limits on the diversity of meanings they can give to a set of stimuli. Yet a great deal of room remains for individual diversity. Their inability to give their attention to more than one thing at a time and their existence in time, space, a group, and a particular environment oblige children to select metaconsciously and consciously between complementary ways of interpreting each moment of their life. These choices begin to constitute individually unique patterns that permeate their existence and thus contribute to individual diversity.

We have at our disposal four basic functions for interpreting stimuli. They are essentially complementary in that they each in their own way can grasp something of reality that the others cannot as easily or not at all. Our finitude, however, tends to reduce their complementarity. They become alternatives to some degree. The interpretation of stimuli involves interrelating the four functions in the context of our being. It is limited by the experience of time, space, the group, and the environment. We need to examine this in some detail.

Take visual perception as an example. As a baby learns to use her senses, a variety of options unfold to her. On one end of the spectrum of possibilities, visual attention would be distributed over as wide an area as possible to examine something in all its relationships with its environment while, on the other end, all visual attention would be concentrated on the object alone to note each and every detail. Of course, a baby would generally function somewhere between these two extremes given a limited time before something else demands attention. She will learn to combine some of each of the two extremes in a unique way. In a group, she can be encouraged to pursue her curiosity for a shorter or longer time or she may be taught to observe things in more or less detail, and this too will oblige her to develop a certain style of distributing her visual attention as a compromise between the above two extremes. The nature of the environment also plays an important role. To survive in the jungle, for example, requires paying constant attention to the whole environment which is not as important if one grows up mostly indoors, as do people living in a very cold climate.

A similar argument can be developed for hearing. In the presence of multiple sound sources, one is also obliged to choose between taking in as much of the available information as possible or selecting one of the sound sources for detailed consideration. Each child learns to develop what psychologists call a cognitive style, although we shall use this concept in a somewhat broader sense.

The basic argument developed for perception can be extended to the function of thought. By means of thought, elements of a moment of life can be related to elements of other experiences, be they past or present, real or imagined. These additional relationships can affect the meaning of that moment of our life. Once again, the number of additional relationships that can be added by means of thought is potentially unlimited but restricted in real life. A person may not have the time to think a situation through or the environment may demand that attention be shifted elsewhere. As children are socialized by a group into the symbolic universe of their speech community, they may be encouraged to think things out and take a critical attitude towards their world or they can be encouraged to be the opposite – to accept the world 'as it is,' not ask questions, and take life as it comes. This may greatly affect the role thought plays in relation to the other three functions. If it plays an important role, immediate impressions obtained by means of perception are not that important. It is necessary to go beyond them to really understand the world. If it does not, immediate experience is valued more to enjoy the way things look, sound, feel, taste, and smell. Here again a spectrum of possibilities is open from which someone learns to make typical choices, thus extending their cognitive style to include a balance between perception and thought.

The argument can be extended still further to the functions of feeling and intuition. No person normally systematically exploits the full potential of all the four functions to come to the deepest possible understanding of a relationship. Most people delimit all the possibilities in unique ways. The causes for this delimitation in part come from the group and the environment. As a child, a person may have been encouraged to feel out their social relationships to become very sensitive to others or, on the other extreme, have learned to distrust these feelings and to be more 'rational' in this respect. As an adult, the person may learn to develop the feeling function further if she works with very young children or adults who are unable to articulate their needs. Similarly, as a child a person may have been encouraged to be creative and to take intuitions seriously. The opposite may also be the case, in which the individual regards intuitions simply as nonsense. Our cognitive style, therefore, tends to include a unique balance between what the four functions typically contribute to an experience.

While the challenges of existing in space, time, the group, and an environment oblige us to develop a particular cognitive style, the characteristics of our mind also have a substantial influence. There exists a diversity of ways in which paradigm-based operations can be carried out by the mind. This directly affects and is affected by the characteristics of the cognitive style related to perception and thought, while indirectly influencing the functions of feeling and intuition. Significant structural differences can occur between equivalent systems (composed of paradigms or concepts) of the structures of experience of the members of a culture. These differences are due to variations in the number of neighbours from which the average paradigm or concept is directly differentiated. This will be called the relational density of such a system.

The meaning of a paradigm or concept depends on the relationships it enters into. Each additional relationship adds a new dimension of meaning to it. In other words, the greater the number of neighbours from which a paradigm or concept is directly differentiated, the more the corresponding sensation, Gestalt, or concept will be rich in detail and meaning. This was illustrated by children learning to recognize four-footed animals. The larger the number of four-footed animals they learned to distinguish and the greater the range of circumstances in which they observed them, the more refined and rich in detail the sensations of the animals became. Experience leads children into an increasingly more differentiated world. A similar development occurs for their systems of concepts. It must not be concluded, however, that two children, even if they had the same exposure to four-footed animals, would develop clusters of perceptual paradigms or concepts of the same relational density. The chances of this happening are almost non-existent because the two children are likely to make different compromises necessitated by their existence in space, time, a group, and an environment.

Cognitive styles that attempt to take in as much of the available information as possible tend to emphasize the broad patterns and structures of experience and grasp details in reference to them. On the other hand, cognitive styles which select portions of the available information for detailed consideration tend to emphasize the details of the elements of experience at the expense of grasping the broad patterns. Neither tendency in its extreme form would permit a person to cope with the complexity and variety of daily life. People develop a habitual set of cognitive styles to meet the demands of a variety of situations. It is nevertheless possible to speak of a person's cognitive style because the range of his habitual styles generally shows a clear bias towards one or the other general tendency.

A person who customarily uses a cognitive style emphasizing the broad patterns of experience will develop the systems of his structure of experience related to the function of perception with a higher relational density than a person having a cognitive style emphasizing details. When the systems of a structure of experience related to perception and language have a high relational density, they are composed of what shall be called divergent paradigms or concepts. If, on the contrary, they have a low relational density their components shall be called convergent paradigms or concepts. The former systems are associated with a divergent cognitive style, but in the latter case they are associated with a convergent one.

To illustrate the consequences that convergent or divergent paradigms have on the functioning of a system of a structure of experience, consider a simple example. Suppose two people, one with a divergent and the other with a convergent cognitive style, enter a room with an unusual window which immediately attracts their attention. The person with the convergent cognitive style will carefully look the window over and notice its unique features. The person with the divergent cognitive style, on the other hand, will be more attentive to the window in its setting. He will therefore notice how well the window lights the room, how it integrates the room with the outside world, how it makes the room look larger or smaller, cosier or more formal, and so on. What makes the window unusual for him may not be its features in relation to other windows but the relation between some of the window's features and the room as a whole. Each person emphasizes different but complementary aspects of the perceptually available information.

When this incident is typical of how these two people tend to use their perceptual function, it is clear that the consequences of their cognitive styles are considerable for the systems of perceptual paradigms and for the way these systems in turn affect their perception. A window seen as unusual in itself is typically what is perceived by means of a system of visual perceptual paradigms with a low relational density, whereas a window seen as unusual in relation to its whole setting is generally what is observed via a system with a high relational density.

The structural characteristics of the system of perceptual paradigms interact with those of the system of concepts because they are built up and used in relation to each other. As a consequence, for the person with the convergent cognitive style the concept of window primarily symbolizes something that lets in light so that it is directly differentiated from doors. For the person with the divergent cognitive style the concept of window will symbolize different aspects of the same reality since the window is related to and directly differentiated from doors, walls, ceilings, and floors, while it is also associated with ideas like the atmosphere of a room in relation to the way it is lit and integrated with the outside world. However, the person with the convergent cognitive style will have noticed many more details of its appearance and construction than the person with the divergent cognitive style.

Since concepts also serve as instruments of thought, it follows that the relational density of the system of concepts affects the system of thought paradigms and vice versa. People with convergent cognitive styles tend to be convergent thinkers, while people with divergent cognitive styles tend to be divergent thinkers. The practical consequences of such differences are considerable. Divergent thinkers have at their disposal divergent thought paradigms that are broadly focused, making them applicable to a wide range of situations without any modifications. They will therefore have relatively few difficulties in relating widely varying data or recognizing patterns of similarity among different objects or events. They tend to have a potential for giving original solutions to problems because their thought paradigms can be readily interrelated in novel solution patterns. The price they have to pay for this facility is that the structural features of their system of thought paradigms could hamper them in precise, logical, and detailed analysis.

Divergent thinkers often do not compensate for the limitations of their thought function, but their feeling and intuition functions tend to be well developed. They typically have a strong creative potential but may experience difficulties in ironing out some of the precise details to make their ideas work. Convergent thinkers, on the contrary, will exhibit the opposite tendencies. Their precisely focused convergent thought paradigms can be applied to a narrow range of situations only, but their lack of generality is compensated for by a great precision in their application. They will have more difficulty than divergent thinkers in relating widely varying data or recognizing patterns of similarity among different objects or situations. They are less likely to come up with new solutions, but this limitation is somewhat compensated for by an ability to carry out a precise analysis of the situation. When all conventional ways of solving a particular type of problem fail, they are in a better position to analyse the situation to see why this is so and to do something about it. They are less likely to come up with radical new solutions, but they are able to push conventional solutions to their possible limits. While divergent thinkers can easily get stuck for lack of a new idea, convergent thinkers are able to carry on thanks to their ability to undertake a precise analysis. Divergent thought paradigms result in a greater creative potential, while convergent thought paradigms give rise to greater analytical potential.

It must not be concluded, however, that analytical potential necessarily excludes creative potential or vice versa. We have again sketched two extremes of a spectrum. The structure of experience of a person is able to execute both analytical and creative operations using the same system of thought paradigms. Neither should it be expected that the relational density is roughly identical for all the clusters of thought paradigms. Creative and analytical activities are only two of many possible ways of adaptive behaviour necessitated by situations that are not normal (in the sense this term was defined earlier). Particularly in a highly differentiated society, children may be encouraged to develop certain kinds of adaptive behaviour in the school, another kind in the home, and still another in the peer group. Hence different relational densities could develop in a number of clusters of thought paradigms if these clusters are primarily used for one of the environments only. Hence both convergent and divergent tendencies coexist in most people, but one of them typically predominates. However, these tendencies are influenced by a person's motivation, interest level, emotional condition, or any other expression of the self, with the result that considerable variations can occur from moment to moment and from activity to activity.

The socialization of children can greatly encourage or suppress convergent and divergent tendencies according to what a society perceives as necessary for its project of existence. We will consider a well-known phenomenon to illustrate how the educational system in a modern society tends to develop the genetically established individual diversity of each generation to reflect what society considers necessary for its continued existence. The systems of education of industrial societies expanded steadily during the twentieth century. This development moved psychologists to develop psychometric techniques to predict a child's likely performance in the school system.[23] Intelligence and achievement tests were devised to measure a narrow range of skills required in school and abilities unrelated to school tasks were largely ignored. The tests were composed of questions to which there was a standard right answer. The educational systems attempted to develop the capacity of a student to be able to give a variety of standard answers to a variety of standard problems, and teachers were generally biased against students who interrupted the planned classroom routine with questions that sought out new relationships or who responded to questions with non-standard answers. The situation implied that students conformed to what was presupposed about human nature in naive stimulus-response views of human behaviour.

The development of science and technology and the way they permeated an increasingly greater number of spheres of activities in the industrially advanced nations, particularly after the Second World War, led to rapid changes on all fronts. Everyone's daily experience was that yesterday's standard answers were not necessarily valid today or tomorrow. The world appeared to be caught up in rapid change which demanded much more adaptive behaviour. All this resulted in profound changes in the symbolic universes of industrial societies. They now implied a different view of human nature.

Psychologists who experienced the changes in the symbolic universe of their society became interested in creativity. These new interests were reinforced in the United States by the shock of the Russians launching their Sputnik which demonstrated a certain technological superiority over the Americans. The security of the nation in the face of Russian competition became increasingly seen as partly related to the state of development of the physical sciences and the creative and imaginative application of their results. Creativity became an educational and scientific bandwagon.

In psychology the research into creativity showed up the shortcomings of the stimulus-response model. Creative behaviour presupposes that something happens within the human mind that cannot be grasped directly by the traditional approach. Attention now had to be turned to what was happening in the mind. A number of mental operations were therefore isolated by means of factor analysis, and the intelligence and creativity of a person were derived from their scores on newly devised tests. These new tests drew a distinction between convergent and divergent thinking, which now became tested separately.[24]

In passing, we should note that above an IQ level of 120 there appears to be no correlation between a person's creative and intellectual abilities as measured by these tests.[25] This would appear to confirm what we said earlier, namely that divergent and convergent thinking are two possible modes of exploiting the system of thought paradigms. For creative excellence, a person must have a system of thought paradigms that has at least a certain intellectual capability. However, a person with an IQ level of 130 may be as creative as a person having one of 180.

The impact of the theoretical developments in psychology and the new awareness of the importance of creativity for a nation's security and economy were partly responsible for making divergent thinking synonymous with social usefulness and convergent thinking with being closed to reality in a way that was socially harmful. To be sure, these are extreme views, but they were part of a general trend which had a big impact on the school system. Schools now had to become 'progressive,' permitting the student to participate creatively in the classroom situation. The schools play an important part in moulding the 'natural' diversity of each generation into the cultural diversity required by the project of existence of industrial societies, particularly since the Second World War.

The tendency of people to be convergent or divergent in their perception and thought also affects the other two functions of feeling and intuition. Just as it is easier for divergent thinkers to relate widely varying data or to uncover patterns of similarity among different things, it will also be easier for their metaconscious to integrate elements of experience differentiated by divergent paradigms into metaconscious patterns of experience. This facility is particularly important for the patterns having greater metaconscious depths, since they integrate highly diverse elements of experience. The potential of the functions of feeling and intuition are therefore increased, provided the genetic system has endowed the brain system with the characteristics necessary to permit a high level of development of one or both of these functions of the mind. The tendency of paradigms to be either convergent or divergent therefore affects all the parts of the structure of experience and thus the four basic functions.

It is now becoming apparent that in one aspect individual diversity ranges from extreme convergent to extreme divergent modes of functioning of the structures of experience. The compromise individuals arrive at is probably largely determined by the genetic system. Whatever tendency the brain system may have, it only develops as the structure of experience forms in the brain. Consequently, the challenge of existing in space, time, the group, and an environment encourages or opposes whatever tendency the brain system may have towards either mode of functioning. To sum up the differences between the two, we might say that people with divergent tendencies emphasize the third dimension of differentiation while people with convergent tendencies emphasize the fourth dimension of differentiation. In other words, a convergent paradigm emphasizes the unity within its diversity, while a divergent paradigm emphasizes the diversity within its unity. People with convergent tendencies live in a neater and more clear-cut form of the symbolic universe than people with divergent tendencies. The latter will be more sensitive to its complexity and ambiguities and hence either have to learn to accept them or face a great deal of nervous tension and anxiety.

The way in which the brain carries out paradigm-based operations also affects a person's ability to learn. This accounts for important differences between individuals. The issue in psychology of how a child learns and individual variations in learning processes will be discussed only in relation to the present theory of the structure of experience. In view of the limited and highly fragmented knowledge about the functioning of the brain, we shall assume that the genetic system equips it with the ability to form and interrelate paradigms. Certain characteristic tendencies (such as forming convergent or divergent paradigms) can be expected to be present at birth. However, the experience of space, time, the group, and an environment affects a person's potential because the structure of experience (built up from experience) interacts with the brain (built up by the genetic system) and vice versa. Learning is an on-going process that coincides with experience. Each time a paradigm is used it learns something, provided it is not involved in the interpretation or generation of an endlessly repeated sequence of identical or nearly identical stimuli. We have cited evidence that, when the paradigms of a structure of experience cannot 'learn,' a number of defence mechanisms intervene to protect them, and that when these fail a deterioration in a person's structure of experience can occur. Learning is, therefore, as essential for a structure of experience as air, food, and drink are for the body as a whole. A constant flow of meaningful information is required to combat disorder and prevent deterioration.

The basic learning functions can be developed from the discussion in chapter 4. We shall first consider the learning operations on the level of a single paradigm. The most common learning operation is generalization, in which the scope of a paradigm is 'stretched,' enlarging the range in which it can operate. Generalization is delimited by a paradigm's neighbours in the system. When generalization goes too far negative interference may occur. In the case of a perceptual paradigm, it may interpret different sets of stimuli as being sufficiently similar to be enfolded by the same paradigmatic operation. The result is that some sets of stimuli are necessarily distorted since something of other sets of stimuli is imposed on them, causing a person to perceive two different things as being essentially alike. Further experience eventually rectifies the situation, obliging the paradigm to reorganize itself by breaking up to form two or more. In this case, positive transfer takes place, since some of the 'knowledge' of the old paradigm is transferred to the newly formed ones. The breaking up of a paradigm causes a sudden change in perception or permits a new mode of behaviour to emerge. A paradigm may be considered as a self-organizing way of performing a specific range of operations of the structure of experience. A paradigm always collaborates with others to enable a person to perceive something, to execute any form of behaviour, or to perform functions like thought. The paradigms associated with the most comprehensive tasks are the ones related to experience, language, and thought.

A great many situations or problems require the use of a sequence of experience, language, or thought paradigms that form a set when each paradigm in the sequence prepares for and leads to the next, welding them into a kind of 'super paradigm' related to a particular situation or task. Here again positive and negative transfer can occur. For example, positive transfer occurs when a person solves a problem by treating it like one he has already learned to solve, while negative transfer occurs when he cannot solve a problem because he treats it like one he knows, which prevents him from seeing it as being fundamentally different. Until he learns to see the problem in a different light, he will not turn to a different range of thought paradigms. For example, when given a postcard and asked to cut a hole in it large enough for a person to pass through, many people will have the idea of cutting the card into a spiral in order to make it larger, but they get stuck because they look for ways to keep the two ends of the spiral joined together. Once they look at the spiral as a strip of paper, the solution becomes obvious: all they have to do is cut a long slit down the centreline of the spiral leaving the ends intact, open it up, and pass through it.

The microlevel learning processes just described are the learning operations of one or more paradigms. They can therefore be affected only indirectly by the context in which they occur, namely the functioning of the structure of experience as a whole. In other words, they can be affected by a person's experience of space, time, the group, and an environment. We need only remember the case of the boy resocialized by Dr Itard to realize how fundamental a person's experience of a group is and how it affects the potential to learn inherent in his brain system. In previous chapters we have extensively described the influence the group has via language on the learning processes at the level of the perceptual paradigms of a child, but a similar influence can arise from ideas resulting from thinking, feeling, or intuitions, which in their turn can be influenced by the group.

Consider once again the case of negative transfer which prevents a person from solving a problem because she treats it as if it were fundamentally like a problem she knows. If she could see it in a new light other solutions might emerge because different paradigms impose themselves. Brain-storming is one of the means available to a group to help people see a problem in a new light. During a brain-storming session, the participants uncritically relate a problem to any 'solution' that comes to mind. Any of the suggested relationships may give the problem a new meaning and place it in a different light, enabling solutions to suggest themselves.

Here we touch on another aspect of a person's creative potential which is not directly dependent on her convergent or divergent tendency. A person may enact a kind of brain-storming technique in her own mind by permitting it to wander uncritically to create new relationships. To be sure, this process will be facilitated by a divergent tendency in her system of thought paradigms, but it is far from being dependent on it. An individual's personality is probably a much more crucial factor in determining to what extent she is able to do so creatively. This means that she defers working out a feeling or intuition about a new idea so as not to prejudice herself against it and to evaluate it only after having let it run its full course. The personality of some people may permit them to do this naturally, while others can be trained to do so to some degree. The latter possibility has been demonstrated by many experiments.[26]

Some experimenters have investigated the relationship between various personality traits and high creative ability.[27] To achieve creative excellence a person appears to require a strong divergent tendency and an above-average level of intelligence as well as suitable personality traits to exploit them. No direct correlation may therefore exist between creative excellence and extreme divergence. Studies of highly creative people do not prove that others do not possess strongly divergent tendencies, which because of their personality traits may remain undeveloped. Creativity is partly a matter of overcoming negative transfer.

Although paradigms are self-organizing, learning can be effective only when a person is presented with new material in a certain way or when he has learned to organize it himself. Sound teaching begins with something with which students are familiar. It then goes on to new material which is added to their structures of experience via existing paradigms. The process continues in a step-by-step fashion, since the teacher cannot assume any flashes of inspiration on the part of the students. This sequence of learning operations involves the expansion of existing paradigms and concepts or the creation of new ones. Failure to understand something occurs when a student can no longer relate it to his structure of experience. Analogues, models, charts, and similes are some of the means a teacher can use to facilitate understanding by 'stretching' existing paradigms. A sound pedagogy consists of making the best possible use of positive transfer in learning processes. Kuhn has illustrated the use of positive transfer in scientific education, where a physics student learns to solve new problems by learning to see them like ones with which he is already familiar.

In view of the fundamental importance of learning, it is clear that a person's inherited ability to learn and the way she learns to develop it is fundamental for her whole being. Living and learning go together. A person is at least metaconsciously aware of her capacity to learn, since it is implied in her prior experience. This awareness will have a considerable impact on her behaviour. It will affect her decision whether or not to undertake something, whether to resort to one or another kind of strategy to reach a goal, the self-confidence with which she goes about something, her attitude to new and unknown things which may require more learning, and so on. A person's convergent or divergent tendency may in some instances aid learning and, in others, render it more difficult. Neither tendency has a clear overall advantage. It follows then that people's learning abilities contribute substantially to individual differences.

We have seen how the cognitive style of a person includes a typical balance between the contributions made by the four functions of perception, feeling, intuition, and thought. However, each of these functions can be used in two complementary ways. They can be used to have people enjoy the world and express themselves by the way they act and live in it, which is the extrovert mode of functioning. They can also be used to get at the deeper meaning of experience and to enrich the meaning of people's lives by developing their structure of experience, which is the introvert mode of functioning. The extrovert mode is an out-going orientation while the introvert mode implies a relative withdrawal from the external world. Although the two modes are essentially complementary, the challenge of time and the demands of the material and socio-cultural environment (past and present) cause people typically to use one at the expense of the other. Extroverts tend to be influenced by their environment, which generally makes them practical, sociable, involved in interpersonal relationships, and interested in trying and manipulating things. People who, on the contrary, predominantly rely on the introvert mode tend to be unsociable and shy, preferring reflection and inner experiences to action. Extroverts largely take the external world as it is, while introverts tend to project a great deal of meaning derived from their 'inner' world onto it, making their four basic functions more subjective than those of extroverts. Introverts may also generate a great deal more nervous tension because things do not turn out as they had imagined or anticipated in their 'inner' world. Here again we find a source of individuality. People range from extreme extroverts to extreme introverts, with, at the centre, those individuals who have struck a balance between the two attitudes.

Another way in which people differ is related to the wholeness of their structures of experience. We have discussed the extreme possibility of a structure of experience breaking up into two or even three relatively autonomous parts to produce a double or triple personality. Between these extreme cases and a well-integrated whole structure of experience lies a range of possibilities. We are here concerned with the part of this range spanned by people whose mental health is considered normal. Within this spectrum, variations of wholeness in the structure of experience can occur because of its highly decentralized organizational character. It permits some parts of a structure of experience to overplay their normal roles by being excessively interrelated to other parts or to underplay their roles by not being sufficiently related to other parts. In the former case, the density of relationships with other parts is excessive, so that the corresponding meanings are distorted by over-emphasis, while in the latter case the density of relationships with other parts is insufficient, causing the corresponding meanings to be distorted by a lack of definition and clarity.

In all these situations the argument set out earlier – namely, that the meaning of a component in a system of a structure of experience depends on the relationships it enters into – has been extended to cover the case of entire parts of a structure of experience. A lack of wholeness in a structure of experience may develop in the course of a person's life. It causes a structure of experience to be divided against itself to varying degrees. The internal tensions that inevitably result permeate a person's emotional and psychic condition, and, when this process goes too far, mental health may be affected.

The reasons for a lack of wholeness in the structure of experience of a person whose mental health is considered normal can vary considerably because they reside in his whole existence. Consider the well-known causes of neurosis. Repressed infantile sexual impulses (studied by Sigmund Freud), the difficulties of mastering the infant's aggressive impulses (studied by Melanie Klein), a drive for power to compensate for feelings of inferiority (studied by Alfred Adler) presumably play a role in the lives of a great many people, but on a scale small enough so as not to cause neurosis. In such cases, a normal part of a person's experience takes on excessive proportions in relation to other parts. This results in a lopsided metaconscious image of the social self which affects a person's behaviour and consequently propagates the problem. At the same time, however, his behaviour represses something of his total self in the unconscious; he hides this from himself without being able to avoid the tensions it provokes. In many of these cases it is the experience of the group that brings about a lack of wholeness.

Jung, on the other hand, concentrated on neuroses appearing in older people for entirely different reasons, often related to unsuccessful integration of the different spheres of a person's life. This can occur in well-educated individuals who have read a great deal and thought they understood life. This knowledge may not correspond to the picture their metaconscious has built up of their own life and that of their culture. A conflict between who a person consciously believes himself to be and his metaconscious picture of the person he is and what his life is all about implies a lack of wholeness due to internal divisons of his structure of experience. A person who has spent the better part of his life on his profession overdevelops some parts of his personality at the expense of others. He develops his function of thought at the expense of other basic functions, which may lead to a feeling of emptiness and lack of meaning at a later age, because the structure of experience is insufficiently interrelated in some areas. A similar conflict between the conscious and the metaconscious can occur when a person's work is so void of opportunities to use his mind or to take initiative and responsibility that it brings about a lopsided development in the opposite direction. The price a society has to pay for excessive specialization in terms of wasted human potential is therefore bound to be considerable.

INDIVIDUALITY AND CULTURE

In the previous section we attempted to show that we are unable to exhaust all the resources of our structure of experience to get at the meaning of each moment of our life. Complementary ways of doing so often become alternatives and these may be severely limited under the pressure of time, space, the group, and the environment which threaten to determine us. From the very beginning, babies and children must constantly assert themselves against a variety of determinisms. As they enfold their being into reality they must continue to unfold something of themselves by making use of the functional indeterminism of their structure of experience. As they succeed in transcending some determinisms they encounter others, and they develop their being in reality in relation to them. This process leads, as an adjustment to themselves and the world, to the emergence of a personality which is both individually unique and yet typical of their social position, culture, and time. By asserting themselves in relation to the functional indeterminism of their structures of experience, their personalities include a compatible set of tendencies in the functioning of the structure of experience rather than one kind of tendency in one range of situations, another for a different range, and so on. Even the most routine actions unfold something of our personality, as is evident, for example, in the uniqueness of everyone's handwriting. We may say that activities permitting little or no expression of one's personality are alienating. When we cannot enfold something of ourselves in a relationship, we live it mechanically as a spectator and suffer the consequences that even a momentary destruction of the integrity of our being brings about.

The functional indeterminism of our structure of experience allows a personality to be enfolded into it as an integral part of the unfolding and enfolding of our being in reality. Hence, the psychological differences described in the last section must be interpreted as dimensions of personality.[28] It is then possible to systematize our findings in terms of the eight personality types described by Jung.[29] These are, of course, ideal types which serve as useful analytical instruments for understanding some aspects of interpersonal relations. The classification is based on two principal observations made by Jung. The first is that people tend to be predominantly either introvert or extrovert; and the second that most people are inclined to use their strongest and most basic function to dominate others. This second observation yields four types that can each be either introvert or extrovert, giving a total of eight ideal types. We shall discuss them only very briefly.

If the function of perception is dominant, people take the world as it comes. Thought, feeling, or intuition are used only occasionally to get at the deeper meaning of experience. What matters to these people is the simple pleasure of the experience, which can make them easy-going and pragmatic. What counts for the extrovert-perception type of people is what causes the experience, while for the introvert-perception types it is the 'inner' experience. Many artists and musicians are of this type.

People of the extrovert-thinking type are mostly interested in facts about the outside world and only concerned with ideas in so far as they derive directly from reality. They tend to be swamped by facts which they have difficulty relating in meaningful ways. To create some order they often resort to oversimplifying the facts. They are inclined to be strong in logic, have strong principles and a sense of duty, but lack warmth and tolerance and typically ignore what does not fit their ideas. The introvert-thinking type, on the other hand, tends to be interested in ideas and theories to give a deeper meaning to facts, and gather facts as evidence and not for their own sake. They are often convinced their ideas are useful to the world, although they may share them only with those they know well.

People who rely predominantly on their feeling function feel a situation, place a value on it, and behave accordingly. People of the extrovert-feeling type tend to be directed towards the world and hence at ease in their milieu, while people of the introvert-feeling type are often governed more by subjective factors than the external world.

Finally, people of the extrovert-intuition type tend to live through situations by means of their intuition. Consequently, what is important about the situation is its possibilities, and customs, traditions, and the feelings of others are less so. Once they are sure of the success of an idea, these people can often have difficulty persisting until they have worked out all the details. People of the introvert-intuition type tend to be preoccupied with the collective metaconscious rather than the outside world, which may make them mystical or prophetic about what is to come.

This basic classification scheme could be expanded by including other dimensions of individuality such as the degree to which a personality is well integrated and its strength. It can also be refined. Highly integrated personalities may use two functions rather than one to dominate the others. Many outstanding painters, for example, appear to have perceived something of what is to come by their introverted intuition which makes them sensitive to new patterns linking up in their collective metaconscious. They express something of these patterns by their introverted perception function. (It should be stressed that this classification scheme is largely based on the observations Jung made mostly of people of his time and culture. Its usefulness for non-Western culture or for other epochs may well be limited. This is particularly true when considering cultures in which personality development is related to somewhat different kinds of determinisms than those characterizing Jung's culture and time.)

The individual diversity in a speech community or a group is of vital importance for its existence. Different personality types often clash when they see only each other's weak points. However, there is also the possibility of different personalities complementing one another on a deeper level, and this is particularly important for maintaining the dialectic of relations essential for any group. To illustrate this point, consider the situation of two people who have watched a movie together. Had their structures of experience been exactly identical in content and mode of functioning, they would have nothing to say to one another. Each person would know exactly what the other had experienced so that any communication would be superfluous and with it all the unique human characteristics associated with language. They have things to say to each other precisely because they were born as unique beings which unfold to varying degrees due to their experience of space, time, the group, and the environment. Since both the content and functioning of their structures of experience are different, they do not experience stimuli generated by the movie in the same way despite the fact that they live within the same symbolic universe. The differences between their structures of experience are sufficiently large to permit meaningful communication but not too different to render communication difficult or impossible. This is what we mean when we speak of the diversity of their structures of experience remaining within the unity of their culture. The dialectical tension between the two people who watched the movie is due to the dialectical tension between their structures of experience, which is rooted in the experience of reality.

Individual diversity can play another role important for the survival and well-being of a group. We have seen that our links with the world are not direct, which implies the risk of losing contact with a changing reality. We have also seen that no individual exhausts the meaning of any relationship or phenomenon. It follows, therefore, that in a well-functioning group individual diversity converts a partial understanding of things into a more complete understanding by means of communication. If, however, there is inadequate communication, the tensions between individual members may grow to the point that individual diversity leads to the break-down of the group.

The role of culture as a social ecology allows individuals to interact, which creates, maintains, and adapts the diversity of their structures of experience within a cultural unity. Their symbolic universe is, therefore, not a fixed image of reality as it is known to them but a meta-language – that is, a symbolic structure that transcends language to interpret and organize a diversity of ways of experiencing things in a meaningful way. A symbolic universe supports this diversity while seeking to maintain a cultural unity.

We have here a partial answer to the problem of why the languages of even the materially most destitute people are enormously complex. A language must be able to designate symbolically the diversity of experience of the members of a culture, which means it must have a very large vocabulary. Different words must exist to designate many aspects of a constituent, event, or relationship of the symbolic universe. This is essential if a language is to be capable of expressing the differences in the ways the members of a culture experience a specific constituent, event, or relationship. A language with a limited vocabulary would be unable to express the dialectical tensions between the members of a culture that spring from their structures of experience forming a diversity within a cultural unity.

When we go beyond a particular speech community or group, the relation between the role culture plays as a social ecology and its relation to individual diversity becomes more complex. Because our links with reality are not direct, they require the mediation of a culture. In the same way, the links between a society and reality need to be culturally mediated. This means that the role of culture as a social ecology does not stop with giving meaning to the life of individuals. It must also make it meaningful for individuals to belong to their society. Hence the role of culture as a social ecology is inseparable from a way of life of a culture, which we have called a project of existence. It involves, as we noted, many dimensions of mediation. Individuals and their speech communities do not all participate in the project of existence in the same way with equal responsibility or power. The result is a social hierarchy of clans, tribes, castes, classes, or social strata. Individuals internalize the project of existence of their society from different social positions within this hierarchy. As a result their metaconscious patterns related to the project of existence will be highly detailed in some areas and less so in others. These differences greatly affect individual diversity. Individual differences arising from social diversity are not just a matter of a division of labour, however, in which different segments of society carry out various complementary functions necessary to maintain a project of existence. Functional complementarity is indissociably linked to antagonisms between segments of a society as a result of the exercise of power and accompanying exploitation, particularly when a society faces severe challenges.

Since culture as a social ecology plays an increasingly important role in the lives of children during socialization, it follows that some of their potentials will be developed and others suppressed according to the value they have for that part of the project of existence in which their speech community is engaged. Consequently, the 'natural' diversity is adapted to specific needs associated with the project of existence of a culture. The individual diversity of a society is, therefore, intimately related to its social diversity.

When we compare individual diversities associated with different cultures, important differences become evident. In everyday experience we observe this when we note that someone's behaviour is typical of his particular culture. We might say that associated with each culture is a unique cultural character which underlies individual differences. The term 'cultural character' refers to that part of a personality which is largely shaped by culture rather than heredity. We will consider only three such types found in Western societies. They are drawn from Riesman,[30] but we will reinterpret them somewhat by relating them to the way the members of a culture use their structures of experience in relation to the nature of the project of existence of their society.

People who have a tradition-directed cultural character tend to use their structures of experience primarily as a mental map. They act as though their structures of experience are not merely the result of internalizing their life in society but as though they were a normative map showing at the same time the past, the present, and the basis for the future. Consequently their structures of experience function as a 'natural' code of behaviour for all situations. This cultural character predominates in Western traditional societies whose projects of existence are designed to maintain the traditional ways of life. In these societies individuals do not seek to alter fundamentally this condition, and a better future is unthinkable. Individual potentials are used to make the best of the situation without essentially altering them. Because of their myths, traditional societies interpret change as being non-fundamental for as long as possible.

People who have an inner-directed cultural character tend to use their structures of experience less as a mental map and more as a kind of gyroscope. They generally have strong and well-defined goals designed to make them successful in the social order. The goals set the course for their lives, and they rely on their 'inner' resources to pursue them. This cultural character tends to be individualistic and not easily influenced by changes in the socio-cultural environment. It becomes common when a traditional project of existence begins to be transformed. Its members encounter many situations for which their structures of experience cannot function as mental maps. No one is entirely sure how to behave in the many new situations. Competing styles of life emerge, and some are clearly more successful than others. Although the new emerging project of existence may not yet be well defined, strong values and ideals are relied on to give direction.

The third kind of cultural character type is called other-directed. In this case, people tend to use their structures of experience more like a radar than a mental map or a gyroscope. They cannot turn to a tradition for guidance, and they experience values and ideals as being too relative to set the course for their existence. Instead they use their structures of experience to pick up signals from others and to shape their behaviour accordingly. What is uppermost in the minds of these persons is to be well adjusted to their social environment, and they constantly scan the reactions of others in order to be able to adjust their behaviour. Because they use their structures of experience as they do, these people are very flexible and able to live in a world whose complex and rapid changes they often do not understand. This cultural character is prominent in modern mass societies.

In Western civilization the tradition-directed cultural character type appears to have been predominant until the project of existence which characterized the last part of the Middle Ages began to make way for a new one. During this slow transition from a traditional to an industrial society, the inner-directed cultural character type came to be common, while the other-directed type emerged after the Second World War. Each of these cultural types was encouraged by certain ways of socializing children and the kinds of determinisms children and adults have to deal with. Before we can further examine the relation between individual diversity and the structure of a society, we need to focus first on society as a system.

SEVEN

Cultural Unity

INDIVIDUALS IN SOCIETY

In the previous chapters we have examined how the members of each new generation learn to mediate their relationships with reality on the basis of culture by unfolding something of themselves while enfolding their existence into the collective being of their society. The 'natural' unity and diversity present in each generation is transformed into a cultural unity and diversity of individual beings. This brings us to the study of cultural unity.

Such a study requires a shift in our frame of reference, thus far attached to the individual as the primary whole under investigation, to the next larger wholes, including society and civilization. It is important to be clear about the relationships between these larger social wholes. Just as the lives of babies and children are enfolded into those of the members of earlier generations, so also the lives of these members were and continue to be enfolded into one another within an institutional framework. Consequently, the social wholes constituted by the members of a society are also enfolded into one another. The structure and organization of a society refer to the ways in which a culture achieves this to create a cultural unity. It includes the way the structures of experience of the members of a society are enfolded into one another via groups and institutions as well as the flows and currents of ideas, opinions, theories, actions, and goods that help constitute and pass through the network of relationships.

In a society people interact within an institutional framework and relate to one another and the world by means of a diversity of structures of experience delimited by the unity of their culture. Cultural unity and individual diversity in a society are the result of two kinds of forces operating on a society. The first tends to increase individual and social uniqueness and hence diversity. If these forces went unchecked, individual differences would grow to the point where cultural unity would be eroded. The symbolic universe of the culture would fall apart first into various group worlds and ultimately into a set of private worlds. Communication between different groups and individuals would become increasingly difficult, leading to the fragmentation and collapse of a culture.

The forces of the second type create individual and social conformity and hence cultural unity. If these forces were not delimited by those of the first type, the members of the groups in a society would have little to say to one another. Each member would largely know what the others experience, think, or feel. The resulting break-down of communication would go hand in hand with the stagnation of various groups and eventually the whole culture, since the members would no longer feel that they belonged to the common unity (community) of a society. It is clear that a society cannot exist if one type of force dominates the other. There must be a constant tension between them. The tension between the forces that increase individual and social diversity and threaten cultural unity, and those that strengthen individual and social conformity and cultural unity at the expense of diversity, will be called the dialectic of a culture.[1]

The dialectic of a culture obliges a society to evolve and to have a history by preventing it from stagnating. In order to understand the threat stagnation poses to a society, we need to recall the fundamental importance of change for a structure of experience. Meaning is at the heart of the functions of the structure of experience. When the possibility of meaning is lost because of lack of change or endless repetition, a structure of experience defends itself as best it can. We have already touched on what happens if a person listens to a word repeated indefinitely or tries to say the same word for any length of time. Similarly, when there is no change in the field of vision (which can be achieved only under special laboratory conditions) what is seen may fade from view only to reappear later.[2] In daily life we have difficulty fixing our attention for any length of time on something that does not change, because attention weakens and inevitably shifts to other things, as explained earlier. Highly subdivided and rationalized work is monotonous, repetitive, and hence meaningless; it produces nervous fatigue.

Consider an extreme case of perceptual deprivation achieved in an experiment in which subjects wore translucent goggles, passing only a blur of light, and long cuffs which prevented them from touching anything.[3] The subjects lay on a bed in a room in which they could hear nothing but the monotonous buzz of machinery. At first they slept a lot, then they became bored and restless. They experienced loss of power of concentration which in some cases progressed to complete disorientation, thought became incoherent, and frequent visual and auditory hallucinations appeared. In another experiment the subjects were placed in a completely dark and silent room.[4] In this case, the lack of perceptual variation was replaced with nothing to be perceived, and there were few hallucinations and little change in thinking. Apparently, meaningful perceptions are essential for a structure of experience.

Consequently, even the most routine of human behaviour is never purely mechanical repetition. Some creativity and imagination is required to produce the variations. Life cannot deteriorate into endlessly repeated cycles. What is true for the individual is equally true for a society. Since its members are not directly linked to reality by means of stimuli, a society can exist only by means of a project of existence which is meaningful – that is, it must undergo change and have a history. This, however, creates an enormous potential for individual diversity to increase.

Consider the two types of forces involved in the dialectic of a culture. We have already seen that the process of socializing the members of each new generation into the culture of a society transforms their 'natural' unity and diversity into a cultural one. Once socialization is completed, however, the forces increasing individual diversity appear to be everywhere, while forces of the other type seem almost absent. As the members of a society go about their daily lives they will sooner or later encounter situations that are anomalous. They can deal with them only by creatively using the resources of their structures of experience which will enfold these situations into their being in new ways. To be sure, most of the adaptations made by adults in the course of their daily lives are paradigmatic extensions of their prior experience, concepts, and thought paradigms. But a great number of these adaptations, mini-inventions, and mini-creations can link up into new patterns of metaconscious knowledge that may break into consciousness. Systematic intellectual work can also create new meaning structures by placing constituents, events, and relationships of the symbolic universe into new contexts, which may be the beginning of new patterns of relationships. In all these cases, some aspect of one individual's structure of experience develops in a non-cumulative way and thus may diverge further from the structure of experience of other members of the culture.

It is quite likely therefore that, after individuals have been socialized, they may discover or create constituents, events, or relationships that are new to the symbolic universe of their culture. They may also come to look at parts of the symbolic universe in new ways and work them out by creating new concepts, ideas, or theories. If they keep these to themselves and if their actions do not reveal them, their findings cannot enter the symbolic universe directly. If, on the contrary, they pass them on to others, a process of diffusion could begin in which language is once again fundamental.

The flow of new discoveries, ideas, or theories along the network of social relationships of the culture is highly complex. When people become acquainted with something new, they must relate it to their structure of experience in order to understand it. Due to individual and social differences their reactions can vary considerably, even to the point of being complete opposites. As a result, individual and social differences are at least reinforced if not amplified. As far as the symbolic universe of the culture is concerned, anything new must be enfolded into it if its effect is to be lasting. This process begins with some individuals changing their thought and action in some respect, and when this spreads, some form of institutionalization may result. Whatever the new findings may be, they are not born in a vacuum but in a symbolic universe that has been made concrete in institutions embracing the many domains of a society. They will consequently be attenuated by this milieu as it proves to be an insurmountable obstacle to the implementation of some of their aspects, a moderate obstacle to other aspects, while facilitating the implementation of still others. The coherence of the symbolic universe could thus be progressively weakened.

Countless examples can be given. The theory of Keynes related in new ways some of the constituents, events, and relationships of the economic domain of the symbolic universe of the industrialized nations of the West.[5] His theory diffused only slowly at first, but when it was eventually implemented, it helped to transform the economic life of these nations.[6] It was inspired by the economic conditions of the time, which Keynes analysed; his creative faculties established a new network of relationships which, when applied, transformed the very conditions that inspired the theory.

The discovery or creation of anything anomalous with respect to the symbolic universe of a culture is, of course, not the only source of increasing individual and social differences. Just the fact that millions of people live together in a society while each person's life is evolving in ways that involve constant adaptation to situations that are never exactly identical to those of the past would be sufficient to undermine the unity of a culture in a matter of years or decades. To this we must add the disputes, conflicts, prejudices, and hatred that further divide the members of a society. Also, the exercise of power, often leading to exploitation, converts what might have been relations of individual and social complementarity into antagonistic ones.

When we begin to look for forces creating individual and social conformity and hence cultural unity, the first candidate that comes to mind is the unity created by socialization. Unless this unity is actively reinforced, however, it will be slowly eroded. Can the environment in which a society lives largely impose a project of existence and hence stabilize the symbolic universe associated with it? We will touch on this matter in the next chapter. For now we will simply point out that environmental determinisms cannot impose a cultural unity, at least not by themselves, since different societies have existed in the same environment in very different ways. Yet somehow a radical departure from the unity of a culture must be rendered almost unthinkable and virtually impossible to put into practice. Otherwise millions of people with all their differences would never be able to live together in a society.

This fact – that the members of a culture live in the same symbolic universe depicting the order and meaning of their being in reality – cannot account for cultural unity either. Even under the most ideal circumstances (where, by effective communication and the absence of relationships of power and exploitation, the differences between them become purely complementary and functional in mutual respect and love), cultural unity could not be sustained. Nothing we have noted thus far makes the order of that universe normative. The possibility of dissent remains, as does that of creating alternative ways of life. In addition, the regularity, order, and meaning which a culture experiences is subject to change partly because of the gap between reality and reality as it is known. Even those world views rendered normative by means of an ideology, philosophy, or theology never endure sufficiently long or are accepted widely enough to support the life of a society in reality.

The enormous complexity of possible activities that remain open to the members of a culture would, if they could freely choose from them, result in a chaotic diversity of experience developing in all directions. Instead of a process of cultural evolution, which presupposes a measure of unity, a process of cultural deterioration would take place because the diversity of the structures of experience of the members would increase without bounds until the cultural unity was completely eroded. Moreover, the limitations imposed by the symbolic universe in which the members of a culture find themselves are far from rigid. The effects that these limitations have depend in some measure on how the members perceive them and to what extent they bring their creative, imaginative, and intellectual faculties to bear on them to attempt their transformation. Whether certain conditions are seen as real limitations and are accepted as such or whether they are considered temporary because they can be changed depends on the structures of experience with which they are regarded. For example, the economic problems of the Western nations in the 1930s seen through the eyes of a classical economist or through the eyes of Keynes became two different things.

It is impossible to imagine a symbolic universe without norms and values because all thought and action would be equally good or bad, useful or useless, beautiful or ugly, and so on. In other words, it would be a universe without human life as we know it. Suppose that at each moment of one's life countless possibilities for action and thought came to mind, while there were no values to guide one's choice between them. Once a choice was made it would be just as meaningful as any other – that is, without any meaning at all. Choices could just as well be made randomly for there would be no possibility of meaning. Life would be a random sequence of events, a complete chaos, which would be existentially unbearable. Freedom would be unlivable. Individual existence would be impossible, let alone life in society. No stimuli could take on a meaning because they would simply be noise. Meaning, as we have seen, is related to order and regularity.

This shift in our frame of reference from the individual to society is beginning to reveal one aspect of the development of the structures of experience of babies and children that needs to be examined more closely. A society living within a symbolic universe requires collective values and norms to guide the lives of its members. These values and norms must be enfolded into the being of every person and their foundation must be unshakable. To explore how a culture might achieve this, consider the following analogy. The order of a symbolic universe must perform a function that in some respects may be compared to that of the rules of a game. Each game has a game universe comprising a 'material' domain (such as a room containing two chairs and a table with a chess board and pieces, or a football field, or a tennis court) and a 'cultural' domain, comprising the rules of the game. The order of the game universe encompasses both domains. In the chess game, for example, the rules assume that gravity will keep the pieces on the board, and the rules of tennis remain within what is physically possible. Since the 'material' domain of the game universe permits countless activities within the constraints that its material reality imposes, a person must be socialized into the game universe: that is, the domain of the possible bounded by the physical and physiological reality must be reduced further if a game involving two or more people is to take place. The players must know what they can expect from one another. They must become alike but also different. The rules of the game perform this function. Without determining the game, they delimit the sphere of freedom for thought and action within the game universe. Each player can creatively think of new game strategies and carry them out within this sphere of freedom.

If a game involves two teams, the rules must sufficiently delimit the number of possibilities of each player at each moment to allow one player to anticipate the strategy that one of his teammates is initiating, thus permitting the collaboration of the members of a team. The rules provide the players with an aim, which permits a large diversity of strategies by players and teams and allows competition between players of the same team as well as opposition between players and teams, all without disturbing the order of the game universe. Their striving remains within the same overall aim. The rules must also include sanctions against violations of the order of the game universe, which, if left unchecked, would threaten that order.

In a similar manner, the order of a symbolic universe must orient those who live within it by delimiting the sphere of possible activities and by providing guidance for choosing between the alternatives that present themselves in order to create a diversity within a unity. The order is effective only when the members of a culture are motivated to remain within it, so that those who go beyond its bounds receive social disapproval or are dealt with by a judiciary system. This means that violations must remain the exception rather than the rule.

The analogy between the order of a symbolic universe and the rules of a game is even more instructive when we analyse its limitations. One has the option of joining a game, and doing so implies a voluntary submission to the rules. This is not the case for a society into which one is born. Furthermore, the diversity of activities guided by the order in a symbolic universe of a society is qualitatively different from those guided by the rules of a game. To attempt to formulate the life of a society in terms of a set of rules is impossible. Even if we accepted that an explicit social contract could be formulated, it is clear that each member of the society would have to be an amateur lawyer to cope with it, not to mention the problem of transmitting it to each new generation and of enforcing, elaborating, and updating it. There is another difficulty. If the members of a society simply established an explicit social contract for their life, they might feel free to withdraw from it if it began to impinge too severely on their interests, beliefs, or convictions.

They might then wish to enter into another contract. A subsociety might emerge, which in turn might break up if another dispute arose.

If the order of a symbolic universe of a society is to be effective in maintaining cultural unity, its foundations must be laid in the metaconscious of children as they are socialized into a culture to act as a kind of internatized guidance system in relation to which they develop their personalities. As a result, alternative courses of action would cease to be of equal value and hence of no value at all, while others would become unthinkable. The metaconscious foundations of the order of a symbolic universe would give it a radically different character from the rules of a game.

If we suppose that the foundations for cultural unity are formed in the metaconscious of children as they are being socialized, the gradual reduction of their playful openness to the world can be explained. Their metaconscious, which points them to deeper and deeper levels of meaning, begins somehow to exhibit the foundations of the culture. At this moment their playful openness to the world decreases sharply, to be replaced by a relational potential. It specifies a fairly stable realm of things, events, and relationships to which they can meaningfully relate. Beyond this horizon nothing meaningful can be experienced. These limits are, of course, not fixed for life. They are constantly shifting in time, contracting on some fronts and expanding on others. The gradual transformation from a playful openness to the world to a fairly stable relational potential is most clearly manifested by the fact that, once socialization is complete, they experience the symbolic universe of the culture as reality itself. Of course, they know that they do not know everthing about that reality, but the unknown is no longer threatening. It can extend their symbolic universe or add details, but it cannot radically call it into question. The symbolic universe of their culture has become the one and only real world. Everything either has or can be given its proper place within it. Given the extraordinary diversity of symbolic universes in history, each of which have supported the lives of millions of people, we are led to the conclusion that somewhere and somehow the structures of experience of the members of a culture must metaconsciously *absolutize* their experience of reality. In other words, the symbolic universe of a culture must imply a going beyond experience to exclude anything that cannot be related to its order. This order would thus be firmly founded, and everything could be valued in relation to it.

Before we examine the kinds of developments in the structures of experience of children that pave the way for the above state of affairs, we need to note that because of individual and social diversity the relational potential of a culture is greater than that of its individual members. The way it can make use of it depends on how well it can exploit individual diversity by means of its social structures and institutions. This also sets limits for the sphere of the dialectic of a culture, although these are, as we will see, by no means the only ones. For example, when the European settlers killed off the bison in North America and took over most of the land, the project of existence of many native people was destroyed along with the dialectic of their culture. The limits of what was possible for the culture to absorb had been exceeded. We will return to this problem in the next chapter.

When a society is evolving normally, its relational potential shifts constantly. If the members of a culture resign themselves to the situation in which they find themselves, thinking that it determines their fate, they risk stagnation and eventual collapse of their culture. The motivation to cope intellectually and creatively with the situation is lost, with the result that the forces tending to increase the diversity of the structures of experience of the members of the culture are weakened and largely paralysed, and the capacity of the culture to relate meaningfully to a complex and changing reality is reduced. The members of a culture must be protected from an excessively fatalistic interpretation of their situation. Within the symbolic universe, a culture must provide its members with a reason for living and motivate them by means of a project of existence. When this happens, the challenges a culture faces will stimulate the creative, imaginative, and intellectual faculties of its members, causing the diversity of their structure of experience to increase, thus enhancing the culture's chances of meeting these challenges.

THE EXISTENTIAL FIELD

Because of the way the lives of the members of a society are enfolded into each other, particularly via the patterns of the collective metaconscious, we may speak of a collective existence. Cultural evolution is the unfolding and enfolding of that collective existence. Its modes cannot be generalized or schematized. They are as diverse as the cultures that have appeared in history. There exist no universal forces that maintain cultural unity or that weaken it. Any force of either type becomes what it is in relation to a symbolic universe. Is it possible then to form a generalized view of what cultural unity is? Yes, if we consider cultural evolution in terms of the way a society relates to reality. The evolution of a culture implies a journey through time and reality. A society is engaged in living in a reality that it neither entirely knows nor dominates and where the reality constantly imposes itself. We mght say that every society must build a home in reality or, rather, it must pick up the building of that home where the members of past generations have left off.

The symbolic universe of a culture may be regarded as its home within reality and time. For this to be possible, the structures of experience of those living within it must include an 'existential' basis that performs four principal functions: 1) to lay and secure the foundations of the culture's home; 2) to provide a plan which the members of each new generation can use to repair and maintain their cultural home, to replace parts that are no longer occupied, and to alter and expand it to suit new needs without undermining its structural soundness or overloading its foundations; 3) to bind the members of a culture together by making their existence inseparable from their cultural home so that they will not abandon it to adopt or construct another when difficulties arise; and 4) to exploit the potentials with which individual members are born to create a diversity of skills within the unity of the task of maintaining, modifying, and expanding their cultural home in reality.

There must, as we have argued previously, be order in the home of a culture. All the functions of the structures of experience of the members of a culture must be carried out in relation to this order. If this order was enfolded in the structures of experience of the members of a society, it would form the immediate context for all functions, including creativity and imagination. All thoughts and actions would emerge in relation to this order, and all constituents, events, and relationships that are new to the symbolic universe of the culture and all new ideas and theories of any kind would be interpreted and evaluated in relation to it. This would include the metaconscious images of oneself and society. In other words, if the structures of experience of the members of a culture contained an order in relation to which all their experience and activities of any kind were initiated, executed, and interpreted, the evolution of a culture would become a coherent complexity of activities within the cultural home. Such an order of the symbolic universe would then constitute a powerful force able to establish and maintain the unity of a culture.

Another analogy can clarify the way a society relates to reality by means of its culture. The collective being of a society constitutes a kind of existential field that may be compared to a magnetic field. The process of a child's socialization into a culture may be considered as rendering his structure of experience 'magnetic' in relation to the 'existential field' of his culture. The direction of his existence aligns itself relative to that field just as the needle of a compass aligns itself to the earth's magnetic field. He is able to change that alignment by means of a force that originates from his creative, imaginative, and intellectual faculties or through the influence of others who have managed to realign their existence. Any such realignment must be maintained if the cultural field is not to return the alignment of a person's existence to a direction compatible with the field. This phenomenon is analogous to the one where the needle of a compass realigns itself to the earth's magnetic field when someone's finger no longer deflects it in a different direction.[7]

The cultural field is generated by the existential fields of the structures of experience of its members. If a group of members realigns their existence in a new but similar direction, they form a subcultural field that makes it easier for those who live within it to maintain their new existential orientation in spite of the fact that the subcultural field continues to interact with the cultural field. This interaction can lead to a realignment of either field. In other words, the evolution of a culture is not a sort of tug-of-war between the forces that increase the diversity of the structures of experience of the members of a culture and the forces that attempt to maintain cultural unity. The structures of experience are normally aligned in the direction of the cultural field, and it is only by the application of some force that they can be aligned differently. When this force is withdrawn they tend to return to an equilibrium position of being aligned with the cultural field. Since this field is dynamic as a result of cultural evolution the new equilibrium position is not necessarily the same as the former one.

When we put these two images of culture together, the double function of the structures of experience of the members of a culture becomes clear. The members of a culture are placed within a cultural home in reality and provided with an existential compass that shows them how to live in it. The existential basis of their structures of experience makes both these functions possible. In order to understand how it performs them and how it is constituted, we will consider the micro- and macro-level stability of a structure of experience as it performs its multiplicity of functions. This will lead to an understanding of what constitutes the order of a symbolic universe and the existential basis. We begin by examining the micro-level stability.

We have already shown that the meaning of each component of the systems that together constitute a structure of experience depends on its neighbours in the system, with the result that any sphere of experience is differentiated and endowed with meaning via a cluster of interacting components. The local or micro-stability of the systems is assured because of these structural features. We have already touched on this matter in relation to the variations that can occur in the ways different cultures differentiate colours, and why once a particular way of differentiation is acquired by a process of socialization it tends to remain unchallenged. Another example of the micro-stability of the structure of experience is the playing-card experiment. Had the subjects been exposed to the anomalous cards with less persistence, they would not have noticed them. Another remarkable example comes to us from paintings. A certain way of picturing a galloping horse was handed down from civilization to civilization for over three thousand years, until it was proved in 1879 by means of photography that in fact this particular gallop did not exist.[8] It is impossible to assert, therefore, that the micro-stability of the domains of a structure of experience that derive most directly from experience is due to their undisputed factuality. Yet in the absence of anomalies, these domains are borne out in daily-life experience allowing us to live as if reality coincides with reality as it is known.

The situation changes somewhat with those domains of the structure of experience that are abstract and whose relationship with experience is more complex. Very few people will have the occasion to debate if the colour blue that they are looking at is really blue, but nearly everyone has debated if her own or another country is democratic in relation to some issue, or has discussed what democracy really is. Particularly when cultural evolution is obvious to everyone, equivalent domains of the structures of experience of different individuals will exhibit a diversity within a unity. This is part of daily experience. These domains are not experienced as being purely factual, consequently they more readily invite intellectual scrutiny. For them, the diversity of the structures of experience of the members of a culture must be sufficiently delimited so that their unity can be taken as being reality itself. The unity underlying the diversity must, therefore, form a stable foundation that appears sufficiently factual and self-evident so as not to attract the daily-life attention of people's creative, imaginative, and intellectual faculties.

Whether the components of a system derive from experience directly (such as the visual perceptual paradigms of colours) or indirectly (such as the concepts designating forms of government) they are suspended in equilibrium positions determined by the third and fourth dimensions of the process of differentiation operating between themselves and their neighbours in the system. When we use the simple spatial model of the systems of a structure of experience developed in previous chapters, the situation may be pictured as follows. The larger the diversity of a particular component of the structures of experience of the members of a society, the larger the locus of possible equilibrium positions on the system surface will be. The locus of equilibrium positions may thus range from a point to a small area on the surface. The area is delimited by the areas of neighbouring components. Whatever the case may be, any component together with its neighbours constitutes a structural equilibrium. This protects the components from arbitrary or ill-founded changes, thus ensuring the micro-stability of a structure of experience.

This micro-stability is further reinforced by the fact that a particular component in one system interacts with the components of other systems. We have already seen this for the perceptual paradigms within various dimensions of experience that derive from the same constituent, event, or relationship in the symbolic universe and the corresponding concepts in the system of concepts. The systems of a structure of experience mesh in such a way as to reduce an unintelligible complexity of stimuli into an intelligible complexity of experience. Consider once again the example of a person's experience of the world of four-footed animals. If the stimuli from these animals are to be interpreted consistently, the clusters of relevant perceptual paradigms in the various dimensions of experience must differentiate these animals in compatible ways. For example, a person's visual and aural sensations of dogs must be associated with and only with the concept of 'dog.' Otherwise the experience of hearing a dog's bark and then seeing it come around the street corner would not make sense. Similarly, the cluster of concepts of four-footed animals can only have their value if they simultaneously represent perceptual differences between these animals and the different relationships they have with their natural milieu, other animals, and people. A person's countless experiences with four-footed animals become an intelligible complexity by the way the various systems in the structure of experience mesh. The experience Gestalts of an animal are integrated by means of a concept. The concept symbolizes each animal's nature, biological structure, and relationships with the other constituents of the world as being distinct from that of other animals. The cluster of concepts of four-footed animals is an instrument to reduce a person's experience of the world of four-footed animals to an intelligible complexity.

The external consistency of the various systems that comprise a structure of experience is due to the way they mesh as they are developed and utilized. It is clear that the meshing of these systems further reinforces the equilibrium position of each system component and consequently the micro-stability of the structure of experience.

The micro-stability of a structure of experience does not ensure its overall or macro-stability. It makes a person relatively resistant to anomalies that necessarily occur between the symbolic universe of the culture and reality. However, there remain many other ways in which the micro-stability of a person's structure of experience can be disturbed. We have already studied them for the period of a person's life during which she is socialized into a culture. To be sure, the frequency with which the micro-stability of her structure of experience is disturbed drops off sharply towards the end of that period, but incidents of that type continue to occur. When they do they can present a serious threat to the macro-stability of her structure of experience. The person's attitude towards incidents of that sort has changed. She no longer lives playfully in her world which as a child she knew not to be coextensive with the world of adults. The reaction of the subjects unable to identify the anomalous cards in the playing-card experiment illustrates this point quite well. In that case, the anomaly was part of an experiment. In daily life, somewhat similar situations may occur. A person may then think her senses are fooling her, begin to doubt the sense of something, or even question the meaning of her life. These reactions are quite foreign to children. The result is that an adult may follow up an incident, in which the micro-stability of her structure of experience is disturbed, with her creative, imaginative, and intellectual faculties. In such a case, a disturbance of the micro-stability can easily lead to a large-scale disturbance or to a disturbance of the macro-stability in an extreme case. The reason is that the structural features that provide a local stability can also propagate a disturbance through the whole system. When a change in a component imposes itself by disrupting the micro-stability, the component's neighbours can be affected, which may in turn affect their neighbours and so on. A chain reaction can be produced when these successive disturbances are worked out by experience and thought. In extreme cases this can lead to political, religious, or ideological conversions.

The price we have to pay for the micro-stability of our structures of experience is the risk of disturbing their macro-stability. Conversion experiences take a great deal of effort to be worked out because they change the world in which one lives and the meaning of one's existence in it. To be faced with this possibility even on an occasional basis would be existentially unbearable. Furthermore, for a culture this situation would be catastrophic because the unity that delimits the diversity of the structures of experience of its members would constantly be broken.

The structural features that ensure the micro-stability of a structure of experience pose another potential threat to its macro-stability. The meaning of each system component is to a certain degree circular because it depends on all the other components, while their meaning in turn depends on its meaning. The meaning of each component is therefore relative rather than absolute, since it has its being only in its relationship to all the others and not in itself. Yet if a culture is to endure – that is, if a unity within the diversity of the structures of experience of its members is to be maintained – this relational circularity must be broken to reduce the probability of conversion experiences, which are the primary threat against the macro-stability of a structure of experience. It is for this reason that every culture has had to introduce an absolute into its symbolic universe, to form the foundation of its home in reality.

MYTHS AND THE SACRED

To recognize the need for an absolute within the symbolic universe of a culture is only a first step on the way to discovering how this absolute functions. It must be internalized into the structures of experience of the members of a culture. But how? Each component of a structure of experience examined thus far has not been absolute because it depended on the others for its meaning and function. To resolve this apparent impossibility, let us recall some of the basic features of a structure of experience. In previous chapters we have insisted on the fact that sensations, Gestalts, experience, and language Gestalts take on their meaning by being placed in the context of a larger whole. In other words, the macro-stability of the systems within the structure of experience ultimately depends on the largest context in which they operate. Consequently the macro-stability of the structures of experience of the members of a society depends on the patterns of metaconscious knowledge having the greatest depth.

We have called these patterns the collective metaconscious since they are shared by members of a culture and because they reflect something of the 'nature' of human cultures. Since the meaning of all experience of the members of a culture is directly or indirectly incorporated into these patterns, they may express the very basis of a culture. They embrace everything that has a meaning for a given structure of experience and nothing has a meaning outside these patterns. For a culture, they form the ultimate context in relation to which everything appears to have its being and outside of which nothing is. These patterns also tend to depict what permitted their formation – namely, what the meanings of all domains of experience have in common as parts of the project of existence. They point to a culture's meaning of meaning, which could, if certain conditions are met, function as an absolute for a culture. It is in reference to such an absolute that a culture could order its existence in reality and establish its cultural unity, because outside this absolute nothing could take on a meaning. The collective metaconscious constitutes the skeleton of the body of experience of the members of a culture. We are now very close to identifying the foundation and structure of a culture's home in reality.

The patterns of the collective metaconscious as we have described them thus far require something more before they can constitute the cultural unity we are looking for. We are still faced with the threat of the relational circularity of a structure of experience. This circularity needs to be broken precisely on the level of the patterns of the collective metaconscious because these patterns increase the probability of a micro-level disturbance growing into a conversion experience. The very scope of the patterns of the collective metaconscious that embrace the totality of a culture's experience causes them to be vulnerable. Any event or discovery that cannot be incorporated into them might eventually threaten them because it cannot be related to them. The coherence of these patterns can be challenged, thus endangering the macro-stability of the structure of experience. They must therefore be protected if a culture is to endure.

The patterns of the collective metaconscious do have a certain capacity to defend themselves. By being located at the very depths of the metaconscious they are beyond the reach of our intellectual faculties. They can be threatened only by anomalies slowly filtering into the metaconscious via the systems of a structure of experience. Most events in our daily lives are of a short duration and affect few others. They contribute to those patterns of metaconscious knowledge having the least depth and are located just beyond the surface of consciousness. Other events endure much longer and affect a great many phenomena in a society. Examples are economic recessions or wars. These events can penetrate much greater metaconscious depths. Finally there are still more fundamental events which may last a century or more and which involve fundamental changes in the project of existence of a society. These can be understood only by going still further beyond immediate experience. These events affect the patterns of the collective metaconscious and hence the way a culture regards itself and its existence in reality. For example, this happened at the end of the Middle Ages in Europe. It also occurs when any traditional society industrializes. Cultural evolution involves the reciprocal interaction of all these levels of change.

The evolution of a structure of experience may be compared to some of the phenomena that occur in a large body of water. At the surface it is greatly affected by everything that goes on in its environment: storms may whip up large waves, but as one goes a little way underneath the surface things rapidly get calmer and, near the bottom, the water is undisturbed. There is a dynamic stability there that appears not to be greatly affected by what goes on at the surface. What is true for the evolution of a structure of experience is equally true of the evolution of a culture as a whole, since the latter is reflected in the patterns of the collective metaconscious.

Suppose now that an anomalous phenomenon begins to penetrate a structure of experience. Even if it has a sufficient scope to reach the deeper patterns of the metaconscious, its impact will be moderated by the fact these patterns become less sharply delineated as their depth increases. This is the case because they represent a diversity of experience within a cultural unity and because one set of patterns is typically disintegrating as a new set is linking up. Furthermore, as the phenomenon is differentiated and integrated into a structure of experience, its anomalous character is attenuated as it enters into different relationships. As we have already noted, any constituent, event, relationship, idea, or theory is interpreted by being related to the structure of experience so that its meaning is a function of both its proper characteristics and those of the structure of experience. The patterns of the metaconscious thus tend to align the meaning of elements of experience to be as compatible with them as possible. The most comprehensive patterns (the collective metaconscious) affect every interpretative function of the structure of experience. The result is that they never encounter anomalies directly. Since these patterns change only very slowly in comparison to the flux of daily experience, they form a framework for the interpretation of and involvement in these experiences. In order for them to constitute the basis for cultural unity, the mind must modify their character. How this may be done becomes evident when we examine some of the characteristics of the patterns of the collective metaconscious.

If a culture is to have a future, the patterns of the collective metaconscious of its members as derived from internalized experience must be open-ended and incomplete. They are in effect fragments of patterns. Only when a culture is beginning to stagnate and repeat itself will these patterns exhibit a tendency to become closed and complete in themselves. Under all other circumstances, the fragments of patterns will be more or less developed depending on the corresponding development of the project of existence. They will be relatively embryonic when the project of existence is undergoing a major transformation and more highly developed if the project of existence is already well established. If a society is to have a future, however, the patterns of the collective metaconscious must not merely be incomplete; they must exhibit a tension between themselves, thus forming the metaconscious foundation for the cultural dialectic. These two characteristics are a threat to cultural unity because they allow for a variety of courses of cultural evolution. The patterns of the collective metaconscious must therefore be extended and unified to imply only one possible course of evolution. This extension cannot be derived entirely from internalized experiences; hence something more is required.

Another characteristic of the patterns of the collective metaconscious becomes evident when we recall the two complementary modes in which a structure of experience determines the meaning of a person's existence. The systems of a structure of experience organize and integrate the dimensions of experience by means of processes of differentiation, while the metaconscious integrates the results of these processes into patterns. The deepest patterns constituting the collective metaconscious take distance from the subjectivity of personal experience. They appear as objective by the members of a culture. Both modes of structuring experience affect the interpretation of subsequent experience. Despite their complementarity, there exists a tension between the micro- and macro-stability of a structure of experience. This tension causes it to evolve beyond what is necessary to interpret the immediate experience of daily life. Its evolution takes the form of a reciprocal interaction between the systems that result from the processes of differentiation and the patterns produced by the processes of the metaconscious. Their mutual conditioning attempts to eliminate any possible contradictions, but this can never be entirely achieved.

It is evident that due to these internal tensions the metaconscious will attempt to include all experience in a set of patterns which, depending on their scope, will reside at different metaconscious depths. We have already noted that the patterns of the metaconscious are incomplete and that they cannot be closed. They are really only segements of patterns. Due to the cultural dialectic, these segments that have been formed cannot simply be extrapolated to meet each other across remaining gaps. All that can be expected is a series of pattern segments that have been oriented as much as possible into a configuration, but gaps, contradictions, and areas of ambiguity remain. The situation would remain this way if the existential basis of the structure of experience did not intervene. If a culture stopped here, it could not withstand the forces that threaten its cultural unity because it is in a real sense already internally fragmented. To withstand the test of time a culture must not be divided against itself; it must be whole or at least appear to be whole to its members. The endurance of cultures over long periods demonstrates that the human mind has to a very large measure been able to overcome these obstacles.

Due to the tensions between the two complementary modes of getting at the meaning of experience, the human mind extrapolates, adjusts, and smooths out the segments of metaconscious patterns to arrive at an internally relatively coherent system of patterns. Those of the collective metaconscious are the most comprehensive. This is achieved by a system of myths, which are an indispensable part of any culture. Myths explain what reason or experience cannot explain, they mediate the problems of a culture, they make permanent the existence of a culture and human existence in it, they influence the culture's situation although they were constituted by it, and they can form a global motivating image. Myths extend the symbolic universe into a global image outside of which nothing can exist that could serve as a point from which the members of a culture could launch a critique against it. All these characteristics of a system of myths[9] are exactly what is necessary to gain a relatively coherent and closed set of metaconscious patterns of experience including those of the collective metaconscious.

To illustrate this point, consider the simple analogy of a scientist performing an experiment. When he plots the results on a graph the points might form two curved segments and a few scattered points. When extrapolating the curved segments towards one another they appear to form a parabola, and the scientist deduces that the parabola shows the relationship between the two variables. The scattered points have now become noise or stray points for which he can usually find some reasonable explanation. In doing so, he has gone beyond his experimental evidence but at the same time has strengthened his confidence in the data because they now exhibit a completed smooth curve.

A system of myths performs much the same function. It goes beyond the body of experience of a culture and in doing so it does not weaken a culture's confidence in it but on the contrary strengthens it. Since the pattern segments on the different levels of metaconscious depth must be operated on simultaneously and systematically, myths never occur in isolation from one another. They must form a system that operates simultaneously on all levels of the metaconscious ranging from the collective metaconscious to the commonplaces, ready-made images, ideas, and formulas that are far from being based on experience only.

We have demonstrated earlier that the patterns of the collective metaconscious tend to reveal the ultimate context in relation to which every aspect of the life of a culture takes on a meaning. This meaning of meaning becomes transformed into an absolute by the system of myths. Everything in a culture derives its meaning from it, and outside of it nothing is. It appears as a kind of providence which for traditional societies is called a 'sacred.' We will also use the concept to designate the equivalent in modern so-called secular cultures.[10] In an interrelated reality nothing can exist in itself, independent of everything else. The only possible exception would occur if there existed a transcendent being. Hence, if the meaning and function of something in the structure of experience of the members of a culture has a meaning in itself, we know that a system of myths must be involved. A sacred supported by a system of myths breaks the relational circularity of the structures of experience of the members of a culture.

At this point a strange reversal takes place. No longer are the sacred and the system of myths necessary extensions and projections of the body of experience of a culture, but it is as if they existed before and outside the culture that created them. They no longer appear as necessary creations of the metaconscious but as absolutes that give everything its meaning. Rather than being self-evident projections and extrapolations of experience into domains unfathomed by it, they appear as what made possible and what ordered that experience in the first place. It is precisely this reversal that permits the sacred and a system of myths to constitute the foundation of the symbolic universe of a culture and to order everything within it.

For the sacred to be an effective foundation and support-structure for a culture's home in reality, it has to embrace everything. It therefore has to be organized in terms of pairs of opposites: the powers that can give meaning and life and those that can destroy them; the known powers and the dark unknown ones; a time of order and a time of limited disorder (as during feasts); a domain of the sacred and a domain of the profane; the pure and the impure; the past, present, and future; life and death; and so on. The sacred delimits the sphere of action and orients people within it. A sacred does not eliminate the cultural dialectic, but causes it to operate within the unity of a culture. It provides a culture with an order to which its members submit and by which they live and act in the world. Because of the sacred, nothing in a symbolic universe is any longer completely relative. Everything takes on a value in relation to the basis for cultural unity as established by the sacred and the system of myths. This happens as this basis, founded in the patterns of the collective metaconscious, pemeates the whole structure of experience of the members of a culture.

In the light of what we have said earlier, it may be thought that the inclusion of a sacred and system of myths in the patterns of the collective metaconscious will prevent a culture from evolving. This is not the case, however. Consider a culture undergoing a transformation in its project of existence. At first some new activities and ideas will relate only to the fringes of the symbolic universe. Their impact will be limited in scope and involve only a small part of a society. The people involved in these activities will internalize these experiences and new fragments of patterns may begin to link up in their metaconscious. If these new developments continue and if they prove to depart in a fundamental way from the traditional symbolic universe, the new patterns will develop as traditional ones disintegrate. Since these persons continue to live in a society based on the old patterns, the scope and depth of the new pattern fragments can grow only very slowly and may not reach the collective metaconscious in the lifetime of these people. It may take several generations before a potential new project of existence permeates the lives of a particular segment of society. At this point new myths may begin to develop and eventually a new sacred may emerge. If the new way of life diffuses throughout the society it will slowly displace the former project of existence. This generally is accompanied by fundamental conflicts between the sectors which stand to lose from the disintegration of the old project of existence and the ones which have strong vested interests in the new project of existence. After the transition period, the new patterns of the collective metaconscious including the sacred and the system of myths will again be shared by the entire society.[11] This does not, however, eliminate relationships of power and exploitation, but the conflicts will no longer challenge the new cultural unity to its very depth.

In the course of these transformations, the sacred and system of myths do not close off the future because they do not eliminate the dialectical tension between the two modes of relating to reality based on differentiation and integration. This allows for minute departures from a project of existence. When these accumulate over several generations and when they begin to link up into comprehensive new patterns able to support a new way of life, the culture gradually enters into a new epoch of its history. At first, myths may be little more than metaconscious extrapolations of new trends. Slowly life then becomes unthinkable without them as they permeate all experience. Myths may be regarded as the basic implicit hypotheses about reality and human life on which a culture is founded. Since these hypotheses are arrived at metaconsciously, the members of a culture are largely unaware of them. The deepest metaconscious patterns thus become absolutized in the sense that alternative hypotheses become unthinkable, unimaginable, and – most importantly – unlivable, at least during a certain epoch in the history of a culture. Myths convert the symbolic universe of a culture into reality itself by absolutizing the patterns of the collective metaconscious by means of a sacred.

THE SACRED AND RELIGION

Since the sacred of a culture is so deeply embedded in the collective metaconscious of its members, it cannot be studied directly. In a society, it manifests itself by means of religious phenomena and we shall therefore examine them in some detail, beginning with the theories formulated by Feuerbach, Marx, and others.

Because we are not directly linked to reality by means of stimuli, we need to mediate all relationships via a culture. In doing so, we go beyond immediate experience to become neither totally natural nor entirely artificial. On the level of the deepest patterns of the collective metacons- cious where we come closest to understanding the nature of our existence, we discover that we are never entirely adapted to our milieu, and this gives birth to a profound anxiety and fear. How does one know for sure that one is really in touch with the universe and that one's way of life is meaningful? Somewhere in reality we need to find a foundation for our life, an absolute certainty and meaning. We have already implied that, to make life possible, the members of a culture metaconsciously project everything that is socially good and useful in their experience onto what appears to order and maintain their society. This projection is accomplished by a system of myths and leads to the establishment of a sacred. A reversal takes place and, when it works itself out in the structures of experience of the members of a culture, religious phenomena suggest themselves. Had human beings been adapted to reality the way animals are, this phenomenon would not have occurred.

A religion built on the sacred of a culture makes the human condition tolerable. In a religion a culture elaborates its relationship with its sacred. The society metaconsciously serves this sacred with whole-hearted devo- tion trusting that it will calm its fears, take away its difficulties, and fulfil its hopes. A society no longer needs to be preoccupied with the ultimate problems of its existential condition. They will be looked after provided it serves the sacred. In traditional societies this is very clear. By personifying a sacred, these societies reassured themselves they were not totally lost in reality. The world was no longer full of phenomena over which they had no control and which they did not understand. Life and death were no longer unbearable. All this became possible because a culture could put itself in contact with the powers of the universe by personifying a sacred as spirits and gods. In creating a religion these powers could be influenced and even manipulated by rituals, ceremonies, prayers, and sacrifices. Nature ceased to be the arbitrary force which gives and destroys life. By giving these forces sacred value, hope was born and even death could be conquered. The religions of traditional societies performed many socio-cultural functions of fundamental importance, including solidifying the unity of a culture in the daily life of a society. For example, by means of prayers, rituals, and good works, the powers of the universe could be obliged to have the soul of a deceased person come to their abode. The nature of death was thus transformed, provided one participated in and submitted to the order of a culture. Religion helped to make death existentially bearable and socially constructive.

In traditional societies, religion invested the order of a symbolic universe with authority. As a result, cultural unity was greatly strengthened. Who would not submit to an order which one's collective metaconscious had rendered self-evident and 'natural'? Who would challenge this order and risk having the life-giving and life-sustaining forces turn against them, their group, and their society? Religion explained the possible consequences. To violate that order was to threaten the life of the group, and not to violate it meant to be inseparably bound to it. The sacred made social life possible. For the sacred to perform its role, nothing should be able to exist and have meaning outside it. It had to embrace not just reality as a culture knows it but all reality so that no unknown and hidden powers or gods could threaten society. The sacred told traditional cultures what could be expected from their symbolic universes, which it made coextensive with reality.

By way of illustration, consider first the cultures totally embedded in nature, such as totemic societies. We have already noted that so-called primitive people did not regard nature as a collection of only superficially related constituents. Their conception of nature is the key to understanding their whole symbolic universe. These people were competent observers of nature. Their strong scientific attitude was focused in a way that was quite different from that of modern science, but its results were equally impressive. Without them civilization could not have emerged: agriculture, animal husbandry, pottery, weaving, conservation of food, and the discovery of many useful natural materials were all essential. Imagine, for example, the systematic research that went into the discovery of the possible uses of the countless available varieties of plants, which was so extensive that we have added little since them.[12] These cultures realized how interdependent the natural world was. For them nature was a whole that could be understood by paradigmatically extrapolating their most immediate experience, namely that of the human group. Nature thus became an extension of the human world. Hence, the physical world was not mute: it was populated and controlled by other forms of life with which communication was possible.

For totemic societies, the natural milieu was the life-giving and life-sustaining force which provided them with everything they needed but also constituted everything that threatened them. This milieu directly or indirectly affected almost every experience in the structures of experience of these people. It traced the boundaries of what was possible and necessary, of what was good and bad, and dominated their whole existential condition. The natural milieu so permeated all human experience that it became a means of organizing the experience of totemic societies. The sacred of the natural world was not a result of people's contemplation of the beauty of nature or of their awe for the natural powers. It was their experience that justified the sacred. Symbols formed in their metaconscious which represented the sacred. The moon, for example, could for some cultures symbolize the sacred, possibly because the importance of the lunar cycle symbolized the role of nature in human life or because it could overcome the powers of darkness and symbolize life.

The emergence of a natural sacred in the first societies led to attempts to integrate the natural and the cultural order to reflect one solidarity of life. The zoological and biological classifications included the human order. Totemism is in fact a system of classifying human experience by incorporating it into the natural diversity of animals and plants. Cultural relations were regarded as a projection or reflection of nature. The structure of such a world has been described by Levi-Strauss.[13] Totemism was of immense practical value. When at the dawn of history societies began to be constituted, new possibilities opened up. By pooling resources and knowledge, a society could do things that were beyond the capabilities of the small prehistoric groups. But almost everything that could be undertaken depended on an adequate knowledge of the natural milieu, be it in order to find a better protection from dangers or to make better use of the natural inventory. This led to the massive scientific effort described above, and under these circumstances totemism was an effective way of organizing society to mobilize its resources for the acquisition, preservation, and transmission of knowledge of the natural milieu. Society was organized in terms of clans, each having a totem. By associating, say, an animal and plant with a totem and giving the clan a special association with them, each clan became a group of specialists in some of the constituents of nature. A division of scientific labour thus became possible. In their early phases of evolution, totemic societies appear to have acted as large scientific communities drawing everyone into this scientific undertaking.

The role of totemic science was severely restricted by religion and magic. In the solidarity of life depicted by the totemic symbolic universes, the regularity of natural phenomena was dependent on the will of the relevant powers. As we noted earlier, scientific knowledge was of little use if these powers did not endorse and support a given human project. The possibilities of technology were equally limited. Much more could be achieved by manipulating the powers of nature by means of magic than by means of technology, although the former certainly does not exclude the latter. In totemic symbolic universes magic was the technology par excellence. Take a simple example of the hunting of large animals. By means of magic a contract could be made with the spirit having power over the kind of animal to be hunted. In a ritual the animals were symbolically given over into the hands of the hunters. The outcome of the hunt was assured, and this gave the hunters the courage to tackle animals that were much stronger than they were. This clearly did not eliminate the need for good hunting techniques and weapons, but their potential value was limited.

It is impossible to classify these and other traditional societies on the basis of their materials and technology and to come to a fundamental understanding of early history by means of concepts like the stone, bronze, and iron ages. This is to assume that these societies put all their efforts into technology as *the* means to a better future, so that the level of technological development would be an accurate indicator of their overall development. However, this is to project something of our own symbolic universe on these peoples. If, however, modern technology happens to lead us to total war and the destruction of our world, it may well produce the greatest tragedy in human history. Science and technology could not become what they are now until at least the natural sacred was destroyed to make way for a mechanistic symbolic universe and project of existence.

It should not be concluded that totemic religions were merely functional. They fundamentally alienated these societies from their true condition. By turning to the powers of the universe for help and hope, they trusted in the non-existent gods they had created. Furthermore, since these powers were the projection of everything that was socially good and useful in these cultures onto an absolute, these societies were deprived of what could have helped them in coming to terms with their real situation – namely, that their gods could do nothing for them and that they appeared to be on their own. To make matters worse, religion also burdened these people with feelings of guilt and sin. When faced with a natural disaster or the premature death of a loved one, they necessarily felt responsible somehow. In their symbolic universe, the cause could never be purely natural. Their gods controlled nature and, being the projection of what was socially good and useful, they would not harm them without a reason. They must have been angered somehow by what someone or the group had done, so that the responsibility for the disaster or the premature death lay with society. Rather than putting all their energies into finding natural causes and doing what they could to protect themselves, they looked elsewhere for the causes. They tried to find out if someone had angered the gods, if the number of sacrifices needed to be increased, or whether some aspects of the rituals needed to be redesigned. Religion set totemic societies on the road of an endless empirical science of pleasing the gods; this alienated them from their real situation.

In making their situation existentially bearable and permitting their cultures to endure, religion prevented them from acting on the very situation that necessitated it in the first place. Religion treated the symptoms rather than the real disease of alienation. The more a religion reposes on experience, the greater is its capacity to suppress the symptons of the disease of alienation and hence the more dangerous it is for a society, because this makes it all the more difficult for the people to see their real situation and do whatever they can under the circumstances.

This brief sketch of the world of totemic people is, of course, highly rationalized; consequently it can be fundamentally misleading. We may, for example, ask how it is possible that these so-called primitive people, being capable of systematically analysing nature, did not know the futility of magic. In posing such questions we touch on the difficulty of abstracting and analysing an aspect of another culture by means of our own culture. The coherence of a symbolic universe does not depend on the factuality of any aspect. So-called primitive people knew very well that magical techniques often failed but accounted for this failure as being the result of the counter-magic of hostile tribes or to adverse circumstances related to the ritual. To understand a symbolic universe we must, as it were, attempt to live inside it and try to understand it in terms of itself. Since childhood we have learned that nature cannot respond to us. Of course, nobody may have explicitly told us so. Few have ever set out to prove it scientifically and those who did have made some interesting claims. Any symbolic universe based on a sacred and a system of myths becomes incoherent, primitive, and irrational when regarded via a structure of experience belonging to another culture based on a different cultural unity.

Can our findings derived from totemic societies be generalized for all cultures? Have we not come of age, and is religion not increasingly a relic of an age we have left behind? To shed some light on these questions, we will briefly consider some aspects of the industrial societies of the nineteenth century. From the present-day transfer of technology to the Third World, we are increasingly learning that the industrialization of a traditional society is not merely a matter of affecting some sectors but a radical transformation of all the structures of society. The name Industrial Revolution is misleading because industrialization is a transformation of the entire project of existence of a society. Beyond the technological, economic, social, legal, political, moral, and religious changes, there lies a larger pattern of change of which these specific changes are an integral part.

The nineteenth century saw the establishment of what we generally call capitalism, which designates a historically unique structure and organization of the industrial societies of that time. Capital became the life-blood of society. Everything was organized for the accumulation and growth of capital. Everything happened by means of money, not only in the economy but also in the other spheres of life, and everything could be expressed in terms of it. Society was essentially divided into two sectors: one constituted by those who developed the project of existence (which we may call industrialization) and reaped most of the riches that it produced, and the other contained those who increasingly had to submit to the new order created by capital and many of whom sold their labour for money, with everthing that implied. Capital became the sacred of society. The experience of these societies was increasingly no longer permeated by nature but by the physical and socio-cultural milieu created by the life-blood of capital.

Along with the sacred of capital, a new system of myths evolved. At its nerve centre, we find the myths of happiness and progress. Happiness became the motivating central image. Earthly happiness could be achieved by what we would call economic development. By constantly raising the level of production, the poor would also eventually be made happy. The myth of happiness converted material well-being into general well-being. People could not accept that all the energies and resources being poured into production would yield only things and nothing else. Only by means of a myth could something more be achieved. Prestige and social status were based on the things one owned, and everything could be bought with money. The myth of happiness was supported by other myths. Comfort, for example, was transformed into its material dimension.[14] Comfort relaxed the hard-working person who became happy by possessing material objects. It excluded all physical effort.

While the myth of happiness linked being to having (one is what one owns), it did not stem from private property. There have been other civilizations based on private property which did not have a myth of happiness. Private property in the nineteenth century was the natural consequence of a project of existence bent on what we would call economic development by transforming and dominating the world. The world was made for humanity and for its happiness. But this could only happen by means of action and hard work. The limits traditional societies had placed on action fell by the wayside. This led to the myth of progress.

The myth of progress came from a belief in human goodness. Action and work would lead to progress. No longer was there progress on a limited scale in a particular sphere, and no longer did this progress have positive and negative aspects. Progress became good in itself, and this could happen only by linking experience to a sacred. History became the progress of humanity by economic development. Civilizations could be classified simply on the basis of their materials and tools. Progress was obvious everywhere. Abundance would replace poverty, science would replace religion, democracy would replace oppressive regimes, and so on. All this could be achieved simply by economic development. Poverty resulted from not contributing to progress and work. Everything was assimilated by the myths of progress and happiness.

Although another sacred and system of myths have sprung up since the nineteenth century, they still contain many of the above elements, although they are integrated in a different way. We therefore begin to uncover some of the roots of our own existence, and this is threatening. Nobody likes being uprooted. Our reaction may well be: 'But things have always been this way! Which civilization was not interested in happiness and progress?' Yet this is not the case, at least not in the manner of the nineteenth century. The fact that we have difficulty depicting a civilization which was not interested in happiness and progress reveals the fact that we too are to some extent still held by these myths. Myths transform something which is relative and hence temporary into an aspect of human nature which is permanent. By looking at the past via our structures of experience, we project our myths on it. Other civilizations have had quite different pursuits, and happiness had a totally different content. In the Middle Ages, happiness was a just relationship with God. In other religions it may be a just relationship with the world or the universe. Different conceptions also occur in utopias. In the Christian new creation, happiness is being reconciled with God. Many other paradises and utopias have also been void of nineteenth-century happiness.

The same could be argued about the myth of progress. In the Middle Ages, for example, before the myth of progress was born in the Western collective metaconscious, the concept of revolution means to revolve, that is, to come back to the point of departure. Generally speaking, political revolutions at that time were just those kinds of events, namely, revolts of the people to attempt to restore the trusted traditions from which their rulers had departed. When the myth of progress was born, the meaning of the concept of revolution changed to its opposite, namely, to destroy tradition by moving forward, often in a violent manner. Yet it can hardly be claimed that the Middle Ages were against economic development by means of technology, especially in the monasteries. But any new development was subjected to a set of values to see if it was just; it was not automatically good in itself. It is still an open question if economic development is sustainable because of limited resources, the ecology, and the growing problems of the developed and underdeveloped worlds. If a conflict erupts over access to scarce resources, for example, and if such a conflict would lead to total war, we may well destroy human civilization.

The sacred of the nineteenth century is evident from the transformation of the religion of the industrial nations. Hand-in-hand with the secularization of the sacred came a secularization of the Christian religion. But this does not mean humanity is becoming of age. It simply shows that, when the sacred of a society is transformed, the religion built on it also changes. Feuerbach and others tried to save the Christian religion by eliminating its dependence on the existence of God. It was to be reduced to those elements which were purely socially useful. All its horizontal aspects were exploited in ways that are well known. Everything that contradicted the new rationality had to be eliminated if Christianity was to have a future, and whatever belief in God still existed was used to advance the new project of existence. Christianity became a morality, a ceremony, and a theology. At the end of this process God was proclaimed dead. The development of liberal Christianity is well known and will not be elaborated here.

The new sacred, the system of myths, and religion were accompanied by a new morality. Moral values were closely related to work, which led to happiness and progress and thus to the good posed by the sacred. Riches and success were distributed by God as a blessing to those who were good – that is, those who worked hard to take advantage of what creation offered to achieve earthly happiness and progress for all. After death, heavenly happiness would be offered to those who had worked hard and been good (economic) stewards of creation. Work was the mother of all virtues and laziness the father of all vices. The choice of an occupation was of the highest importance for life. A career led to the making of money, and with money everything could be had.

We have given a very rough sketch of the symbolic universe of the industrial societies of the nineteenth century. It is, of course, highly simplified and rationalized, yet together with the earlier example it helps to illustrate the role religion plays in society. This may be summed up in the words of Karl Marx: 'Religion is the general theory of the world, its encyclopedic compendium, its logic in popular form, its spiritual point d'honneur, its enthusiasm, its moral sanction, its solemn complement, its general basis of consolation and justification. It is the fantastic realization of the human being inasmuch as the human being possesses no true reality ... Religious suffering at the same time, is an expression of real suffering and a protest against real suffering. Religion is the sigh of the oppressed creature, the sentiment of a heartless world and the soul of soulless conditions. It is the opium of the people.'[15]

While we have come to very similar conclusions as Feuerbach and Marx, we have also gone beyond them. The members of a society take what the patterns of their collective metaconscious reveal as socially and individually good and extrapolate it to the absolute. They therefore rob themselves of this good and live expecting great things from this sacred. In return, the symbolic universe becomes existentially bearable. It becomes the ultimate explanation and the heart and spirit of a world full of inhumanity. While religion is a necessity, the price a society pays for it is alienation.[16] Religion reconciles a society with its world and makes it virtually impossible for its members to grasp the nature of their existential situation. The ultimate integration of the structure of experience leads to a condition of alienation, and this condition appears to be a part of every culture. It is not caused only by capitalism, socialism, or any other system but by any project of existence based on a sacred, a system of myths, and a religion. The latter are of the order of necessity and are related to the way we are linked to reality. Alienation, therefore, goes much deeper and is much more permanent than Marx thought.

A sacred, system of myths, religion, and morality have their origins in the body of experience of a society. Since nothing in human experience is absolute, however, reality keeps impinging on them. Hence the evolution of a society, and indeed that of humanity as a whole, appears to be bound up with an endless process of sacralization and desacralization. We will briefly sketch this process for Western civilization.

When Christianity began to permeate the Roman Empire, it desacralized the basis of that world. But in the course of this process it helped build a new sacred, namely that of the Christian religion, which was a confusion of the natural sacred and the religious constructions of the Roman Catholic Church. To live openly outside that sacred was to risk such consequences as being burned at the stake. This sacred began to disappear in the seventeenth century with the rise of science, but it only disappeared fully in the commercial and industrial bourgeoisie. At that point there was as yet no replacement so that monarchs, even when they no longer believed in the Christian sacred, continued to lean on it because there was nothing else. Even Napoleon after the French Revolution said that there can be no authority without the sacred and that there was no other sacred than the Catholic religion.

The rise of science, commerce, and industry changed all that. Science showed itself capable of explaining a great many things that had traditionaly been explained by religion. There was nothing to indicate that this trend would not continue, with the result that the patterns of experience of the people of the time could be extrapolated to go beyond their experience. New patterns of the collective metaconscious began to link up, but since science did as yet not affect the daily life of society to any great extent, it could not constitute a new sacred. But many people placed their hopes in what was implied in the new patterns of experience. The capabilities of science became extrapolated in their minds far beyond what experience could justify. Science became a sacred belief. People trusted in science to lead them to the 'truth,' to free them from religion and the power of the Catholic Church. It would enable them to enter into and live in a rationally explicable universe free from all supernatural beings. This belief was intuited and accepted by many people because of the metaconscious extrapolations of their experience in a manner that was fully supported by all the trends. They hoped science would deliver them from what had alienated society for centuries.

As self-evident as the extrapolations were, however, they became just as religious in character as the ones made by totemic societies, which in their situation were equally self-evident. Science desacralized the explanatory role of the sacred created by Christendom and in doing so eventually contributed to a new sacred. We may smile at the identification of science with 'Truth' which, according to current theories of science, is a myth. But we have firm experience where the people of an earlier epoch had only tendencies. Science did not, however, replace the sacred created by Christendom in so far as it was the foundation for the social, economic, and political order of society. Another sacred would take the place of that function of Christendom's sacred. It was at that time that economic development became the new project of existence in the West. At this point capital became the new sacred.

The above description of the pattern of desacralization and resacralization is only an outline, but it shows the essential features. When new pattern fragments in the collective metaconscious begin to link up and when they grow to the point where they appear to be able to embrace the experiences of the members of a society, they are extrapolated by means of myths to constitute an absolute. A reversal takes place as the new sacred permeates the structures of experience of the members of a society. As this happens the consequences are elaborated in a religion which, together with the sacred and the system of myths, constitute the basis for a new project of existence and hence the unity of a culture. As reality inevitably imposes itself on what is not real and as creativity and imagination create new forms of action and thought, a process of desacralization gets underway which eventually leads to a new sacred and system of myths. A culture's journey through reality and time appears therefore to have a spiritual dimension – namely, the endless search for a form of a sacred.

Because of the nature of the sacralization-desacralization process, a new historical epoch in a culture is entered into in a very continuous way. A new upcoming sacred develops in the symbolic universe dominated by another sacred and, once the latter has been desacralized, it lingers on as an important constituent of the patterns of the collective metaconscious. As a result, each culture has a very strong collective memory of its history.

By identifying a sacred and a system of myths in a culture, we render them explicit and abstract them from an internally coherent universe. In other words, we are really taking this world apart. Consequently, the sacred and the system of myths lose their vitality and meaning. The reasons are evident. A system is more than the sum of its parts. Each time even one of the relationships between the constituents of a symbolic universe is destroyed by a process of abstraction, something of the meaning of these constituents and of the symbolic universe is lost. The process is exactly the reverse of how a structure of experience is built up – that is, it is destructive of all meaning. This explains the normal reaction of a person who refuses to believe that a particular sacred and a system of myths could have founded the order of a culture during a certain epoch in its history. It may be hard to accept that all members believed in the foundation of their culture without questioning it. The classical solution is then to think of these cultures as being less rational, scientific, or developed because they were supposedly more 'primitive,' superstitious, and religious than the culture of the observer. A culture can only be truly appreciated by attempting to imagine what it was like to live within it and not by judging it in terms of criteria that are foreign to it, because they dismantle it into a collection of unrelated fragments to make non-sense of the lives of those who lived within it.

It is possible to begin to appreciate another culture only when one begins to grasp the internal 'logic' of its design for living and how its elements coherently and consistently enfold into one another and, furthermore, only when one becomes aware of the mythical basis of one's own culture. The home of a culture in reality must be entered and lived in to be fully appreciated. The working hypothesis most likely to minimize distortions in viewing another culture through the eyes of one's own is to realize that, had one been born into it, one would have lived in it with the same certitude of its validity and soundness that one has for one's own culture. People have never been able to substitute their own mediation with reality (thus creating their own symbolic universe) for the culture of their society, except in cases of mental disorders.

In permitting the creation of the order of the symbolic universe of a culture, a sacred, a system of myths, and a religion become the foundation and main support structure of a system of values, norms, and a morality. Everything is related to the order of a symbolic universe, and the implications of those relationships for that order are expressed in terms of norms and values. All human actions when related to the order of a symbolic universe within a person's structure of experience take on a moral aspect, which together constitute a morality. While in many cases norms, values, and a morality are explicitly formulated by a culture, they have their foundation in the structures of experience of its members. The relationships between any constituent, event, and relationship and the order of a symbolic universe are first created in a structure of experience which is capable of detecting any tensions that they may create within the body of experience. This permits a structure of experience to act as an internal 'gyroscope,' causing a person to do almost 'instinctively' what for the culture is the right thing. All spontaneously obeyed laws have the support of the system of values and norms and the morality that are implied in the structures of experience of the members of a culture. Simplistically we might say that everything that supports the order of a symbolic universe is good, valuable, and moral, and all that is contrary to it is bad, without value, dangerous, or immoral.

In conclusion, there are two matters with respect to the phenomenon of religion which need to be dealt with. The first is its relationship to science.

August Comte, in his theory of the three stages, proposed that the relationship between science and religion is a complementary one, causing the latter to recede as the former advances. In the nineteenth century, his theory appeared well supported, but subsequent developments have shown the theory to be invalid, however, for two main reasons. First of all, it places science and religion on the same plane and consequently overlooks the fact that religion, unlike science, is primarily social and existential. Second, Comte's theory implies that science progresses to a complete knowledge of reality in a cumulative way. This view of science is, as we have seen, untenable. The relationship between science and religion is more complex. Religion has its roots in the way we are linked to reality. It does not arise from a lack of science or from the existence of transcendent beings, but from the necessity of a culture to build a symbolic universe to enable it to exist in reality. It is thus related to its social and existential condition. Science can affect this condition, and when it does so it can affect the religion of a society. The process is one of reciprocal interaction between two entities operating on different planes.

The decline of traditional religions cannot be interpreted as a decline in the religious phenomenon. In industrial societies, the sacred is no longer associated with the natural, and traditional religions decline. But the sacred does not disappear; it only changes its form. As it does, new secular religions spring up. As the modern state continues to expand its role and directly or indirectly organizes nearly all aspects of industrial societies (democratic or socialist), it helps constitute the patterns of the collective metaconscious and the modern sacred. On this sacred of the state, secular religions can be built. Neither national socialism, communism, nor democracy created the sacred of the state, but they all exploit it to varying degrees to create a secular religion. There are also many other forms of secular religions today, but an analysis of them would require a detailed study of the structure of contemporary industrial nations, which goes beyond the scope of this work.

There is one other question to deal with. We have tried to demonstrate that religion is a purely socio-cultural phenomenon, but does this prove that no transcendent being exists? We will deal with this matter for the case of Christianity only (although the argument could be extended to other religions) and consider the views of a believer and an opponent.

The position of Karl Marx is highly instructive. Although Marx was very insightful in exposing the basic presuppositions of his contemporaries, he never criticized the myth of progress which helped guide his culture. When it came to religion therefore, the matter was quite straightforward:

Christianity was the religion of the most highly evolved societies and therefore the most highly developed religion. If it could be shown that it was a purely socio-cultural phenomenon, as Marx believed, then the case was closed for all religions. Yet Marx recognized that a final verdict in the matter could not be reached scientifically. In a letter he wrote to his friend Max Rugge towards the end of his life he said that when all the political foundations of religion are wiped out, when the organization and the institution of the church are destroyed, then normal religious faith – Christian faith – would have to disappear.[17] But it is not out of the question that religious faith will survive. This would mean that there is a religious reality that does not depend solely on the social and the institutional, and under these conditions we would have to heed this reality, which is not in the category of traditional religion. In other words, Marx leaves the door open. Faith may be a fact, but we will not know this until its socio-cultural basis is destroyed.

Within the Christian community, an opposition between faith and religion has been drawn in the works of Karl Barth. Faith is not purely socio-cultural but the result of the existence of a living God who reveals himself to humanity. However, those who receive this faith remain subject to the socio-cultural processes that lead to the formation of religion. Hence, wherever Christian faith enters a culture there is a strong tendency for it to be transformed into a religion. It becomes an attempt to take possession of God. This was the case, for example, in the theology of good works, designed to force God to save people because they were good. Today again, Christianity takes on new forms that correspond to the socio-cultural necessities imposed by our society. It is clear, therefore, that from this perspective a coherent explanation of what Christianity has been and is can be developed, which in no way contradicts the theory of religion as a purely socio-cultural phenomenon. Christianity as a religion is from this perspective the opposite of Christian faith.[18]

TRANSMITTING CULTURAL UNITY

Since the basis for the unity of a culture is deeply embedded within the collective metaconscious of its members, it is transmitted only indirectly from one generation to the next. This transmission is remarkable because the members of a culture are normally unaware of the existence of a sacred and a system of myths, let alone the fact they pass them on to each new generation. These processes probably make the most extensive use of the enfolded characteristics of a structure of experience.

Communication between adults and children being socialized into a culture involves the interaction of two frames of reference. Both are constituted by structures of experience, but those of the children are only partially based on the unity of the culture, while those of the adults are fully based on it.[19] Children use language to represent things in their 'worlds' while the others use it to represent things in the symbolic universe of the culture. Because of the structure of the system of concepts and a system of language and the way they are enfolded into the entire structure of experience, the language Gestalts used by the child or the others necessarily enfold something of the world of the child or the symbolic universe respectively. Language is a system that symbolizes not reality itself but reality as it is known. It is for this reason that it refers to experience via the symbolic universe of a culture. The language Gestalts of the members of a child's speech community imply the sacred and the system of myths in the way situations are approached and talked about, in the way things are singled out for attention, and in the way some possibilities are never entered into. We shall consider several facets of this transmission by implication.

We have already noted that children are drawn beyond their immediate experience when the metaconscious begins to develop in their structures of experience. These developments are dependent in a fundamental way on the contact with the adults of their speech community because they present them with the order of the culture's life in its symbolic universe. Children do not merely learn to differentiate their experiences in a neutral fashion. They learn that experience Gestalts lived by the same experience paradigm, for example, can be ranked according to one or more standards of perfection, values, norms, customs, tradition, or institutions. There are good and poor ball games, beautiful and ugly dogs, honest and dishonest salesmen, and so on. Children learn this as they learn to interpret stimuli. When a child spills his food he will soon notice his mother's displeasure. He learns that 'my mother does not like me to spill food.' When he discovers that other people do not appreciate it either, he learns that 'food is not to be spilled.' Gradually, the subjective disapproval of his mother becomes an objective norm. This example is paradigmatic. By differentiating the situations in which the modes of behaviour of the members of the child's speech community are more or less identical for a given type of event, children implicitly learn the standards of perfection, values, norms, customs, and institutions of the speech community as well as the unique ways in which individuals enfold their lives into them. Since all these developments interact with each other as they contribute to the formation of the patterns of the metaconscious, children begin to get some sense of the integrality of the order of the symbolic universe of their culture.

Language plays a crucial role in the above developments. It can be used to focus on a variety of dimensions of a situation (social, economic, political, moral, legal, religious, and so on). When this is done consistently by the members of a culture in accordance with the values, norms, customs, and institutions that help constitute the order of a culture's symbolic universe, children will implicitly learn this via the processes of differentiating and integrating their experiences. They will metaconsciously learn the hierarchy of values that relates different spheres of activities and eventually the system of myths and the sacred that orders the project of existence of their culture. In the example of a child learning the meaning of the concept of freedom, the father's explanation that he is not free from work implies that the kind of activities he does in his free time are more enjoyable than work. The fact that other situations are characterized by other concepts also implies something about their interrelationships. Because the metaconscious acts as a meta-language in both children and adults, the dialectical tension between them makes the implicit transmission of the cultural order possible.

What language is *not* used for is equally significant. A culture may systematically avoid making certain interconnections in its symbolic universe, although these connections may be perfectly obvious to another culture. To the first culture these relationships are unthinkable; they simply do not come to mind. This not only affects the meaning of some constituents and phenomena of the symbolic universe but also, when enfolded into the structures of experience of children being socialized into the culture, something of the system of myths emerge. Myths shield a culture from certain aspects of reality which would threaten the basis of its cultural unity. Possibilities that are systematically never talked about, or are never talked about in certain ways, therefore also symbolize the foundation of a culture. There are other matters that are implied which are never dealt with explicitly or critically. They are so self-evident that they cannot be talked about. But in an interrelated reality nothing is that self-evident.

At the stage where the above processes yield only embryonic results in the structures of experience of children, they begin to sense that the world of adults has some kind of order. Children then use language to explore these intuitions. For example, a child may want to know the why of everything. She may ask her father why her mother has to go to work; he replies that she has to help earn money so that she can buy food and other necessary things. Being unsatisfied with such an answer, she may next ask why money is necessary to buy things. By posing chains of these questions, the child learns something about the order of the symbolic universe of her speech community. The stage of development of a child during which she wants to know the 'why' of everything soon passes. Presumably this means that her questions have largely been answered. When we think about the kind of answers she has received, we must conclude that no system of final causes giving an account of the social and cultural 'why' of reality has been given to her. In fact, every adult trying to answer the chains of questions the child poses during this period has experienced that at some point reason seems to give out, so that all one can do is to answer that things simply are that way. While the child may not be particularly happy with this answer, the adult recognizes that he cannot go any further with reason.

This does not make the father question the order of his symbolic universe as though it were unfounded. On the contrary, he affirms his belief in that order when he gives such an answer. What then accounts for the difference in the behaviour of the child and the adult? The adult's structure of experience contains a cultural foundation while that of the child does not. By answering her questions, the members of a child's speech community help her go beyond her immediate experience. The child's world becomes increasingly endowed with a 'deeper' meaning, which permits the patterns of her metaconscious to be linked up at increasingly greater depths. The need for a system of myths then manifests itself as an apparent interest in causal relationships. When these processes have caught up with the level of development of her structure of experience the stage during which she wants to know the why of everything has come to an end. From now on the cultural foundation appears to develop hand in hand with her structures of experience.

Language makes a child enter into a new universe that requires different explanations. Somewhat analogous situations occur in science. When scientists believed the world to be corpuscular, any accepted explanation of a phenomenon related to the size, shape, motion, and interaction of corpuscles. This belief about the nature of the universe placed distinct limits on how far causality had to be explained. Modern science operates in a different universe, with the result that identical phenomena now receive quite different explanations. The explicit, and more important, implicit hypotheses about the nature of reality that are embedded in a scientific discipline during a stage in its development perform a function analogous to that of the order of a culture for the adult replying to the why-questions of the child.

Gradually children's structures of experience permit them to enter and exist in the symbolic universe of their culture. Their playful attitude diminishes as they acquire absolute confidence in their knowledge of the world. As the sacred and system of myths begins to develop in their structures of experience, reality as they know it is transcended and absolutized so that it is experienced as reality itself. The situation is somewhat analogous to that of a science student. While science is supposed to be based on facts, the student must enter the world of science by believing in it. No student performs all the experiments necessary to see if what his professor or textbook says is true. Even if he wanted to he could not, because he would in fact have to be an extraordinarily competent scientist. He must first believe that what he is taught is largely correct, which does not exclude the possibility that he may later come to doubt some or all of it. The same holds true for children. They enter and grow up in the symbolic universe of the culture into which they are born without ever doubting it.

In most societies (with the exception of the so-called industrially advanced societies in which new patterns of socio-cultural developement are beginning to emerge) the parents and particularly the father exemplify and enforce the order of the culture. They present the child with the 'you shall' and the 'you may not.' Depth psychology indicates that children cannot live and develop themselves without internalizing the 'law' of their culture. The moral order and the cultural foundation on which it is based and to which the parents adhere must be internalized by children. If the parents are unable or unwilling to perform this role, the children are socialized into a symbolic universe that is relatively neutral to human life with all the consequences mentioned earlier. In this case the structures of experience of children become other-directed and function as a kind of social radar system.

The transmission of a culture from one generation to another can never be a process in which children merely copy the members of their speech community. We have already noted that nothing can have a meaning for children unless they can relate it to their structures of experience and that the meaning taken on is largely determined by prior experience. Children can be helped indirectly by others, but it is impossible for the latter to directly transmit meaning to them. Meaning is created in the structures of experience by processes of differentiation and integration. In societies evolving only very slowly, there is a great deal of continuity between the structures of experience of different generations. When this evolution becomes very rapid or when a transformation in the project of existence is under way, discontinuities or generation gaps may occur. This is because the structures of experience of older generations tend to cover over what is new when its paradigms have been extensively used and thus reinforced. They may therefore lag behind the developments in a society. In a rapidly changing society, growing old is often synonymous with a growing alienation from its project of existence rather than with a satiation with life as occurred in traditional societies. The generation being socialized in a society will detect this problem as reality imposes itself on them. They may feel the older generation is out of touch with reality and unable to help them to find their way in building a coherent symbolic universe. But they too, typically, cannot face the reality of their condition and thus alienate themselves perhaps even further.

The establishment of what constitutes the foundation of a culture within the structures of experience of children has important consequences. Their structures of experience become a non-neutral way to relate to reality. While children become united with the members of their culture, barriers are thus created between them and other cultures. This is an endless source of division and conflict in human history. First consider a simple example. Suppose that a person visits a culture which does not distinguish between the colours green and yellow. Once he notices that his host culture does not make this distinction, he has to try to imagine how these people perceive colours in order to use the names of colours in the other language correctly. This is not a problem of simple translation. Direct translation is possible only when the clusters of the appropriate concepts in the two languages correspond. When this is not the case, the problem enters the cultural domain. The visitor is obliged to attempt to enter into the world of colour of the symbolic universe of his host culture and think in terms of it. This is difficult because one cannot unlearn the perceptual distinctions, which are involuntary. The problem becomes even more difficult for abstract concepts since they are more bound up with the way the two cultures regard the world and their existence in it. If these problems are frequent all the visitor can do is to attempt to enter the symbolic universe of the host culture by learning its language from daily-life situations in the culture.

This amounts to building a second symbolic universe, which is somewhat like an adult going through some of the same stages children do when they enter the symbolic universe of their speech community by learning their mother tongue. It is only by this process that the visitor can become largely integrated into the host culture. Even when he cuts all ties with the culture into which he was born, however, it will be almost impossible to become fully integrated into another once a first set of patterns of the collective metaconscious has formed. A complete conversion is almost impossible.

These patterns evolve much more slowly than the flux of daily experience, and they form much less easily for a second time because of the interference of the first set. Furthermore, even when a person has lived in another culture for a sufficiently long time that new patterns of the collective metaconscious have linked up, they will coexist with fragments of the old patterns which continue to have their impact. The older people are, the more extensively the patterns of the collective metaconscious are elaborated, with the result that their adaptation to another culture will be longer in duration than that of children or younger persons. Beyond a certain age it becomes almost impossible for people to adapt to and feel at home in another culture.

Opposite kinds of phenomena can occur when people temporarily move into a different culture or when they are deported. The experience of the new culture will link up into metaconscious patterns that threaten those derived from their own culture. They may sense a threat to their identity. These feelings may be intensified as the depth of the new metaconscious patterns increases to the point that they begin to affect the patterns of their collective metaconscious. The very roots of their existence in reality are threatened, and in such a case these people may fall back on the sacred of their culture. We see this, for example, with North Africans working in France, who face the threat of being assimilated by their Western host culture. In order to protect their existential roots these people fall back on Islam and religously reaffirm the sacred on which their culture is founded. In so doing they reaffirm the very foundation of their existence and become stronger adherents of Islam than they ever were in their home country. Similar phenomena can be observed in North America, particularly in those ethnic groups striving to maintain their identity.

When people regard another culture through the eyes of their own – that is, via their own structures of experience – they will necessarily impose on it the sacred, the system of myths, the values, norms, and so on of their own culture. The other culture is necessarily distorted, which can lead to prejudice, social conflicts, and discrimination. Consider some examples. Early Victorian observers of so-called primitive people were so convinced that these people were only half human that they were hardly willing to credit them with having a language. Not until a clergyman, possibly convinced that his God had created all people equal, set out to document a vocabulary of over 30,000 words while he lived with a tribe of natives on Tierra del Fuego between 1861 and 1879, did the West realize that so-called primitive people do indeed possess highly developed language.[20] The West's image of so-called primitive people has been upgraded ever since, to the point where there are now occasional tendencies to idealize them somewhat.

Similar tragic distortions occur when a cultural minority is interpreted in terms of the language, values, beliefs, myths, and the sacred of a dominant culture. The first generation of a cultural minority that enters the dominant culture is obliged to adopt its language in order to communicate with its members. At the same time its old culture is frequently maintained within the community and particularly the home. As a consequence, an interaction occurs between the domains of their structures of experience derived from either culture. New metaconscious patterns are formed, with the result that the cultural minority enters a symbolic universe which may at first sight appear as a degraded form of that of the dominant culture but which in fact is a mutation typifying a subculture. This process may take several generations, but once it comes about the cultural minority can maintain a unique identity for a very long time, provided the conditions for cultural evolution are met. In some cases this situation may give birth to a new language as an act of cultural self-defence. This happened in the case of the Jewish people in central Europe – they created Yiddish.

Yet many observers have concluded that such cultural minorities speak the language poorly, cannot think logically, and on the whole are culturally deprived because they evaluate the minority in terms of their own culture. This evaluation distorts the culture of the minority and makes it incoherent, giving the overall impression of its being on a lower cultural level. To administer intelligence tests designed in terms of the symbolic universe of the dominant culture to children of a cultural minority is a sure way to demonstrate their intellectual and cultural inferiority. Furthermore, when these children enter a public school system geared to the cultural majority, they enter a new symbolic universe that is not their own. Labov[21] has exposed some of these problems with a great deal of clarity in relation to the black subculture in the United States. By culturally translating from one symbolic universe into the other, he shows how a completely different picture of the cultural minority emerges. This demonstrates that the symbolic universe of the cultural minority is just as coherent and culturally meaningful as the dominant one.

Cultures having a Western conception of time, which is linear and mechanical, have often judged members of cultures having a different conception of time as being lazy or procrastinators. Nothing of the sort is true, however. We are not dealing with personal qualities but with the way these people exist in reality by means of their culture. Considering the large number of social conflicts and the prejudice and human suffering that arise from the co-existence of different cultures, the problem of cultural translation has received remarkably little attention. Cultural translation cannot be done purely scientifically because it is profoundly existential. The incapacity of a cultural majority to translate culturally may lead a minority to seek political independence. Cultural boundaries form natural political boundaries for obvious reasons.

Some factors contributing to the idea of human progress in history are now becoming visible. The more another culture differs from our own, which generally has some relationship with the length of time that separates it from ours, the more difficult it is to appreciate its coherence and the sacred and system of myths on which it was built. Consequently, the older the culture is, the lower its level of cultural development appears to be. It was all too tempting to extrapolate Darwin's theory of evolution to social evolution. Another factor that has contributed to the illusion of human progress is the confusion between material and human progress. If one is willing to credit other cultures with being capable of having other projects of existence than economic development because they do not link overall human well-being so strongly to material development, then they cannot be judged by their tools, machines, or industry in general. Each culture has its project of existence, and to assume it is following our own is to distort it into something it is not. There is therefore no single set of criteria according to which all cultures can be ranked on a progressively evolutionary scale. To hold up our own project of existence of economic development (whatever the ideological cloak it may be dressed up in) as a standard of reference is to affirm the superiority of that goal. As long as the threats to human survival directly related to economic development are not eliminated, however, there would appear to be little intellectual honesty in that position.

The current situation is unique. The project of existence of the industrialized world has steadily intensified the contacts between all cultures. Since they dominate the world scene, the sacred and system of myths of the projects of existence of economic development are increasingly undermining the traditional sacred and myths of other cultures, to the point where the basis for their traditional way of life is destroyed. In some cases this was accomplished by violent means, but in others force was nearly absent. Many traditional cultures now wish to set out on the road of economic development. For the first time in human history, cultures are no longer simply different in their projects of existence. They can now be ranked by a common scale and grouped into what are erroneously called the fully developed, developing, and underdeveloped nations. But this was not possible, for example, at the time of the Chinese, Egyptian, or Roman empires.

The current situation is potentially a threat to humanity from the point of view of culture as a social ecology. In the past, civilizations disappeared when their project of existence collapsed, but this did not threaten humanity as a whole because many others with different projects of existence survived. If the current tendency towards one globally shared project of existence continues, the situation may well alter. As the plurality of cultures decreases, any difficulty that prevents modern cultures from functioning as a social ecology could threaten humanity as a whole. The tendency for the plurality of cultures to decrease does not, of course, guarantee peace, as two world wars have demonstrated. A third world war could emerge out of a dispute over increasing scarce resources vital for economic development.

Culture and History

CULTURE AS DIALECTICAL MEDIATION

Based on a unique organization of the human mind, a culture produces the patterns of internal and external regularities in the lives of the members of a society, in so far as these patterns are not hereditary in origin. It is, of course, impossible to establish the dividing line between 'nature' and culture. The mental structures built up from experience graft themselves onto those established genetically, and the two become inextricably related. Hence, what is natural in human beings is transformed by the cultural element. As a result, there is no longer a spontaneous evolutionary adaptation to the natural environment. Whether we draw the distinction between human beings and animals on the basis of language, tools, work, or religion is not important here; what matters is that societies, by means of their cultures, introduce something non-natural into nature that cannot be integrated into it – namely, an element of choice and free will.

There are thus two contradictory elements in human experience. On the one hand, human beings experience a distance between themselves and the world, obliging them to make decisions regarding their existence in it (presupposing a certain freedom), while, on the other hand, they constantly experience how much they are determined by that world. Faced with this contradiction, human beings have never acted as if their power to make decisions were mere illusion, giving them no choice but to resign themselves to live on the level of immediate experience. They have never accepted things for what they are. The contrary has always been the case. Human beings assert the will to be free precisely because of their experience that they are not. Human groups and societies constantly set out making conscious and metaconscious decisions as if they were free, and they translate these decisions into cultures with liveable projects of existence. Were human beings as spontaneously adapted to their environment as animals, no fundamental decisions regarding human existence would be required, and were they totally free there would be no need to want freedom.

Human groups and societies typically hope to find freedom in a social and physical milieu of their own making. They seek to create a milieu in which they are secure in the hope that, as its creators, they will be able to eliminate all threats and alienation. All groups and societies have searched for such a milieu by means of a culture.

For prehistoric groups totally immersed in the natural milieu, to set out on a course rejecting things as they were was a radical undertaking. The experiences of these people and hence the patterns of their collective metaconscious must have been largely determined by nature. Consequently their project of existence may at one point have resembled the way some animals lived, with one fundamental difference. No matter how 'natural' their culture may have been, it could not have been entirely so; a human choice, no matter how limited, was implied. Moreover, the resulting cultural order was made normative, and this is not the case for animals. There can be no natural morality, no natural law, and no natural theology, because even though nature may hold out a certain order to human beings, it never commands them to obey it. These prehistoric groups exercised an element of human freedom. Consequently they had already introduced something non-natural into reality.

It would appear that the human decision to create a non-natural milieu and a culture-based group was considered so all-encompassing and defiant of all determinisms that nothing could be left to chance. An inventory of the natural and social milieu had to be made. The meaning of everything had to be known and related to that decision. By means of language, everything the group experienced was drawn into a new order by the act of giving everything a name. Via the magic of language, prehistoric groups placed themselves in their own symbolic universe, which was not merely a systematic interpretation of the experience of its members but also its transcendence by means of a sacred and systems of myths and values. As a result, the project of existence founded in the patterns of the collective metaconscious no longer appeared as one of many possible ways to mediate the distance between the groups and reality. It became existentially valid for all times. The introduction of an absolute into the culture rendered it perfectly self-evident and 'natural.' There was simply nothing else the members of the group could think or do that was meaningful. In this way the culture created a 'human nature,' for how could the group be otherwise? This 'human nature' matched the project of existence.

It is clear that already in prehistory human groups introduced something non-natural or artificial into nature by exercising their free will.[1] But what are the limitations to the freedom introduced into reality by the human element? A culture's project of existence creates a non-natural balance between human desires, the possibilities and limitations of the natural and social environments, and the means available. Human freedoms must be understood as being dialectically related to the possibilities and necessities of reality mediated by culture.

In prehistory, the primary limitations to human freedom derived, of course, from the natural milieu in which the human group was immersed. However, by means of agriculture and the domestication of animals, human groups decisively intervened in the natural order to expand their non-natural order within it. In fact, these developments were the mere outward manifestation of how human groups were trying to impose their order on nature. By means of language, magic, and religion, reality had already been symbolically transformed into a human world. The natural milieu became populated with spirits and powers with which the groups could not only communicate but also negotiate to have nature work their way. The symbolic universe of these groups was established by interpreting nature on the analogy of the better understood experiences of human life.

As the non-natural order established in the natural milieu expanded further, the groups could grow in size and societies began to emerge. The structures of experience of the human beings involved were now increasingly constituted by experiences of the social milieu rather than those of the natural milieu. A mutation in the kind of sacred and system of myths could now take place, although the natural sacred persisted for a long time in agrarian societies. The limitations of human freedom were increasingly less associated with the natural milieu. As the social milieu became the primary milieu, the principal limitations and challenges also came from that milieu. The human power collectivized in society called for a political master – namely, the state – and with this master came a new slavery.

The emergence of societies greatly reinforced the artificial character of the human community and its members. As 'human nature' is largely a cultural product, no fixed 'human nature' exists. But it may be objected that most groups and societies have contacts with others. Did this not make them aware that in fact 'human nature' and the project of existence vary with each culture? This is not the case, since members of one society necessarily interpret another culture via their own. This distorts the other culture and its project of existence, rendering it incoherent and hence unliveable for them. It is only with the guidance of a great deal of training and thought that one can attempt to place oneself within another cultural universe. If one can judge it on its own terms, one can begin to appreciate it, but to really live that culture is virtually impossible. When contact with another culture destroys the myths of a society, its culture mutates or disappears.

It will now become evident that the concept of a cultural dialectic as introduced in the last chapter needs to be expanded. The introduction of the human phenomenon into reality upsets the evolutionary scheme. There now exists an artificial or cultural sphere which cannot be absorbed into nature, while it cannot be detached from it either. There is a fundamental contradiction between the cultural order and reality. As reality keeps on imposing itself, it obliges the society to evolve. The reason is simple. In order to maintain a cultural order in reality, its unity must be safeguarded or replaced with an alternative one as the previous one disintegrates. Everything must be brought into the order established by the sacred and system of myths. This is clearly impossible given the contradiction between culture and reality, because the former is based on an absolute which cannot exist in an interrelated reality. The only solution is to give this contradiction a place within a culture – that is, to build the culture around it. Each culture is necessarily built on this dialectic, and we will therefore expand our concept of a cultural dialectic to include it. We will briefly explore the structure of the cultural dialectic as it now stands.

The building of a symbolic universe by means of language introduces one aspect of artificiality into reality, which is inherent in the 'nature' of language, itself in part determined by the natural characteristics of the human brain. The process of differentiation organizes the world of perception by establishing oppositions between paradigms. Language names these paradigms by means of a system of differentiated concepts. We noted that a colour has no meaning apart from the other colours, while the world of colour receives its meaning by being differentiated from other kinds of visual characteristics of objects. Similarly, on the level of experience, we also find a dialectical structure of differentiated experiences. The metaconscious foundation of language is therefore profoundly dialectical in character. It can be expected to reflect (with a time lag) the micro-structure of the cultural dialectic of a society.

On the conscious level, the meaning of a concept can be expressed as a definition which is an ideal type.[2] It helps to make reality intelligible, but also contributes to falsifying it in some way. Since a language is used systematically, it orders the disorder in the system which results from the contradiction between culture and reality. In this sense, language can furnish the basis for an ideology. Language reflects the micro-structure of the cultural dialectic. This finds its ultimate expression in the dialectical structure of the sacred, comprising the order of the culture as one pole and the violation of that sacred in an order of transgression as the other pole.[3] In its dialectical structure the sacred grasps something of the contradiction between the order of culture and reality.

The symbolic universe of a culture thus expresses the contradiction between culture and reality as experienced by the members of a society. The cultural dialectic orders this contradiction and locates it at the centre of the project of existence. It permeates all human experience and all levels of the life of a society. For example, it manifests itself in the ambivalence of thought and action, in the tension between the underlying intentions and the results of human activities, in the contradictions between the symbolic universe and reality, and between individual action and the project of existence of the society. By grafting itself onto the natural, a culture restructures the natural in both the group and the environment into a dialectical whole composed of contradictory elements. Culture cannot exist except in relation to the natural, while the natural has no meaning without the cultural. The latter was clearly seen by Lewis Mumford when he said: 'It is only through the light of consciousness that the universe becomes visible, and should that light disappear, only nothingness would remain. Except on the lighted stage of human consciousness, the mighty cosmos is but a mindless nonentity. Only through human words and symbols, registering human thought, can the universe disclosed by astronomy be rescued from its everlasting vacuity. Without that lighted stage, without the human drama played upon it, the whole theater of the heavens, which so deeply moves the human soul, exalting and dismaying it, would dissolve again into its own existential nothingness, like Prospero's dream world.'[4]

Because the project of existence of a society is founded on a cultural dialectic, it tolerates and uses a certain level of disorganization for its own evolution. A society can therefore never be regarded as a mere structure or mechanism or a system of functions, nor can the cultural dialectic be reduced to the contradictions between the forces and relations of production. If a society becomes too much like a mechanism, it passes its own death sentence. It is a dialectical whole in which the creativity of its members must constantly be exercised to respond to the challenges arising from its own contradictions, from other societies, or from its physical environment.[5]

The maintenance of a society's cultural home in reality is therefore much more complex than a struggle for survival in the material sense. Since a project of existence is a human creation based on a sacred and a system of myths on which reality constantly imposes itself, it can be called into question by on-going experience. A society must be busy maintaining its cultural home in reality or it will slowly lose its sacred coherence and eventually disappear. Physical survival is therefore only a part of cultural survival. The complexity of tasks necessitated by cultural survival is far greater than those imposed by the economic activities of a society. We see no reason why economic activities should be the master activity in human history. In fact, the birth, life, and death of civilizations appear in many cases not to have been caused by economic factors in the first place.[6] If a project of existence is to mediate the relationship with reality, it requires a variety of dimensions of mediation, some of which can be readily identified.

A society must have adequate knowledge of its environment in order to be able to construct and maintain its symbolic universe. It also requires a diversity of technologies to satisfy the needs associated with its way of life. The needs depend in part on the 'human nature' created by its culture. These technologies are a part of a system of production whose output requires a system of distribution. Each new generation needs to be socialized to transform a natural diversity into an individual diversity based on a cultural unity, which in turn must yield the social diversity required to perform all tasks related to the project of existence. The events of human life, such as birth, marriage, and death, need to be integrated into the social fabric of society. A political master must be found for the collective human power created by a society and choices between political options have to be made. The normal activities of a society need to be distinguished from others by means of values. The former need to be institutionalized and violations of these institutions need to be dealt with. A society also has to settle the question of right and wrong. It needs to relate to the powers which, according to the collective metaconscious, shape the project of existence. Frequently, cultures also have ways of expressing something of what the patterns of the collective metaconscious reveal about that society and the existential condition of its members. In other words, together the dimensions of mediation constitute a whole which forms the basis for mediating all relationships the members of a society enter into. Some of these dimensions are the scientific, technological, economic, social, political, legal, moral, religious, and artistic. This list is not comprehensive, however. The number of dimensions and their individual and collective configurations vary according to the project of existence by which a culture mediates the relationship between the society and reality.

No single dimension of mediation mediates a specific set of relationships the members of a society enters into, to the exclusion of all others. This is evident when one attempts to classify the activities of daily life according to the dimensions of mediation. It will become evident that the activity of buying something in a bakery, for example, has an economic as well as a social dimension. The concept of dimensions of mediation is an ideal type for analysing the socio-cultural fabric of a society.

CHALLENGES TO A CULTURE

Insight into the roles the various dimensions of mediation play in helping to build and maintain a society's cultural home in reality can be gained by examining some of the challenges that society will face. Consider the challenges first of time, and then of space and the group.

If a culture is to create a stable project of existence in reality, it must adequately mediate the influence of time. Time is a threat to any project of existence because the relationships the members of a society enter into change constantly, and little by little these changes can call into question many aspects of daily life and eventually the entire project of existence of a society. If a project of existence is to be at least partly successful at overcoming determinisms, it must aid the members of a society in mastering time. We have already seen how myths can mediate the effects of time. Religion can also help dominate time by removing the finitude of human life. It also provides explanations of what was and what is to be. In some cultures time is made cyclic: although what was is no more, it will come back. Time can also be halted by language in the sense that past experiences can be relived in the present when they are recorded in writing or retold from memory.

Social institutions can also help mediate the effects of time. Some societies believed that the cultural order of their society degraded with time. The belief was that at the origin of the world there was a chaos in which all energies were concentrated and that the order which emerged from this chaos used up energy. If the social order was to be preserved, a society had to periodically be plunged back into the primitive chaos to renew its energies. This took the form of a feast in which total disorder had to reign. In primitive Rome, for example, during the annual feast of Saturnalia all institutions had to be renewed by being negated. For three days slaves became masters and masters became slaves; men took on the roles of women and vice versa. For three days a slave was placed on the throne and given unlimited power, but when the feast was over he was killed. During that time, the king, if he was found, was put to death. After the feast, the institutions had renewed their energies and life could go on as before.

All these measures are inadequate to create a cultural order on the level of daily life. People need durable relations that can stand the test of time. It is for this reason that all societies for thousands of years have created legal dimensions of mediation.[7] By setting up a system of juridically founded institutions a culture creates artificial relationships which pretend that nothing changes, and the legal dimensions of mediation sanction those who cause a relationship to change. For example, in a marriage relationship both partners change in unpredictable ways, but once they enter this institution they know what they can expect from each other and the society knows what it can expect from them. Their relationship takes on a measure of predictability. By the institution of marriage, the legal dimension of mediation obliges the members of a society not to let these relationships be dominated by circumstances. In this sense it limits the possible ways marriages can evolve so as to make the future predictable, and it sanctions those who disturb the artificially imposed order by causing a divorce.

Another example is business relations of any kind. When a member of a society enters into a contract with another member, the legal dimension of mediation gives these relationships an artificial predictability which ignores all changes due to the passing of time, or it makes these changes conform to a model. Regardless of whether one of the parties becomes ill, loses his job, moves to another location, or of any other change that may occur, he is not absolved from his responsibilities. The legal dimension of mediation stabilizes the relationship to make it predictable in time, and it sanctions those who change its form. A legal dimension of mediation thus permits a society to create an order in all its domains of activities by providing a system of models of behaviour. One knows what one can expect from the other members of the society and what they expect in return. In this way the legal dimension of mediation helps a society master time.

The legal dimension of mediation also helps a society to meet the challenges of space. For a project of existence to be workable in daily life, a society must establish stable predictable relationships with its environment. This may appear a trivial matter to modern people who, with an extensive scientific knowledge, are able to predict much of what can be expected from nature. It has already been noted that a knowledge of regularities in nature is synonymous with predictability only if nature is believed to be like a gigantic mechanism unable to do anything but follow the 'laws' inscribed in it; in that case a knowledge of those laws makes nature predictable. But a general belief that nature is free from gods and spirits or other supernatural powers is barely five hundred years old. If a society believes nature to be governed by supernatural beings, knowledge of its regularities is not synonymous with predictability, for the supernatural beings could always change the behaviour of nature at any instant if they wished to do so. All prior regularity of behaviour was thus no guarantee for the future, and a knowledge of nature could be applied with confidence only if some contract with the supernatural powers had been established. If the members of these early societies were to have orderly and predictable relationships with their environment, they had to enter into an agreement with the supernatural powers. Since natural phenomena are generally spatially localized, it was generally believed that each supernatural being had a specific competence in a limited territory.

For a traditional society to establish a project of existence, it had to mark out a specific territory and make a contract with the local supernatural beings. These rituals had a religious but also legal character. The legal dimension of mediation modelled and stabilized the relationships with the supernatural powers as it did in the case of social relations. This ensured that the experience of the local environment would be stable and predictable. Only when the contract with the local supernatural powers had been juridically and religiously founded, entered into, and maintained by appropriate rituals was it possible for a society to establish a cultural order to replace the natural one, because the gods had consented to co-operate with the human order. Outside this territory other supernatural beings reigned over nature, and since the members of the society had no relationships with them, anything at all could happen there. For any expedition outside their territory, they required the services of a magician who was in contact with the supernatural beings of the surrounding territories. The magician, being in contact with these powers, lived outside the order of a society, and was therefore both a necessity and a threat. Magic was a dimension of mediation complementing religion.

Within the territory, the society ordered all the relationships necessary for its project of existence. An example of a juridically instituted relationship is furnished by property relations. Contrary to what is often believed, the original reason for their institution was not in the first place to protect people from theft but to protect them from the powers of nature reclaiming what people had appropriated. Here we see how the legal dimension of mediation set up a space and within it ordered all the relationships necessary for the maintenance of a project of existence by means of a system of institutions. This is still the case today. Most cultures have been constituted into nation-states within a carefully designated territorial boundary. Their borders delimit a space within which a legal system orders all relationships directly relevant to their project of existence.

To gain further insight into how legal dimensions of mediation are necessitated by the daily-life experience of the group, we need to reinterpret briefly some aspects of the process of socialization studied earlier. All meaningful relationships into which the child is able to enter have a dialectical tension between a normal and a non-normal component. For example, all communication must situate itself between a message containing already known information and complete randomness or noise. In other words, it presupposes systems of paradigms. Any communication must have a previously determined component corresponding to a paradigm to interpret the stimuli and a non-previously determined one to provide new information. This is also valid for any relationship the child learns to have with her environment. The system of paradigms acquired by a child corresponds to a diversity of normal relationships which make sense to her and to the other members of her speech community. They are therefore normative to the culture in the sense that they can take on a meaning only within the scope of a paradigm. The child continually discovers that, if she makes up her own words or behaves differently from the normal pattern of a relationship, she will not be understood by others and risks receiving disapproving reactions. She thus gradually internalizes the metaconscious foundation for the laws of her culture.

Because the structure of experience acts as the metaconscious foundation for the institutional framework, individuals live almost spontaneously in accord with the institutions of their society. The paradigms in their structures of experience provide them with models of behaviour. All this presupposes, of course, that the process of socialization did not occur too far on the fringes of a society or was not undermined by serious dificulties. Deviant behaviour and juvenile delinquency can be the result in such cases. A highly permissive childhood environment can seriously interfere with this aspect of the development of the structure of experience. We should note that in many societies, the end of the process of socialization was marked by a ritual of initiation. The youngsters became new persons, as it were, equipped with the 'human nature' of their cultures. They were now able to accept the responsibilities of full members of society.

While the structures of experience of individuals permit them to think and act in accordance with the internalized project of existence, difficulties necessarily arise on the level of a society. Individual diversity, even when it remains within the cultural unity, can cause social tensions which must be resolved if the project of existence of a society is to function in daily life. This is the inevitable consequence of a society not being part of the natural order. It needs to establish and maintain its own order if it is to survive. The problem we need to explore next is the following: how well are the structures of experience of the members of a society able to mediate all relationships in accordance with the social order?

First consider normal situations in which members can spontaneously fall back on their paradigms. In these situations the diversity of individual behaviour is already considerable, but it generally remains within the order established by a project of existence. However, despite the fact that these paradigms have a normative character, a person can always convince himself that on the basis of the non-normal component of the situation, a non-normal response to the situation is called for. Imagine what this means for a business transaction between two members of a society. No matter what has been explicitly agreed upon, there always remains an implicit part of the agreement, and it is this part that can cause problems when it is used by one member to justify a non-normal course of action. The other member may feel cheated because her understanding of the agreement was different. Both members may be acting in good faith in accordance with the ways they have internalized the paradigms and values for the situation, making the conflict all the more difficult to resolve. If these kinds of conflicts become commonplace the social order of society could eventually be threatened.

For non-normal situations, the risks are even greater. The fact that a society evolves because of a variety of challenges on both a macro- and micro-level leads necessarily to new situations to which existing paradigms cannot easily be extended. If the distance between the culture's values internalized in the structures of experience of the members of a society and a non-normal situation is small, most members spontaneously behave in a way that is comprehensible and acceptable to their fellow members, so that conflicts tend to be relatively rare. Suppose, however, that no value relates directly to a situation. It is then possible, consciously or metaconsciously, to apply one of several values, none of which has a clear priority over the others. Contradictory interpretations of the situation can give rise to different members engaging in contradictory courses of action, paving the way for serious conflicts. The situation is often complicated further by the way power is mediated in the society. The more these situations are decisive in the evolution of a society, the more these conflicts are a serious threat to the cultural order. This can lead to attempts to rectify the situation by an abuse of power, which may produce a schism in the body social.

What happens in these situations is that the distance begins to grow between the project of existence as internalized in the patterns of the collective metaconscious of the members of a society and the fabric of daily life. Language as a dimension of mediation is no longer able to reduce the conflicts to the level of disorganization necessary for cultural evolution of the system. We have already noted how the deepest patterns of the collective metaconscious evolve only very slowly while the patterns of a lesser metaconscious depth can evolve much more rapidly. Consequently, the latter can become less and less compatible with the former if conflicts and the relations of power distort the fabric of daily life to the point where the values implied in the project of existence no longer adequately mediate. This is where the legal dimension of mediation can intervene once again. It can help work out the artificiality of the cultural order right down to the level of daily experience. If the law-makers of a society discern the situation they can legislate solutions to the problems threatening the social order. If the laws anticipate events sufficiently and if they clearly embody the values derived from the myths and sacred of the culture without excessively favouring the powerful sectors of society, they may be widely recognized as just and appropriate for the situation. When this does not happen, the law-makers can attempt to lean on the sacred they represent and on which their authority is normally founded. In some societies they can warn the people that disobedience of these laws can anger the gods or the powers of nature. As long as the people believe in that sacred – that is, as long as the religious dimension of mediation adequately mediates the distance between the sacred and daily-life experience – their laws will generally be obeyed, at least for a while. Laws must find ways and means for realizing the values of the culture of a society, particularly in situations where this does not happen spontaneously.

If, on the other hand, new laws do not correspond to the values held by the members of a segment of society or a society as a whole, they will be considered unjust. Depending on the level of force that is used, the degree to which the laws violate the values alive in the structure of experience of the members of a society, and the strength of these values, the laws could be spontaneously and massively disobeyed. This will render them inapplicable because no non-totalitarian political authority has the means to deal with such a situation.

It should be noted that the role of the legal dimension of mediation varies according to the phase of evolution a society is in. In an early phase of its evolution, when a society has just stabilized itself after its genesis, the distance between the project of existence and the daily-life experience of its members is quite small, the former still largely being founded on myths that are largely metaconscious extrapolations and interpolations of the patterns derived from the latter. The result is that the social order can largely be mediated by its religion. The legal dimension of mediation is generally of the common-law type since the values implied in the structures of experience of its members readily and spontaneously apply to virtually all situations. The common-law system is strongly internalized by all members of society, and where differences of opinion arise between members they can be settled relatively easily by negotiation with or without the aid of a third party. Any proposed solution which clearly embodies the values of the society is easily recognized as just and accepted as self-evident.

As the society continues to evolve, it grows in complexity because of the many challenges it has to overcome. The answers to these challenges both on the macro- and micro-levels are only partly in harmony with the sacred and the system of myths deeply embedded in the collective metaconscious. Hence the values implied in the patterns of the collective metaconscious with a lesser metaconscious depth become more fuzzy and less well defined. The integrality of the structures of experience of the members of society decreases and the cultural symbolic universe becomes less well mediated by the sacred. Individual members can increase their distance from the body social somewhat. They appear to have an identity apart from the group. Consequently, the possibility of social conflict increases while at the same time values become less well defined and hence less able to mediate. Conflicts cannot as easily be mediated by third parties because they will have greater difficulty finding solutions which embody the values clearly and unequivocally. The religious authorities step in or are asked to step in to arbitrate since they represent the highest value. They will seek to mediate, and the judgements handed down may become widely accepted because of the sacred the authorities represent. As a result, these judgements may become models for resolving other disputes and pass into the common-law system, provided they sufficiently embody the weakened values of the society.

The above developments lead to another challenge. When there is no centre of authority in a society other than a religious one, it is obliged to assume a diversity of activities that are in fact political. Because of conflicts and other challenges, choices need to be made which are fundamental enough to be capable of affecting the society's future evolution for some time to come. If on the basis of the values of that society each of the alternatives has good and bad implications, then the system of values cannot mediate between them. When no one option imposes itself as the best one, a decision of a political nature must be taken. It is here where religious authority representing the sacred sooner or later runs into difficulties. It represents the absolute and cannot afford to make mistakes. Yet their religion cannot give infallible guidance. Mistakes will be made, and no ideological constructions can in the long run explain a growing number of decisions which succeeding events show to be in error. Slowly but surely a sphere of thought and action begins to escape the religious authorities precisely because religion is only a partial mediation between the sacred and daily-life experience. In the political sphere new leadership emerges and a political dimension of mediation becomes institutionalized. It is then necessary for the religious authorities to recognize this leadership and vest its authority in religion, for the sacred would be called into question if another authority could establish itself independently from it.

When a political authority emerges, a society enters another phase in its evolution. A political and a religious authority each delimit one another in such a way that together they mediate between the project of existence and the daily-life experience of the members of a society. The two authorities necessarily delimit each other as long as they both derive their ultimate authority from the same source. However, if the state becomes the sacred of a society, the balance between religious and political authority is destroyed. The political authority increasingly penetrates the traditionally religious sphere. At this moment political authority takes on a religious character.

Thus, the legal dimension of mediation of a society is a response to the challenges of time, space, and the group. However, a society encounters many other external and internal challenges to its project of existence. Some of these challenges and the contributions the various dimensions of mediation can make in overcoming them become evident when we examine the evolution of a society.

CULTURAL EVOLUTION

In the previous sections we found that, when a society establishes an artificial order in reality, it embarks on a process of cultural evolution distinct from natural evolution. Because of the dialectical tension between them, the process of cultural evolution is an on-going attempt to establish a dynamic equilibrium between the cultural order and reality. This equilibrium causes and encounters new challenges. A response to these challenges must then be found. If a successful response emerges, a new dynamic equilibrium will be established which in its turn will be disturbed by new challenges. In the course of cultural evolution, the social dimension of mediation is faced with the challenge of continually transforming the 'natural' unity and diversity of each new generation to an artificial individual and social unity and diversity in accordance with the evolving culture and project of existence.

Let us first consider the distance between the daily experiences of the members of a society and the project of existence. Although the latter is internalized in the patterns of the collective metaconscious, it is available to those individuals only to the extent that they are sensitive to these patterns. However, this sensitivity is very limited for most people, and even where it does exist, it expresses itself only indirectly, as in art.

The distance between the daily-life experiences of the members of a society and the project of existence is large, for the reasons we can recall from our earlier analysis. In the first place, the metaconscious processes of integration, which establish the patterns of the collective metaconscious including the sacred and the system of myths, are infinitely slow compared to the flux of daily experience. In the second place, these patterns have an anonymous and collective character, while daily experience remains personal no matter how widely it may be shared with others. Finally, these patterns are the result of a historical process to which many generations contribute, while daily experience is personal and immediate.

The problem is not merely to bridge the distance between the daily-life experiences of the members of a society and the project of existence, but to do so in a non-uniform manner so as to create a social diversity within a cultural unity. The social dimension of mediation must organize and harmonize the diversity of daily activities of the members of a society while keeping them on the course of evolution of the project of existence. In other words, the social dimension of mediation must allow the project of existence to condition the daily experiences of the members of a society differently, while leaving room for human freedom and creativity, without which no cultural evolution is possible.

In each new generation the social diversity and cultural unity required for a project of existence can be recreated in a variety of ways that together constitute a spectrum. At one of its ends we find societies that limit social mobility as much as possible so that children follow in their parents' footsteps, while on the other end we find societies with a maximum of social mobility. By means of an educational system, children are classified according to how essential their abilities are for the development of the

280 Culture and History

project of existence. They are trained for those social positions where their abilities can be best put to use. It should be pointed out that these two extremes are, of course, ideal types.

The position a society takes in this spectrum is largely dictated by the kind of knowledge base it has – that is, how it organizes its scientific dimension of mediation. Most traditional societies had severely limited social mobility because their knowledge base was embedded in experience and could not be separated from it. Knowledge embedded in experience can be transmitted only by a kind of apprenticeship arrangement of learning things by doing them. For example, in agrarian societies where the extended family is an important societal unit and work is not separated from the family, children grow up exposed to and often participating in the activities of their parents. The knowledge they acquire will not be lost to society if social mobility is restricted so that they take up the social positions of their parents. The transmission of the culture's knowledge base and the re-creation of the social diversity necessary for the culture's project of existence are thus assured, provided there are no serious demographic changes. In these societies the process of socialization yields structures of experience in each new generation which are very detailed with respect to everything related to the position a person will occupy in the social hierarchy, and far less detailed in relation to the activities associated with other positions. The children of a baker, for example, will have structures of experience that are very detailed about being a baker and much less detailed about being part of the nobility. They will, of course, learn enough about other segments of the project of existence to be able to relate to the members of society involved in them. Because they will generally interact most extensively with people in the same stratum of the social hierarchy, their structures of experience tend to have more in common with these people. In fact, each social stratum can be characterized by certain internal and external regularities in the lives of their members, which, although generally recognizable as belonging to a specific culture, are unique to that stratum. These unique characteristics are based on the specificity of the structures of experience of the persons involved.

Present-day industrial societies, on the other hand, require a great deal of social mobility, and once again the reason is related to the character of the principal knowledge base. Modern science and technology are founded on knowledge that has been separated from experience in the sense that it can no longer be acquired by doing things. A construction worker can put up steel structures all his life, but he will not learn stress analysis from this experience. The new knowledge base is transmitted only in the classroom.

In industrial societies an educational system differentiates between people on the basis of certain intellectual abilities relevant to the primary knowledge base and prepares them for different positions in the project of existence according to these abilities. Ideally, the range of social positions open to an individual does not depend on one's position at birth, but on one's achievements in the educational system. In order for this process to function, many traditional barriers to social mobility had to be eliminated as much as possible. Once again social diversity depends on a diversity of individual structures of experience, but the nature of this diversity is highly complex.[8]

The specific forms the social dimensions of mediation have taken all throughout history are extraordinarily diverse. The reasons are clear. If there is no master activity in human history, there is no common denominator between the projects of existence of past cultures. Hence the distance between each project of existence and the 'natural' diversity of each new generation needs to be mediated differently in each case. However, the situation in our time is beginning to change radically as societies increasingly adopt similar projects of existence based on economic development by means of a universal science and technology.

The social dimension of mediation must also respond to the challenge of cultural evolution. As the project of existence of a society evolves, the unity and diversity of structures of experience of the members must evolve with it. This is a matter, of course, for those segments of the society directly involved in developing the project of existence. Their position in the social hierarchy is central with respect to this development. Hence the members of these segments, more directly than the people in other segments, internalize the current status of the project of existence in the course of their daily experience. If they also respond creatively to the challenges encountered by the culture, they constitute what Toynbee has called a creative minority.[9] Other segments of society are not as centrally involved in the project of existence; hence their structures of experience do not necessarily evolve along with those of the creative minority. A potential threat to social unity is therefore indissociable from cultural evolution. The diversity of the mental maps of the members of a society must constantly be adjusted while maintaining the cultural dialectic. This challenge will be studied next in some detail.

When the development of the structures of experience of children was examined earlier, a distinction was drawn between cumulative and non-cumulative developments. We reintroduce this distinction here in relation to the cultural evolution of a society. After completion of the process of socialization – that is, after the establishment of the deepest patterns of the collective metaconscious – the structure of experience of a person continues to develop as a result of countless new experiences. These experiences can be arranged along a spectrum in accordance with the implications they have for the sacred and system of myths embedded in the patterns of the collective metaconscious. Towards one end of the spectrum we find experiences that were lived simply by paradigmatically extending the relational capacity of the person's structure of experience according to the sacred and system of myths. We will call these experiences culturally cumulative.

On the other end of the spectrum we find experiences that were lived by introducing further contradictions into a person's structure of experience because they are in some way incompatible with the sacred and system of myths. Experiences of this kind do not, of course, threaten the basis of the culture's unity as it exists in that person's collective metaconscious, and they therefore do not threaten the roots of that individual's life. They do, however, create a growing level of disorganization in the structure of experience, rendering it internally less consistent. The development of these structures as wholes remains essentially culturally cumulative despite the occurrences of what we will call culturally non-cumulative experiences. However, when a significant number of these culturally non-cumulative experiences begin to link up to form new metaconscious patterns not necessarily compatible with the deeper patterns of the collective metaconscious, the roots of a person's existence may be threatened and the evolution of her structure of experience may become culturally non-cumulative.

Just because the development of an individual's structure of experience is culturally cumulative or non-cumulative does not mean that the evolution of a culture as a whole is the same. The latter is based on the interaction of a great many structures of experience. Individual and social diversity render the problem highly complex. Consider first the situation in which the creative minority is faced with a series of micro- or macro-level challenges. If these challenges can be met by a variety of culturally cumulative experiences which extend and refine the project of existence without changing the configuration, a local development of the culture takes place. A general development in the culture occurs if the creative minority gives leadership to the other segments of society and if the latter follow the lead because the people involved consciously or metaconsciously recognize that the successful responses embody some of the values and myths of the culture. The society as a whole then evolves in a culturally cumulative way.

We will say that it is in a developmental period in its history when the society's project of existence is being extended and refined on the basis of its sacred, system of myths, and values. During these periods, the various segments of the body social share the same sacred, myths, and values. This is not to say that there are no power struggles between different segments or that one segment does not exploit another. On the contrary. However, these conflicts do not call the project of existence into question because they remain based on the sacred and system of myths. They concern aspects of the project of existence rather than its very basis. During a developmental period the social structure of a society may therefore be conceptualized as a continuous hierarchy of social strata such as the spectrum of upper, middle, and lower classes, for example. There are other periods, however, when this is not possible.

Although the structures of experience of the members of society evolve mostly in a culturally cumulative fashion during a developmental period, culturally non-cumulative experiences do occur as a result of the cultural dialectic and some of the challenges. As these experiences begin to link up into metaconscious patterns and as these patterns begin to threaten those of the collective metaconscious, individuals face a challenge to the very roots of their existence and society as a whole faces a deterioration in its cultural integrity. If this problem cannot be solved on the basis of its sacred, myths, and values, the developmental period draws to a close and a period of transition sets in. The latter is culturally non-cumulative.

The end of a developmental period in the evolution of a society can also come prematurely if a major challenge to its project of existence appears which cannot be resolved on the basis of the sacred, myths and values. The experiences of attempting to deal with the challenges are culturally non-cumulative and, if the challenge persists over a long period of time, they may link up into metaconscious patterns that threaten those of the collective metaconscious. The result is much the same kind of situation as we just described. In both these cases, the behaviour of the various segments of society begins to change dramatically. People begin to sense a loss of meaning in their lives because the roots of their existence are being threatened. The members of the creative minority who have power over their condition, because they are not dominated or exploited by other segments, may seek to find new meaning for their existence. They will typically use every opportunity to attempt to restore a greater measure of cultural integrity in their lives. If the resulting metaconscious patterns link up with those resulting from the earlier culturally non-cumulative experiences, two related processes may result. One is a process of desacralization as the sacred and system of myths deteriorates, and the other is a process of resacralization as the former basis of the culture is reconstituted around a new sacred. Many of the old myths may be reincorporated into the new system of myths. These processes characterize a culturally non-cumulative evolution in what we shall call a transition period.

This process of transforming the collective metaconscious takes many generations. It is not always begun by the creative minority. In fact, if it responds to the situation in a non-creative manner and seeks to maintain the status quo by means of force, another segment of society may take the initiative. Unless the society breaks down,[10] this other segment may eventually become a new creative minority provided the old creative minority does not reawaken to pursue the new direction of cultural evolution that has been opened up.

Other segments of society may respond quite differently to an imminent transition period. Their members may sense the crumbling of the sacred and system of myths while not as yet experiencing that a new basis for their existence is in sight. In the extreme case some of these people may act as if their world is coming to an end and, culturally speaking, this is of course true. They do not see the new doors that are being opened as the sacred and some myths disintegrate. This may be the case because their position in the social hierarchy has not exposed them as much to what is happening as the creative minority. Other members of these segments may see the new possibilities but strive to preserve the old ways. Since these segments have little power, the efforts generally come to nothing. As the creative minority continues to implement the new direction for cultural evolution, the members of the other segments of society will increasingly be confronted with a loss of meaning in their lives. The very roots of their existence are threatened as the patterns of the collective metaconscious continue to disintegrate while no new patterns have linked up as yet to any significant degree.

Anomie[11] sets in because there is movement in the cultural foundations. The incidence of suicide, violence, mental disorder, alcoholism, vandalism, arson, and other such problems will increase because the social selves of people are inextricable intermingled with their culture. Disturbances in the latter will therefore affect the former. The above problems are symptoms of an illness in the body social and point to the need for a healing dialectical transformation. People who cannot cope with the enormous contradictions and who see their lives as decaying into non-sense may lose hope and resort to desperate acts. Others may find consolation in new ideologies or religious movements. As time goes on, however, new patterns of the collective metaconscious will also emerge in the members of the less creative segments of society. A new body social will be constituted on the basis of a new sacred, system of myths, and values.

During a transition period the body social can no longer be conceptualized as a hierarchy of social strata that are more or less functionally complementary within a common project of existence. We now find a number of classes in fundamental conflict with one another because they no longer fully share the same sacred, system of myths, and values. In the nineteenth century, for example, the traditional project of existence was gradually replaced by one based on the sacred of capital, which founded a cultural order of material progress and the 'happiness' this would bring. A number of classes emerged in the strict sense of that term, as elaborated in the works of Karl Marx. There were classes who responded to the instabilities in the putting-out system. They also addressed the challenges of the many developments that had eroded the traditional structures of the economic, social, political, moral, and religious dimensions of mediation ever since the collapse of the medieval project of existence.[12] These classes were actively promoting what we would call industrialization. However, there were classes who saw the new machines and the order they helped create as a threat to everything they stood for, including their means of existence. They responded to the same challenge by seeking to preserve the traditional way of life by finding solutions on the basis of the traditional sacred and myths. The members of these classes were the last to embody the new cultural order in the collective metaconscious because of their indirect and passive involvement in it. This did not happen until well into the twentieth century. During the transition period the body social had thus broken up into several fragments based on opposing projects of existence with mutually exclusive bases. There was a fundamental conflict over the kind of society they wanted, although no single class could evolve without the others because of the link between the processes of sacralization and desacralization.

As the new project of existence increasingly affected all areas of society, transforming traditional pre-industrial into industrial societies, the structures of experience of all the members of the culture were increasingly again based on the same sacred, system of myths, and values. At that point power struggles and exploitation do not cease, but they are transformed. There is no fundamental opposition at the level of the collective metaconscious. We shall thus make a distinction between social classes and strata on the basis of the relationship they have to the process of cultural evolution of a society. We shall speak of social classes during transition periods and of social strata during developmental periods.

In modern societies the values once limited to what Marx called the bourgeois class have now spread throughout society.[13] The conflicts are no longer centred on whether or not industrial technology and the kind of society that comes with it are good or bad and should be accepted or rejected by means of revolution. They are now centred on who will make the decision concerning the exploitation of technology and the distribution of its benefits, disbenefits, and risks.

Developmental and transitional periods in the evolution of a culture can be distinguished in another way. During the former, the structures of experience of the members of a society evolve in the same direction because the sacred, system of myths, and values act as a social gyroscope. There is little or no negative feedback in the cultural system because of the absence of a point of reference that exists outside of the sacred order.[14] The course of evolution is maintained until a series of culturally non-cumulative experiences arising from various challenges begins to threaten the patterns of the collective metaconscious. Attempts are made to make minor corrections to the course of evolution on the basis of the sacred, myths, and values. If these fail, a transition period begins. The social gyroscope is reset to a different course associated with a new sacred, system of myths, and values. It is important to note that some kinds of structures of the collective metaconscious make it more difficult than others for culturally non-cumulative experiences to link up. They therefore expose their culture to a greater risk of becoming out of touch with reality, which would lead to cultural stagnation and eventual collapse. Because of a weakening sacred, periods of transition are characterized by a lessening degree of alienation and hence a relatively higher level of negative feedback at the expense of a lesser social coherence. Some personalities thrive in this situation.

There is an alternative possibility to a period of transition, namely the break-down of a culture. Let us briefly retrace our steps to see the reasons for this. We have seen that any society encounters a variety of internal and external challenges to its artificial project of existence. In most cases a society evolves by finding a successful response to these challenges. If it does so on the basis of its sacred and system of myths, its evolution is essentially cumulative and all segments of the body social continue to evolve together. During these periods there is a tendency towards a growing level of disorganization in the system due to culturally non-cumulative experiences. Suppose, however, that these experiences do not have enough in common to form metaconscious patterns. There is then no basis from which a new cultural order can be built to replace the current one, and a society can break down. The segments of society increasingly have no basis for belonging together, so they grow apart. Society begins to be divided against itself, and a time of trouble [15] sets in. Because this is a difficult situation, there is a tendency for a segment of society to establish a temporary political solution in the form of a strong state. The other segments typically welcome this as a relief from the time of troubles. This external order has no basis in the structures of experience of the members of society. The state is not an external manifestation of an inner order founded in the collective metaconscious. It can last only as long as it allows the segments of the broken-down society to coexist.

A cultural break-down can also occur if a society cannot successfully overcome a challenge on the basis of its sacred, system of myths, and values. The unsuccessful attempts yield culturally non-cumulative experiences. If these do not point to a new order by forming new metaconscious patterns, a cultural break-down occurs.

Whether the mode of cultural evolution of a society is developmental or transitional affects not only the social dimension of experience but all others as well. We can illustrate this by completing our analysis of the legal dimension of mediation.

During periods of transition from one developmental epoch to another, we typically find the formulation of theories of natural law by the political and religious authorities to prevent the legal system from crumbling along with the cultural edifice. This is an attempt at maintaining a spontaneous obedience to the law. Nevertheless, the handwriting is on the wall. As the members of a society begin to sense a weakening of the sacred manifested by a greater disorder in their structures of experience, they begin to question their religion and start to ignore those laws that no longer correspond to the values that remain alive in their metaconscious. Laws making excessive religious demands fall into disrepute. The people take the political and religious authorities less seriously. They seek to settle their own problems by asking counsel of those who have proved themselves able to settle disputes in ways considered just and acceptable to most people because these settlements embody the values they still hold. A new system of common law generally appears during the periods of transition. Law then appears as a social fact.

When a society breaks down, it enters a time of troubles which, as we have noted, often ends up in the establishment of a strong state. Under these circumstances, the state typically places the common law on record and assigns itself the responsibility for maintaining and updating it. This occurred in the West as part of the expansion of the power and domain of the authority of the state until it became so all-embracing that it constituted a sacred. At this point the distance between the project of existence of that society and the daily-life experience of its members had become very large. Ideally the state should regulate social problems by designing a system of institutions by which the values implicit in a culture can be realized. It cannot create these values itself for they arise spontaneously in the structures of experience of its citizens. The state must invent ways and means that, on the one hand, anticipate social developments and, on the other hand, embody the values recognized by the society. If it succeeds the laws will be recognized as being just and consequently will be readily obeyed. The sanctions set out for the offenders will have to be applied only in exceptional cases, permitting the police and the courts to do their work. If a law does not embody the values of a society it may be ignored by the people, which makes it inapplicable. If the law misjudges a social reality it may be inapplicable because it does not correspond to anything.

When the laws made up by a state embody the values of justice, equality, and order, it is clear that the ways of enforcing them must also embody these values. Laws designed to create social justice and order cannot be enforced by a police force which is corrupt, disorderly, and violent without the public losing respect for the law. The more a state expands its power to become involved in nearly all spheres of activity the more difficult it becomes to make laws which embody the values of the society on the one hand and which correspond to the needs of social reality on the other. The legal system may then deteriorate into little more than a means for organizing society. The state will then have little choice but to lean more heavily on its sacred character by means of political religions or theories of natural law. There is a distance which establishes itself between the state and the legal system it has created since its laws, once explicitly set out, can be used against it. The law may thus turn against the law-maker and delimit the freedom to act arbitrarily. The legal dimension of mediation can therefore never become purely organizational.

On the basis of the distinction we have established between the two modes of cultural evolution, we can begin to draw some simple generalizations. A society is culturally healthy when its project of existence makes extensive use of the structures of experience of its members as fundamental elements of the social gyroscope for the cultural system. In this case, the structures of experience of the members of a society evolve almost spontaneously along with the system because of the dialectical tensions within it. A society which no longer develops this way because it has broken down cannot rely on the structures of experience of its members. It has to design extensive external controls which can usually be put into place only by a powerful and oppressive state. We will need to examine some of these matters in greater detail in the next section, but it is already evident that the degree of cultural integrality can vary greatly depending on the nature of the project of existence, the division of labour it requires, the institutionaliza-tion of its dimensions of mediation, and the phase of cultural evolution it is undergoing. Modern urban mass societies are perhaps the least well integrated on the basis of the structures of experience of their members, but they have the strongest external controls. However, these societies will be examined in a later book.

As far as the integrality of a project of existence is concerned, a great deal depends on how the dimensions of mediation are anchored in the sacred and system of myths. When human groups were submerged in nature, they used human reality with which they were most familiar as an analogy to conceptualize nature. The result was a nature full of spirits and gods. With this mythical conception of nature, the religious, magical, scientific, and technological dimensions of mediation were closely intertwined. In socie-ties preoccupied with technology, the mechanical part of experience has become the paradigm depicting nature and society. As a result, quite different relationships emerge between the above dimensions of mediation. Some of them are inseparable from the culture while others, such as technology, can diffuse to other cultures more easily. These are important matters when examining the evolution of civilizations as systems of societies.

CULTURE, CIVILIZATION, AND HUMANITY

From the perspective developed thus far, the genesis, evolution and death of a society can be understood in terms of the establishment, evolution, and disintegration of a cultural order in reality which acts as the basis for social existence. Since these processes occur in the context of and by interacting with neighbouring societies, a society generally forms an integral part of a civilization. A civilization is constituted of a group of interacting societies having somewhat similar cultural sacreds, systems of myths, and values which allow for and result from processes of diffusion.

Both the possibility and necessity for the artificial order of societies and civilizations stems from the way human beings are linked to reality. If we can speak of a 'human nature' at all, it would certainly include the human decision not to live on the level of immediate experience, but to go beyond it. By symbolically mediating all relationships by means of a culture, human groups transform themselves into artificial societies with a unique 'human nature.' Cultural mediation needs to include certain possibilities and exclude others by means of an absolute or sacred. The price humanity pays for millions of people being able to live together with a measure of meaning and harmony is their being fundamentally alienated by a sacred. A dialectical tension between freedom and alienation thus appears to be a part of any 'human nature.'[16] The profound conscious and metaconscious allegiance to a sacred renders religion (traditional or secular) an integral part of any culture. The mythologies of past societies may be seen as attempts to penetrate the deeper metaconscious levels of human existence, which is possible only by creating a unique mode of communication.

These mythologies tell us something about the roots of social life in an interrelated reality. People are a part of this reality, while at the same time they introduce an element of freedom and self-determination into it. By means of culture, societies appear to have asserted the will to freedom and self-determination in the face of a host of forces seeking to determine their existence. By establishing a non-natural order, they struggle to defend it against the challenges from within and without. In this section we briefly sketch how the various phases in the evolution of a society can be interpreted from the above perspective, as well as the contribution this makes to our understanding of the human phenomenon.

While it is quite possible that during a certain period in the evolution of a society one dimension of mediation may dominate all the others, it is not the same for all times and for all societies. Hence we have rejected the concept of a master activity in human history. Neither religion, politics, technology, nor the economy, as central as they may be to the projects of existence of past or present societies, are master activities in human history. Because so-called primitive societies left us little else but their tools and products of their technologies, we tend to think of prehistoric people as *homo faber*. The classification of societies in terms of their technology and the division of prehistory and history into the stone, bronze, and iron ages and so on, are the consequences of imposing the myths of the nineteenth century onto all of human history. From the perspective of culture as the social ecology of a society, we need to interpret the distinction between prehistory and history in terms of the way human societies mediated their relations with internal and external reality.

The introduction of a culture in reality establishes at least two milieus. The first is the natural milieu, constituted by symbolically mediating all relationships with natural reality. The other is the social milieu, constituted by the non-natural cultural group. Although they become inextricably related in the metaconscious of the members of a society, they nevertheless are not equal in importance. The culture integrates the two milieus into a hierarchy according to their centrality in the project of existence. The primary milieu is the one that dominates the structures of experience of the members of society because most of the metaconscious patterns are based on experiences derived from it. Consequently, it is the one which directly or indirectly provides a culture with everything necessary to sustain its project of existence as well as the principal challenges to it.

For the better part of the prehistoric period, the size of human groups and societies was restricted by a variety of factors, such as the food supply, delimited by the project of existence. As a result, human life was deeply immersed in nature and the natural milieu predominated over the social milieu. The artificiality of the projects of existence of these human groups and societies was particularly limited on the material plane. In fact, we might say that, having taken the decision not to live on the level of immediate experience, humanity had first built up the symbolic bases for culture. It was only after this immense task (about which we know so little) was far advanced that new challenges from the material domain surfaced. Further advances towards a greater freedom from the necessities imposed by the natural milieu could be achieved only by increasing the distance between the human order and the natural order. In other words, immediate experience had to be transcended even further to create more artificial cultural orders. The primary obstacles to a break-through now came from the material limitations of the projects of existence.

It is important not to identify the concept of a growing artificiality of cultures and their projects of existence with that of progress. Not all societies considered the material limitations of their projects of existence as a challenge. The reasons are readily understood. By creating a sacred, cultures alienate themselves from reality by including certain possibilities and excluding others. They are therefore not driven by some mysterious thirst for freedom. Because each step towards freedom is based on a sacred, there is an on-going dialectical relationship between freedom and necessity. There is no human experience of a constantly growing level of freedom but only the on-going encounter of new necessities that accompany newly found freedom. A society that is not faced with challenges will not evolve and may eventually even stagnate and collapse. We clearly see this at the dawn of history. Generally speaking, we may say that civilizations emerged where the existing projects of existence were severely challenged for a variety of reasons, while so-called primitive cultures continued to exist (often until relatively recently) where no serious challenges were encountered or perceived.[17]

The transition from prehistory to history is characterized by the births of civilizations. Civilizations can be distinguished from so-called primitive groups or societies by a reversal of the hierarchy of the natural and social milieus. They are based on projects of existence which are more independent from the natural order and which require large numbers of people for their maintenance. These projects of existence emerge when the social milieu gradually interposes itself between individuals and nature. The necessities of life can now be obtained only if the entire collectivity helps to maintain the project of existence. The primary dangers derive from the social milieu (such as war or political instabilities) since society is better able to defend itself against the dangers associated with the natural milieu (such as wild beasts or drought). The dramatic reversal in the hierarchy of the two milieus also led to new 'human natures' as well as substantial changes in the structure and mode of evolution of society. So-called primitive groups and societies were largely self-regulating because the distance between the project of existence and the structures of experience of the people was small. Hence the interacting structures of experience functioned adequately as a social gyroscope for all dimensions of mediation in a manner similar to the one described for the common-law phase of the legal dimension of mediation.

This is generally not the case for civilizations. Their projects of existence require a more complex division of labour, with the result that the distance between them and the structures of experience of the people increases substantially. Such social systems are far less self-regulating on the basis of the structures of experience of its members. They require a greater complexity of institutions to complement the internalized mode of self-regulation. All this contributed to an increasing distance between nature and culture due to an increased level of artificiality of the latter.

If the transition from prehistory to history hinges on a gradual reversal in the hierarchy of the two milieus, we need to inquire into the reasons for such a dramatic change. Given the interrelated character of culture, it is, of course, not likely that single causes can ever be found. Besides, a specific set of conditions will elicit different responses from individuals and cultures because of human freedom. The usual explanations for the emergence of civilizations are well known, and we will only briefly indicate how they can be reinterpreted from our perspective.

Suppose, in addition to its 'internal' challenges, a society faces a major challenge to its way of life as a result of changes in the climate, for example. Its members then have the choice of facing the challenge and establishing a new project of existence less dependent on the climate or moving to regions where the climate does not necessitate such a change. Suppose a group of people decides to attempt to face the challenge of an advancing desert by cultivating the land adjacent to the swamp of a river delta. It is easily imagined how such a decision could trigger off a chain of challenges and responses, the end result of which nobody could have imagined. Perhaps at first small plots of land adjacent to the swamp were watered by hand. As the desert continued to advance other groups may have been driven to do the same. Soon all the land that could be irrigated by carrying water over a reasonable distance was taken up, but the influx of new groups continued. Under the pressure of this challenge, small irrigation ditches may have been dug to bring water to the land further away from the swamp. Assuming that the level of the land increased with the distance from the swamp, this solution had its limits as well. As more groups continued to be driven to the river delta by the advancing desert, struggles for control of the agricultural land must have broken out. In time a political order must have resolved this problem and forced everyone to participate in extending the new mode of agriculture into the swamps themselves. This project was probably thought of earlier on, but it became feasible only when a central political power had been established.

The civilizations which constructed the massive irrigation works in the deltas of some rivers could have come into existence in part by means of some chain of challenges and responses of the type just described. Regardless of the precise sequence of events, there is a tendency for such chains to be self-reinforcing. The new experiences begin to link up into metaconscious patterns that are likely to yield intuitions. When these are implemented on the basis of the structures of experience in which these new patterns are prominent, the new project of existence is likely to be advanced. Yet we should not underestimate the complexity of the process of the birth of a civilization. Recall that the structures of experience of the people involved function as a kind of mental map in which every experience is situated in relation to all the others. The introduction of a subset of new experiences calls into question the whole structure of these maps. Every experience related to every dimension of mediation needs to be reinterpreted and relocated in the maps. Some of the old landmarks disappear and new ones need to be found. Yet human beings do not easily depart from the traditions that have become an integral part of their lives. The systematic character of a culture makes it resistant to change, but when substantial changes impose themselves they disturb other parts of the system to which they are directly related. When these parts are reinterpreted and restructured to be compatible with the changed segment, a further disturbance in still other parts results. This process continues until the entire system has been transformed into a new dialectical whole. It usually requires many generations before new patterns of the collective metaconscious can establish a new sacred, system of myths, and values; and it is only when this has taken place that the birth phases of a new civilization comes to an end.

The process by which a civilization is born is thus a cultural conversion elaborated by all those who participate in it. It is a chain-reaction type of process in which a successful but culturally non-cumulative response to a challenge leads to another challenge because of the disturbance it causes in the culture, and so on. If most of these creative responses are worked out by a creative minority, the rest of society does not necessarily follow in their footsteps. They may not see the need for change and consequently cling to tradition, or they may feel their social position is jeopardized. When the unity of the body social is broken, the birth process may fail unless a state can impose a political unity.

An equally serious risk to the birth process is the loss of creative power. There is a familiar human tendency to become complacent as a result of past successes. When this happens, the culture's home in reality may fall into disrepair, which again could lead to a social break-down.

There are also some factors, however, that tend to operate in favour of the birth process of a civilization being completed successfully. The challenge triggering the birth process is clearly a substantial one, requiring a strong culturally non-cumulative response. Such a response is therefore not likely to be geographically local. If a large geographical area is exposed to the same challenge, there is a tendency for the integrality of the existing cultures to be severely weakened by their quest for a solution. The cultural differences that existed before the challenge made its appearance now appear less important, with the result that communication, the sharing of experiences, and the diffusion of new ideas, institutions, and other cultural elements become easier. At the same time, competition between groups and societies intensifies. They are no longer fundamentally different because they all struggle to meet the same challenge. Consequently, when one of the groups or societies begins to develop what appears to be a successful response, the others tend to imitate it on the basis of their own culture.

A civilization is generally structured as a group of interacting societies with similar courses of evolution. These societies have developed similar patterns of the collective metaconscious, and hence similar sacreds, systems of myths, and values.[18] The plurality of cultures within the unity of a civilization allows the successful responses created by one society to readily diffuse to the others. A healthy competition can develop, which increases the likelihood of the civilization successfully evolving as a result of the chain of challenges and responses. If the creative minority of one society ceases to be active because of the tendency to become complacent as a result of past successes, another society may take the lead. This is quite evident in the history of Western civilization where almost all societies excelled in creativity at one time or another, so that their influence radiated throughout the civilization. Because of its unique past, its current position in the civilization, or its geographical location, one society may be more capable of responding to challenges than others. While the plurality of cultures thus strengthens the ability of a civilization to meet challenges, it also leads to internal power struggles and exploitation.

It follow that the birth of a new civilization is a hazardous process. Only relatively few civilizations have been born as compared to the much larger number of so-called primitive societies. We have analysed the births of civilizations only schematically, for a detailed examination is beyond the scope of this work. We have sought only to indicate how their emergence can be examined from the perspective presented earlier.

Next we briefly consider the growth and evolution of civilizations. Once the patterns of the collective metaconscious of the member cultures have been established in embryonic form, the growth phase sets in, during which cultural evolution is predominantly cumulative in nature. In other words, the growth phase is a period of self-articulation in relation to the challenges it encounters. A society has to learn to be itself in a host of circumstances by meeting the challenges on the basis of the foundations of the member cultures. If it fails to accomplish this, the integrity of its cultural order will be eroded. The process of growth is not mechanistic, however. In each case the member cultures must recognize the challenge and decide whether or not to respond and to work out that response. There remains an element of human freedom and indeterminism in history. Growth is a process of integrating an increasing range of experiences into sets of patterns which are increasingly comprehensive, flexible, and stable in the face of new challenges. In other words, growth is not characterized by a greater mastery over the environment,[19] but by an articulation of the being of a civilization in relation to its physical and social environments.

During a period of growth there is a lot of activity in the 'soul' of a civilization. It cannot neglect internal disorders in order to concentrate on a greater mastery over the environment. While it is true that initially the challenges may be largely external, there is a tendency for them increasingly to arise from within. A growing number of culturally non-cumulative experiences in the minds of the people weakens both the integrality and foundation of the cultural order. If a society is alert to these internal challenges, it will develop a greater capacity for self-determination. A period of growth is thus a period during which a civilization strengthens the establishment of a plurality of similar interacting cultural orders in reality by reinforcing their internal coherence. Enormous demands are made on the creative ability of a society. Yet this still relatively mysterious human potential appears to come and go. At some periods in the history of a society it makes a culture highly dynamic, while at other times it is present at such a low level that the culture barely holds its own. Here we encounter another important aspect of the structure of a culture: namely, the relationship between the 'human nature' it creates and moulds and the creativity that 'nature' is able to generate and sustain.

During the growth of a civilization, the locus of creativity is typically embodied in one or more creative minorities of the member societies. If these creative efforts are to allow the civilization to evolve, the people in the less creative segments of society must either have similar experiences to those of the members of the creative minorities (which is rarely the case) or they must imitate the externals of these new experiences. The latter process has been studied by Toynbee,[20] who called it mimesis. Either process keeps everyone in tune with the evolution of the constituent society.

In the previous section we have noted that during a developmental period (such as growth) the number of culturally non-cumulative experiences in the structures of experience of the members of the constituent societies of a civilization tends to increase.[21] Eventually, the cultural foundations of one society after another will be threatened. As one of the constituent societies goes through a process of desacralization and resacralization, the others may not yet have entered a period of transition. Again we see how a limited cultural plurality of a civilization can stabilize the process during which one constituent society after another goes through a transitional period. The life of a civilization is thus marked by an alternating sequence of developmental and transitional periods.

Although there is no reason why civilizations cannot go on for as long as history lasts, there is nevertheless the possibility of a civilization breaking down, disintegrating, and eventually disappearing. We consider this from the perspective developed in this work. A civilization is a system only in the sense that it is composed of a set of interacting cultural orders established in reality in ways that are similar enough for cultural exchanges to be possible, and yet sufficiently different to create dialectical tensions to encourage and stimulate these exchanges. Their absolutes are sufficiently similar to create a collective cultural field with various regions. A civilization derives its strength from the similar and hence mutually reinforcing constituent fields. It is frequently not unified politically,[22] and in this sense a civilization is not a system. We have already seen that, under the pressure of major challenges that can launch the birth process of a civilization, societies become closely united on the cultural plane, but not necessarily on the political plane. While this situation invites stimulating competition, it can also lead to endless warfare. This is less likely in the beginning when all societies are busily seeking to meet their common challenges, but once they begin to meet these challenges so that mutual co-operation is less vital, competition can easily degenerate into armed struggle. As the constituent societies grow in strength, this warfare can become increasingly destructive. This is particularly true when these societies mistakenly believe that genuine freedom and self-determination flows from a greater mastery over the physical and social environments. A new challenge of internal conflict brings the rhythm of desacralization and sacralization to an end, producing a break-down. The civilization is tearing itself apart: the disadvantages of cultural unity without a political unity begin to outweigh the advantages.

At this point the time of troubles of a civilization may come to an end. Once again the constituent societies are faced with a major challenge. They must politically unite or they will destroy each other. The challenge can be met by founding what Toynbee has called a universal state. But this response brings with it a new challenge. A centralized state requires a large civil service and a well-paid army. It is established at the expense of local government and local mechanisms of cultural self-regulation on the basis of the structures of experience of the people. As this continues, the state has to pick up an increasing number of problems that are no longer regulated locally, while at the same time the superimposed regulation of the civilization by the state externalizes all kinds of local details, leading to even more problems. It is not difficult to see, therefore, that once the challenge of self-destruction disappears from the horizon of a civilization's experience because of the successful response in the form of the universal state, a new challenge emerges due to the inability of the state satisfactorily to regulate and control the constituent societies. Moreover, the costs of supporting a universal state are high and continue to climb as the role of government expands. The economy can produce the required resources only if it manages to increase its productivity substantially. Yet this is rarely possible. Major economic advances have been relatively rare historical events. If an economic crisis breaks out and some parts of the empire become too impoverished by the tax burden, rebellions may break out, requiring further intervention by the state. A self-reinforcing process may cause the universal state to lapse slowly into 'anarchy.' Many people begin to sense that the blessings of the universal state are now outweighed by the disadvantages. Regions and societies may take up arms to gain self-determination. The whole process may now repeat itself. Once the challenge of widespread armed conflict presses heavily on the people, they may be willing to accept and support the reinstitution of the universal state. The life of a civilization may thus alternate between a time of troubles and periods of political unity maintained by a universal state.[23]

There is another question which needs to be addressed: why do civilizations break down to slide into a time of troubles? The birth, growth, and life of a civilization correspond to a human decision to establish a new artificial order in reality. The cultural order is the vehicle by which societies and civilizations journey through reality. It is the basis for the freedom and alienation of human existence. When this vehicle breaks down a civilization loses its self-determination. Toynbee has shown that a break-down rarely comes because a civilization is being destroyed by outside forces.[24] The main threat comes from within.

A break-down can come because there is a loss of creativity, withdrawal of mimesis, or the inability of the old institutional framework to embody the new socio-cultural forces that emerge. We have already touched on the first problem. A great deal of the life of a civilization is based on routine, custom, and tradition, all requiring little of its creative potential and thus leaving it free to be focused on the challenges that need to be faced. However, the more mechanical aspects can overcome the creative part of life. A creative minority can become a victim of mimesis. If this happens, the second threat to the vitality of a culture can easily follow: there is no longer a leadership that commands respect, hence there is no reason why people should spontaneously follow the now complacent creative minority. As each segment of society begins to go its own way, the body social breaks into fragments.

The third cause for a breakdown occurs if, for a variety of reasons, new social forces cannot be harmoniously integrated into the institutional frameworks of its constituent societies. As a result, the framework for social life can collapse. In any of these cases (examined by Toynbee in great detail) the constituent societies of a civilization will not be able to maintain their cultural home in reality. The civilization may then disintegrate and disappear, as a good many civilizations have.

Our analysis, which began by analysing the way human beings are linked to reality, has thus shed new light on the evolution of societies and civilizations. Many of the processes described by Toynbee and Sorokin[25] can now be understood in greater depth. It is, however, beyond the purpose of this work to work out these implications.

We will close by briefly considering the relationships between civilizations. For a long time civilizations were fundamentally different, pursuing projects of existence that had little in common except the symbolic basis of culture we have examined in this work. The diffusion of cultural elements from one civilization to another was difficult because of the incompatibility of their sacreds, systems of myths, and values, even though these were all related to the culture's primary milieu. Hence civilizations were the key fields of investigation during most of history. There are exceptions, however. When a civilization's cultural foundation is breaking down or disintegrating, the contact with another culture can be decisive. According to Toynbee[26], universal churches constituted by the higher religions play a vital role in the transition period between the disintegration of the second generation of civilizations and the births of those of the third. Each of the latter civilizations are affiliated to an earlier one by means of a higher religion which is fundamental in giving direction in shaping a new sacred and system of myths. While the perspective developed here can shed further light on the important problems Toynbee struggled with in the later part of his work, we will restrict our attention to a recent trend.

I began this work by noting that, as the West became increasingly preoccupied with science and technology, the picture of humanity being composed of largely independent civilizations changed. Gradually the contact between civilizations has intensified. The result has been disastrous for many cultures who have seen their sacred, myths, and values eroded by this contact. Since the Western project of existence of economic development based on technique is increasingly sought after by all the nations of the world, we appear to be entering a new period in human history in which the first universal subculture of technique is transforming virtually every traditional culture. In order to increase our understanding of this transformation, we have analysed the way traditional cultures symbolically mediated their links with reality. This paves the way for the examination of how the universal subculture of technique constitutes a way of relating to reality that is fundamentally different from the ones established by traditional cultures. It is increasingly technique and not culture that constitutes the social ecology for human life. Once that analysis is completed, we will be able to turn our attention to what happens to human societies and cultures once the universal subculture of technique begins to play a prominent role in their evolution.

An understanding of our modern world and the radical transformation of human existence within it cannot be understood simply by gathering and interpreting the 'facts' about it. As is becoming evident from our analysis of the way we are linked to reality, what we perceive as facts depends on our structures of experience (including the way they may have been affected by a scientific or professional training). The theory of culture as social ecology will constitute the principal map to guide us in our forthcoming study of the dawn of the post-cultural era. It will help us to identify new facts and relationships and reinterpret others.

ENVOI

Although the computer and associated techniques are providing us with another generation of mechanistic analogies and metaphors for understanding the 'systems' central to human life, this enterprise of looking for the living among the dead is open to theoretical objections. One of the differences between living and mechanistic systems on which we have concentrated involves the relationship between the whole and the constituent elements. All mechanistic systems come into existence first as isolated parts. These are integrated into sub-assemblies that are, in their turn, interconnected to constitute the system. This is not the case for human' systems,' and we need to know something about this if we are to understand the relationship between technique and human life.

In the 'body-mind system' of a person, for example, what comes closest to the parts of a mechanistic system develop in an enfolded whole which evolves in part by transforming the way it is enfolded into its environment. We thus began our study of the 'systems' central to human life by examining the development of the individual while presupposing the existence of the socio-cultural environment into which the life of a person is enfolded as it unfolds. Metaconsciously the being of a person becomes enfolded into those of others in ways that reflect the society's project of existence. In time this process provides the person with a cultural ground to stand on in the form of a sacred and system of myths. Thus, the relationship between the individual and the larger cultural systems ranging from the family through a society to a civilization is quite different from that between the parts and the whole in a mechanistic system.

When we began the analysis of societies and civilizations, we presupposed the individuals enfolded into them. A society develops by unfolding itself through its members and by enfolding their activities. It enfolds itself into each new generation, whose members unfold something of that society. Early civilizations were generally characterized by the highly enfolded complexity of their knowledge base and institutions, while our civilization especially is characterized by a greatly unfolded complexity. Even in the latter case, however, the relationship between society and its members is not like that between the whole and the parts in a mechanistic system.

By concentrating on the relationship between the individual and society and how each is reflected in the other, we have sought to contribute to the closing of the gap that exists in many of the social sciences between micro- and macro-level studies. By not accepting a mechanistic view, including those based on the analogies and metaphors of high technology, it becomes possible to see how the various systems central to human life are enfolded into one another by means of a culture. We thus begin to lay a foundation for our next study, examining, among other topics, the relationship between micro- and macro-social and economic phenomena.

If this emphasis on the enfolded character of the systems central to human life proves to be fruitful in the long term (and this neither I nor anyone else can assume), then the very conception of what these systems are will change. Already it is clear that their enfoldedness means that no individual system interacts with its environment by means of the kind of feedback mechanisms commonly envisaged. Similarly, terms like 'equilibrium' and many others associated with systems thinking will have to be rethought if not abandoned altogether. What the analogy of superimposed holograms may contribute to the understanding of certain systems, other metaphors and concepts will have to accomplish for the enfolded systems associated with human life.

I have the profound sense that our present concepts allow us to see the mystery of human life only through a dark glass. Owing to the limitations of scientific knowing, this is not likely to change. Between the human reality as we know it and human life itself probably lie many things which, as Einstein suggested, our theories do not permit us to see and which will trigger further changes in our view of human life. But the very process of asking new questions and not absolutizing reality as we know it is vital, not only to keep scientific debates within their proper context, but also to guarantee a genuine intellectual life for us and the generations to come.

Given the central role science plays within the phenomenon of technique there are some very basic issues at stake that we need to address in the future. There is a problem associated with the attempt of contemporary civilization seeking to improve human life by applying the technical operation to determine the one best way of doing things. If reality is mechanistic, such a strategy might not be too problematic. If, on the other hand, human life has an enfolded character even in a highly differentiated mass society, then it becomes clear that many of the successes and failures of technique become inextricably related. In an enfolded human reality the striving for rationality on the micro-level of specific activities, institutions, or socio-technical ensembles is bound to create irrationalities on the macro-level. We are, along with other scientists and intellectuals, forced to re-examine our implicit and explicit conceptions of the 'nature' of reality which in our present context leads to another question that underlies both this and the following works. Can a civilization be born which incorporates technique but which is structured on the basis of a culture not permeated by technique, thus allowing the enfolded wholeness of human life to continue, or will human life become increasingly reified?

In the dialogue over these and other questions we have to remember something about the paradigms we have acquired from higher education. These are much more than the basis for scientific and intellectual activities of invisible colleges. Their ability to play these roles depends on their acting as filters which derive from a highly interrelated and enfolded reality a diversity of phenomena that are seen as being related only in certain ways. However, as filters, they transmit very little information about how everything belongs to an enfolded whole.

If these reflections can contribute to giving new energy to a dialogue within the multi-versity and among intellectuals around science, technology, and technique and their influence on human life, my audacity in attempting a synthesis of such a vast scope will have been worthwhile.

NOTES

1 For an overview of the meaning that the concept of culture has in various social sciences see F.C. Gamst and E. Norbeck, eds., *Ideas of Culture* (New York: Holt, Rinehart and Winston, 1976). Also see R. Wuthnow *et al.*, *Cultural Analysis* (Boston: Routledge and Kegan Paul, 1984). Our own definition of culture will become evident later in this work.

2 I recognize that there is a tendency today to minimize this diversity by assuming that underneath the apparent diversity of languages, for example, lie certain universal characteristics which are based on innate neural structures. This hypothesis is, I believe, a reflection of the current collapse of cultural diversity which masks the earlier diversity. I will seek to demonstrate that such extreme assumptions are not necessary.

3 In a later chapter we will show that mentally healthy adults live their lives with a great deal of integrality and coherence. Each experience is lived in the context of our whole life, which constitutes a metaconscious distinct from the subconscious and the collective unconscious.

4 See, for example, K.A. Dahlberg, *Beyond the Green Revolution* (New York: Plenum, 1979); D. Goulet, *The Uncertain Promise* (New York: IDOC/North America, 1977); J. Ladrière, *The Challenge Presented to Cultures by Science and Technology* (Paris: UNESCO, 1977); L. Peattie, *Thinking about Development* (New York: Plenum, 1981); P.J. Pelto, *The Snowmobile Revolution: Technology and Social Change in the Arctic* (Menlo Park: Cummings, 1973); B. Richardson, *Strangers Devour the Land* (New York: Macmillan, 1975); E.P. Thompson, 'Time, Work-Discipline and Industrial Capitalism,' *Past and Present* , no. 38 (Dec. 1967), 56–97.

5 See, for example, Brace Research Institute and Canadian Hunger Foundation, *A Handbook on Appropriate Technology* (Ottawa: Canadian Hunger Foundation, 1976, 1977); M. Carr, *Economically Appropriate Technologies for Developing Countries: An Annotated Bibliography* (London: Intermediate Technology Development Group, 1976); N. Jéquier, *Appropriate Technology: Promises and Problems* (Paris: Development Centre of the Organization for Economic Co-Operation and Development, 1976). For a more critical view see W. Rybczynski, *Paper Heroes: A Review of Appropriate Technology* (Garden City: Anchor Press/Doubleday, 1980).

6 See, for example,
R. Aron, *Progress and Disillusion* (New York: Praeger, 1968); R. Aron, *Eighteen Lectures on Industrial Society* (London: Weidenfeld & Nicolson, 1967); J. Baudrillard, *La Société de consommation* (Paris: Gallimard, 1970); D. Bell, *The Coming of Post-Industrial Society* (New York: Basic Books, 1973); J. Ellul, *The Technological Society* (1954), trans. J. Wilkinson (New York: Knopf, 1964); J. Ellul, *The Technological System* (1977), trans. J. Neugroschel (New York: Continuum, 1980); J. K. Galbraith, *The New Industrial State*, 3rd ed. rev. (New York: Mentor, 1978); G. Grant, *Technology and Empire* (Toronto: Anansi, 1969); H. Marcuse, *One-Dimensional Man* (Boston: Beacon Press, 1964); R. Richta, *Civilization at the Crossroads* (New York: International Arts and Science, 1969); A. Touraine, *The Post-Industrial Society*, trans. L. Mayhew (New York: Random House, 1971); L. Winner, *Autonomous Technology* (Cambridge: MIT Press, 1977).

7 See, for example.
ART: J. Ellul, 'Remarks on Technology and Art,' *Social Research*, vol. 46, no. 4 (1979), 805-33; J. Ellul, *L'Empire du non-sens* (Paris: Presses Universitaires de France, 1980); F.D. Klingender, *Art and the Industrial Revolution*, ed. and rev. Arthur Elton (London: Evelyn, Adams & McKay, 1968); A. Malraux, *The Voices of Silence* (1953), trans. Stuart Gilbert (London: Paladin Books, 1974); L. Mumford, *Art and Technics* (New York: Columbia University Press, 1952); P.C. Vitz and A.B. Glimcher, *Modern Art and Modern Science* (New York: Praeger, 1984).
MUSIC: G. Friedmann, 'The Role and Place of Music in an Industrial Society,' *Diogenes*, no. 72 (winter 1970), 22–38; R.M. Schaefer, *The Tuning of the World* (Toronto: McClelland and Stewart, 1977); C. Small, *Music–Society–Education* (London: John Calder, 1980).
LITERATURE: G. Graff, *Literature against Itself* (University of Chicago Press, 1979); R. Hoggart, *The Uses of Literacy* (London: Chatto & Windus, 1957); A.B. Kernan, *The Imaginary Library* (Princeton University Press, 1982);

G. Steiner, *Language and Silence: Essays on Language, Literature and the Inhuman* (New York: Atheneum, 1967); W. Sypher, *Literature and Technology* (New York: Random House, 1968).

LANGUAGE: W. Berry, 'Standing by Words,' *Hudson Review*, vol. XXXIII, no. 4 (winter 1980-81), 489-521; T.B. Farrell and G.T. Goodnight, 'Accidental Rhetoric: The Root Metaphors of Three Mile Island,' *Communication Monographs*, vol. 48 (Dec. 1981), 271-300; H. Kenner, 'Machine-Speak,' in *The State of the Language*, Michaels and C. Ricks eds., (Berkeley: University of California Press, 1980), 467-77; C.S. Lewis, *The Abolition of Man: Reflections on Education with Special Reference to the Teaching of English in the Upper Forms of Schools* (New York: Macmillan, 1947); M. Stanley, *The Technological Conscience* (New York: Free Press, 1978).

WELTANSCHAUUNG: J. Berger *et al.*,*Ways of Seeing* (London: BBC and Penguin, 1972); D. Cappon, *Technology and Perception* (Springfield: Charles C. Thomas, 1971); E.J. Dijksterhuis, *The Mechanization of the World Picture*, trans. C. Dikshorn (Oxford University Press, 1961); S. Giedion, *Mechanization Takes Command* (New York: Norton, 1969); A. Kroker, *Technology and the Canadian Mind: Innis/McLuhan/Grant* (Montreal: New World Perspectives, 1984).

RELIGION: H. Botting and G. Botting, *The Orwellian World of Jehovah's Witnesses* (University of Toronto Press, 1984); J. Ellul, *The New Demons* (1973), trans. C. Edward Hopkin (New York: Seabury, 1975); J. S. Glen, *Justification by Success* (Atlanta: John Knox Press, 1979); D. Meyer, *The Positive Thinkers* (New York: Anchor, 1966); V.S. Owens, *The Total Image or Selling Jesus in the Modern Age* (Grand Rapids: Wm. B. Eerdmans, 1980); P. Rieff, *The Triumph of the Therapeutic* (New York: Harper and Row, 1966).

MORALITY AND VALUES: D. Boorstin, 'Statistical Morality,' in *The Collective Definition of Deviance*, ed. F. James Davis and Richard Stivers, (New York: Free Press, 1975), 156-61; J. Ellul, 'Technological Morality,' in *To Will and To Do* (Philadelphia: Pilgrim Press, 1969), 185-98; J.K. Galbraith, *The New Industrial State*, (New York: Mentor, 1978), 119-63; J. Henry, *Culture against Man* (New York: Vintage, 1965); A. MacIntyre, *After Virtue* (London: Duckworth, 1981); A.I. Solzhenitsyn, *A World Split Apart* (New York: Harper and Row, 1979); M.W. Thring, 'Values in Engineering,' *Science and Public Policy*, vol. 8, no. 6 (1981), 444-57.

EDUCATION: R.E. Callahan, *Education and the Cult of Efficiency* (University of Chicago Press, 1962); I. Illich, *Deschooling Society* (New York: Harper and Row, 1970, 1971); J. Kozol, *The Night Is Dark and I Am Far From Home* (Boston: Houghton Mifflin, 1975); J. Spring, *Education and the Rise of the*

Corporate State (Boston: Beacon Press, 1972); V.P. Suransky, *The Erosion of Childhood* (University of Chicago Press, 1982).

LEISURE: F. Balle, ed., *Medias et société* (Paris: Editions Montchrestion, 1980); S. de Grazia, *Of Time, Work and Leisure* (New York: Anchor, 1964); B. Lefkowitz, *Breaktime* (London: Penguin, 1980); D. MacCannell, *The Tourist* (New York: Schocken, 1976); S. Parker, *Leisure and Work* (London: Allen and Unwin, 1983); B. Rigauer, *Sport and Work*, trans. A.B. Guttmann (New York: Columbia University Press, 1981).

SEXUALITY: D. Holbrook, *Sex and Dehumanization* (Toronto: Pitman, 1972); D.H. Merkin, *Pregnancy as a Disease* (New York: Kennikat, 1976); M. Odent, *Entering the World* (London: Marion Boyars, 1984); R. Stivers, 'A Festival of Sex, Violence and Drugs: The Sacred and Profane in our World,' *Katallagete* (winter 1979), 18–25; T. Szasz, *Sex by Prescription* (New York: Penguin, 1981).

PROFESSIONS: B.J. Bledstein, *The Culture of Professionalism* (New York: N.Y. Norton, 1976); I. Illich *et al.*, *Disabling Professions* (Toronto: Burns & MacEachern, 1977); M.S. Larson, *The Rise of Professionalism* (Berkeley: University of California Press, 1977); D. Schön, *The Reflective Practitioner* (New York: Basic Books, 1983).

AGRICULTURE: W.Berry, *The Unsettling of America* (San Francisco: Sierra Club, 1977); R. Burbach and P. Flynn, *Agribusiness in the Americas* (New York: Monthly Review Press, 1980); R.H. Hall, *Food for Nought* (New York: Harper and Row, 1974); US Congress, Senate, Committee on Commerce, Consumer Subcommittee. *Dry Cereals*: Hearings, July 23, August 4 and 5, 1970, serial no. 91–72 (Washington: US Government Printing Office, 1970).

WAR: R. Aron, *War and Industrial Society* (Westport: Greenwood, 1980); M. Kaldor, *The Baroque Arsenal* (London: André Deutsch, 1982); J.U. Nef, *War and Human Progress* (Cambridge: Harvard University Press, 1950); J. Schell, *The Fate of the Earth* (New York: Knopf, 1982); Stockholm International Peace Research Institute, *The Arms Trade with the Third World* (London Penguin, 1975).

8 See, for example, Ellul, *The Technological System*; Galbraith, *The New Industrial State*; R.G. Krohn, *The Social Shaping of Science* (Westport: Greenwood, 1971); W. Krohn, E.T. Layton, Jr., P. Weingert, eds., *The Dynamics of Science and Technology* (Boston: Reidel, 1978); D. Noble, *America by Design* (New York: Knopf, 1979); D.J. de Solla Price, *Little Science, Big Science* (Columbia University Press, 1963). Richta, *Civilization at the Crossroads*; A. Touraine, *Workers' Attitudes to Technical Change* (Paris: Organization for Economic Co-operation and Development, 1965).

9 In his book, *La Technique ou l'enjeu du siècle* (Paris: Armand Colin, 1954), Ellul shows the proliferation of techniques in all areas of life. This proliferation leads to a society organized on the basis of technique, and hence the title of the English translation, namely *The Technological Society*, does not reflect the distinction Ellul draws between technology and technique.

10 This point has been well expressed by P. Freire in *Pedagogy of the Oppressed*, trans. M. Ramos (New York: Herder & Herder, 1970). The political implications the author draws from this point are not the only possible ones.

11 The concept of technique as milieu and system has been developed by Jacques Ellul in *Le Système technicien* (Paris: Calmann-Lévy, 1977), 43–61. The translation (*The Technological System*) erroneously translates the French words 'technique' and 'milieu' as 'technology' and 'environment' respectively. The theory of technique as milieu was further developed in W.H. Vanderburg, ed., *Perspectives on Our Age* (Toronto: CBC, 1981), 59–84. This development includes the theory of the three primary milieus in human history discussed later on.

12 L. Mumford, *The Pentagon of Power* (New York: Harcourt Brace Jovanovich 1970)

13 A. Huxley, *Brave New World* (London: Chatto and Windus, 1932)

14 See, for example, D. Gabor *et al.*, *Beyond the Age of Waste* (New York: Pergamon, 1978); E.J. Mishan, *The Costs of Economic Growth* (London: Penguin, 1969); A. Rotstein, ed., *Beyond Industrial Growth* (University of Toronto Press, 1976); E.F. Schumacher, *Small Is Beautiful* (New York: Harper and Row, 1973); Science Council of Canada, *Canada as a Conserver Society*, Report 27 (1977).

15 We will give only one example, from the food industry: B.T. Hunter, *The Mirage of Safety* (New York: Scribner, 1975).

16 *The Structure of Scientific Revolutions* (University of Chicago Press, 2nd ed., 1970)

17 We will continue using the term 'paradigm' in accordance with what Kuhn originally had in mind. In a later work, we will analyse the structure of paradigms and show that the concept of disciplinary matrix is inadequate.

18 Quoted in T.S. Kuhn, *The Copernican Revolution* (Cambridge: Harvard University Press, 1957), 138

19 *The Philosophical Works of Descartes*, trans. E.S. Haldane and G.R.T. Ross (Cambridge University Press, 1975), vol. 1, 5

20 Ibid., 14.

21 Mumford, *The Pentagon of Power*

22 The process by which competing schools quickly disappear in the physical sciences has been described by Kuhn in *The Structure of Scientific Revolutions*.
23 Mumford, *The Pentagon of Power*
24 J. Ellul, *Métamorphose du bourgeois* (Paris: Calmann-Lévy, 1967)
25 Giedion, *Mechanization Takes Command*
26 W.H. Vanderburg, 'A New Approach to Professional Courses,' *Proceedings, Canadian Conference on Engineering Education*, P.M. Wright ed., Toronto, 1980.; 'The Transmission of Values in Engineering Education,' *Proceedings, Third Canadian Conference on Engineering Education*, G. Wacker, ed., Saskatoon, 1982
27 The analysis that follows in the next few pages is partly based on the work of Edgar Morin, *La Méthode, vol. 1: La Nature de la nature* (Paris: Seuil, 1977), 94–151.
28 L. von Bertalanffy, *General Systems Theory* (New York: Braziller, rev., 1973). For a good introduction to von Bertalanffy's work, see M. Davidson, *Uncommon Sense*. (Los Angeles: J.P. Tarcher, 1983).
29 (New York: Universe, 1972)
30 R. Vacca, *The Coming Dark Age*, trans. J.S. Whale (Garden City: Anchor, 1974); C. Perrow, *Normal Accidents* (New York: Basic Books, 1984)
31 *The Structure of Scientific Revolutions*
32 Particularly for living systems, it is important to draw a distinction between open and closed systems. In the former, the import and export of material and information is not only possible but essential. In closed systems, on the contrary, there are no such transfers across the boundaries of the system.
33 For a critical review of this mechanistic holism, see D.J. Burton, 'Methodology for Second-Order Cybernetics,' *Nature and System*, vol. 3 (1981), 13–27; R. Lilienfeld, *The Rise of Systems Theory* (New York: Wiley, 1978); D.C. Phillips, *Holistic Thought in Social Science* (Stanford University Press, 1976); Stanley, *The Technological Conscience*.
34 The danger of separating human knowledge from the individual or community has been clearly seen by M. Heidegger. For a clear statement of this problem, see H.L. Dreyfus, 'Knowledge and Human Values: A Genealogy of Nihilism,' *Teachers College Record*, vol. 82, no. 3 (spring 1981), 507–20 and 'Holism and Hermeneutics,' *Review of Metaphysics* , vol. 34 (Sept. 1980), 3–23.
35 An excellent study of what is involved in the concept of system has been carried out by Morin in *La Méthode, vol. 1: La Nature de la nature*, 94–151. The discussion that follows is in part drawn from that work but fundamental differences persist in general orientation.

36 See, for example, B. d'Espagnat, *In Search of Reality* (New York: Springer-Verlag, 1983); W. Eckhardt, 'Limits to Knowledge,' *Knowledge: Creation, Diffusion, Utilization*, vol. 3, no. 1, (1981), 61–81.
37 M. Polanyi, *Personal Knowledge* (University of Chicago Press, 1962)
38 *The Structure of Scientific Revolutions*
39 D. Bohm, *Wholeness and the Implicate Order* (London: Routledge & Kegan Paul, 1980); B. D'Espagnat, 'The Quantum Theory and Reality,' *Scientific American* (Nov. 1977), 158–81. For a critical evaluation of the parallels with mysticism, see S. Restivo, *The Social Relations of Physics, Mysticism, and Mathematics* (Dordrecht: Reidel, 1983).
40 Bohm, *Wholeness and the Implicate Order*. The last chapter of this work gives a good non-technical summary of the crisis in physics and its implications for our view of reality.
41 Ibid., 177
42 See, for example, K.H. Pribram, *Languages of the Brain* (Englewood Cliffs, Prentice-Hall, 1971), 140–66, and 'The Role of Analogy in Transcending Limits in the Brain Sciences,' *Daedalus*, vol. 109, no. 2, 1980 19–38; G.S. Globus *et al.*, eds., *Consciousness and the Brain* (New York: Plenum, 1976),317–28; D. Gabor *et al.*, 'Holography,' *Science*, vol. 173 (1971), 11–23.
43 The study we are about to embark on is of a fundamentally different kind from that undertaken by Arthur Koestler (*The Ghost in the Machine*, New York: Macmillan, 1968). We do not believe that our current problems are the consequence of some deficiency in the human brain. Such theories are mechanistic and reductionistic and neglect what more than anything else leads to our current challenges, namely our collective symbolic life based on culture. We are in substantial agreement with Robert Jay Lifton's critique in *History and Human Survival* (New York: Random House, 1961), 247–54.
44 See, for example, E.O. Wilson, *Sociobiology* (Cambridge: Harvard University Press, 1975) and for a critical view M. Sahlins, *The Use and Abuse of Biology* (Ann Arbor: University of Michigan Press, 1976).
45 'Basic Postulates of Analytical Psychology,' *Collected Works*, vol. 8 (New York: Pantheon, 1960), 353
46 A. Petersen, 'The Philosophy of Niels Bohr,' *Bulletin of the Atomic Scientists*, vol. 19 (Sept. 1963), 8–14, and *Quantum Physics and the Philosophical Tradition* (Cambridge: MIT Press), 188
47 'Autobiographical Note,' *Albert Einstein: Philosopher-Scientist*, ed. P.A. Schilpp (Evanston, Library of Living Philosophers, 1949). The second quote can be found in W. Heisenberg, *Physics and Beyond: Encounters and Conversations* (New York: Harper and Row, 1971), 63.

48 We do not use the concept of symbolic universe in the sense of P. Berger and
T. Luckmann in *The Social Construction of Reality* (New York: Doubleday,
1966), but in the sense of E. Cassirer in *An Essay on Man* (New Haven:
Yale University Press, 1944). He argued that individuals do not deal with
reality directly but through a symbolic medium. Human beings therefore
live in a symbolic universe rather than a 'real' world.

49 For a classical treatment (1890) of the role of the brain in animals and
humans, see William James, *The Principles of Psychology*, vol. I (New York:
Dover, 1950), 12–80.

50 A.A. Brill, ed., *Sigmund Freud: Basic Writings* (New York: Random House,
1938); J.A.C. Brown, *Freud and the Post-Freudians* (London: Penguin,
1961)

51 The concept of mental map has been used largely in relation to the geo-
graphic environment by P. Gould and R. White, *Mental Maps* (London:
Penguin, 1974), and R.M. Downs and D. Stea, *Maps in Minds* (New
York: Harper and Row, 1977).

52 J. Ellul, *Histoire des institutions*, vols. 1-2 (Paris: Presses Universitaires de
France, 3rd ed., 1970)

53 Our approach will be different from that of K. Lewin, 'Life Space and Psychological Ecology,' in D. Cartwright, ed., *Field Theory in Social Science*
(New York: Harper and Row, 1951), 306, 308–9.

CHAPTER TWO

1 For a variety of views on this subject, see J. Eccles, ed., *Mind and Brain: The
Many-Faceted Problems* (Washington: Paragon, 1982).

2 Harvey A. Carr, *An Introduction to Space Perception* (New York: Hatner,
1935), 20–23

3 I. Kohler, 'Rehabituation in Perception,' *The Formation and Transformation of the Perceptual World* (New York: International Universities Press,
1964)

4 J.S. Bruner and Leo Postman, 'On the Perception of Incongruity: A Paradigm,' *Journal of Personality*, vol.XVIII (1949), 206–23

5 Ibid., 218

6 K. Lewin, *Principles of Topological Psychology* (New York: McGraw Hill,
1936)

7 For detailed studies in this area we refer the reader to the works of Jean
Piaget. Particularly relevant are: *The Construction of Reality*, (New York:
Basic Books, 1954); *The Mechanisms of Perception* (London: Routledge
& Kegan Paul, 1969); *The Origins of Intelligence in Children* (London: Rout-

ledge & Kegan Paul, 1952); *Play, Dreams and Imitation in Childhood*
(New York: Norton, 1951). See also T.G.R. Bower, *Development in Infancy*
(San Francisco: W.H. Freeman, 1974);K. Kaye, *The Mental and Social
Life of Babies* (University of Chicago Press, 1982).
8 For a related discussion in a different context see L. Wittgenstein, *Philosophical Investigations*, trans. G.E.M. Anscombe, (New York, 1953),
31–6, and T.S. Kuhn *The Structure of Scientific Revolutions* (University of
Chicago Press, 1970), 2nd. ed. 44–5). In perception no explicit criteria for
assessing similarity or difference exist.

CHAPTER THREE

1 The reader is referred to the extensive literature on the psychology of perception or to one of the introductory texts such as M.D. Vernon, *The Psychology of Perception* (London: Penguin, 2nd ed., 1971).
2 R.H. Thouless, 'Phenomenal Regressions to the Real Object,' *British Journal of Psychology* (1931)
3 G.H. Mowbray, 'The Perception of Short Phrases Presented Simultaneously
for Visual and Auditory Perception,' *Quarterly Journal of Experimental
Psychology* (1964)
4 For an introductory overview, the reader may refer to: Ian M.L. Hunter,
Memory (London: Penguin, rev.ed., 1964). The two main approaches to the
psychology of human memory are presented by Charles N. Cofer, ed.,
The Structure of Human Memory (San Francisco: W.H. Freeman, 1976),
and Ulric Neisser, ed., *Memory Observed* (W.H. Freeman, 1982). For a
critical review of current theories of memory, see H.A. Bursen, *Dismantling
the Memory Machine* (Boston: D. Reidel, 1979).
5 For a related treatment of the subject see G. Mandler, *Mind and Body* (New
York: Norton, 1984).
6 For a review of the various theories of emotions, the reader is referred to
P.T. Young, 'Feelings and Emotions,' *Handbook of General Psychology*,
ed. Benjamin B. Wolman (New York: Prentice-Hall, 1973), 749–71;
K.H. Pribram, 'The New Neurology and the Biology of Emotion, '*American
Psychologist*, vol.22 (1967), 830–8; K.H. Pribram, 'Emotion: Steps toward a Neuropsychological Theory,'*Neurophysiology and Emotion*, ed.
D.C. Glass (New York: Rockefeller University Press, 1967).
7 K.B. Madsen, 'Theories of Motivation,' *Handbook of General Psychology*,
673-706. This chapter is particularly amusing in that it condemns the values
implied in some schools of thought even to the point of being nationalis-
tic ('Despite the testimony of Freud there remain psychologists–even

American psychologists – who believe that the motivation of man is fundamentally different from that of animals') while not scrutinizing its own paradigms and value judgements.

8 G.A. Kelly, *The Psychology of Personal Constructs* (New York: Norton, 1955) has attempted to give the conceptions people have about the future a central role in the human personality. His treatment is extremely limited, however, in that it largely neglects several facets of the human personality, such as the subconscious and metaconscious.

9 Some interesting questions in this regard have been raised by J.H. Van den Berg, *The Changing Nature of Man* (New York: Delta, 1961). We will, however, reach quite different conclusions.

CHAPTER FOUR

1 T.S. Kuhn, *The Structure of Scientific Revolutions* (University of Chicago Press, 1970)

2 For an overview of Piaget's works, see H. Gruber and J. Voneche, eds., *The Essential Piaget* (New York: Basic Books, 1977). For a sympathetic critique of Piaget's works, see R. Vuyk, *Overview and Critique of Piaget's Genetic Epistemology 1965–1980* (New York: Academic Press, 1981). For a different critique, see J. Broughton, 'Piaget's Structural Developmental Psychology,' *Human Development* vol. 34, no. 2 (1981), 78–109. These works include a critique of the concept of stage in the development of children. See also G. Matthews, *Philosophy and the Young Child* (Cambridge: Harvard University Press, 1981), and C. Gilligan, *In a Different Voice* (Harvard University Press, 1982).

3 When there are no more tensions or dialectical relationships within a group, there is little to be shared and communicated. Because the members have nothing to say to each other, social ties between them are weakened. There is little internal reason for the group's existence. It will begin to disintegrate unless it is held together by external pressures. The members of the group must experience the reality of their daily lives sufficiently differently to have something to share and maintain communication, but the differences must not be too large or they would live in different worlds, rendering communication impossible. A group must maintain a diversity within a unity. Take marriage as an example. At first the relationship is alive and dialectic. Each partner evolves with regard to the other and is related to the other because of their differences, tensions, and love. If after a long time of marriage the evolution of the man and woman eliminates their differences because, for example, both take on similar habits and

interpret reality in much the same way, they no longer find many reasons for being together, so that the relationship may break up. It is for this reason that virtually all societies attempt to prevent this break-up by external juridical pressures. The marriage can then continue despite a lack of internal reasons. The same is true for a society. For a society to maintain itself, it must meet challenges that force it to implicitly find reasons for its existence. Different groups will give divergent answers, and it is by these differences that a society evolves. A society that does not evolve begins to repeat itself. When this happens it stagnates and disintegrates because people become indifferent and see no reason for belonging to it.

4 The distinction between one's body and the external world is not always correctly made. Some psychotic patients do not identify some of their limbs as their own. For example, a patient may forget to dry them after a bath. W. Russell, *Brain, Mind, Perception and Science* (Oxford, 1951), 35

5 For an unusual case study, see B. Bettelheim, 'Joey, the Mechanical Boy,' *Scientific American* (March 1959).

6 E.T. Hall, *Hidden Dimension* (New York: Doubleday, 1966)

7 Ibid., and A. Kendon, 'Some Functions of Gaze-Direction in Social Interaction,' *Acta Psychologica*, vol. 26 (1967)

8 A. Kendon, 'Movement Coordination in Social Interaction,' *Acta Psychologica*, vol. 32 (1970). W.S. Condon and W.D. Ogston, 'Sound Film Analysis of Normal and Pathological Behaviour Patterns,' *Journal of Nervous and Mental Disease*, vol. 143, no. 4 (1966), 338-47

9 See for example, S. Giedion, *Mechanization Takes Command*, (New York: Norton, 1969) 17–30, 44, 101–13

10 H. Poincaré, *The Foundations of Science* trans. G.B. Halstead (Lancaster: Science Press, 1924), 383–94. For this account as well as other studies on creative processes, the reader is referred to P.E. Vernon, ed., *Creativity* (London: Penguin, 1970).

11 See, for example, Vance Packard, *The Hidden Persuaders* (New York: D. McKay, 1957); W.B. Key, *Subliminal Seduction* (Englewood Cliffs: Prentice Hall, 1973); E. Loftus, *Memory* (Don Mills: Addison-Wesley, 1980)

12 J. Baudrillard, *Le Système des objets* (Paris: Gallimard, 1968), and *La Société de consommation* (Gallimard, 1970); M. McLuhan, *The Mechanical Bride* (New York: Vanguard, 1951); E. Goffman, *Gender Advertisements* (New York: Harper & Row, 1979); P. Dumouchel, *L'Enfer des Choses* (Paris: Seuil, 1979)

13 J.K. Galbraith, 'Economics as a System of Belief,' *American Economic Review, Papers and Proceedings* (May 1970), reprinted in J.K. Galbraith, *Economics, Peace and Laughter* (New York: New American Library, 1972), 56–77

14 J. Ellul, *Propaganda* (New York: Knopf, 1968); G.N. Gordon, *Persuasion* (New York: Hastings House, 1951); D.L. Altheide and J.M. Johnson, *Bureaucratic Propaganda* (Toronto: Allyn and Bacon, 1980)

15 For a general introduction to this quite complex phenomenon, see I. Oswald, *Sleep* (London: Penguin, 3rd ed., 1974).

16 C.G. Jung, *The Practice of Psychotherapy* (New York: Pantheon, 1966); S. Freud, *The Interpretation of Dreams* (London: Hogarth Press, 1953)

17 Somewhat analogous ideas can be found in the works of P.A. Sorokin and Robert Jay Lifton. See for example, Sorokin, *Society, Culture and Personality* (New York: Harper, 1947) and Lifton, *The Broken Connection* (New York: Basic Books, 1983).

18 S. Waldfogel, 'The Frequency and Affective Character of Childhood Memories,' *Psychological Monographs*, vol. 62, no. 4 (1948)

19 E.G. Schachtel, *Metamorphosis* (New York: Basic Books, 1959)

20 For treatment of this problem from a different perspective, see Georges Gurvitch, *Traité de sociologie* (Paris: Presses Universitaires de France, 2nd ed., 1962).

21 John Welwood, 'The Holographic Paradigm and the Structure of Experience,' in Ken Wilber, ed., *The Holographic Paradigm and Other Paradoxes* (Boulder: Shambhala, 1982), 127–36

22 Ibid., 128

23 Ibid., 128–9

24 Ibid., 129

25 See S. Freud, 'Project for a Scientific Psychology,' in *Collected Works*, vol. 1 (London: Hogarth Press, 1966), and K.H. Pribram, *Freud's 'Project' Reassessed* (London: Hutchinson, 1976).

26 From a different perspective, Vygotsky has quite justly criticized Piaget on some of these points. For further details of his important contribution, see L.S. Vygotsky, *Thought and Language*, trans. E. Hanfmann and G. Vakar (Cambridge: MIT Press, 1972).

27 M. Polanyi, *Personal Knowledge* (University of Chicago Press, 1962)

CHAPTER FIVE

1 This is well illustrated in the study by S. Giedion, *Mechanization Takes Command* (New York: Norton, 1969).

2 See J. Baudrillard, *La société de consommation* (Paris: Gallimard, 1970), although we find his conclusions inadequate. For a critique, see J. Ellul, *The Technological System* (New York: Continuum, 1980).

3 L. Mumford in *Technics and Human Development*, vol. 2 of 'The Myth of

the Machine' (New York: Harcourt Brace Jovanovich, 1966) has pointed to the role dreams could have played in the emergence of humanity in prehistory. See in particular chap. 3.

4 J. Ellul, *La Parole humiliée* (Paris: Seuil, 1981)

5 See, for example, E. Cassirer, *An Essay on Man*, (New Haven: Yale University Press, 1944); H.D. Duncan, *Symbols in Society* (New York: Oxford University Press, 1968); G. Gusdorf, *Speaking*, (Evanston: Northwestern University Press, 1965); M. Eliade, *A History of Religious Ideas* (University of Chicago Press, 1968); R. Escarpit, *Théorie générale de l'information et de la communication* (Paris: Hachette, 1976); and A. Leroi-Gouran, *Le Geste et la parole*, vols. 1 and 2 (Paris: Albin Michel, 1964).

6 We will not enter into the debate over the precise origin of language. The reader is referred to the works of Chomsky and Piaget. For an important exchange of ideas between these two men, see M. Piattelli-Palmarini, ed., *Language and Learning: The Debate between Jean Piaget and Noam Chomsky* (Cambridge: Harvard University Press 1980).

7 The explanation of the emergence of language that we will develop in this section can explain, I believe, why recent research shows that the acquisition of a 'mother tongue' follows very similar patterns despite the difference between individual languages. See, for example, D.I. Slobin, *Psycholinguistics*, 2nd ed. (Glenview: Scott Foresman, 1979) and also P. Fletcher and M. Garman, eds., *Language Acquisition: Studies in First Language Development* (Cambridge University Press, 1979). Once again there is no question that innate mental structures related to language exist. The structures built up from experience graft themselves onto the ones established genetically. Ivan Illich in *Shadow Work* (London: Marion Boyars, 1981) has shown that the idea of a mother tongue arose with the nation-state, which created an 'official' language. Following Illich we use 'vernacular' rather than 'mother tongue.'

8 This paves the way for the symbolic reversal to be examined in chapter seven. As we will see, the symbolic foundation of a culture does not rest on immediate experience, as is evident from the vocabulary of a language. While some concepts can be derived directly from immediate experience, others (such as those designating moral values) cannot.

9 For an overview of the various theories of modern linguistics, see Slobin, *Psycholinguistics*. For one of the most influential theories see N. Chomsky, *Language and Mind* (New York: Pantheon, 1975).

10 Particularly good examples of the 'educated' conversational style and a more 'purely conversational' style have been given by W. Labov, *Language in the Inner City* (Philadelphia: University of Pennsylvania Press, 1972),

201-40. This example includes the problem of crossing the boundary between different subcultures, which will be discussed in a later chapter.

11 For a detailed analysis of the media, the reader is referred to Marshall
McLuhan, *Understanding Media*, (New York: McGraw-Hill, 2nd ed.,
1964).

12 W.M. Cook, 'Ability of Children in Colour Discrimination,' *Child Development*, vol. 2 (1931), 303

13 P. Malrieu, 'Quelques Problèmes de la vision des couleurs chez l'enfant,'
Journal de Psychologie (1955), 52, 222

14 J. André, *Etudes sur les termes de couleur dans la langue latine* (Paris:
Klinksieck, 1949), 427

15 This has been brought to light by Claude Lévi-Strauss in *The Savage Mind*
(University of Chicago Press, 1966). He shows that language helps members
of a society to understand the external world by establishing a classification of things. Things have a reality for primitive people when they are well
classified in the universe of language.

16 In fact the basic concept of physical nature is once again being fundamentally questioned, as we noted in chapter one.

17 See Frederick Suppe's introduction and chapter 1 to 5 in *The Structure of
Scientific Theories* (University of Illinois Press, Urbana: 1971), 3–232.

18 Escarpit, *Théorie générale de l'information et de la communication*

19 J. Piaget, *Logic and Psychology* (Manchester University Press, 1953); J.
Piaget and B. Inhelder, *The Psychology of the Child* (New York: Basic
Books, 1969)

20 For an overview, see N. Bolton, *The Psychology of Thinking* (London:
Methuen, 1972).

21 H.L. & S.E. Dreyfus, 'The Psychic Boom.' *Creative Computing*, vol. 6, no.
7 (July 1980)

CHAPTER SIX

1 See, for example, F. Hulse, *The Human Species* (New York: Random House,
1971), 288–92.

2 For some related critiques see H. Dreyfus, *What Computers Can't Do*
(New York: Harper and Row, 2nd ed., 1979); and J. Weizenbaum,
Computer Power and Human Reason (San Francisco: W.H. Freeman,
1976).

3 We will not discuss the valuable and interesting findings of ethology.

4 R. Vacca, *The Coming Dark Age* (New York: Doubleday, 1974)

5 The interaction of some of these systems, particularly in prehistory, has

been examined by E. Morin *(Le Paradigme perdue: la nature humaine* (Paris: Seuil, 1973) in an attempt to explain the genesis of humanity.

6 These reports, together with accounts of other similar cases, are available in Lucien Malson, *Les Enfants sauvages* (Paris: Union Générale d'Editions, 1964). A good account in English can be found in Roger Shattuck's *The Forbidden Experiment* (New York: Washington Square, 1981).

7 A beginning of a deterioration of the structure of experience has been noted in the experiments on partial sensory deprivation. Studies of total sensory deprivation have demonstrated that animals deprived of visual experience from birth for a prolonged period never fully recover their visual capacities R. Melzack and W. Thompson, 'Effects of Early Experience on Social Behaviour,' *Canadian Journal of Psychology*, vol. 10 (1956), 82–90). Children under seven months of age who had been in hospital for one or two weeks appeared almost unaware of objects and people when they were taken home. They spent their time gazing around with blank and bewildered expressions on their faces. This behaviour lasted several hours to two days. They had become set in the monotonous hospital environment where they were rarely picked up and played with, which made it difficult for them to readjust to a normal environment. H.R. Schaffer, 'Objective Observations of Personality Development in Early Infancy,' *British Journal of Medical Psychology* (1958), 31, 174)

8 What we mean by myths will be dealt with in the next chapter.

9 See Helen Keller, *The Story of My Life* (New York: Doubleday, 1902), and in this same volume, Part 3: Supplementary Account of Helen Keller's Life and Education, 315ff. For Laura Bridgman, see Mary Swift Lamson, *Life and Education of Laura Dewey Bridgman* (New York: Arno, 1975). Their cases have been discussed by Ernst Cassirer, *An Essay on Man* (New Haven: Yale University Press, 1944).

10 K. Goldsten, *Human Nature in the Light of Psychopathology* (Cambridge: Harvard University Press, 1940), 48

11 H. Kohl, *The Age of Complexity* (New York: New American Library, 1965) chap. 5

12 In contemporary society, serious internal conflicts in the structures of experience of the members is common, as seen in K. Horney, *The Neurotic Personality of Our Time* (New York: Norton, 1937).

13 Somewhat different cases have been documented in *The Three Faces of Eve* by C. H. Thigpen and H. Cleckley (New York: Popular Library, 1957,) and *Sybil* by F.R. Schreiber (New York: Warner, 1974). See also D. Keyes, *The Minds of Billy Milligan* (New York: Random House, 1981).

14 L. Carmichael, H.P. Hogan, and A.A. Walter, 'An Experimental Study of

the Effect of Language on the Reproduction of Visually Perceived Form,' *Journal of Experimental Psychology* (1932), 73–86

15 See M.L. Johnson Abercrombie, *The Anatomy of Judgement* (London: Hutchinson, 1960).

16 E. Siipola, 'A Group Study of Some Effects of Preparatory Sets,' *Psychological Monographs*, no. 210 (1935), 46

17 R. Levine, I. Chein, and G. Murphy, 'The Relation of Intensity of a Need to the Amount of Perceptual Distortion,' *Journal of Psychology* (1942), 283–93

18 J.C. Gilchrist and L.S. Nesberg, 'Need and Perceptual Change in Need-Related Objects,' *Journal of Experimental Psychology* (1952), 369–76

19 H. Proshansky and G. Murphy, 'The Effects of Reward and Punishment on Perception,' *Journal of Psychology* (1942), 295–305

20 J.M. Levine and G. Murphy, 'The Learning and Forgetting of Controversial Material,' *Journal of Abnormal Social Psychology* (1943), 38, 507–17

21 M. Haire and W.F. Grunes, 'Perceptual Defenses: Processes Protecting an Organized Perception of Another Personality,' *Human Relations* (1950), 403–12

22 M.B. Smith, J.S. Bruner, and R.W. White, *Opinions and Personality* (New York: Wiley, 1956), 251. Freud has also given many examples in his *Psychopathology of Everyday Life* (London: Penguin, 1975).

23 For a critical evaluation, see Albert Jacquard, *Au Péril de la science* (Paris: Seuil, 1982).

24 J.P. Guilford, 'Traits of Creativity,' in H.H. Anderson, ed., *Creativity and Its Cultivation* (New York: Harper, 1959), 142–61

25 D.W. MacKinnon, 'The Nature and Nurture of Creative Talent,' *American Psychology*, vol. 17, 484–95

26 See, for example, A. Meadow and S.J. Parnes, 'Evaluation of Training in Creative Problem-Solving,' *Journal of Applied Psychology*, vol. 43 (1959), 189-94; and S.J. Parnes and A. Meadow, 'Evaluation of Persistence of Effects Produced by a Creative Problem-Solving Course,' *Psychological Reports*, vol. 7 (1960), 357–61.

27 D.W. MacKinnon, 'The Personality Correlates of Creativity: A Study of American Architects,' in P.E. Vernon, ed., *Creativity* (London: Penguin, 1970), 289–311

28 We do not deal with the many attempts to establish a classification of personality types using a statistical approach by means of factor analysis. Since the factors are computed from averages, they tend to be somewhat abstract and less useful for our purposes.

29 C.G. Jung, *Psychological Types* trans. H.G. Baynes (New York: Pantheon,

1964). The brief résumé given here has mostly been drawn from F. Ford-ham, *An Introduction to Jung's Psychology* (London: Penguin, 1953), chap. 2.
30 David Riesman, *The Lonely Crowd* (New Haven: Yale, rev. ed., 1961)

CHAPTER SEVEN

1 As will become increasingly evident in this and later chapters, I am using the word 'dialectic' in a much broader sense than Marx and his successors. The study by C. Castoriadis, *L'Institution imaginaire de la société* (Paris: Seuil, 1975), arrives at conclusions that resemble the ones reached in this study.
2 R. Pritchard, W. Heron, and D.O. Webb, 'Visual Perception Approached by the Method of Stabilized Images,' *Canadian Journal of Psychology*, vol. 14 (1960), 67
3 W.H. Beston, W. Heron, and T.H. Scott, 'Effects of Decreased Variation in the Sensory Environment,' *Canadian Journal of Psychology*, vol. 8 (1954), 70
4 J.P. Zubeck, D. Pushkar, W. Sansom, and J. Gowing, 'Perceptual Changes after Prolonged Sensory Isolation (Darkness and Silence),' *Canadian Journal of Psychology*, vol. 15 (1961), 83
5 J.M. Keynes, *The General Theory of Employment, Interest and Money* (New York: Macmillan, 1936)
6 See, for example, J.K. Galbraith, 'How Keynes Came to America,' reprinted in *Economics, Peace and Laughter* (Boston: Houghton Mifflin, 1971).
7 For an interesting study for the case of science, see D. Bohm, 'On Insight and Its Significance for Science, Education and Values,' *Education and Values*, ed. D. Sloan, (New York: Teachers' College Press, 1980).
8 J. Stoetzel, *La Psychologie sociale* (Paris: Flammarion 1963) originally by S. Reinach, 'La Représentation du galop dans l'art antique et moderne,' *Revue archéologique* vol. 36 (1900), 216–51, 441–50. See also P.C. Vitz and A.B. Glimcher, *Modern Art and Modern Science* (New York: Praeger, 1984).
9 See, for example, R. Caillois, *Man and the Sacred*, trans. M. Barash, (New York: Free Press, 1959); M. Eliade, *The Sacred and the Profane*, trans. W. Trask (New York: Harper and Row, 1961), and *Patterns in Comparative Religion*, trans. R. Sheed (Cleveland: World, 1970); J. Ellul, *The New Demons* (New York: Seabury Press, 1975); C. Lévi-Strauss, *The Raw and the Cooked*, trans. J. and D. Weightman (New York: Harper and Row, 1969); R. Stivers, *Evil in Modern Myth and Ritual* (Athens: University of Georgia Press, 1982); P. Ricoeur, *The Symbolism of Evil*, trans. E. Buchanan (New York: Harper and Row, 1967).

10 Some readers may perhaps be disturbed at the usage of this term. After all, we have 'become of age.' Yet I do not see how a culture can endure without a sacred, a system of myths, and a religion. For a while it seemed that their universal existence was receding, but we shall attempt to show that this conclusion is incorrect.

11 For a study of how this happened during and after the Industrial Revolution, see J. Ellul, *Métamorphose du bourgeois* (Paris: Calmann-Lévy, 1967).

12 L. Mumford, *The Myth of the Machine: Technics and Human Development* (New York: Harcourt Brace Jovanovich, 1967)

13 C. Lévi-Strauss, *The Savage Mind* (University of Chicago Press, 1966)

14 S. Giedion has given some interesting illustrations of what constituted medieval comfort. See *Mechanization Takes Command* (New York: Norton, 1969).

15 'Contribution to the Critique of Hegel's Philosophy of Right,' in R. Tucker, ed., *The Marx-Engels Reader* (New York: Norton, 2nd ed., 1978) 53–4

16 We are using the concept of alienation in its original two-fold meaning, namely a condition of being possessed by someone or something and hence being a stranger to onself.

17 H. Lefebvre, *Morceaux choisis de Karl Marx* (Paris: Gallimard, 1934), 189.

18 For a brief elaboration of these points see: W.H. Vanderburg, ed., *Perspectives on Our Age: Jacques Ellul Speaks on His Life and Work* (CBC/Seabury, 1981)

19 P. Ariès, *Centuries of Childhood* trans. Robert Baldick (New York: Random House, 1965)

20 Mumford, *The Myth of the Machine*

21 W. Labov, *Language in the Inner City* (Philadelphia: University of Pennsylvania Press 1972)

CHAPTER EIGHT

1 Our study brings us to the same conclusion as that reached by J. Ellul in 'Nature, Technique and Artificiality,' in Paul T. Durbin, ed., *Research in Philosophy and Technology*, vol. 3 (1980), 263–83.

2 We are using the concept of ideal type following Max Weber.

3 J. Ellul has shown how the modern sacred is constructed dialectically in *The New Demons* trans. C.E. Hopkin (New York: Seabury, 1975). For a discussion of this matter, see John Boli-Bennett, 'The Absolute Dialectics of Jacques Ellul,' in Durbin, ed., *Research in Philosophy and Technology*, 171–201.

4 *The Myth of the Machine: Technics and Human Development*, vol. 1 (New York: Harcourt Brace Jovanovich, 1967), 33.

5 We are using the concept of challenge following A. Toynbee, *A Study of History* (Oxford University Press, 1933-54). For an abridged version the reader is referred to D.C. Somervell, ed., (New York: Dell, 1978). For a dialogue with his critics and some resulting revisions to his thought, see A. Toynbee, *Reconsiderations* (Oxford University Press, 1961.) Although various details of Toynbee's theories have been criticized, it remains the most recent attempt to give a systematic interpretation of history. We will show that his models can be readily related to the findings of this work.

6 For the study of the genesis, growth, break-down, and disintegration of civilizations, we refer the reader to the works of Toynbee.

7 The following discussion of how legal institutions meet the challenges of time, space, and the group is based on notes the author took in a doctoral course in the philosophy of law taught by Jacques Ellul at the University of Bordeaux in 1977-8. I am grateful to Professor Ellul for permission to include some of this largely unpublished research in this work. Some elements of this research have been published in: 'Sur l'artificialité du droit et le droit d'exception,' *Archives de Philosophie du Droit*, no. 8 (1963), 21-33; 'Sur l'artificialité du droit et le droit d'exception,' part 2, ibid., no. 10 (1965), 191-207; 'L'Irréductibilité du droit à une théologie de l'Histoire,' *Rivista Internazionale di Filosfia del Diritto*, vol. 48, no. 2-3 (1971), 220-39; and 'Le Problème de l'émergence du droit,' *Annales de la Faculté de Droit* (Bordeaux), vol. 1 (1976), 5–15.

8 The relationship between knowledge and experience and the corresponding kinds of knowledge bases a culture can have will be treated in a separate work.

9 Toynbee, abridged version of *A Study of History*, vol. 1, 271–82, 420 ff

10 Ibid., 286–413

11 Since Durkheim, the phenomenon designated by the concept of anomie has grown in scope and depth, particularly in mass societies in which technique has constituted a milieu and system. In a later work we will show that anomie in these societies would be widespread were it not for the rise of a new mode of social integration. Technique fundamentally transforms the roles of the structures of experience of the members of a culture, including their relationship to daily experience. This causes a loss of meaning and a rootlessness that is compensated by the new forces of social integration. Under these conditions movements may arise that may be regarded as 'anti-cultural.' They call everything into question without anything being put in its place. In other words, these movements are not 'counter-cultural,' striving for a mutation in the project of existence, but largely nihilistic. To destroy everything because it has lost all its meaning in the

hope that something new can grow in its place is to yield to a dangerous illusion. Once a cultural desert has been created nothing new can emerge. An example of an anti-cultural movement imposed by force on a traditional society is the Chinese Cultural Revolution. Another example of such a movement was the anti-French propaganda made by the French themselves during the Algerian war. Nihilistic currents can, of course, also be found in various movements in North America.

12 David S. Landes, *The Unbound Prometheus* (London: Cambridge University Press, 1969)

13 See. J. Ellul, *Métamorphose du bourgeois* (Paris: Calmann-Lévy, 1967).

14 The only possible exception can arise from faith which, unlike religion, is the result of a transcendent god who reveals himself to people. If these people work out that faith in their lives, they will live in part outside of the sacred cultural order. Their presence will be iconoclastic as they challenge the sacred (false gods) of their society, thus attempting to prevent cultural stagnation. However, the question of faith or religion cannot, as we have seen, be resolved scientifically and the evidence of iconoclasm based on faith is limited. Many Christians today appear to have withdrawn their faith from the public arena. Others have adapted it to political issues in a way that does not challenge the sacred of the modern state.

15 We are using the concept 'time of troubles' following Toynbee, abridged *Study of History*, vol. 1, 28. We will apply it to a civilization in the next section.

16 The theme of freedom is central in the Jewish Torah which, as the Christian Old Testament, has played a fundamental role in Western civilization. The first commandment the Jews are given by Yahweh after their deliverance from slavery is not to create or worship idols. If we recognize that these idols symbolized something of the cultural sacred and myths, these texts bring an important message about human freedom.

17 Toynbee, abridged *Study of History*, vol. 1, 67-196

18 Toynbee's dilemma as to whether civilizations or 'higher' religions are the primary intelligible units for historical study can be transcended by recognizing that the two are interrelated via the similar sacreds and systems of myths of the societies involved.

19 Toynbee, abridged *Study of History*, vol. 1, 197-285

20 Ibid., 320-413

21 An example is furnished by art in contemporary society. It draws in elements from art derived from earlier traditional cultures which do not reflect the contemporary cultural order. This introduces culturally non-cumulative elements into modern art.

22 An example is furnished by Western European nations which are part of one civilization and yet cannot make much progress on the road to greater economic and political unification.
23 The model we have just described largely follows Toynbee's Helleno-Sinic model in *Reconsiderations*, 186-96.
24 There are exceptions. Some cultures have been destroyed by violence. Islam eliminated with force every culture it conquered during the eighth, ninth, and tenth centuries. It was simultaneously an economic and military power as well as a religious force. For an interesting view see: A.B. Schmookler, *The Parable of the Tribes* (Berkeley: University of California Press, 1984).
25 Pitirim Sorokin, *Social and Cultural Dynamics* (New York: American Book Co., in 4 vols., 1937–41). The work was revised and abridged in one volume *(Social and Cultural Dynamics* (Boston: Porter Sargent, 1957) by the author.
26 Toynbee, abridged *Study of History*, vol. 2, 11-136

INDEX